C L PRINCESS of Beasts

2

Yu Tomofuji

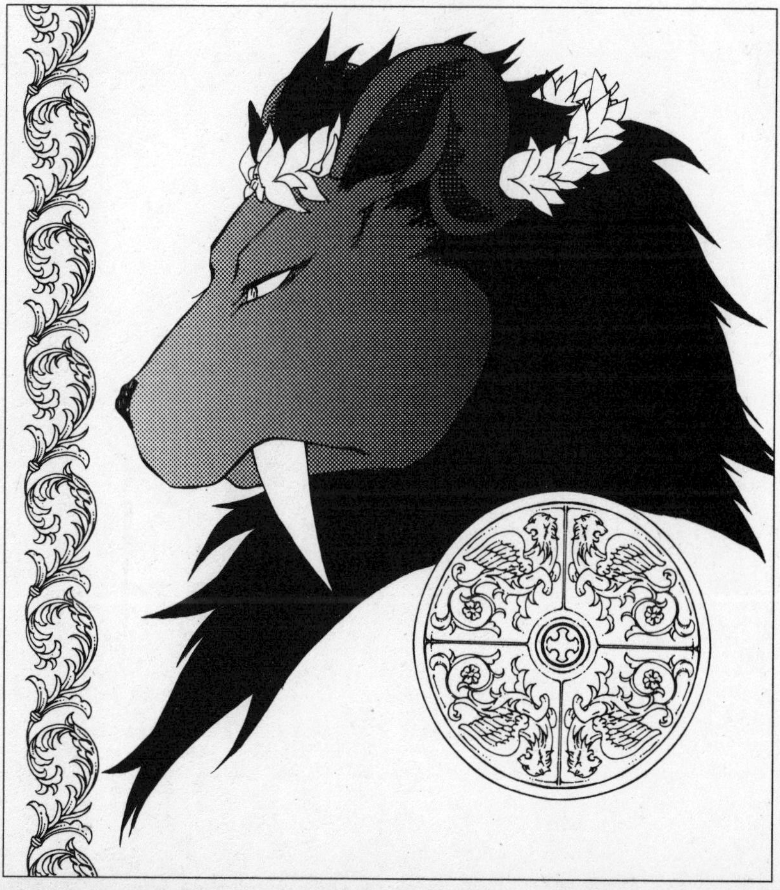

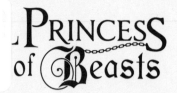

SACRIFICIAL PRINCESS AND THE King of Beasts

2

contents

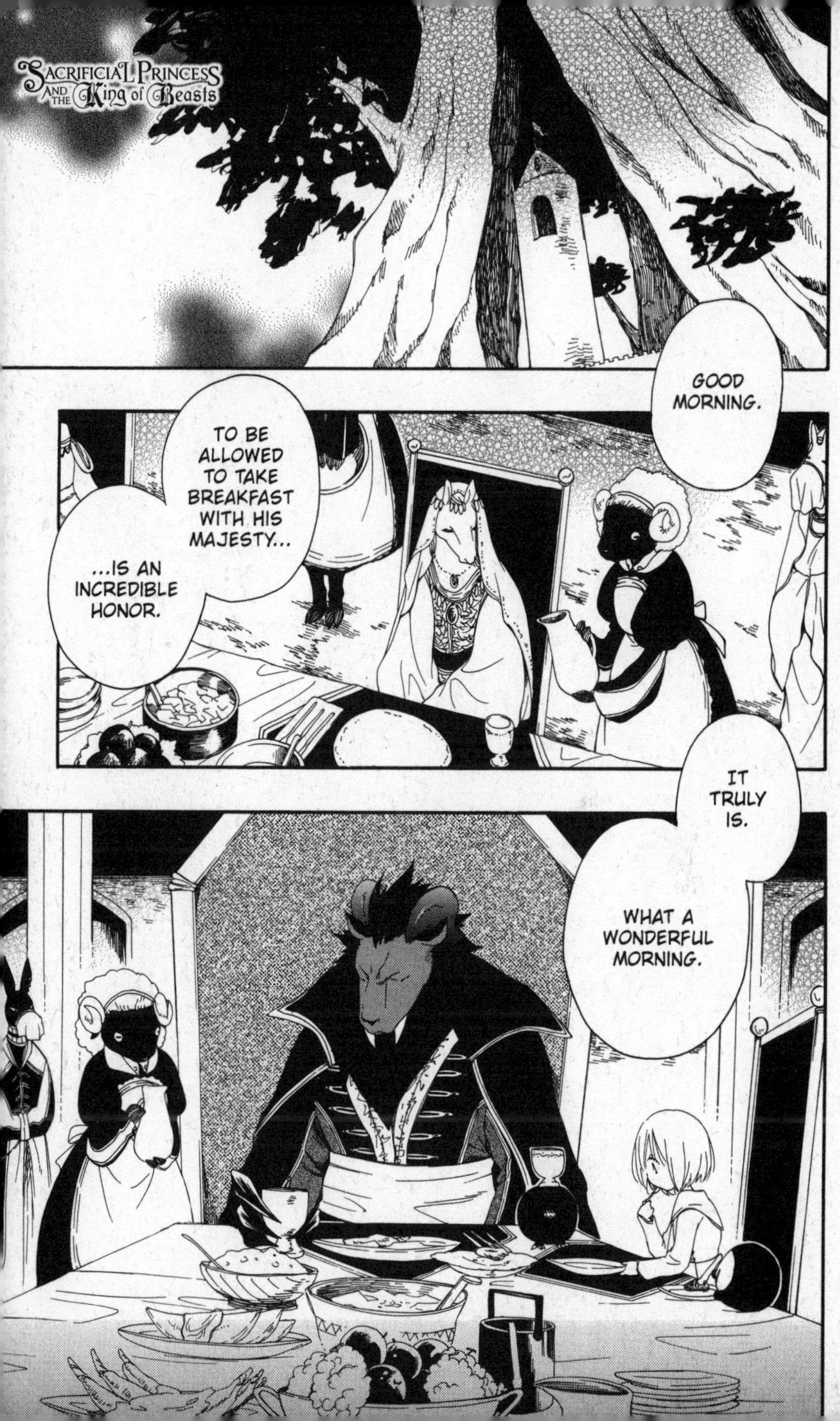
SACRIFICIAL PRINCESS AND THE KING OF BEASTS
GOOD MORNING.
TO BE ALLOWED TO TAKE BREAKFAST WITH HIS MAJESTY...
...IS AN INCREDIBLE HONOR.
IT TRULY IS.
WHAT A WONDERFUL MORNING.

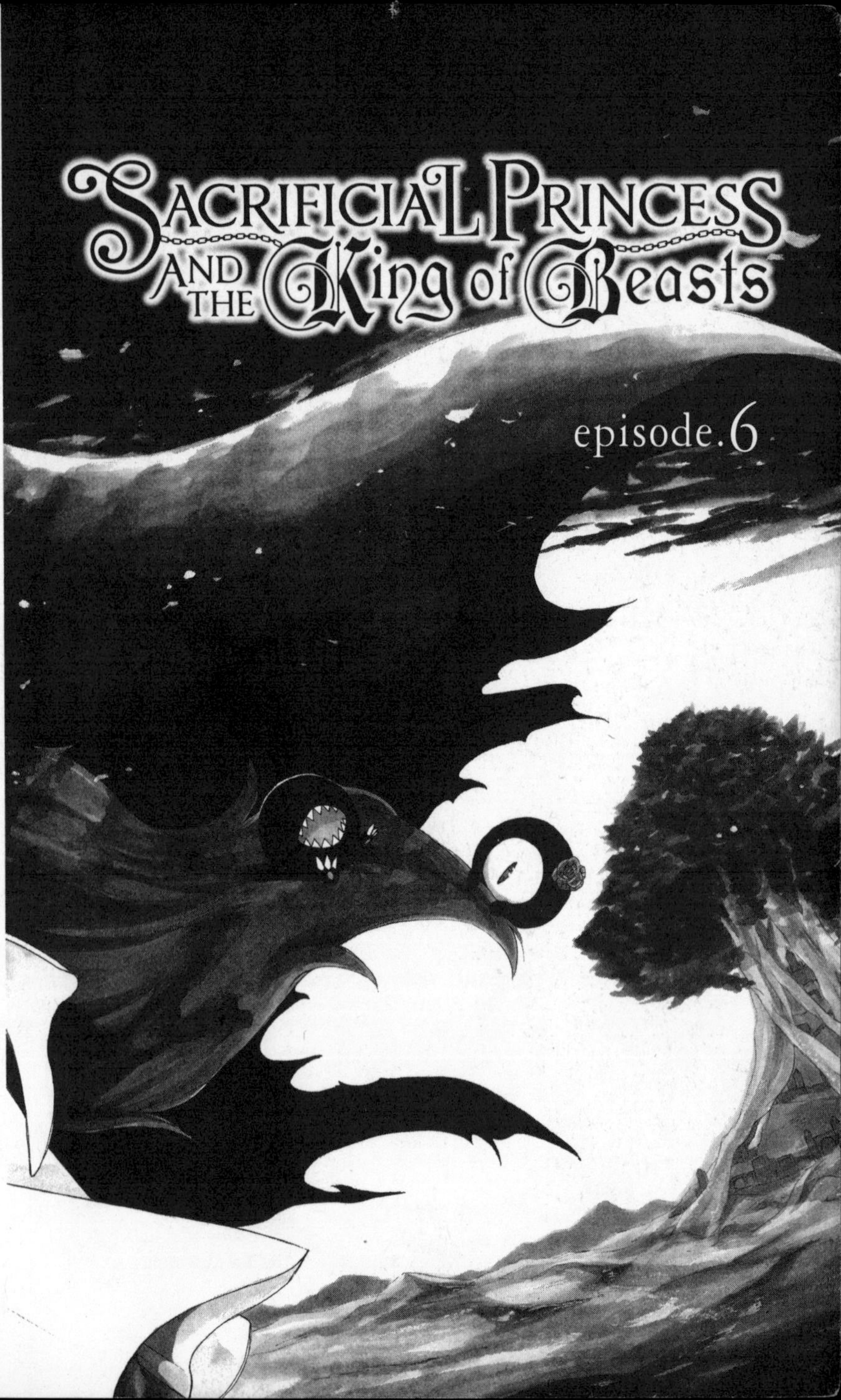
SACRIFICIAL PRINCESS AND THE King of Beasts
episode.6

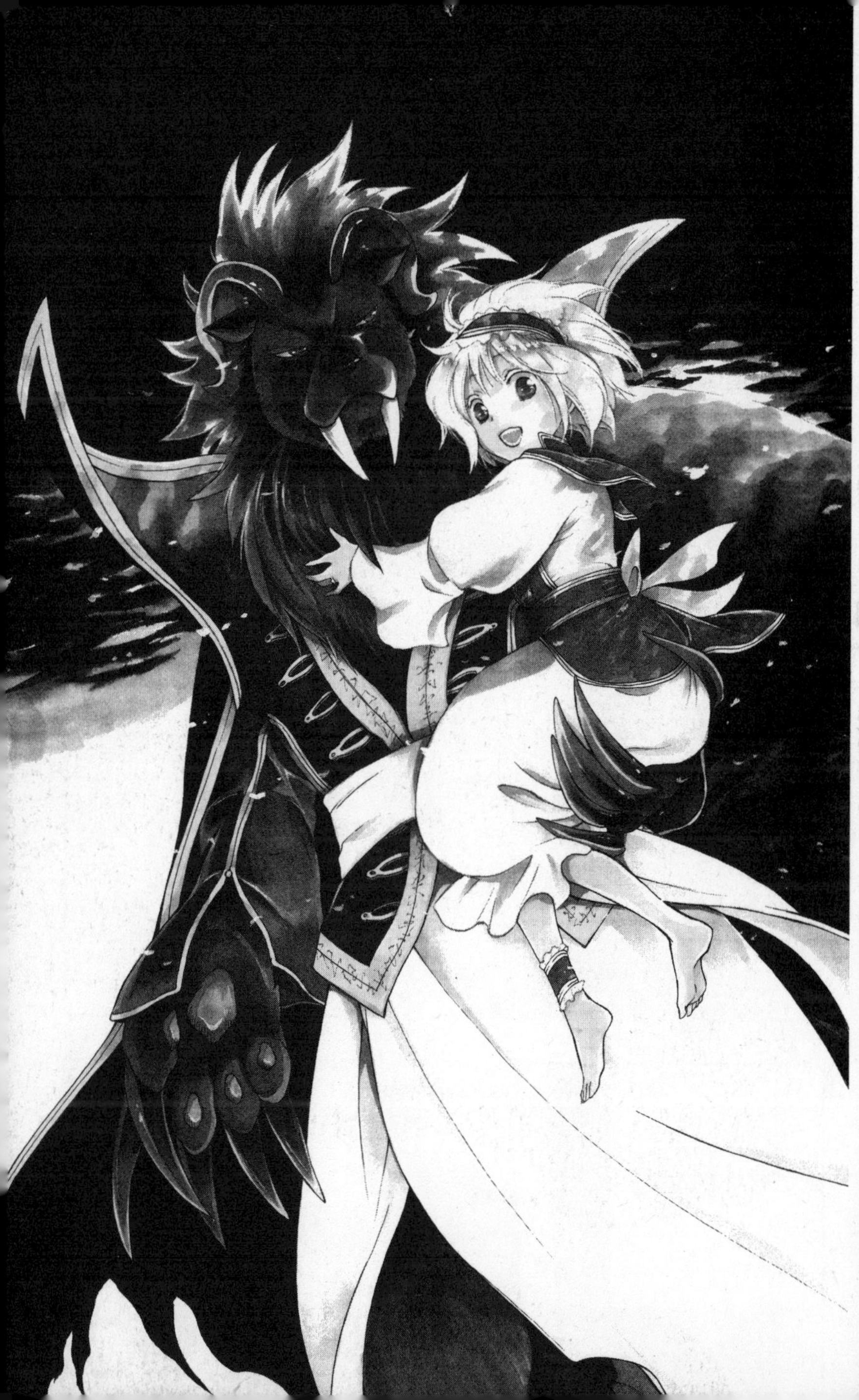

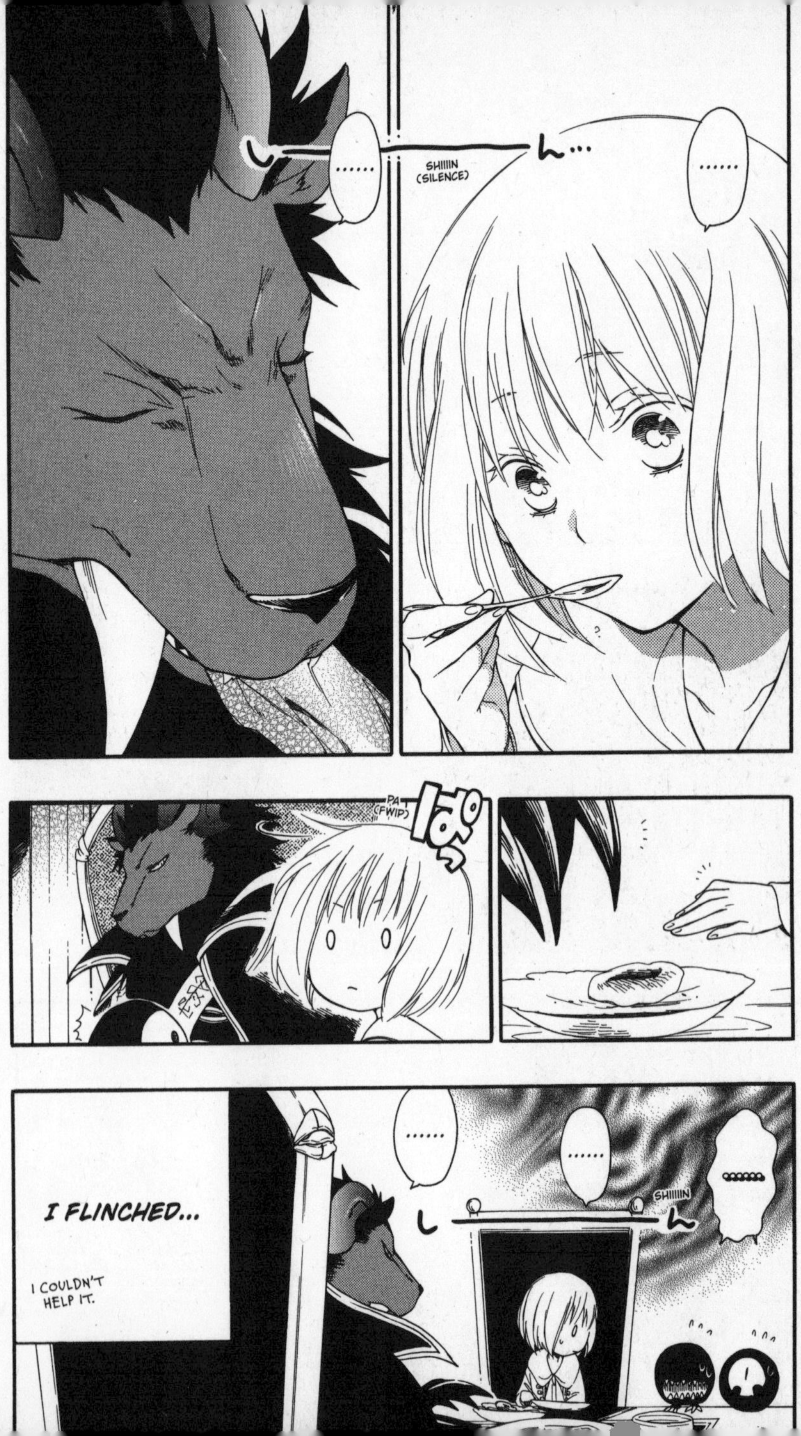
......
SHIIIN (SILENCE)
し——ん…
......
PA (FWIP)
ぱっ
......
......
......
SHIIIIN
し——ん
I FLINCHED...
I COULDN'T HELP IT.

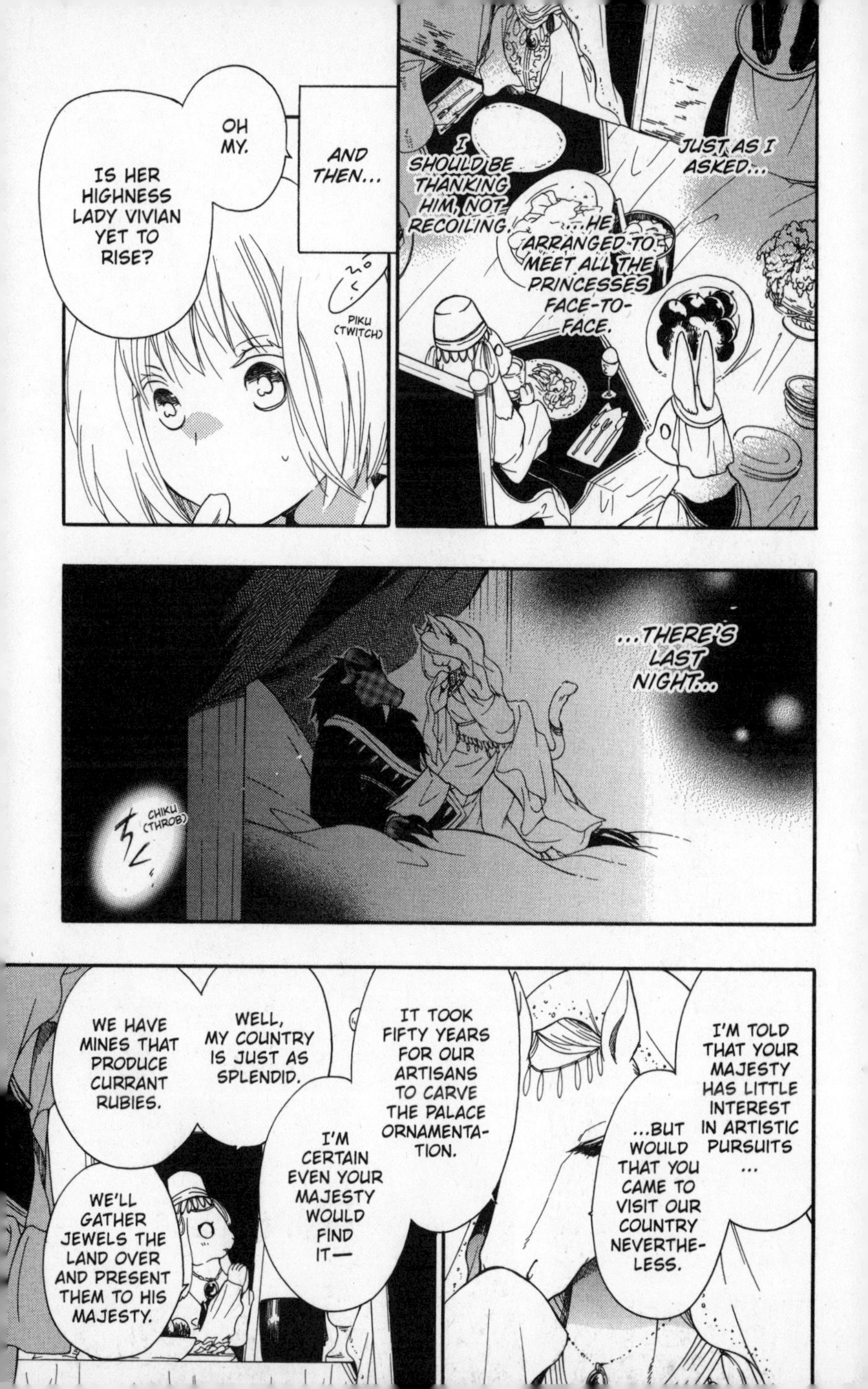
JUST AS I ASKED...
...HE ARRANGED TO MEET ALL THE PRINCESSES FACE-TO-FACE.
I SHOULD BE THANKING HIM, NOT RECOILING.
AND THEN...
OH MY.
IS HER HIGHNESS LADY VIVIAN YET TO RISE?
PIKU (TWITCH)
...THERE'S LAST NIGHT...
CHIKU (THROB)
I'M TOLD THAT YOUR MAJESTY HAS LITTLE INTEREST IN ARTISTIC PURSUITS...
...BUT WOULD THAT YOU CAME TO VISIT OUR COUNTRY NEVERTHELESS.
IT TOOK FIFTY YEARS FOR OUR ARTISANS TO CARVE THE PALACE ORNAMENTATION.
I'M CERTAIN EVEN YOUR MAJESTY WOULD FIND IT—
WELL, MY COUNTRY IS JUST AS SPLENDID.
WE HAVE MINES THAT PRODUCE CURRANT RUBIES.
WE'LL GATHER JEWELS THE LAND OVER AND PRESENT THEM TO HIS MAJESTY.

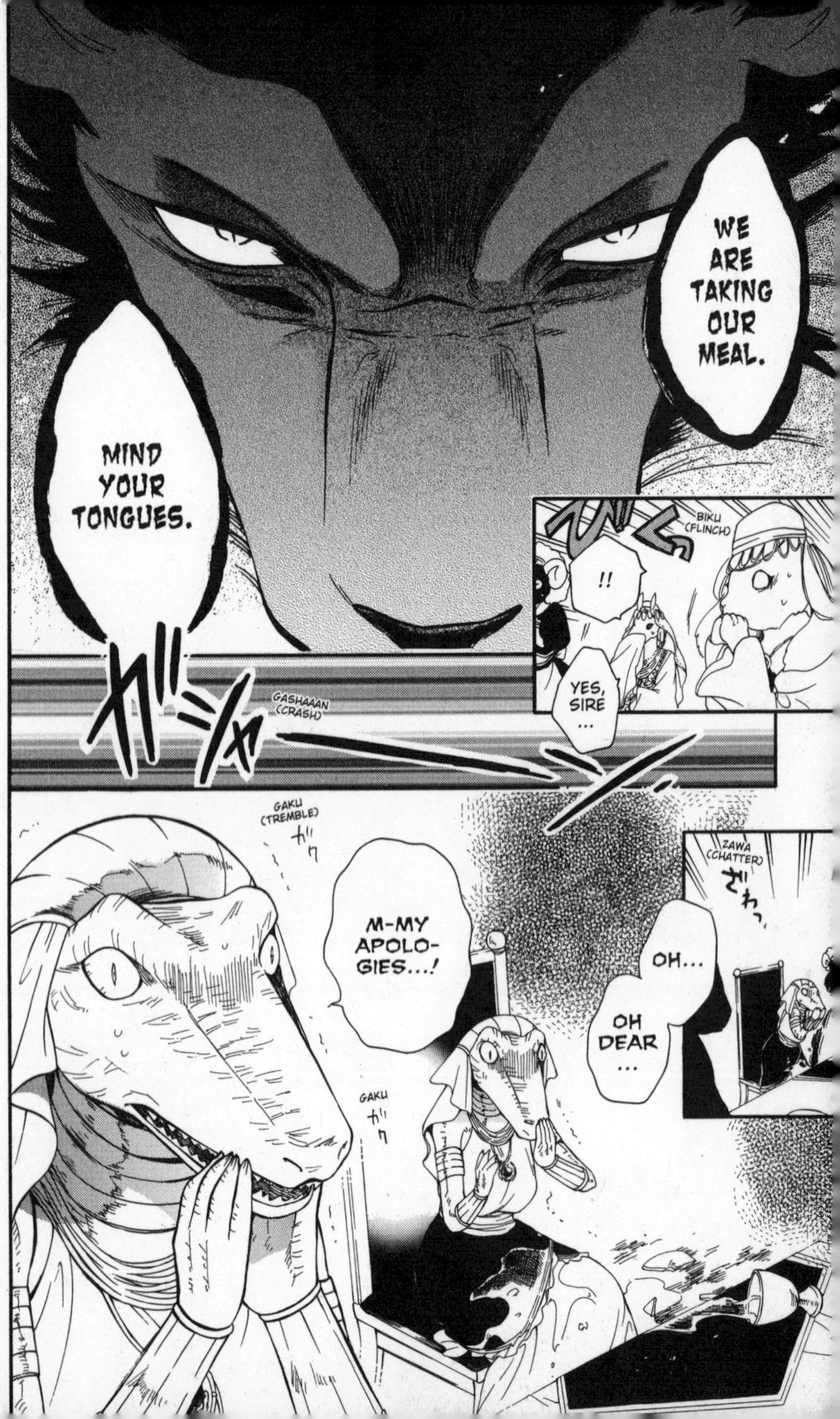
WE ARE TAKING OUR MEAL.
MIND YOUR TONGUES.
BIKU (FLINCH)
!!
YES, SIRE ...
GASHAAAN (CRASH)
ガシャーン
GAKU (TREMBLE)
M-MY APOLOGIES...!
ZAWA (CHATTER)
ざわっ
OH...
OH DEAR ...
GAKU

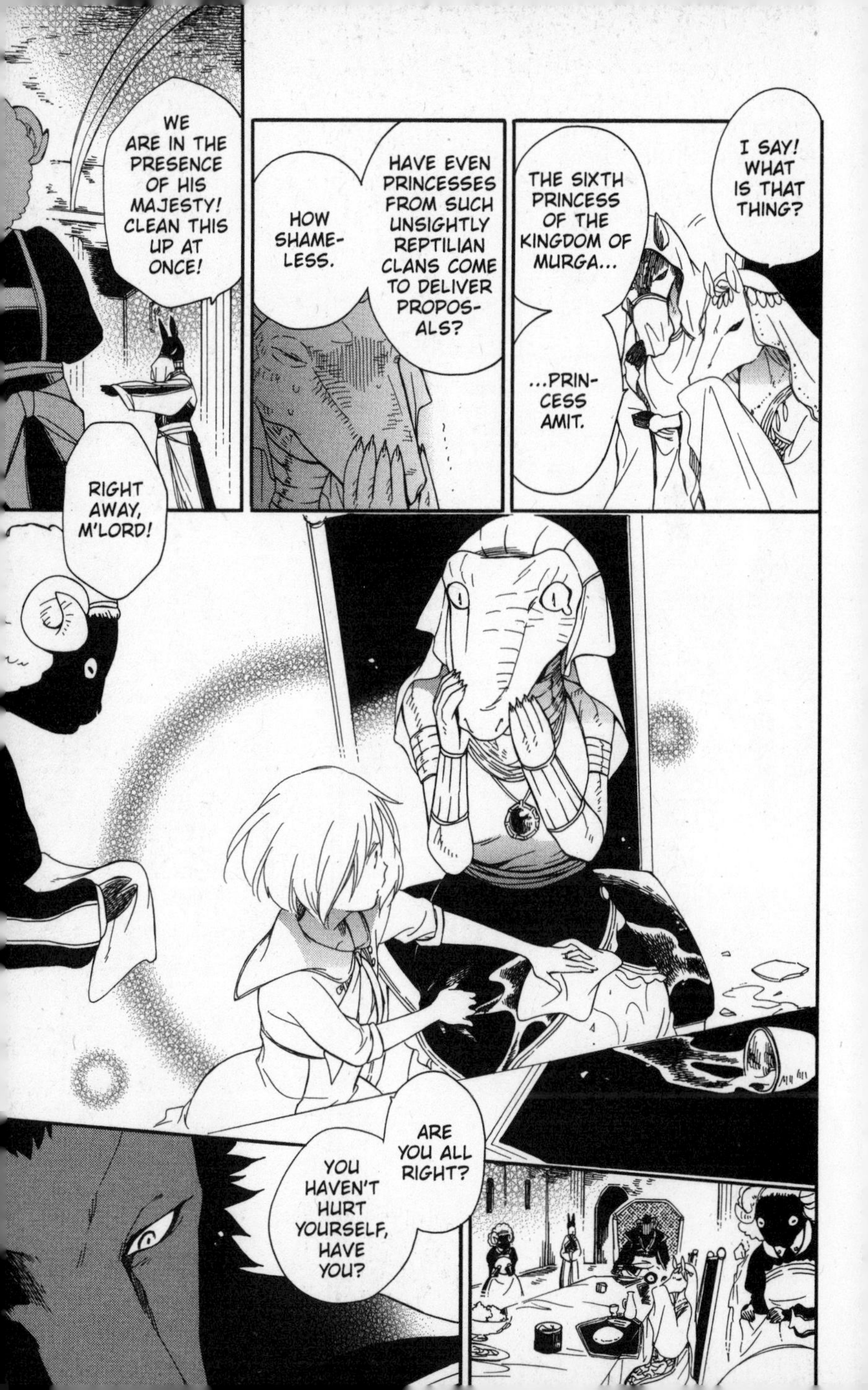
I SAY! WHAT IS THAT THING?
THE SIXTH PRINCESS OF THE KINGDOM OF MURGA...
...PRINCESS AMIT.
HAVE EVEN PRINCESSES FROM SUCH UNSIGHTLY REPTILIAN CLANS COME TO DELIVER PROPOSALS?
HOW SHAMELESS.
WE ARE IN THE PRESENCE OF HIS MAJESTY! CLEAN THIS UP AT ONCE!
RIGHT AWAY, M'LORD!
ARE YOU ALL RIGHT?
YOU HAVEN'T HURT YOURSELF, HAVE YOU?

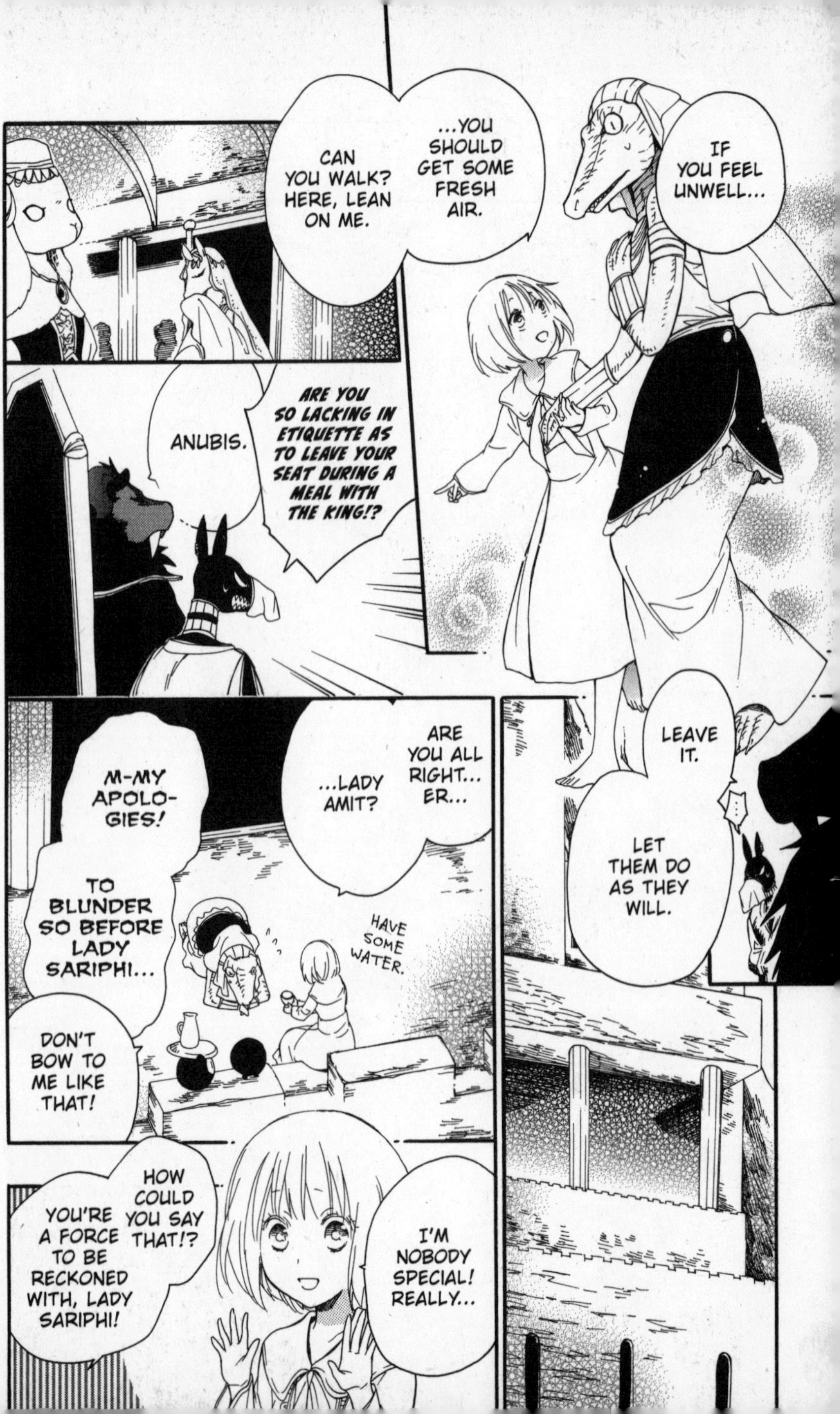
IF YOU FEEL UNWELL...
...YOU SHOULD GET SOME FRESH AIR.
CAN YOU WALK? HERE, LEAN ON ME.
ARE YOU SO LACKING IN ETIQUETTE AS TO LEAVE YOUR SEAT DURING A MEAL WITH THE KING!?
ANUBIS.
LEAVE IT.
LET THEM DO AS THEY WILL.
...
ARE YOU ALL RIGHT... ER...
...LADY AMIT?
M-MY APOLOGIES!
TO BLUNDER SO BEFORE LADY SARIPHI...
HAVE SOME WATER.
DON'T BOW TO ME LIKE THAT!
I'M NOBODY SPECIAL! REALLY...
HOW COULD YOU SAY THAT!?
YOU'RE A FORCE TO BE RECKONED WITH, LADY SARIPHI!

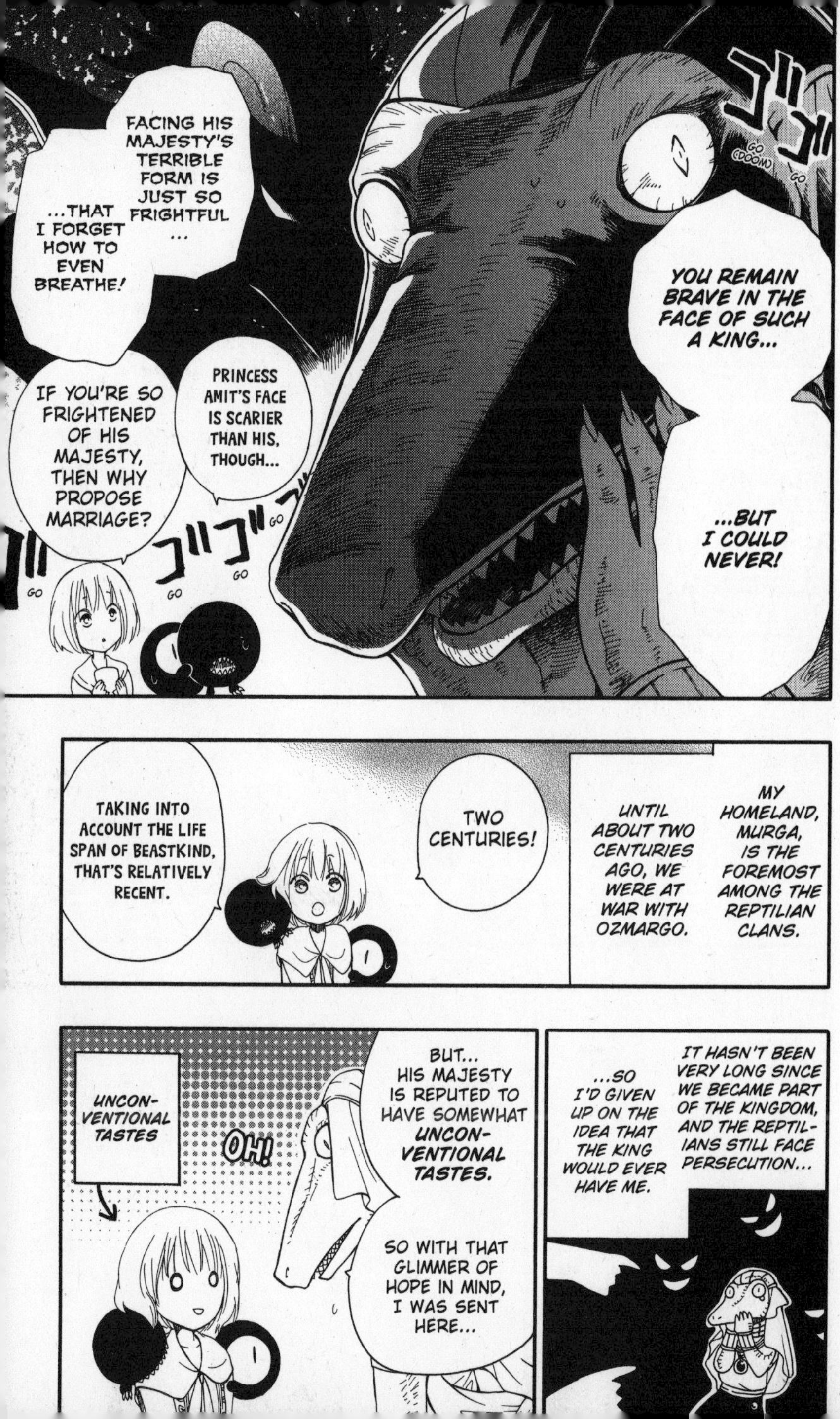
GO (DOOM) GO
YOU REMAIN BRAVE IN THE FACE OF SUCH A KING...
...BUT I COULD NEVER!
FACING HIS MAJESTY'S TERRIBLE FORM IS JUST SO FRIGHTFUL...
...THAT I FORGET HOW TO EVEN BREATHE!
PRINCESS AMIT'S FACE IS SCARIER THAN HIS, THOUGH...
IF YOU'RE SO FRIGHTENED OF HIS MAJESTY, THEN WHY PROPOSE MARRIAGE?
GO GO GO GO
MY HOMELAND, MURGA, IS THE FOREMOST AMONG THE REPTILIAN CLANS.
UNTIL ABOUT TWO CENTURIES AGO, WE WERE AT WAR WITH OZMARGO.
TWO CENTURIES!
TAKING INTO ACCOUNT THE LIFE SPAN OF BEASTKIND, THAT'S RELATIVELY RECENT.
IT HASN'T BEEN VERY LONG SINCE WE BECAME PART OF THE KINGDOM, AND THE REPTILIANS STILL FACE PERSECUTION...
...SO I'D GIVEN UP ON THE IDEA THAT THE KING WOULD EVER HAVE ME.
BUT... HIS MAJESTY IS REPUTED TO HAVE SOMEWHAT UNCONVENTIONAL TASTES.
SO WITH THAT GLIMMER OF HOPE IN MIND, I WAS SENT HERE...
OH!
UNCONVENTIONAL TASTES

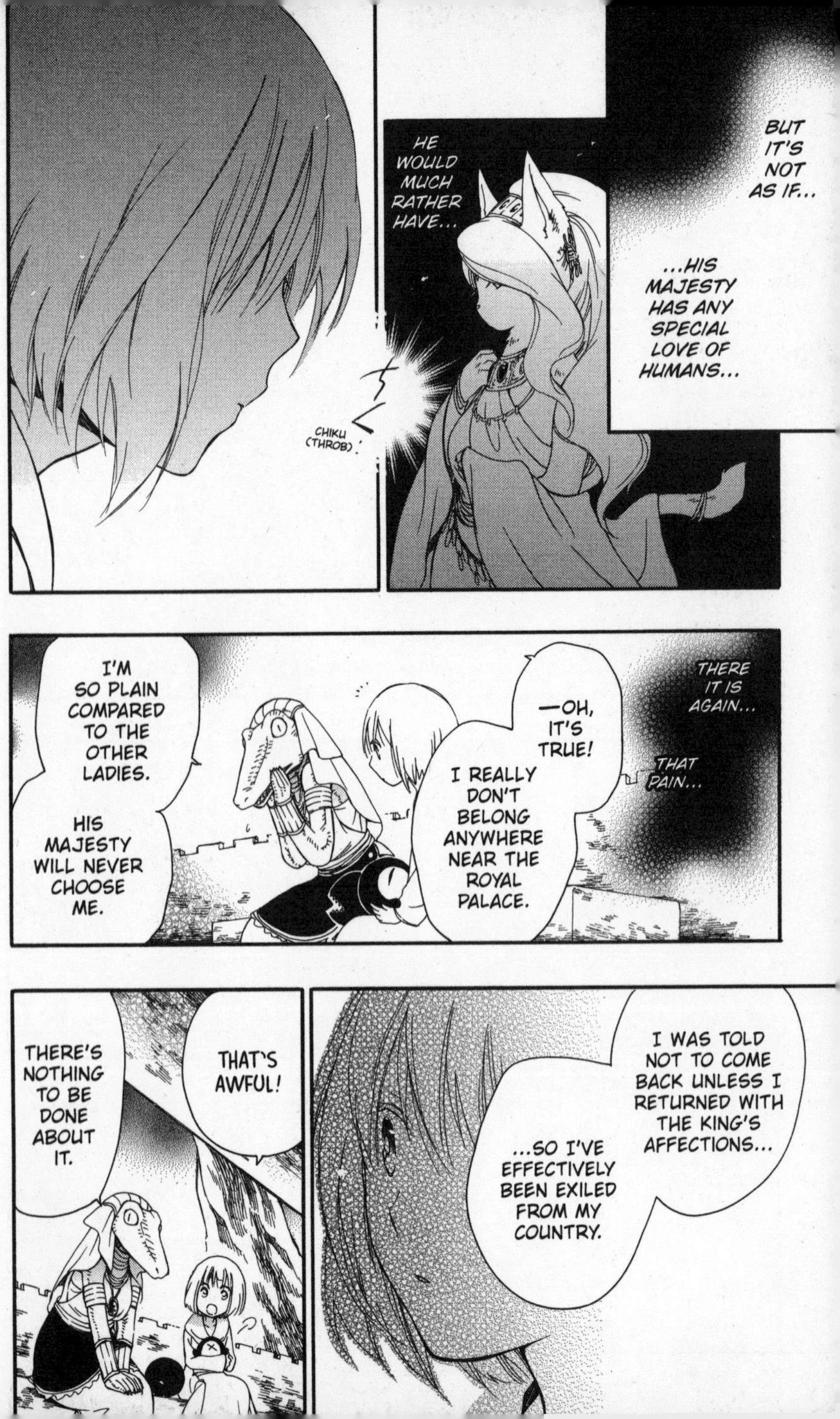
BUT IT'S NOT AS IF...
...HIS MAJESTY HAS ANY SPECIAL LOVE OF HUMANS...
HE WOULD MUCH RATHER HAVE...
CHIKU (THROB)
THERE IT IS AGAIN...
THAT PAIN...
—OH, IT'S TRUE!
I REALLY DON'T BELONG ANYWHERE NEAR THE ROYAL PALACE.
I'M SO PLAIN COMPARED TO THE OTHER LADIES.
HIS MAJESTY WILL NEVER CHOOSE ME.
I WAS TOLD NOT TO COME BACK UNLESS I RETURNED WITH THE KING'S AFFECTIONS...
...SO I'VE EFFECTIVELY BEEN EXILED FROM MY COUNTRY.
THAT'S AWFUL!
THERE'S NOTHING TO BE DONE ABOUT IT.

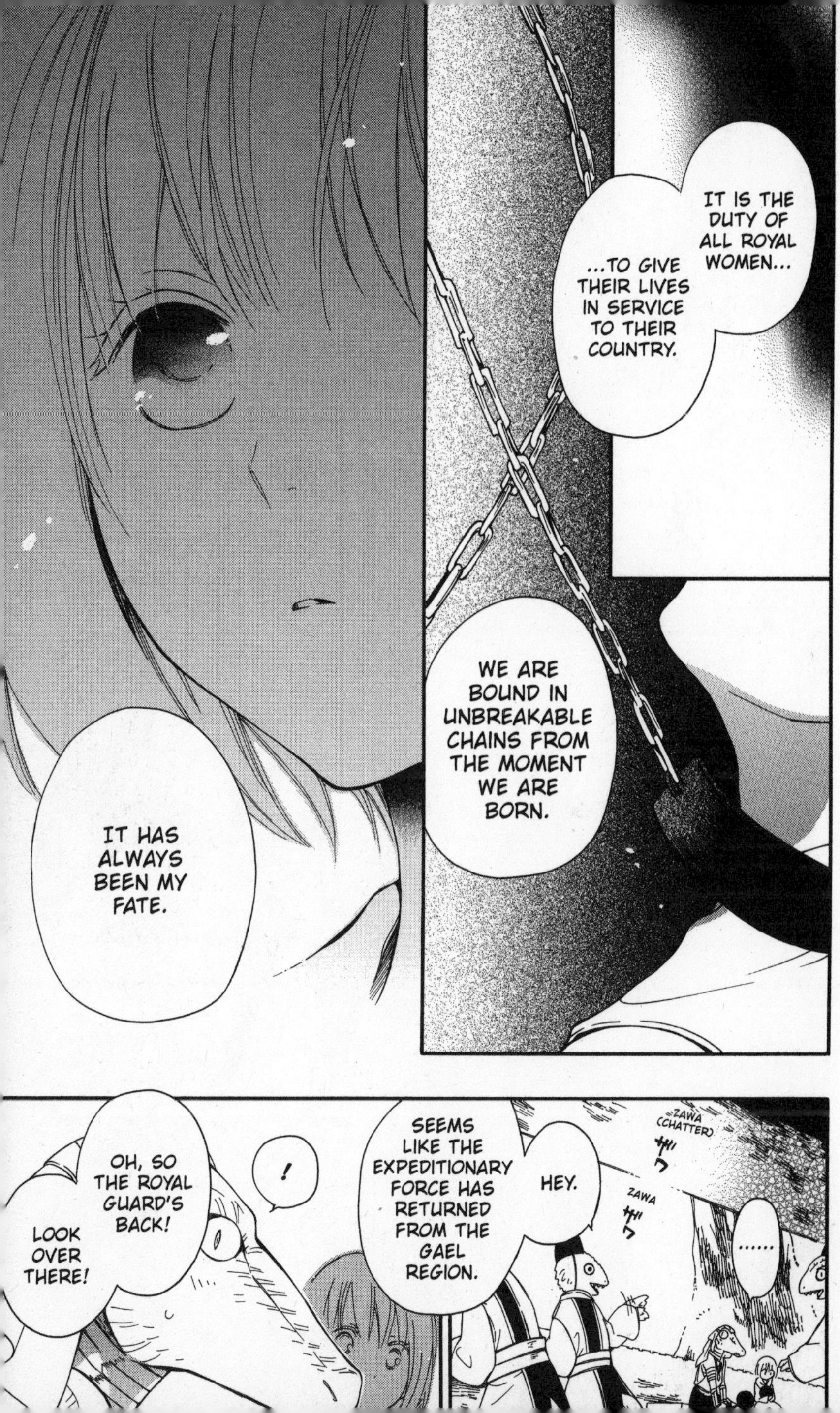
IT IS THE DUTY OF ALL ROYAL WOMEN...
...TO GIVE THEIR LIVES IN SERVICE TO THEIR COUNTRY.
WE ARE BOUND IN UNBREAKABLE CHAINS FROM THE MOMENT WE ARE BORN.
IT HAS ALWAYS BEEN MY FATE.
ZAWA (CHATTER)
ZAWA
......
HEY.
SEEMS LIKE THE EXPEDITIONARY FORCE HAS RETURNED FROM THE GAEL REGION.
!
OH, SO THE ROYAL GUARD'S BACK!
LOOK OVER THERE!

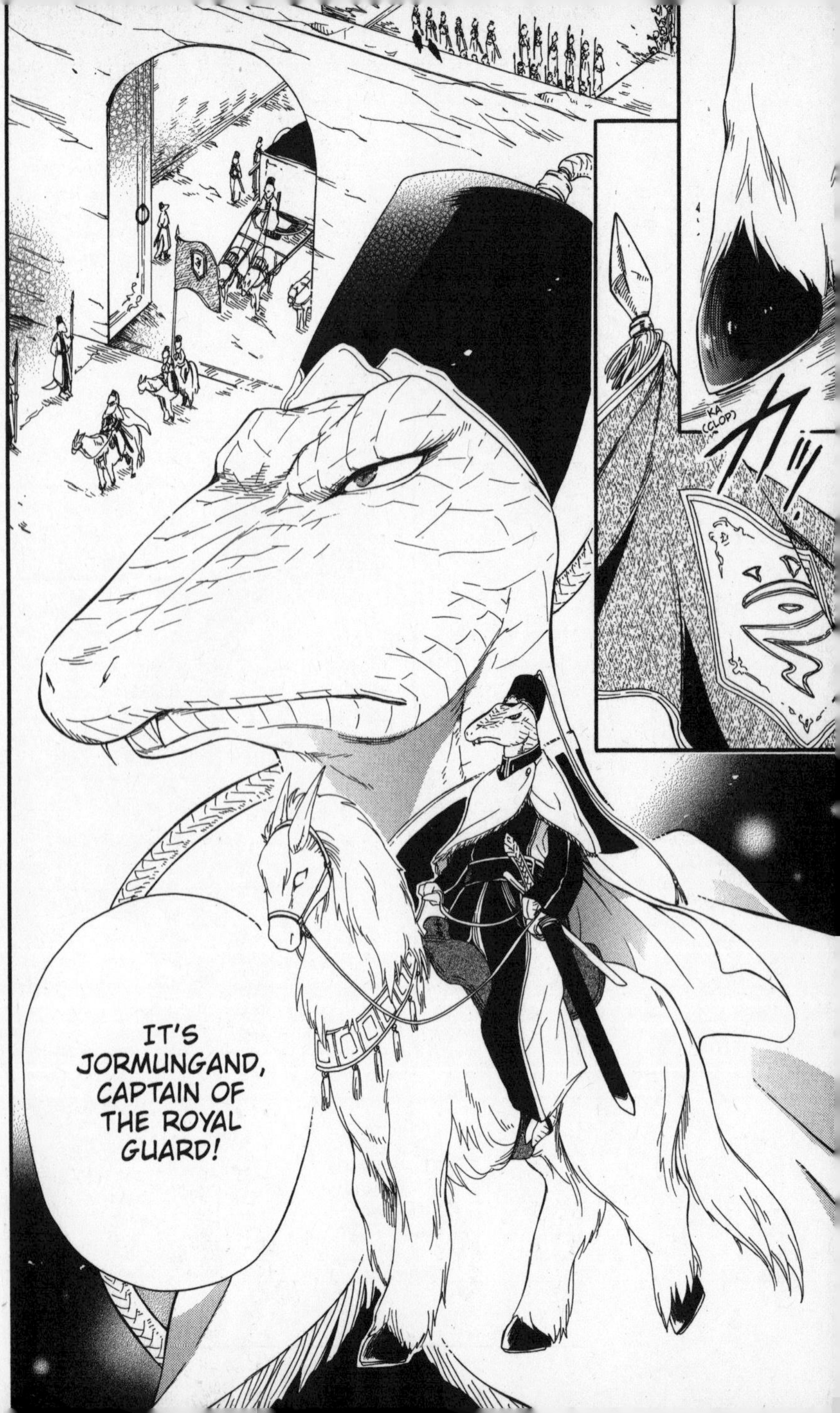
KA (CLOP)
カッ
IT'S JORMUNGAND, CAPTAIN OF THE ROYAL GUARD!

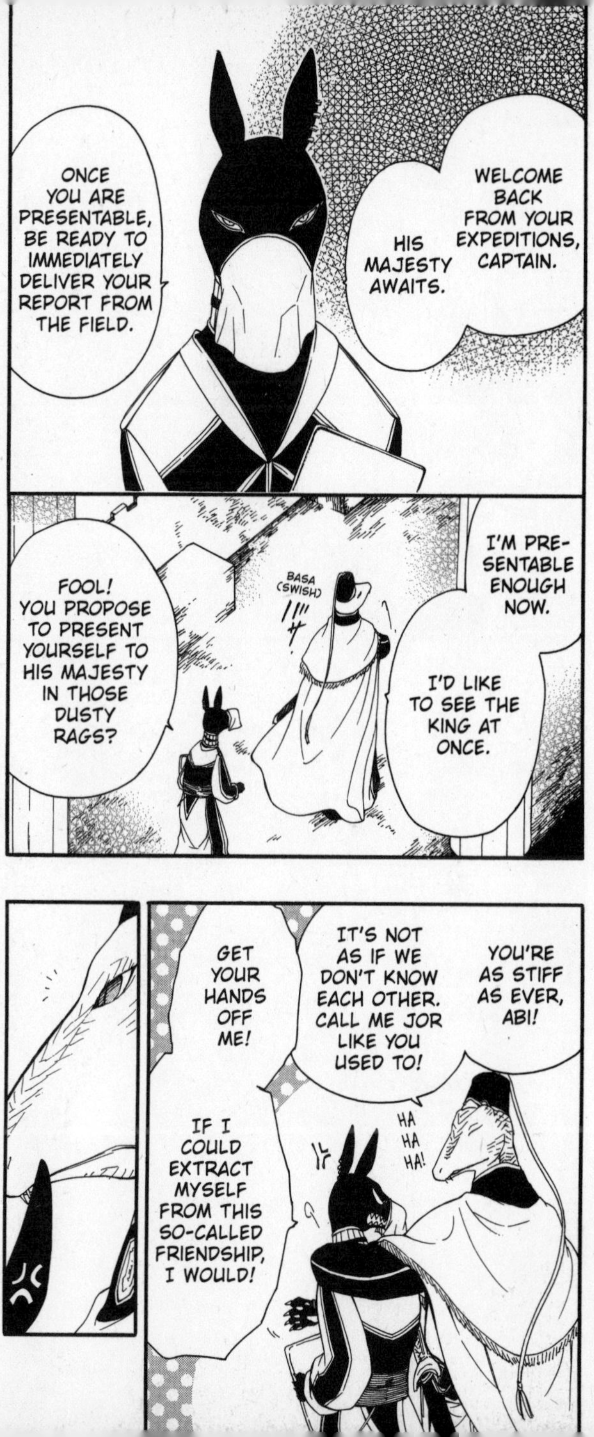
WELCOME BACK FROM YOUR EXPEDITIONS, CAPTAIN.
HIS MAJESTY AWAITS.
ONCE YOU ARE PRESENTABLE, BE READY TO IMMEDIATELY DELIVER YOUR REPORT FROM THE FIELD.
I'M PRE-SENTABLE ENOUGH NOW.
I'D LIKE TO SEE THE KING AT ONCE.
BASA (SWISH)
FOOL! YOU PROPOSE TO PRESENT YOURSELF TO HIS MAJESTY IN THOSE DUSTY RAGS?
YOU'RE AS STIFF AS EVER, ABI!
IT'S NOT AS IF WE DON'T KNOW EACH OTHER. CALL ME JOR LIKE YOU USED TO!
HA HA HA!
GET YOUR HANDS OFF ME!
IF I COULD EXTRACT MYSELF FROM THIS SO-CALLED FRIENDSHIP, I WOULD!

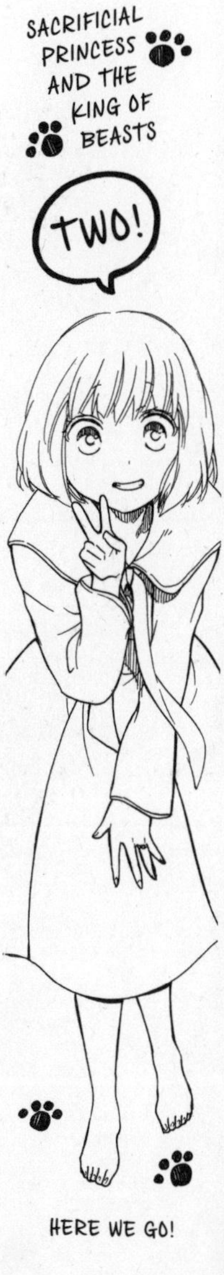
SACRIFICIAL PRINCESS AND THE KING OF BEASTS
TWO!
HERE WE GO!

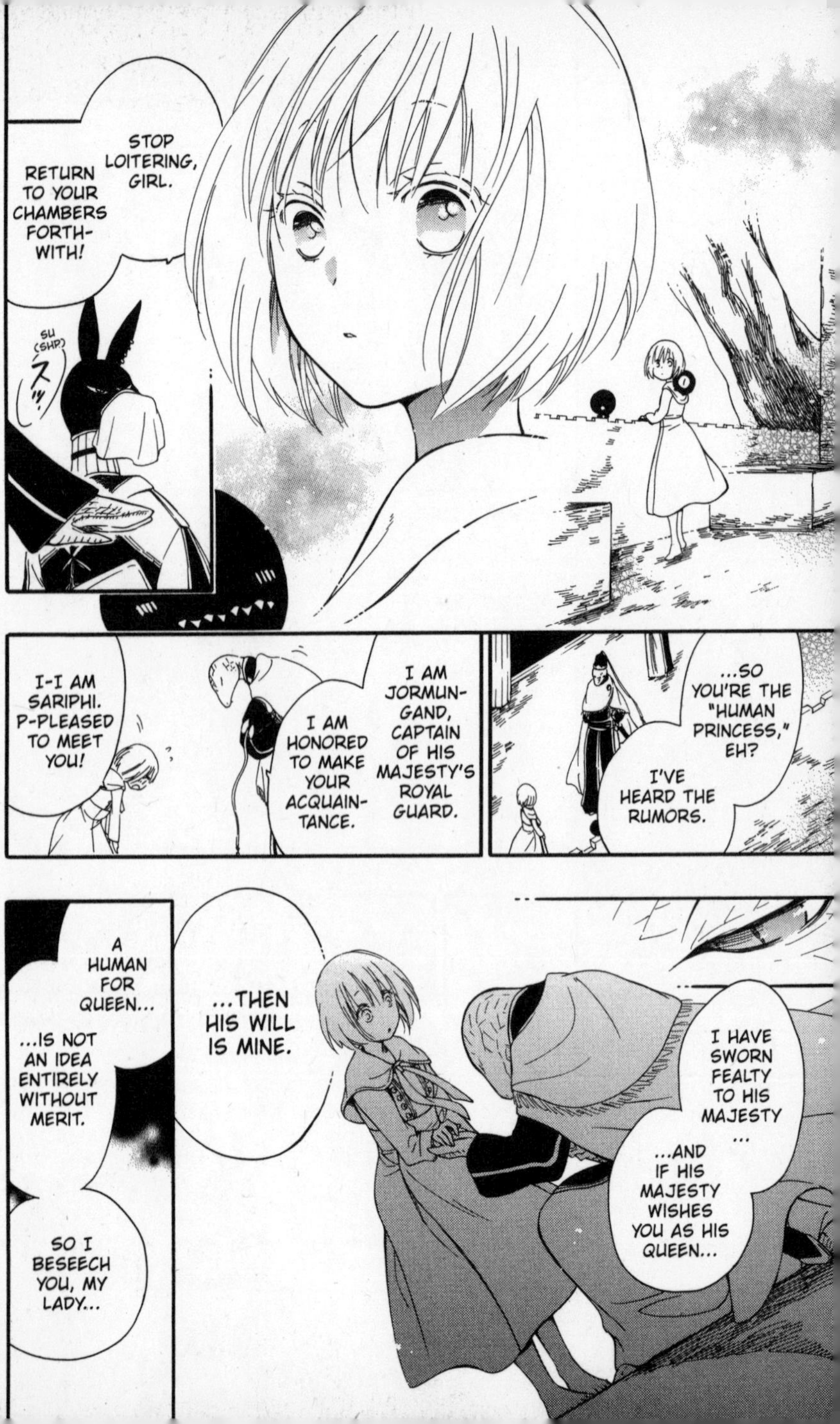
STOP LOITERING, GIRL.
RETURN TO YOUR CHAMBERS FORTHWITH!
SU (SHP)
スッ
...SO YOU'RE THE "HUMAN PRINCESS," EH?
I'VE HEARD THE RUMORS.
I AM JORMUNGAND, CAPTAIN OF HIS MAJESTY'S ROYAL GUARD.
I AM HONORED TO MAKE YOUR ACQUAINTANCE.
I-I AM SARIPHI. P-PLEASED TO MEET YOU!
I HAVE SWORN FEALTY TO HIS MAJESTY...
...AND IF HIS MAJESTY WISHES YOU AS HIS QUEEN...
...THEN HIS WILL IS MINE.
A HUMAN FOR QUEEN...
...IS NOT AN IDEA ENTIRELY WITHOUT MERIT.
SO I BESEECH YOU, MY LADY...

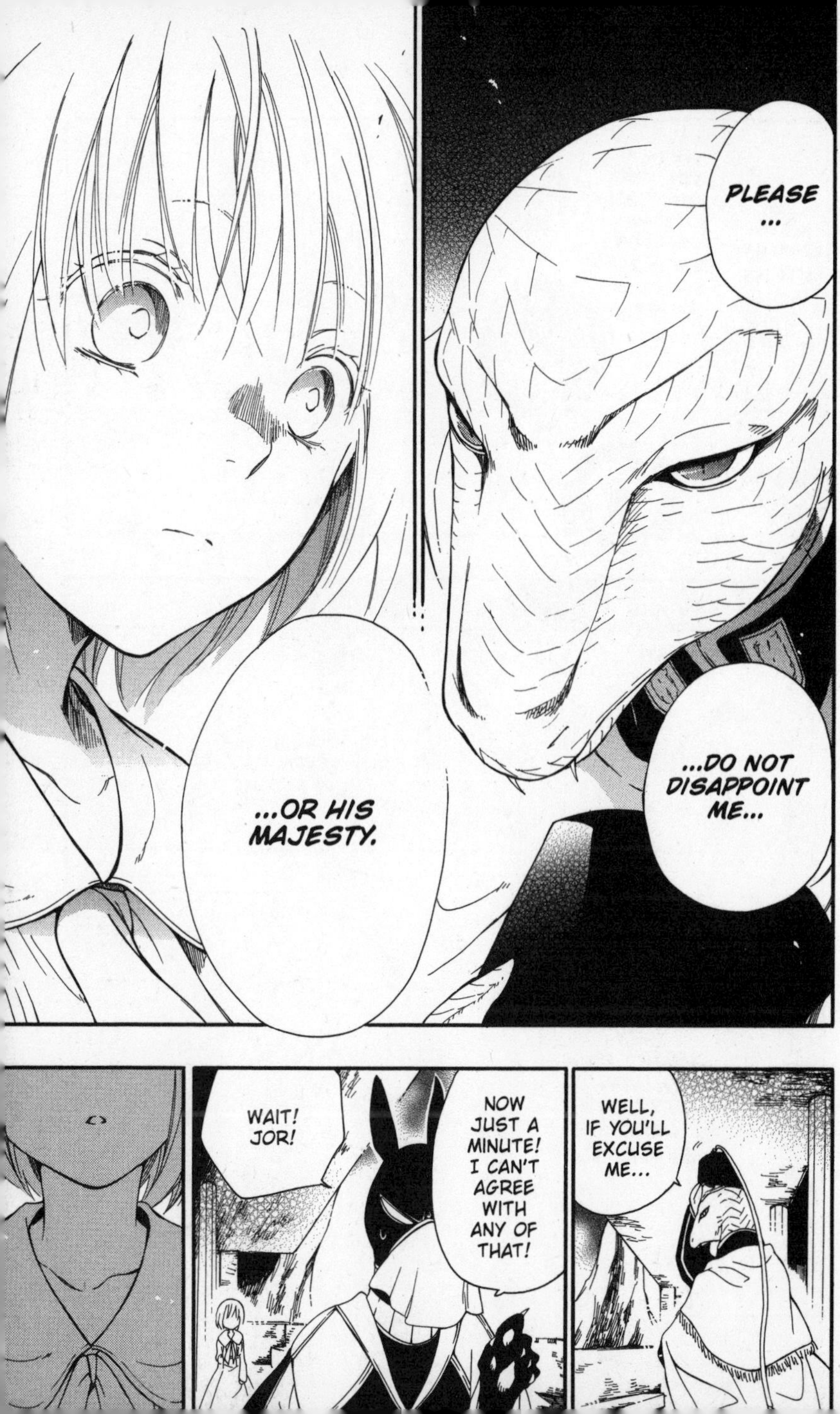
PLEASE ...
...DO NOT DISAPPOINT ME...
...OR HIS MAJESTY.
WELL, IF YOU'LL EXCUSE ME...
NOW JUST A MINUTE! I CAN'T AGREE WITH ANY OF THAT!
WAIT! JOR!

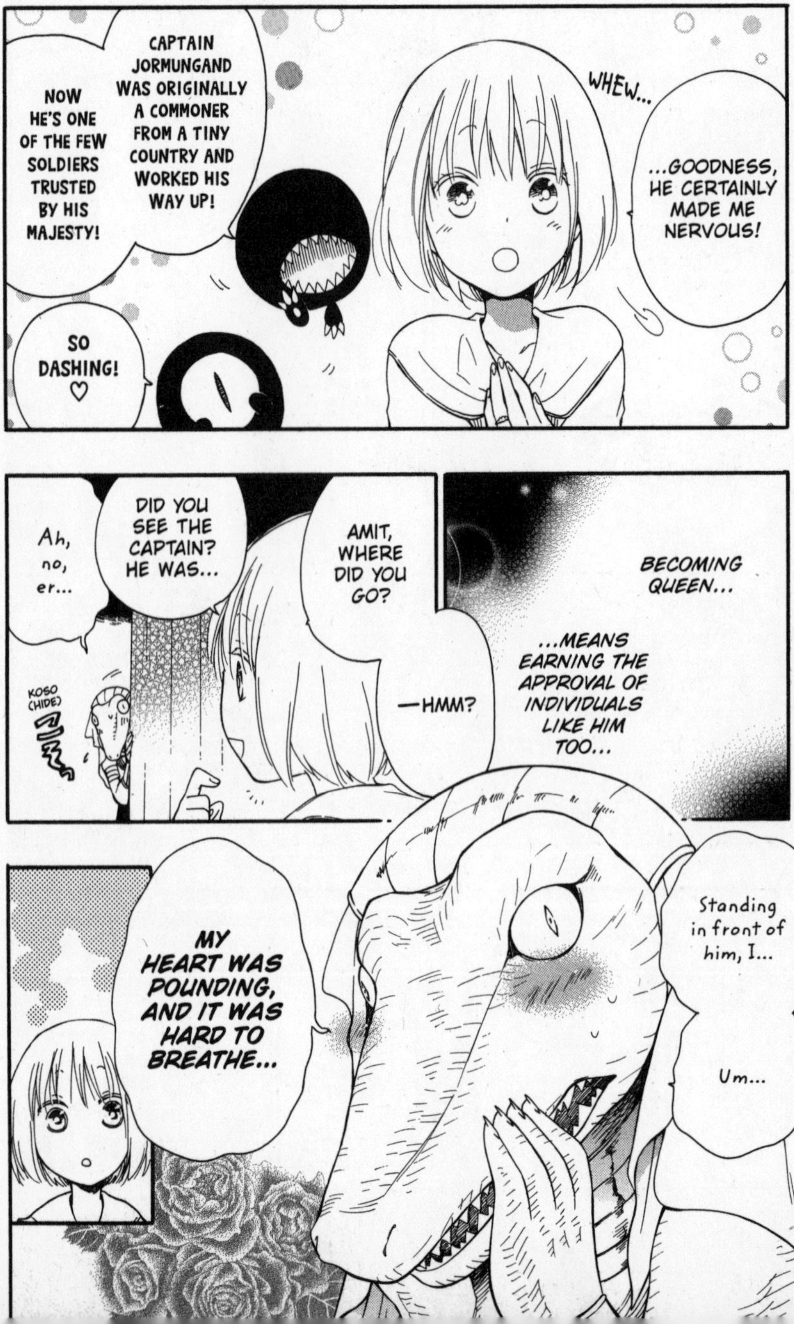
WHEW...
...GOODNESS, HE CERTAINLY MADE ME NERVOUS!
CAPTAIN JORMUNGAND WAS ORIGINALLY A COMMONER FROM A TINY COUNTRY AND WORKED HIS WAY UP!
NOW HE'S ONE OF THE FEW SOLDIERS TRUSTED BY HIS MAJESTY!
SO DASHING! ♡
BECOMING QUEEN...
...MEANS EARNING THE APPROVAL OF INDIVIDUALS LIKE HIM TOO...
AMIT, WHERE DID YOU GO?
—HMM?
DID YOU SEE THE CAPTAIN? HE WAS...
Ah, no, er...
KOSO (HIDE)
Standing in front of him, I...
Um...
MY HEART WAS POUNDING, AND IT WAS HARD TO BREATHE...

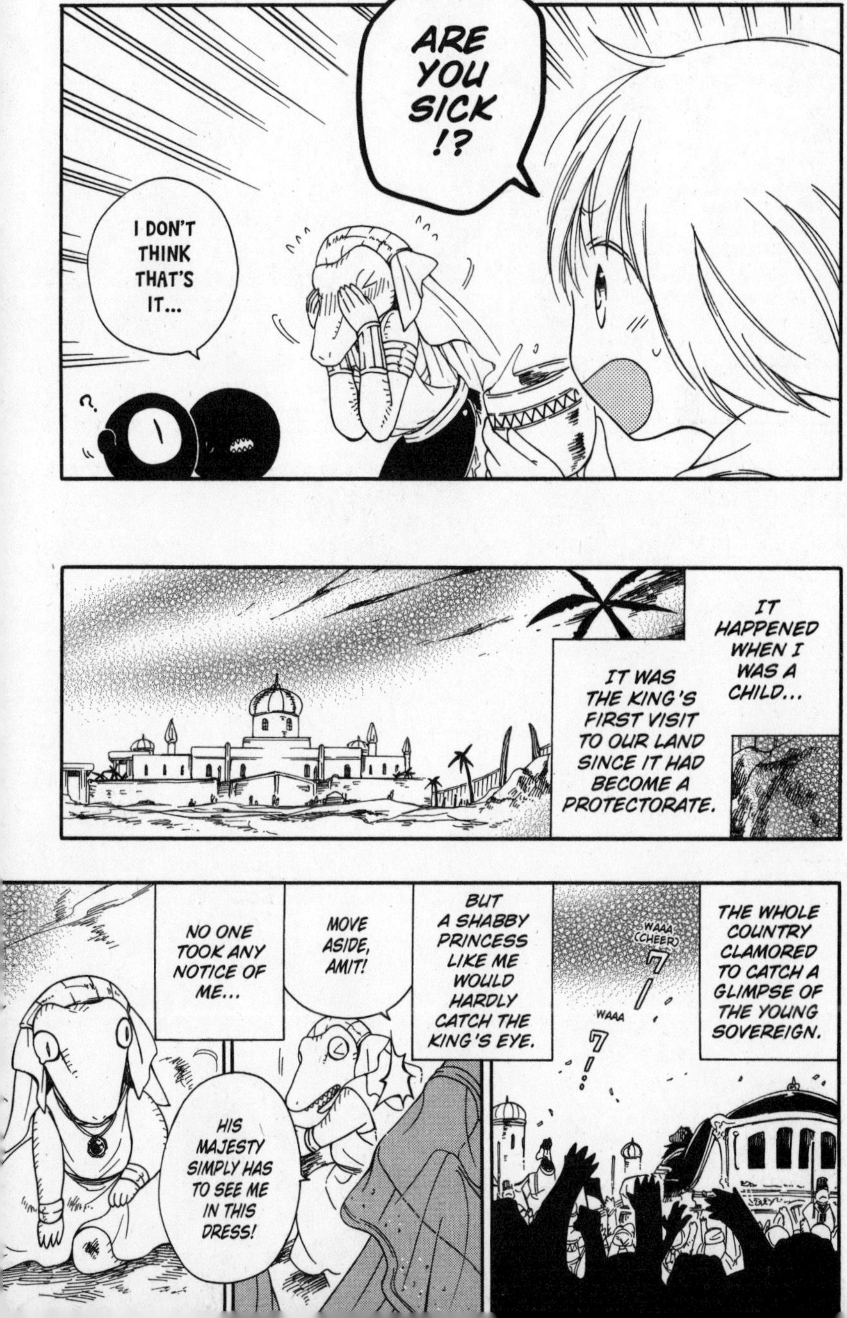
ARE YOU SICK !?
I DON'T THINK THAT'S IT...
IT HAPPENED WHEN I WAS A CHILD...
IT WAS THE KING'S FIRST VISIT TO OUR LAND SINCE IT HAD BECOME A PROTECTORATE.
THE WHOLE COUNTRY CLAMORED TO CATCH A GLIMPSE OF THE YOUNG SOVEREIGN.
WAAA (CHEER)
WAAA
BUT A SHABBY PRINCESS LIKE ME WOULD HARDLY CATCH THE KING'S EYE.
MOVE ASIDE, AMIT!
HIS MAJESTY SIMPLY HAS TO SEE ME IN THIS DRESS!
NO ONE TOOK ANY NOTICE OF ME...

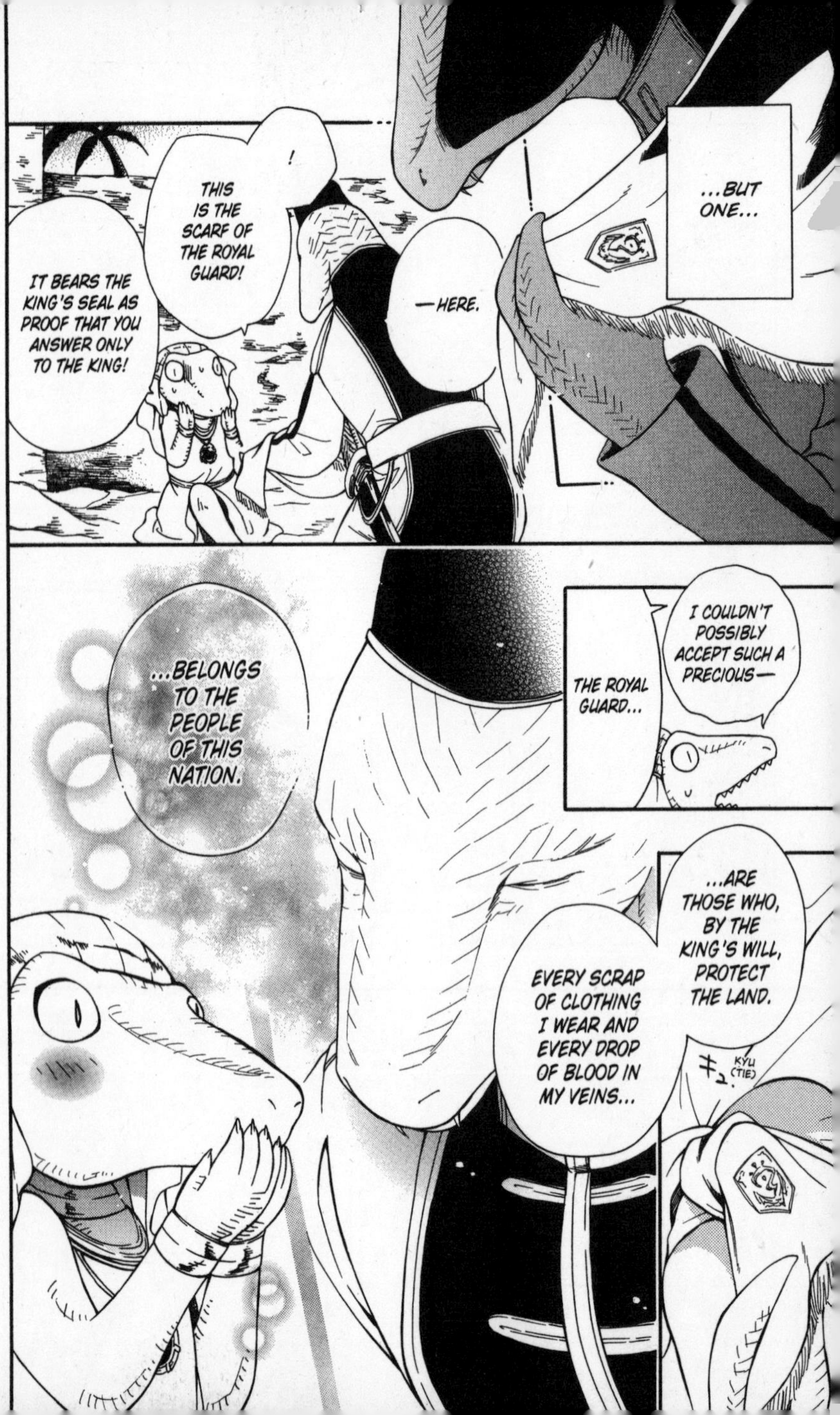
...BUT ONE...
—HERE.
!
THIS IS THE SCARF OF THE ROYAL GUARD!
IT BEARS THE KING'S SEAL AS PROOF THAT YOU ANSWER ONLY TO THE KING!
I COULDN'T POSSIBLY ACCEPT SUCH A PRECIOUS—
THE ROYAL GUARD...
...ARE THOSE WHO, BY THE KING'S WILL, PROTECT THE LAND.
KYU (TIE)
EVERY SCRAP OF CLOTHING I WEAR AND EVERY DROP OF BLOOD IN MY VEINS...
...BELONGS TO THE PEOPLE OF THIS NATION.

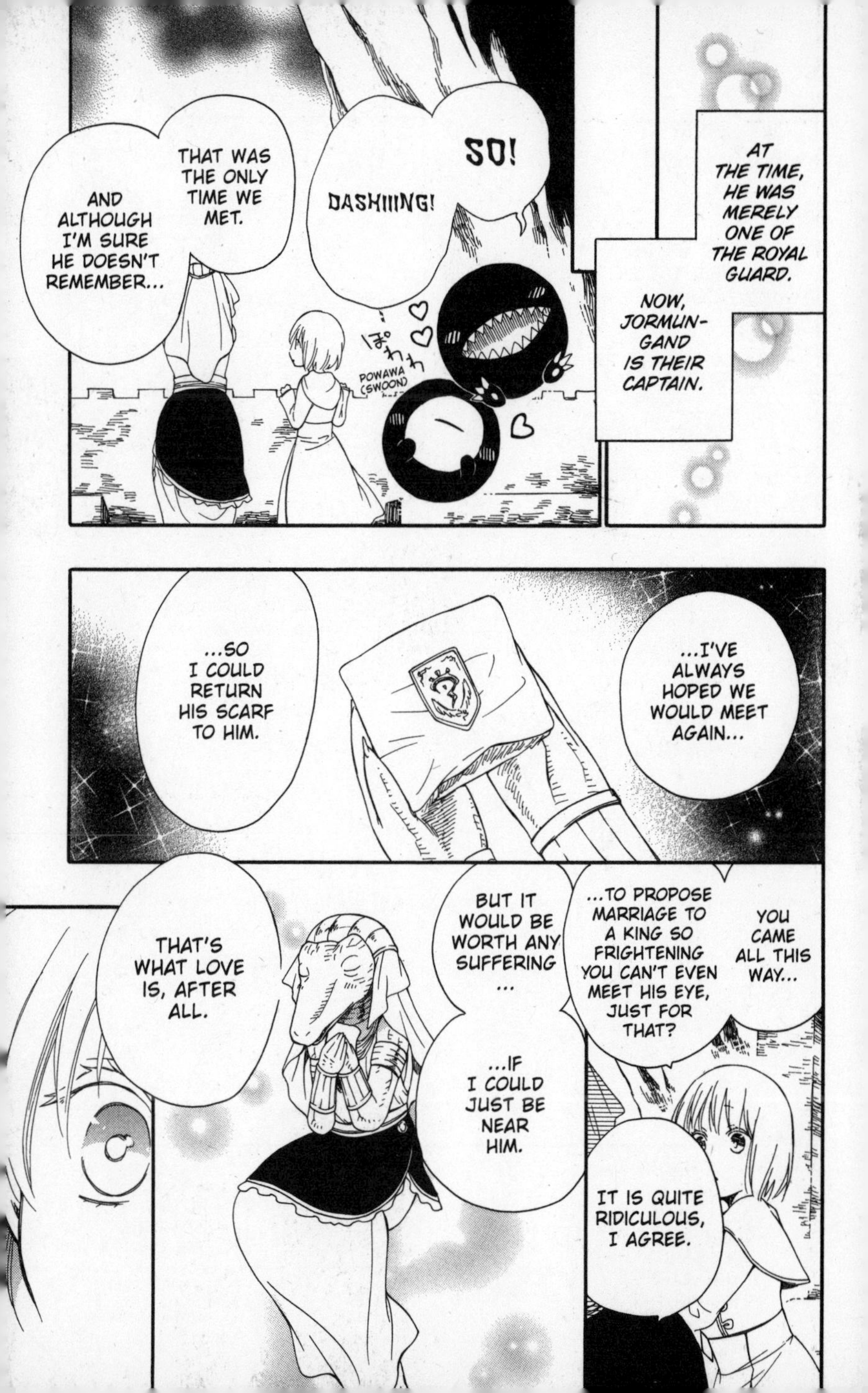
AT THE TIME, HE WAS MERELY ONE OF THE ROYAL GUARD.
NOW, JORMUNGAND IS THEIR CAPTAIN.
SO!
DASHIIIING!
THAT WAS THE ONLY TIME WE MET.
AND ALTHOUGH I'M SURE HE DOESN'T REMEMBER...
ぽわわ
POWAWA (SWOON)
...I'VE ALWAYS HOPED WE WOULD MEET AGAIN...
...SO I COULD RETURN HIS SCARF TO HIM.
YOU CAME ALL THIS WAY...
...TO PROPOSE MARRIAGE TO A KING SO FRIGHTENING YOU CAN'T EVEN MEET HIS EYE, JUST FOR THAT?
IT IS QUITE RIDICULOUS, I AGREE.
BUT IT WOULD BE WORTH ANY SUFFERING...
...IF I COULD JUST BE NEAR HIM.
THAT'S WHAT LOVE IS, AFTER ALL.

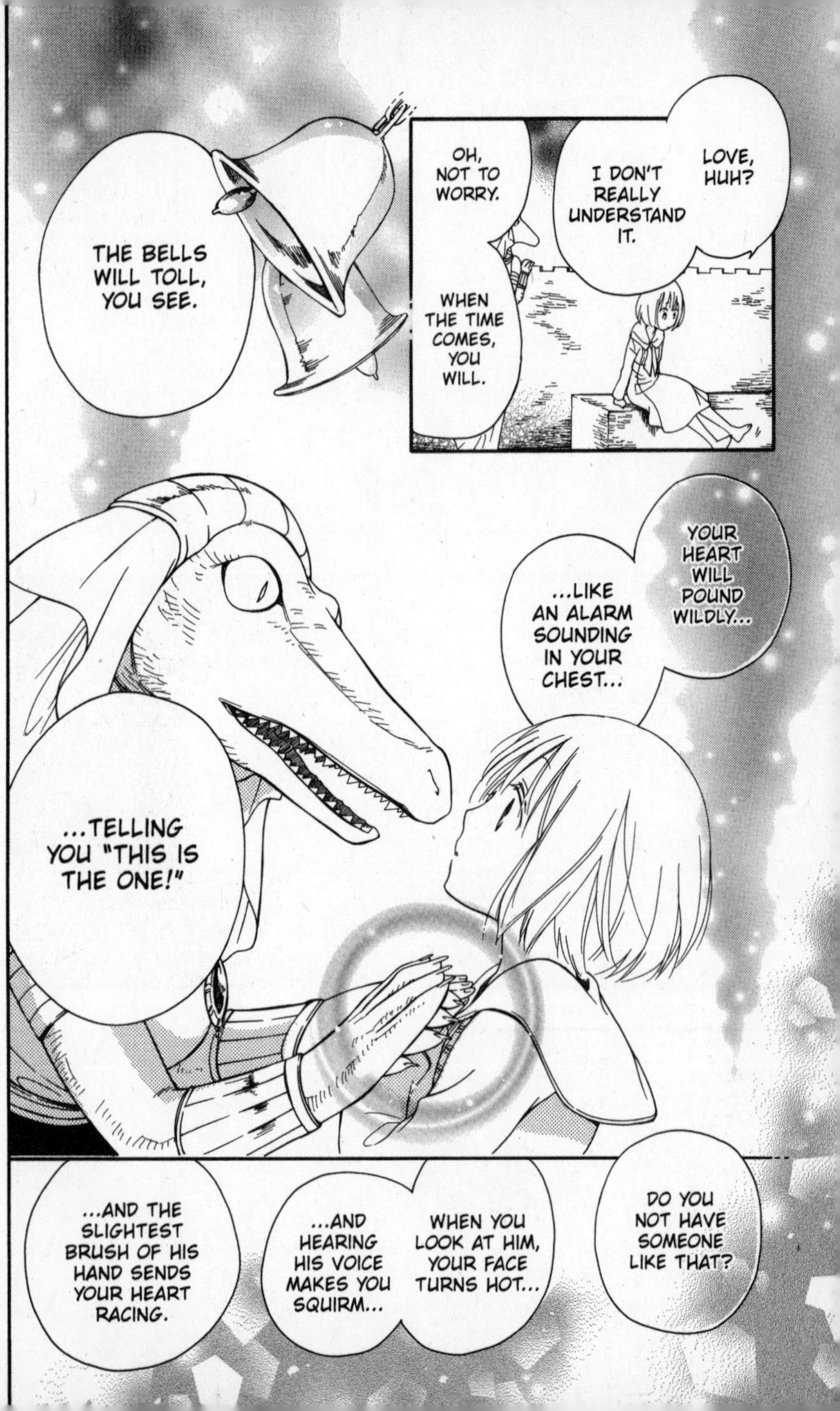
LOVE, HUH?
I DON'T REALLY UNDERSTAND IT.
OH, NOT TO WORRY.
WHEN THE TIME COMES, YOU WILL.
THE BELLS WILL TOLL, YOU SEE.
YOUR HEART WILL POUND WILDLY...
...LIKE AN ALARM SOUNDING IN YOUR CHEST...
...TELLING YOU "THIS IS THE ONE!"
DO YOU NOT HAVE SOMEONE LIKE THAT?
WHEN YOU LOOK AT HIM, YOUR FACE TURNS HOT...
...AND HEARING HIS VOICE MAKES YOU SQUIRM...
...AND THE SLIGHTEST BRUSH OF HIS HAND SENDS YOUR HEART RACING.

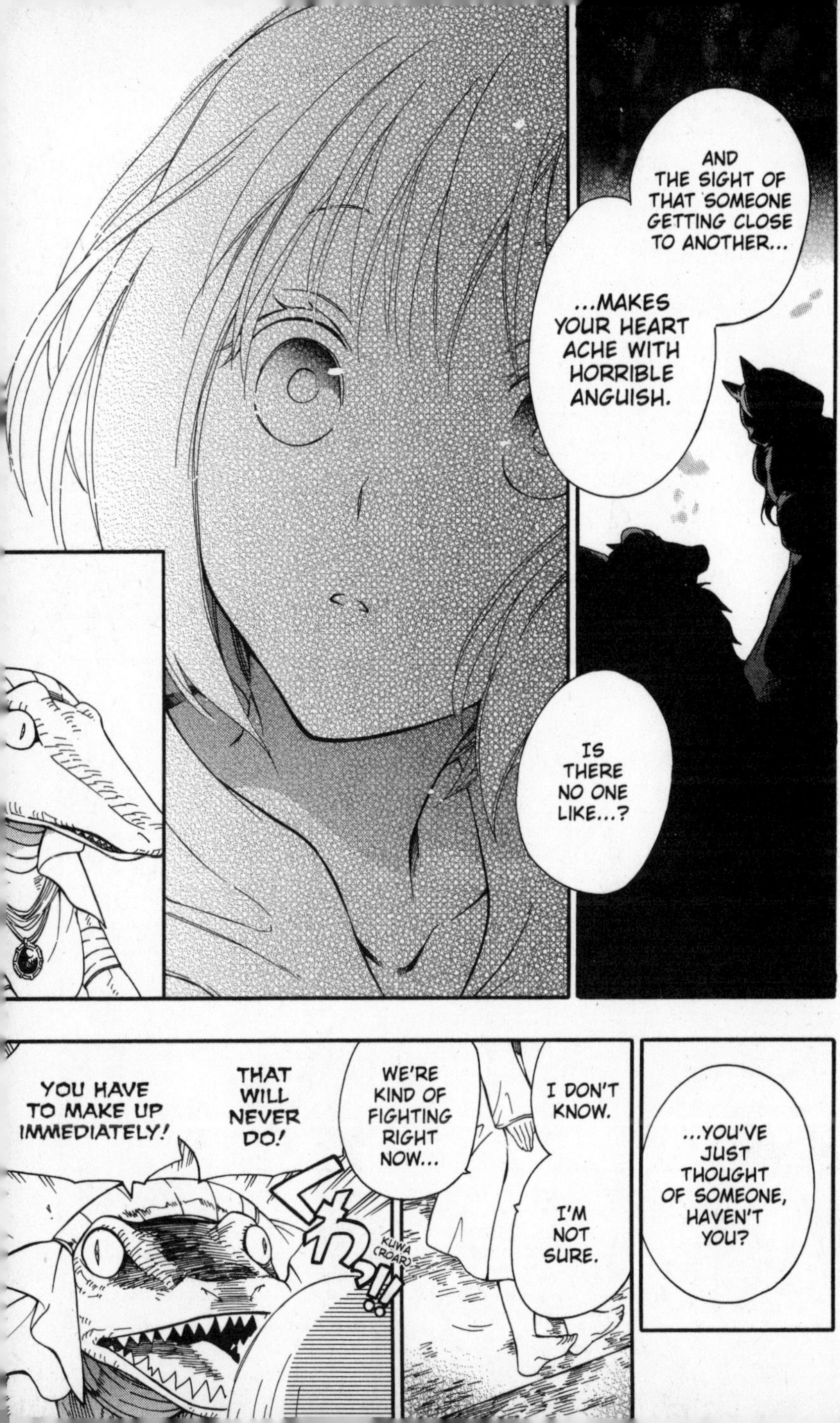
AND THE SIGHT OF THAT SOMEONE GETTING CLOSE TO ANOTHER...
...MAKES YOUR HEART ACHE WITH HORRIBLE ANGUISH.
IS THERE NO ONE LIKE...?
...YOU'VE JUST THOUGHT OF SOMEONE, HAVEN'T YOU?
I DON'T KNOW.
I'M NOT SURE.
WE'RE KIND OF FIGHTING RIGHT NOW...
KUWA (ROAR)
THAT WILL NEVER DO!
YOU HAVE TO MAKE UP IMMEDIATELY!

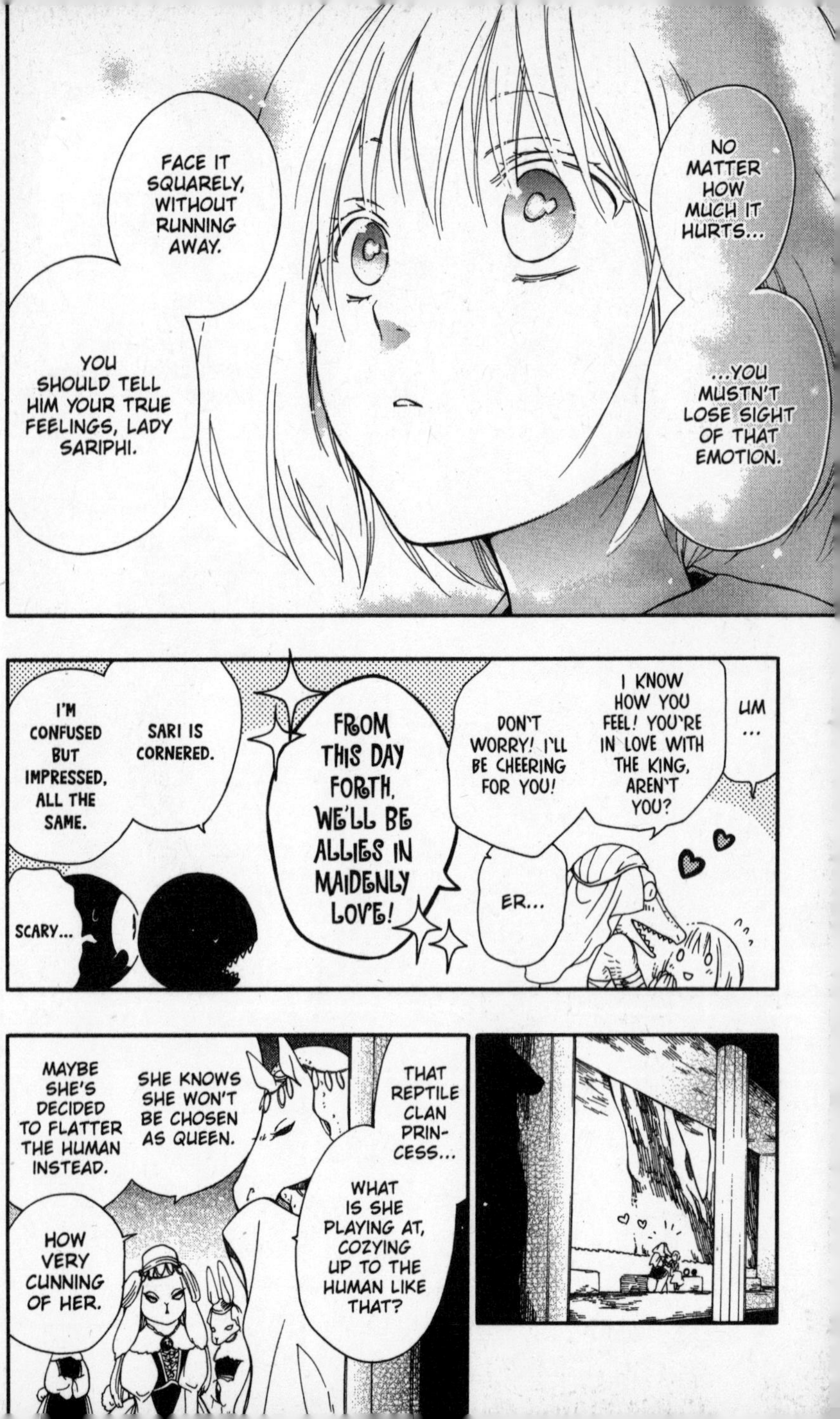
NO MATTER HOW MUCH IT HURTS...
...YOU MUSTN'T LOSE SIGHT OF THAT EMOTION.
FACE IT SQUARELY, WITHOUT RUNNING AWAY.
YOU SHOULD TELL HIM YOUR TRUE FEELINGS, LADY SARIPHI.
UM ...
I KNOW HOW YOU FEEL! YOU'RE IN LOVE WITH THE KING, AREN'T YOU?
DON'T WORRY! I'LL BE CHEERING FOR YOU!
ER...
FROM THIS DAY FORTH, WE'LL BE ALLIES IN MAIDENLY LOVE!
SARI IS CORNERED.
I'M CONFUSED BUT IMPRESSED, ALL THE SAME.
SCARY...
THAT REPTILE CLAN PRINCESS...
WHAT IS SHE PLAYING AT, COZYING UP TO THE HUMAN LIKE THAT?
SHE KNOWS SHE WON'T BE CHOSEN AS QUEEN.
MAYBE SHE'S DECIDED TO FLATTER THE HUMAN INSTEAD.
HOW VERY CUNNING OF HER.

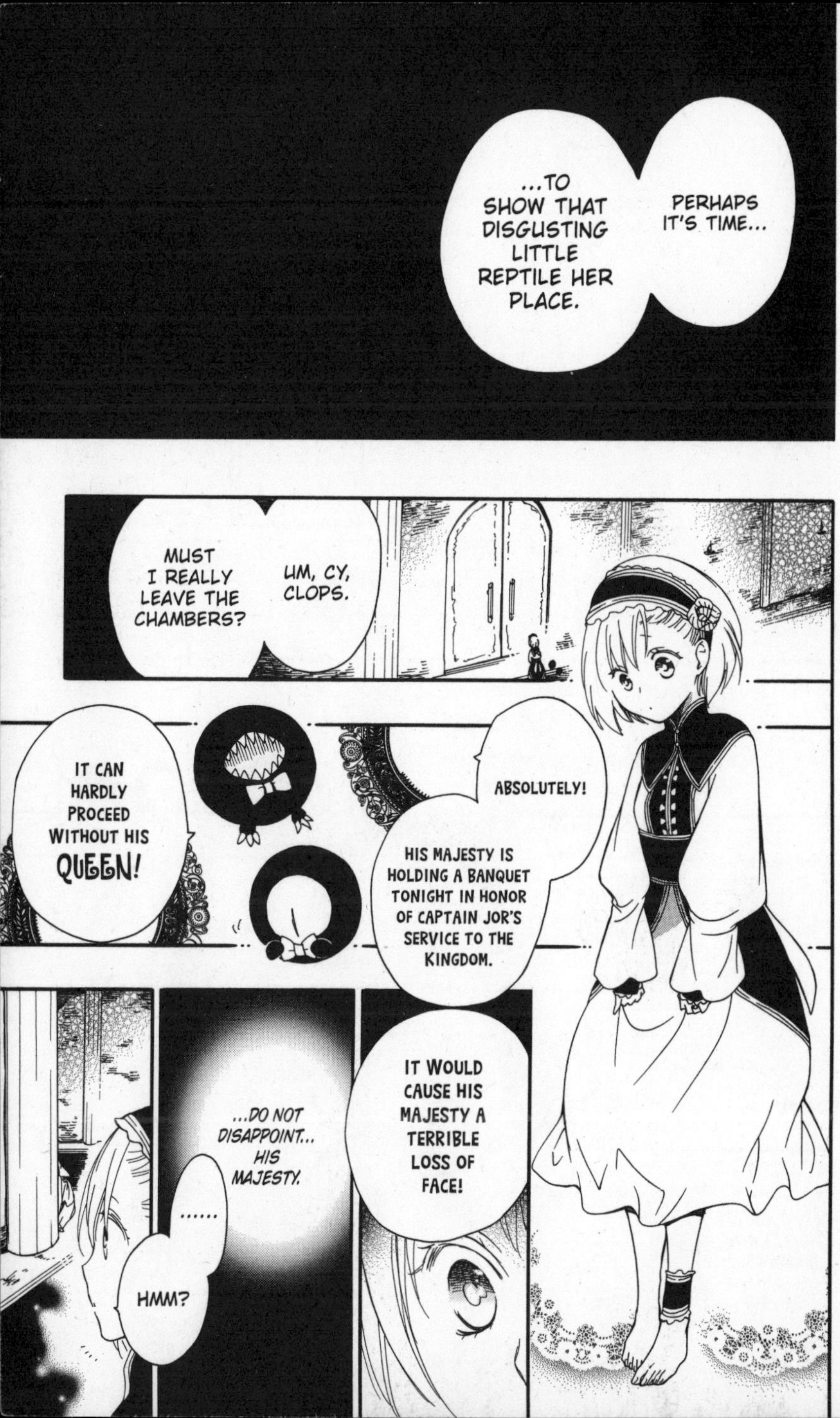
PERHAPS IT'S TIME...
...TO SHOW THAT DISGUSTING LITTLE REPTILE HER PLACE.
UM, CY, CLOPS.
MUST I REALLY LEAVE THE CHAMBERS?
ABSOLUTELY!
HIS MAJESTY IS HOLDING A BANQUET TONIGHT IN HONOR OF CAPTAIN JOR'S SERVICE TO THE KINGDOM.
IT CAN HARDLY PROCEED WITHOUT HIS QUEEN!
IT WOULD CAUSE HIS MAJESTY A TERRIBLE LOSS OF FACE!
...DO NOT DISAPPOINT... HIS MAJESTY.
......
HMM?

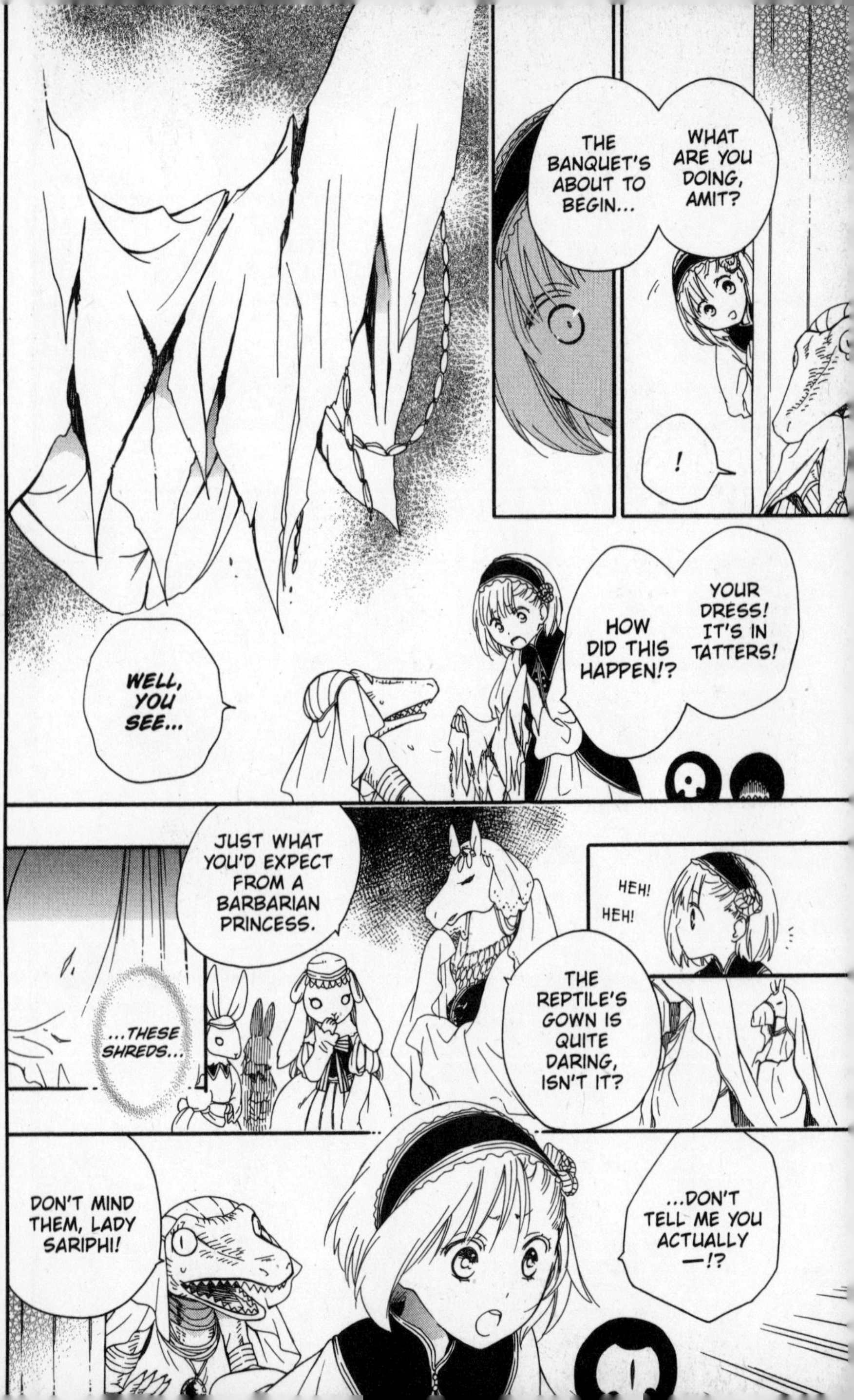
WHAT ARE YOU DOING, AMIT?
THE BANQUET'S ABOUT TO BEGIN...
!
YOUR DRESS! IT'S IN TATTERS!
HOW DID THIS HAPPEN!?
WELL, YOU SEE...
HEH! HEH!
THE REPTILE'S GOWN IS QUITE DARING, ISN'T IT?
JUST WHAT YOU'D EXPECT FROM A BARBARIAN PRINCESS.
...THESE SHREDS...
...DON'T TELL ME YOU ACTUALLY—!?
DON'T MIND THEM, LADY SARIPHI!

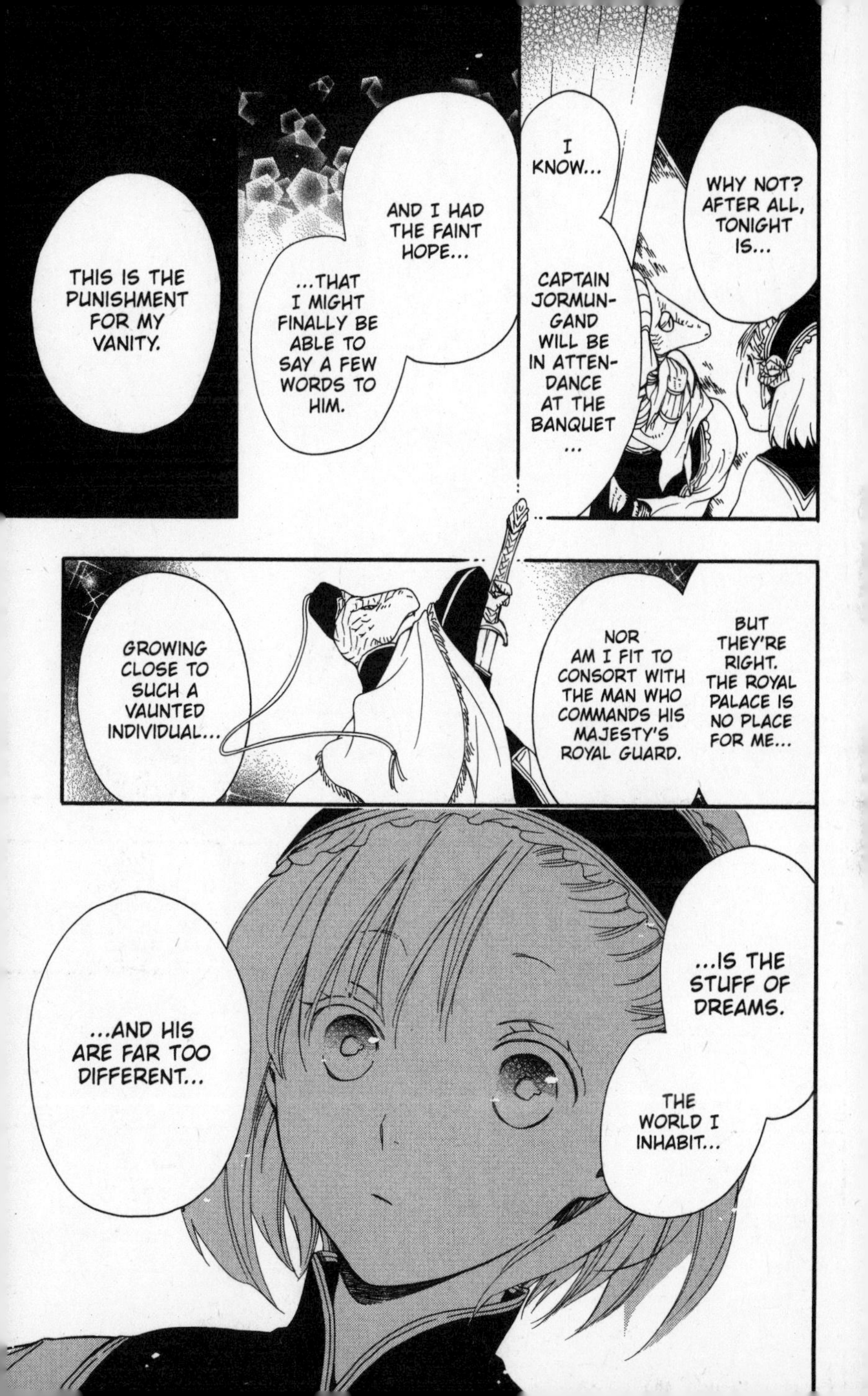
WHY NOT? AFTER ALL, TONIGHT IS...
I KNOW...
CAPTAIN JORMUNGAND WILL BE IN ATTENDANCE AT THE BANQUET...
AND I HAD THE FAINT HOPE...
...THAT I MIGHT FINALLY BE ABLE TO SAY A FEW WORDS TO HIM.
THIS IS THE PUNISHMENT FOR MY VANITY.
BUT THEY'RE RIGHT. THE ROYAL PALACE IS NO PLACE FOR ME...
NOR AM I FIT TO CONSORT WITH THE MAN WHO COMMANDS HIS MAJESTY'S ROYAL GUARD.
GROWING CLOSE TO SUCH A VAUNTED INDIVIDUAL...
...IS THE STUFF OF DREAMS.
THE WORLD I INHABIT...
...AND HIS ARE FAR TOO DIFFERENT...

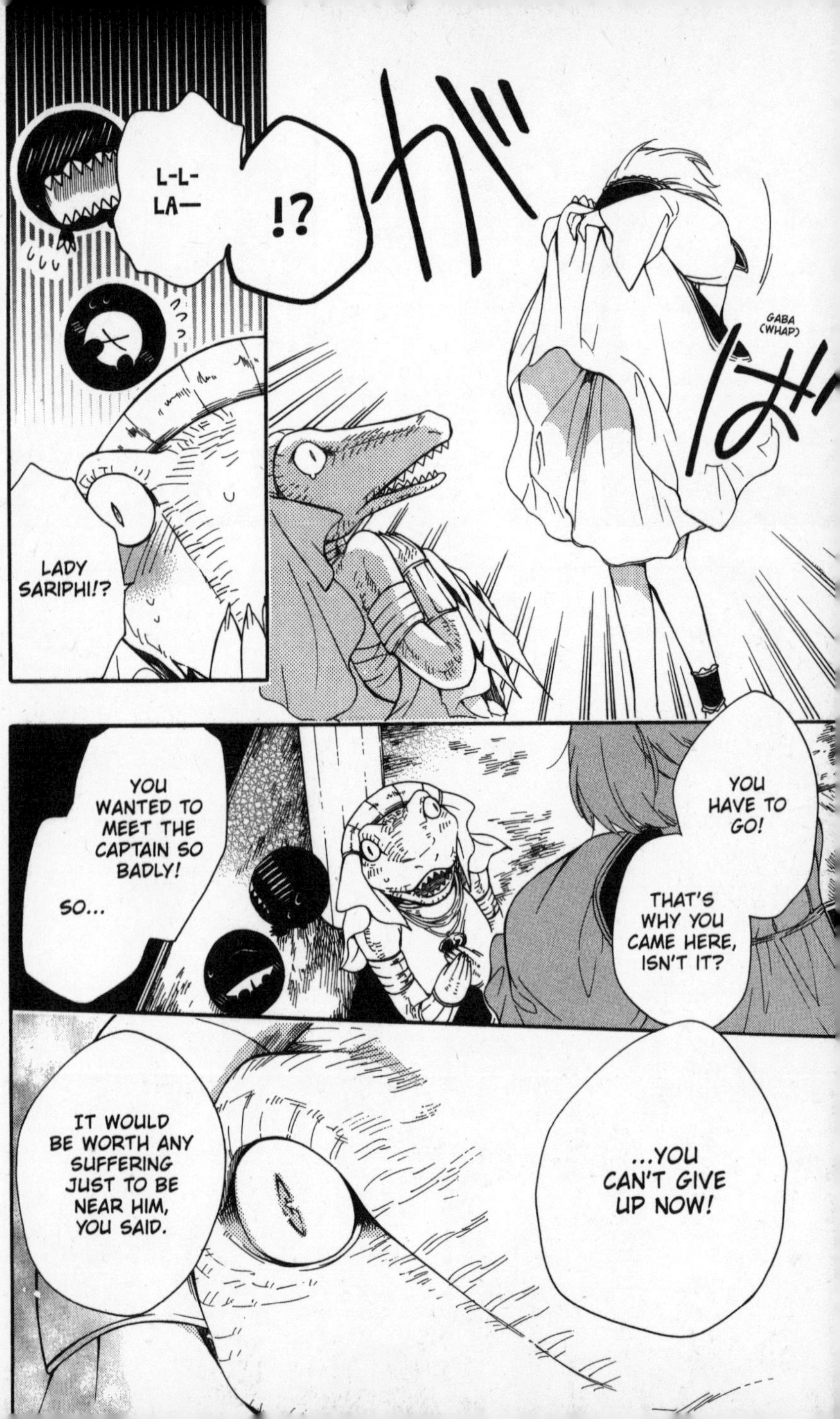
GABA (WHAP)
L-L-LA— !?
LADY SARIPHI!?
YOU HAVE TO GO!
THAT'S WHY YOU CAME HERE, ISN'T IT?
YOU WANTED TO MEET THE CAPTAIN SO BADLY!
SO...
...YOU CAN'T GIVE UP NOW!
IT WOULD BE WORTH ANY SUFFERING JUST TO BE NEAR HIM, YOU SAID.

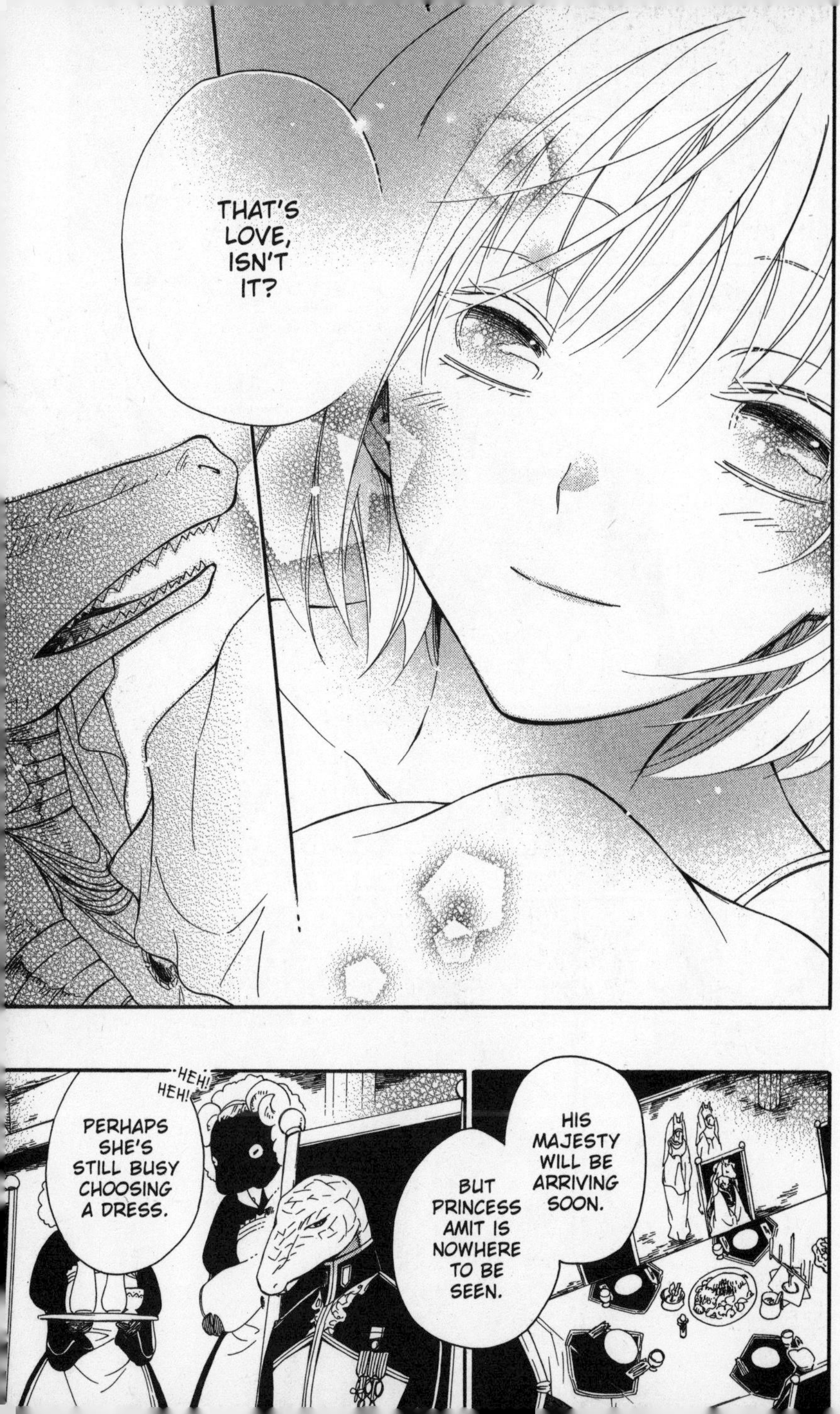
THAT'S LOVE, ISN'T IT?
HIS MAJESTY WILL BE ARRIVING SOON.
BUT PRINCESS AMIT IS NOWHERE TO BE SEEN.
HEH! HEH!
PERHAPS SHE'S STILL BUSY CHOOSING A DRESS.

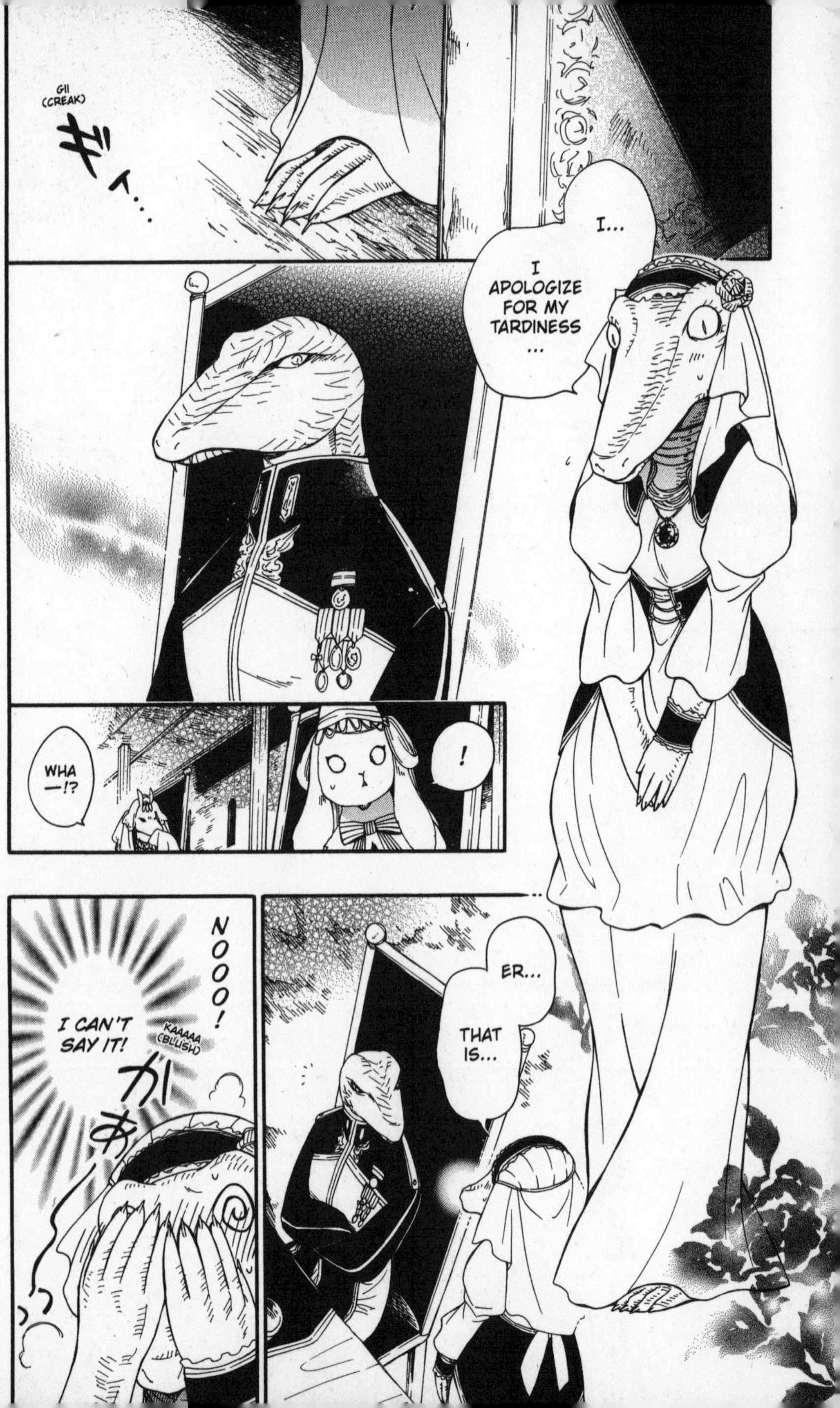
GII (CREAK)
ギイ…
I...
I APOLOGIZE FOR MY TARDINESS ...
ER...
THAT IS...
!
WHA—!?
NOOOO!
I CAN'T SAY IT!
KAAAAA (BLUSH)
かあ

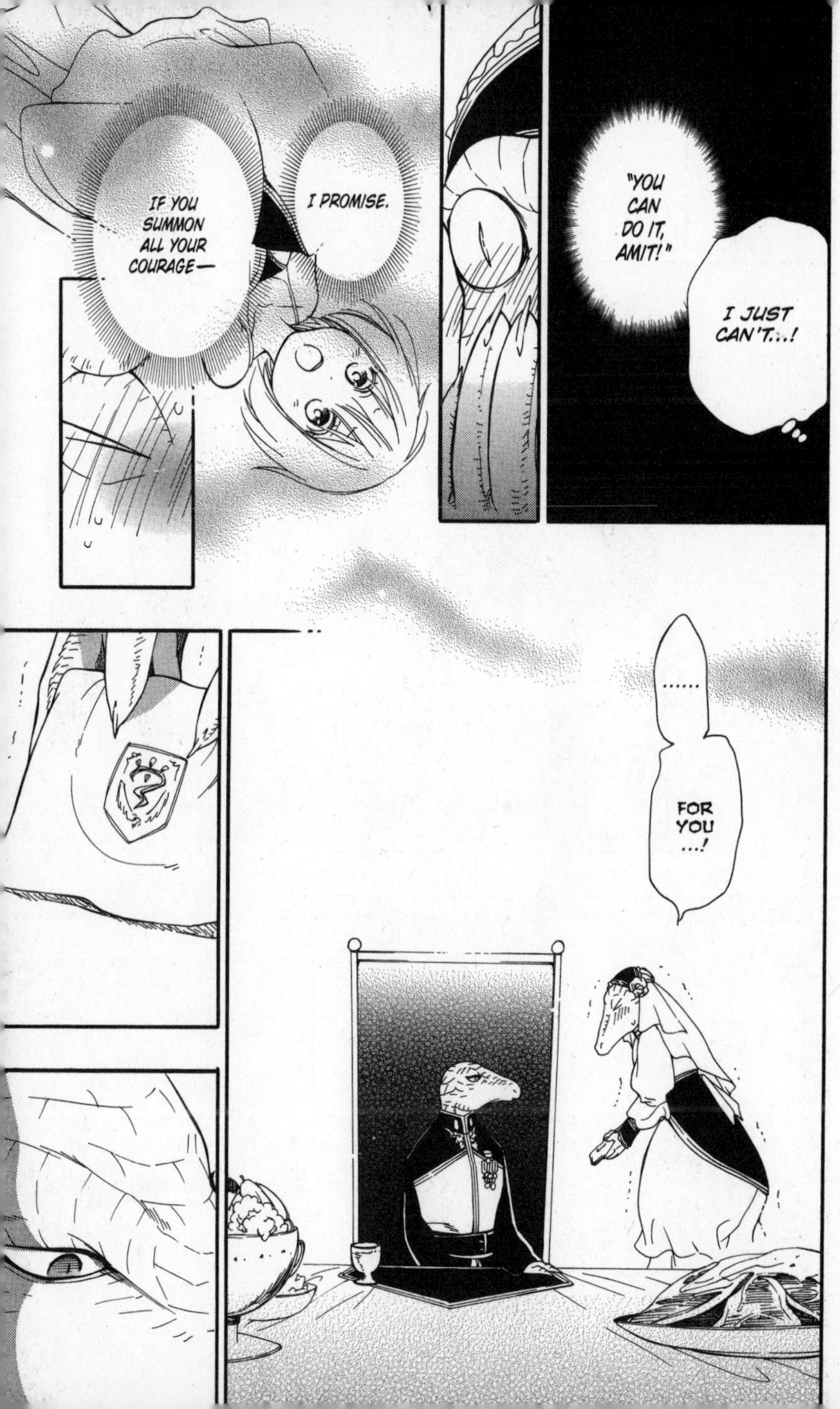
"YOU CAN DO IT, AMIT!"
I JUST CAN'T...!
I PROMISE.
IF YOU SUMMON ALL YOUR COURAGE—
......
FOR YOU...!

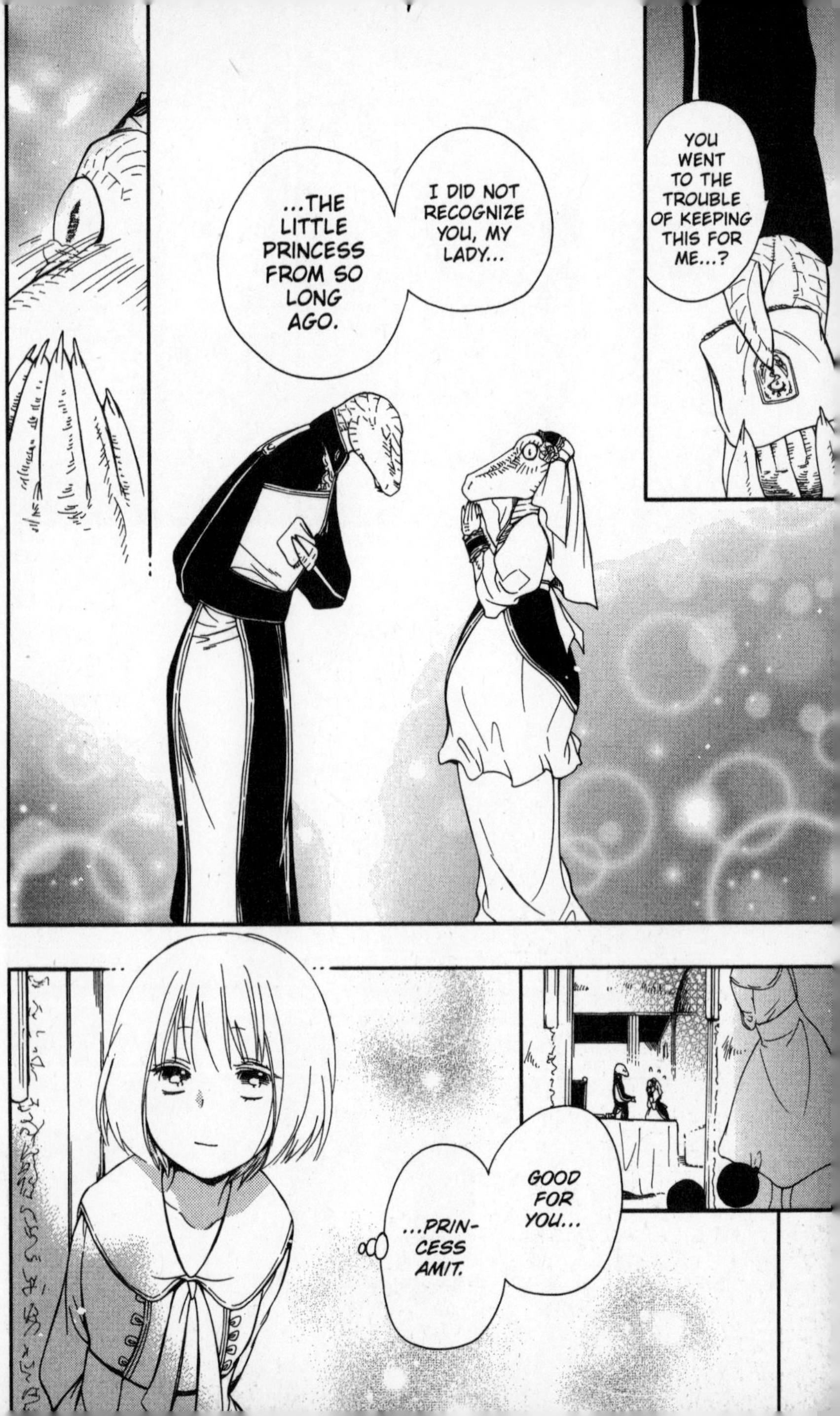
YOU WENT TO THE TROUBLE OF KEEPING THIS FOR ME...?
I DID NOT RECOGNIZE YOU, MY LADY...
...THE LITTLE PRINCESS FROM SO LONG AGO.
GOOD FOR YOU...
...PRIN-CESS AMIT.

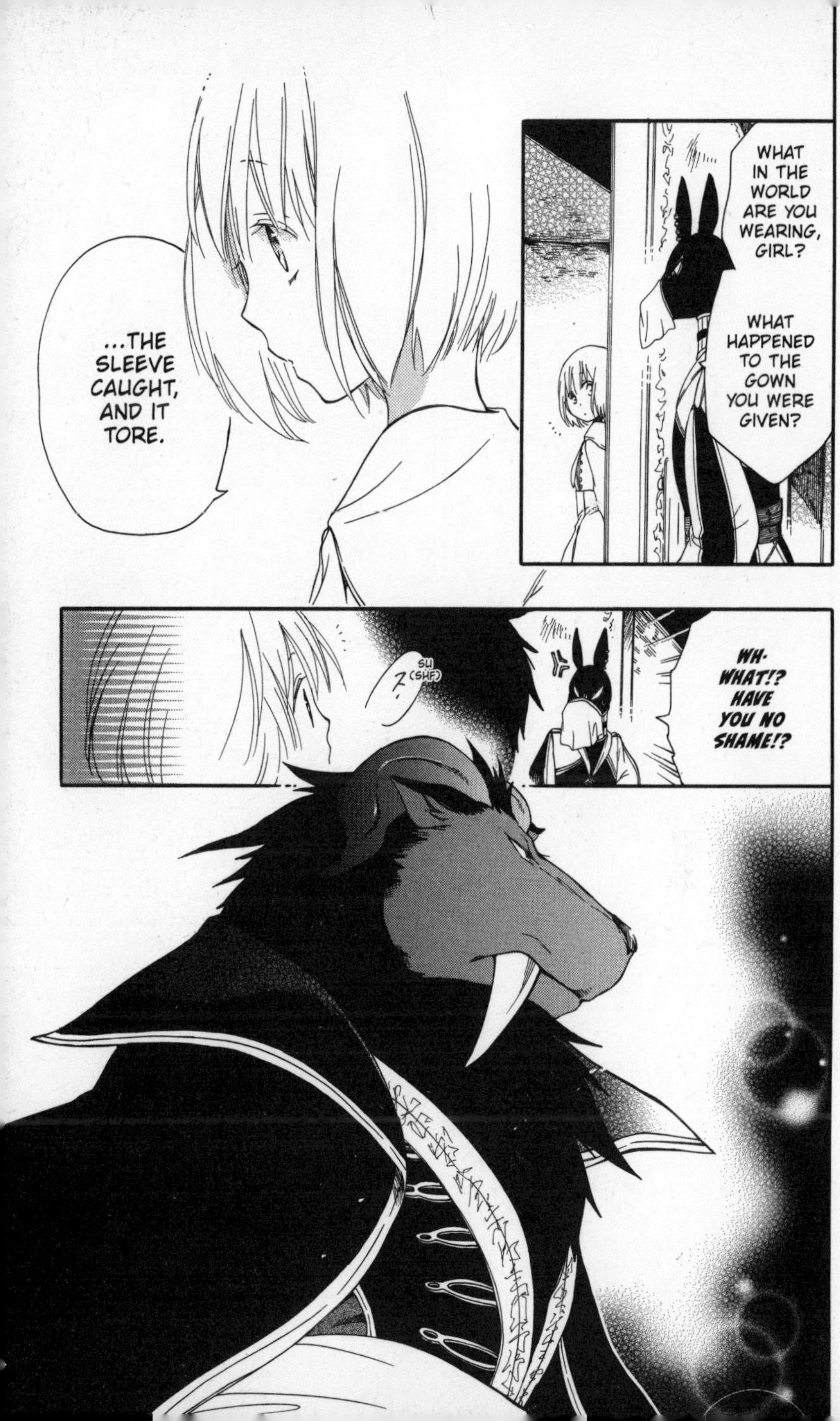
WHAT IN THE WORLD ARE YOU WEARING, GIRL?
WHAT HAPPENED TO THE GOWN YOU WERE GIVEN?
...THE SLEEVE CAUGHT, AND IT TORE.
WH-WHAT!? HAVE YOU NO SHAME!?
SU (SHF)

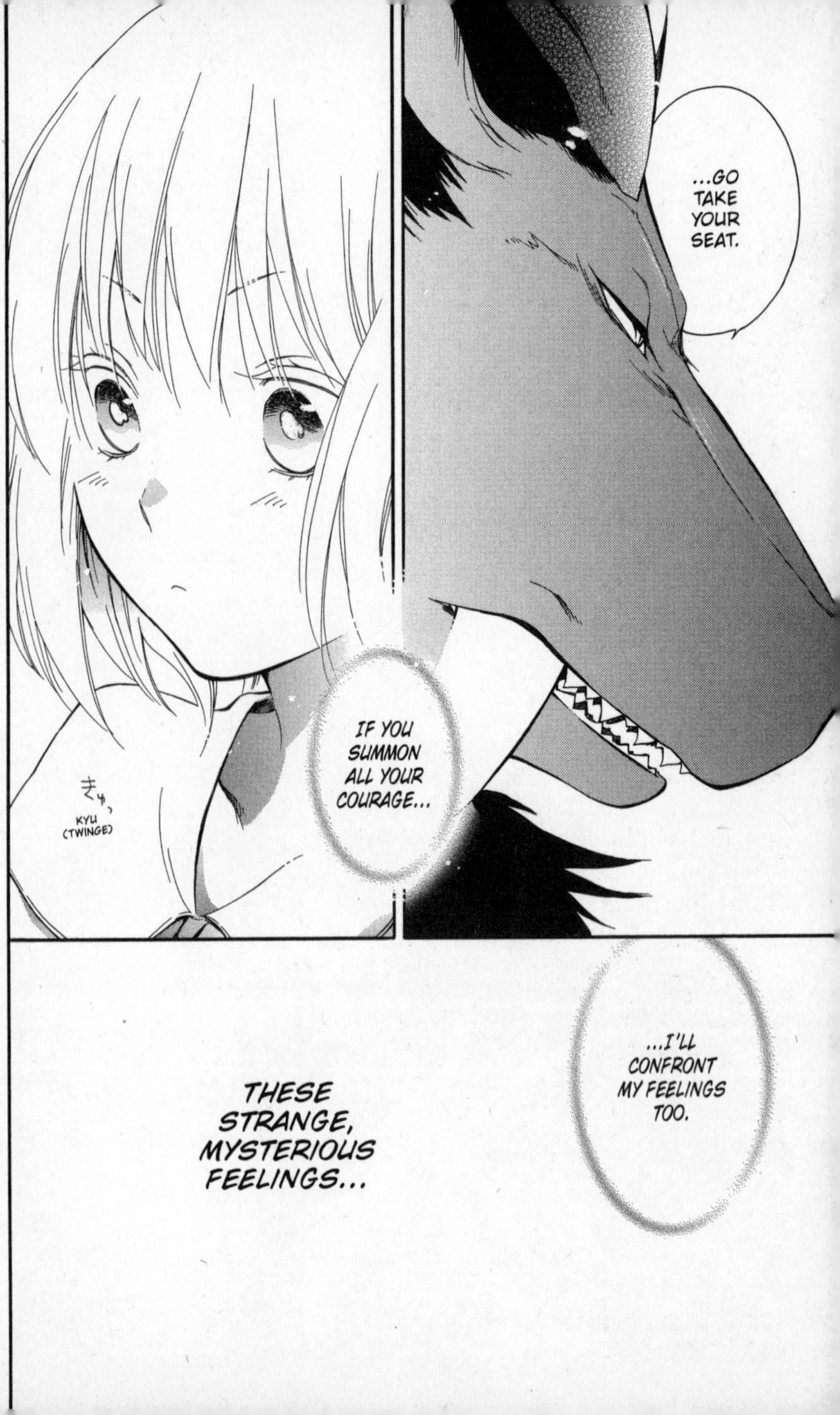
...GO TAKE YOUR SEAT.
IF YOU SUMMON ALL YOUR COURAGE...
きゅっ
KYU (TWINGE)
...I'LL CONFRONT MY FEELINGS TOO.
THESE STRANGE, MYSTERIOUS FEELINGS...

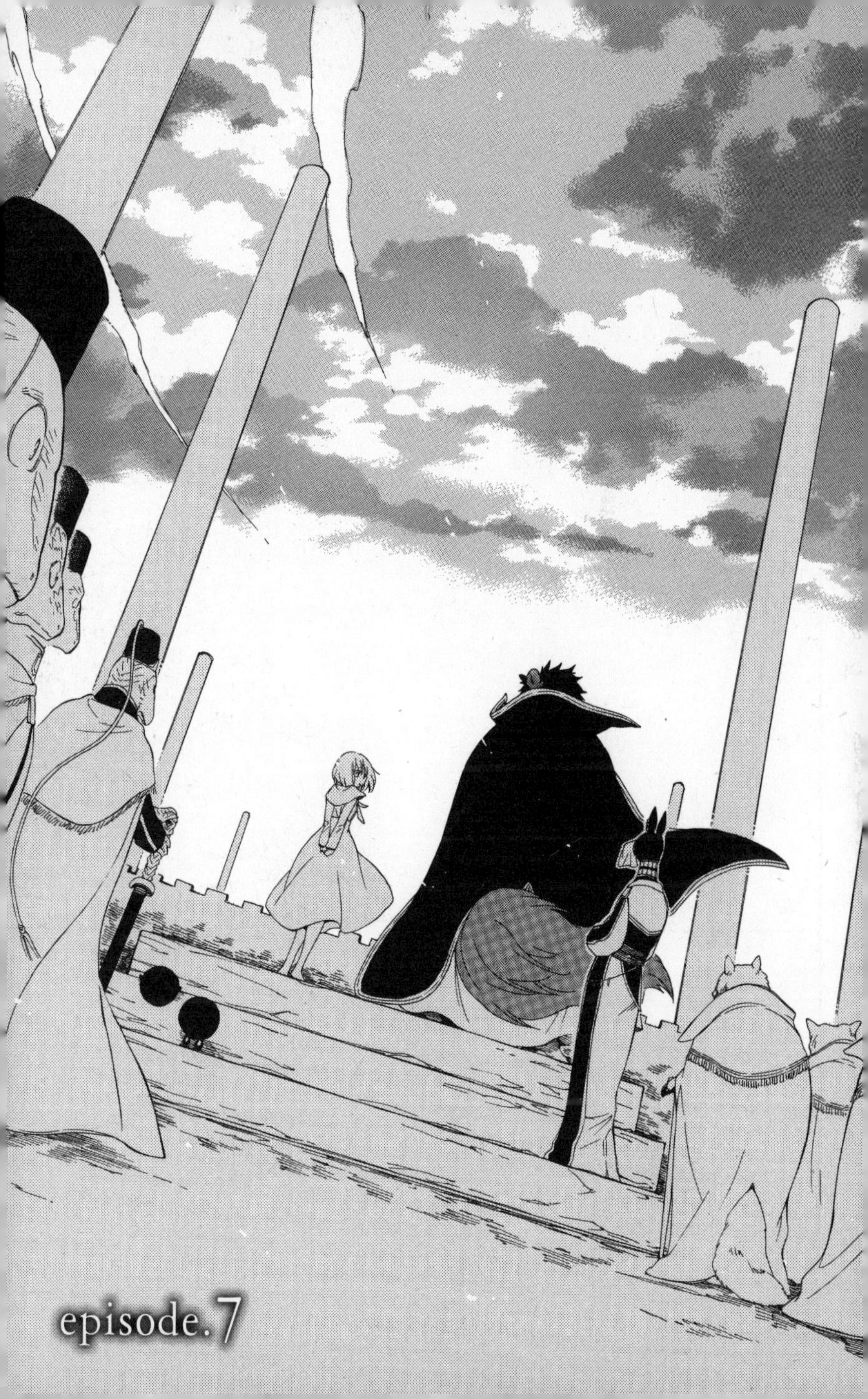
episode. 7

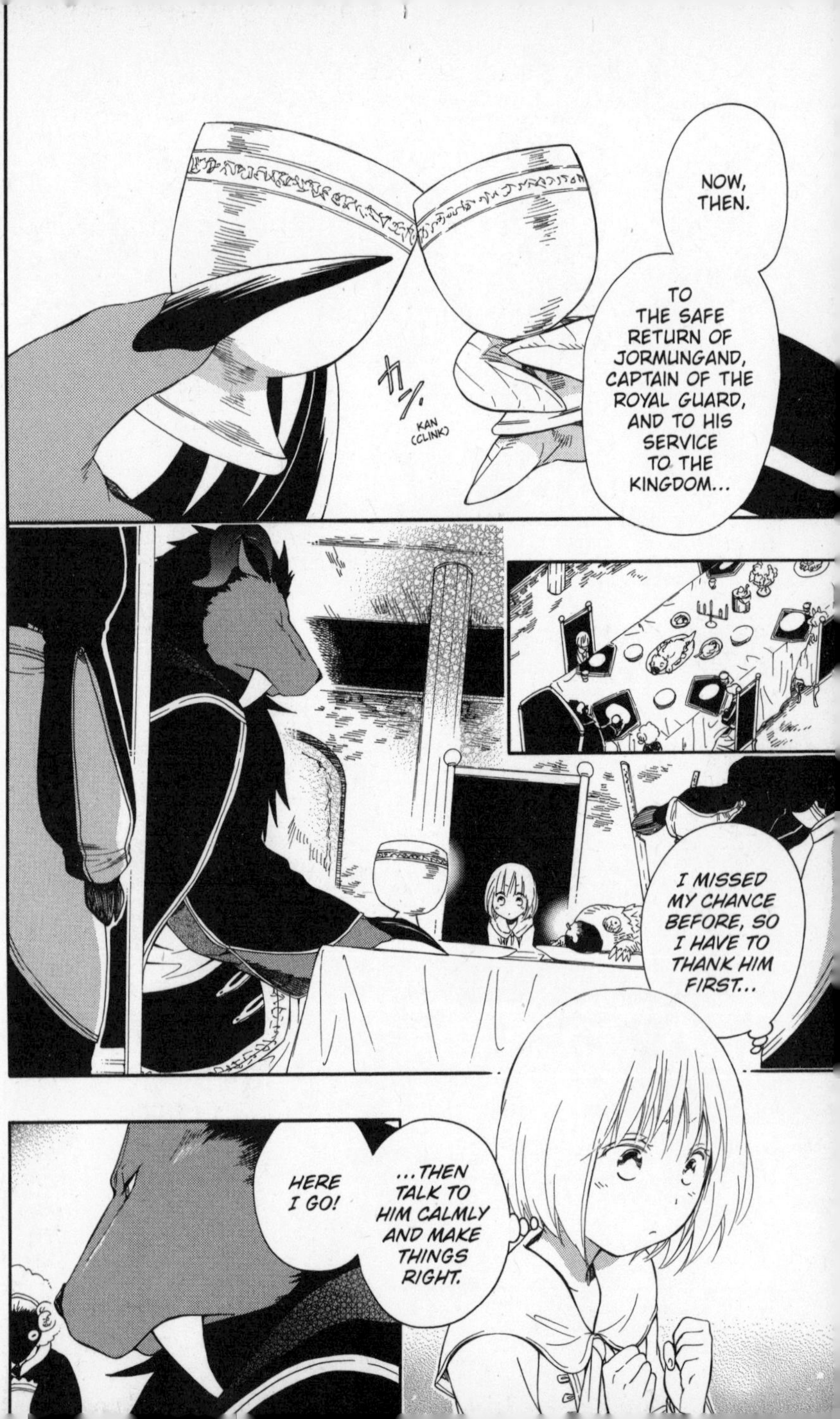
NOW, THEN.
TO THE SAFE RETURN OF JORMUNGAND, CAPTAIN OF THE ROYAL GUARD, AND TO HIS SERVICE TO THE KINGDOM...
KAN (CLINK)
I MISSED MY CHANCE BEFORE, SO I HAVE TO THANK HIM FIRST...
...THEN TALK TO HIM CALMLY AND MAKE THINGS RIGHT.
HERE I GO!

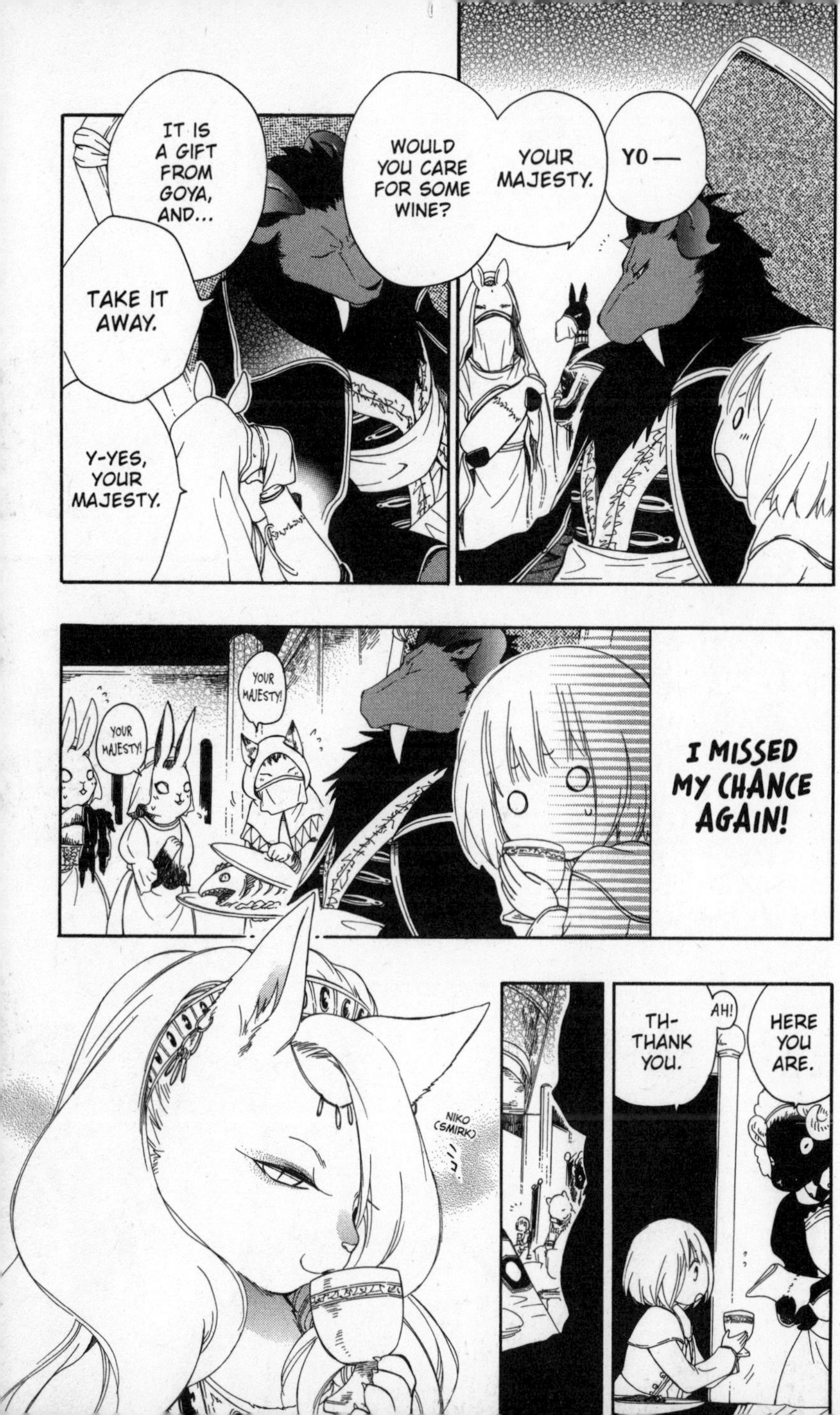
YO—
YOUR MAJESTY.
WOULD YOU CARE FOR SOME WINE?
IT IS A GIFT FROM GOYA, AND...
TAKE IT AWAY.
Y-YES, YOUR MAJESTY.
I MISSED MY CHANCE AGAIN!
YOUR MAJESTY!
YOUR MAJESTY!
HERE YOU ARE.
AH!
TH-THANK YOU.
NIKO (SMIRK)

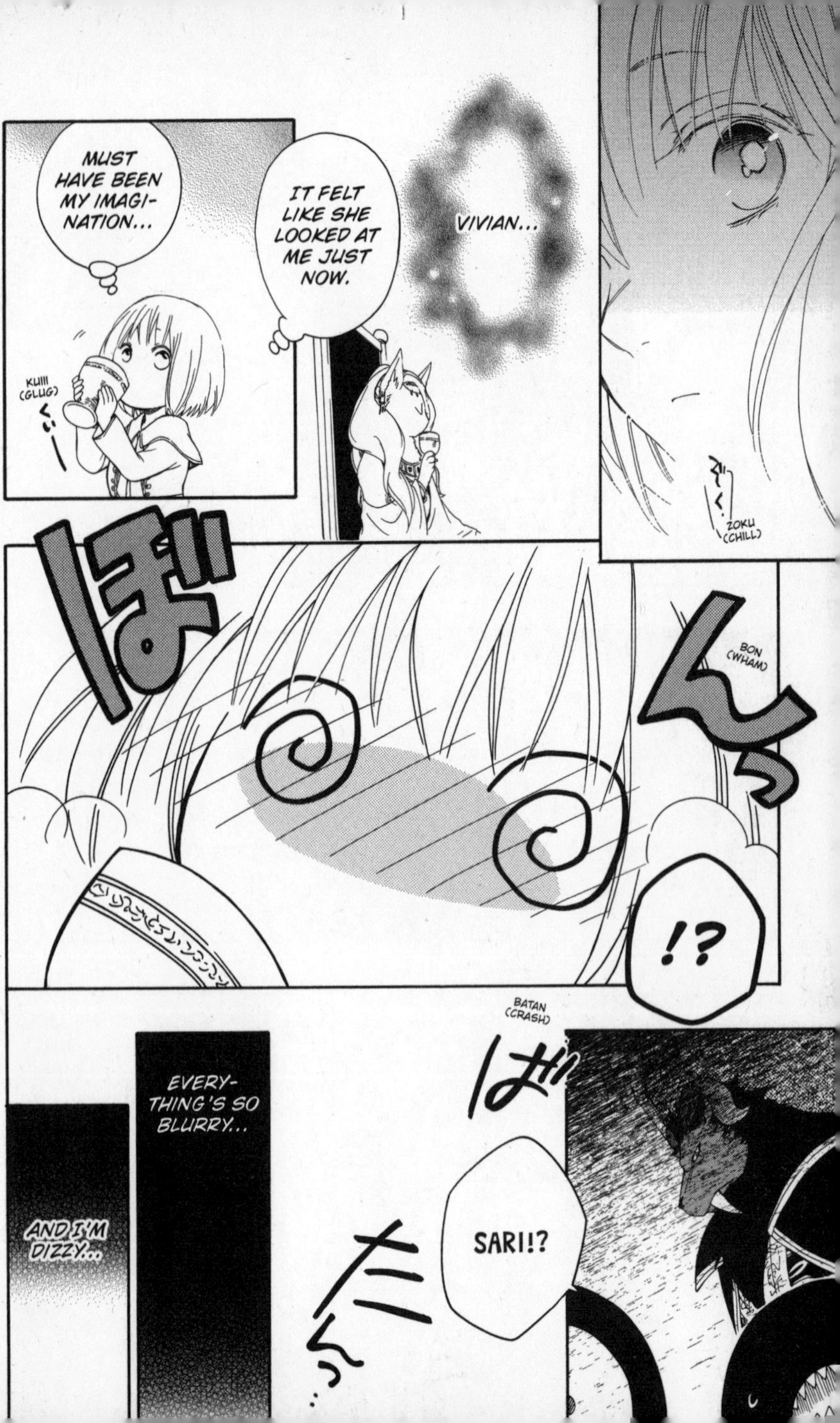
ZOKU (CHILL)
VIVIAN...
IT FELT LIKE SHE LOOKED AT ME JUST NOW.
MUST HAVE BEEN MY IMAGINATION...
KUIII (GLUG)
BON (WHAM)
!?
BATAN (CRASH)
SARI!?
EVERY-THING'S SO BLURRY...
AND I'M DIZZY...

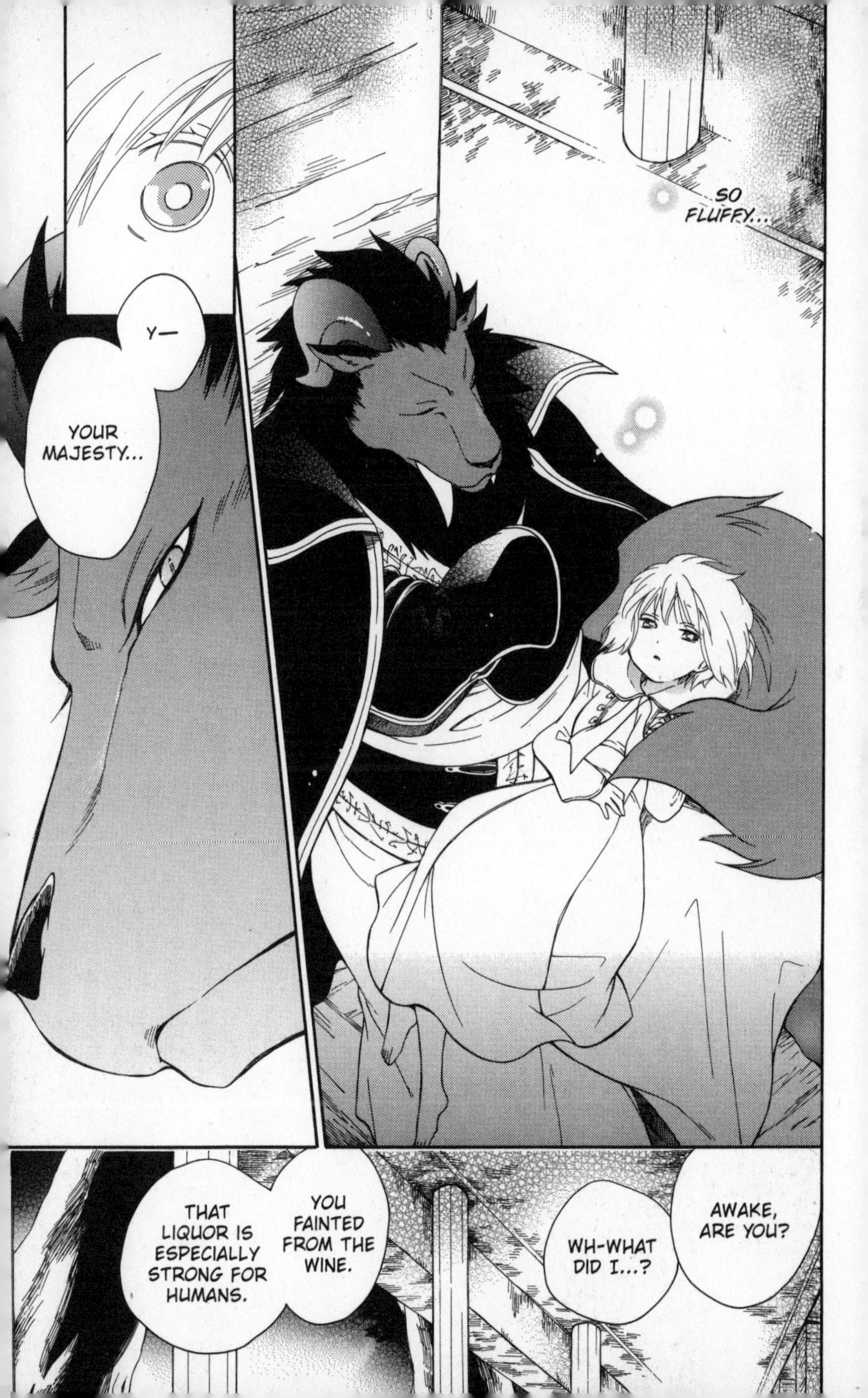
SO FLUFFY...
Y—
YOUR MAJESTY...
AWAKE, ARE YOU?
WH-WHAT DID I...?
YOU FAINTED FROM THE WINE.
THAT LIQUOR IS ESPECIALLY STRONG FOR HUMANS.

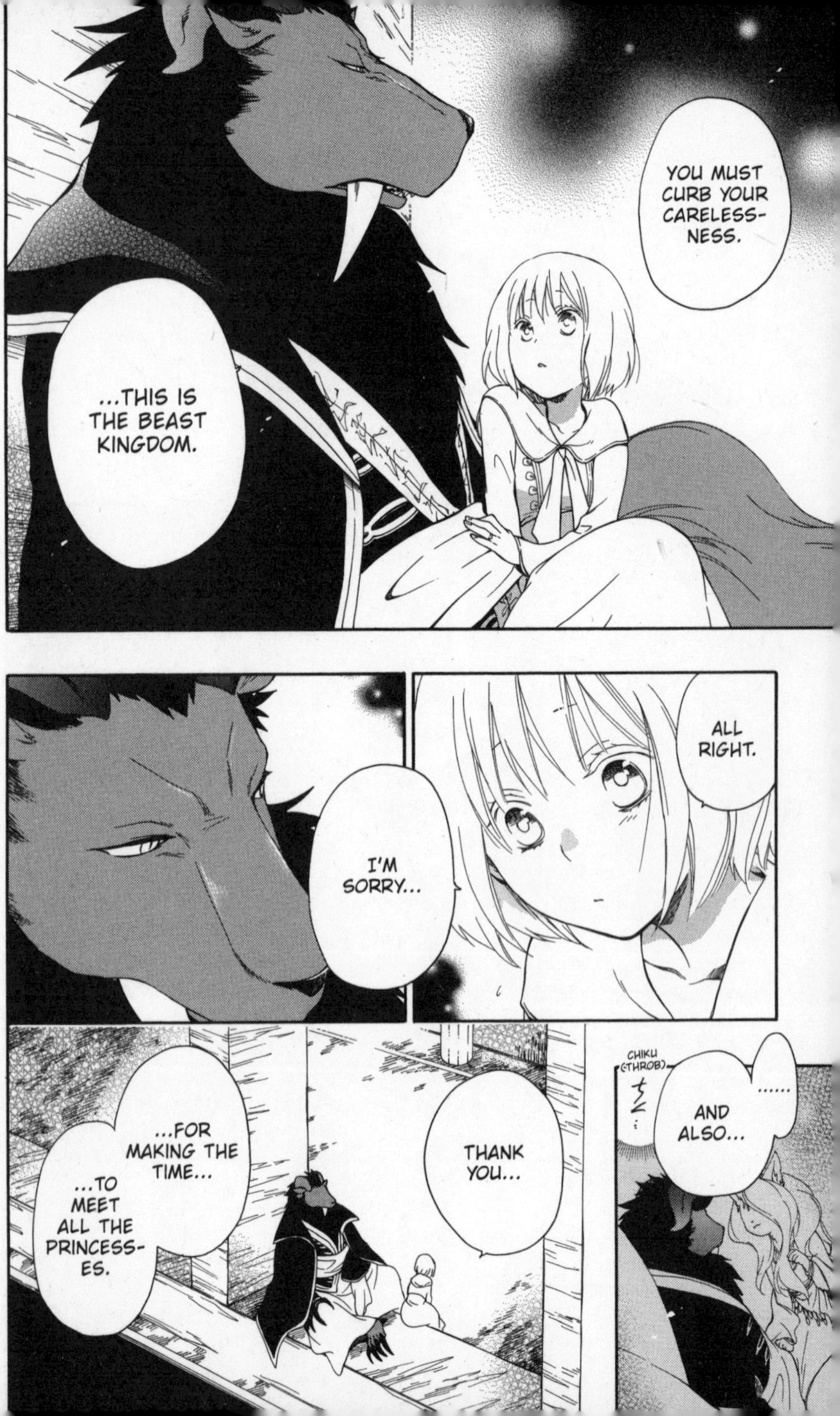
YOU MUST CURB YOUR CARELESS-NESS.
...THIS IS THE BEAST KINGDOM.
ALL RIGHT.
I'M SORRY...
......
CHIKU (=THROB)
AND ALSO...
THANK YOU...
...FOR MAKING THE TIME...
...TO MEET ALL THE PRINCESS-ES.

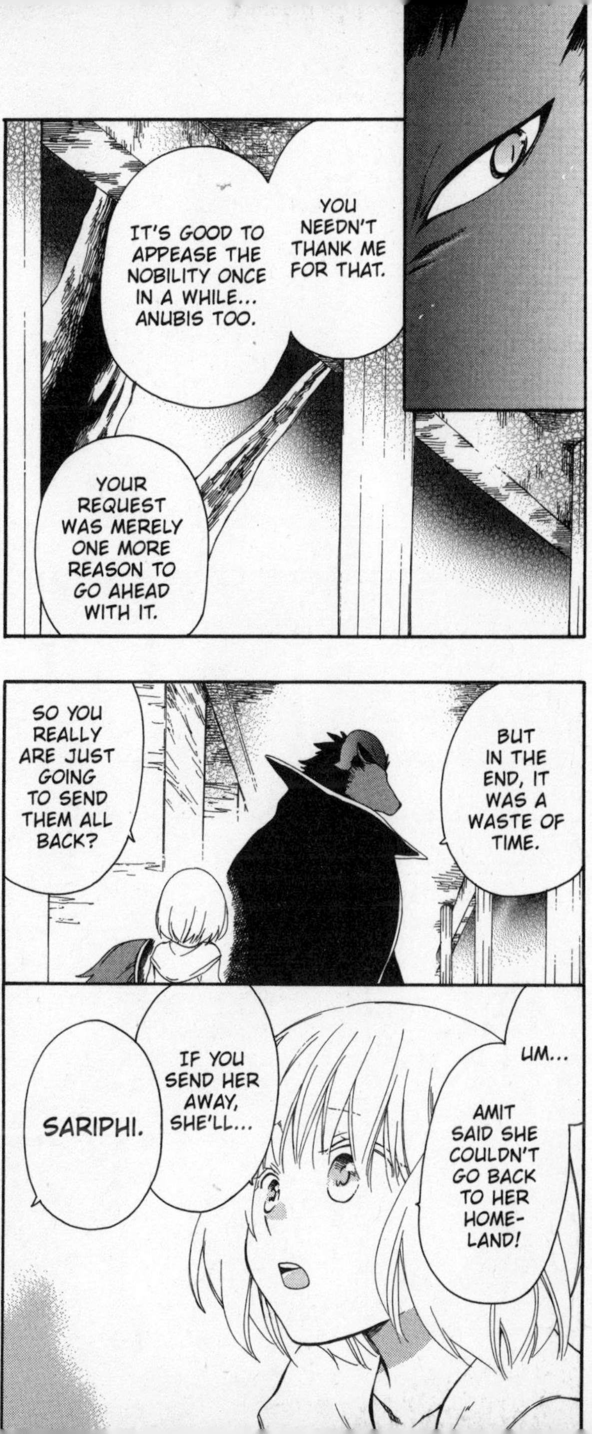
YOU NEEDN'T THANK ME FOR THAT.
IT'S GOOD TO APPEASE THE NOBILITY ONCE IN A WHILE... ANUBIS TOO.
YOUR REQUEST WAS MERELY ONE MORE REASON TO GO AHEAD WITH IT.
BUT IN THE END, IT WAS A WASTE OF TIME.
SO YOU REALLY ARE JUST GOING TO SEND THEM ALL BACK?
UM...
AMIT SAID SHE COULDN'T GO BACK TO HER HOMELAND!
IF YOU SEND HER AWAY, SHE'LL...
SARIPHI.

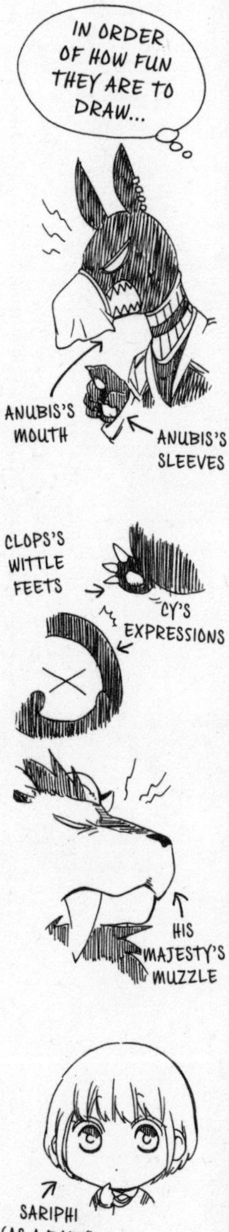
IN ORDER OF HOW FUN THEY ARE TO DRAW...
ANUBIS'S MOUTH
ANUBIS'S SLEEVES
CLOPS'S WITTLE FEETS
CY'S EXPRESSIONS
HIS MAJESTY'S MUZZLE
SARIPHI (AS A BABY)

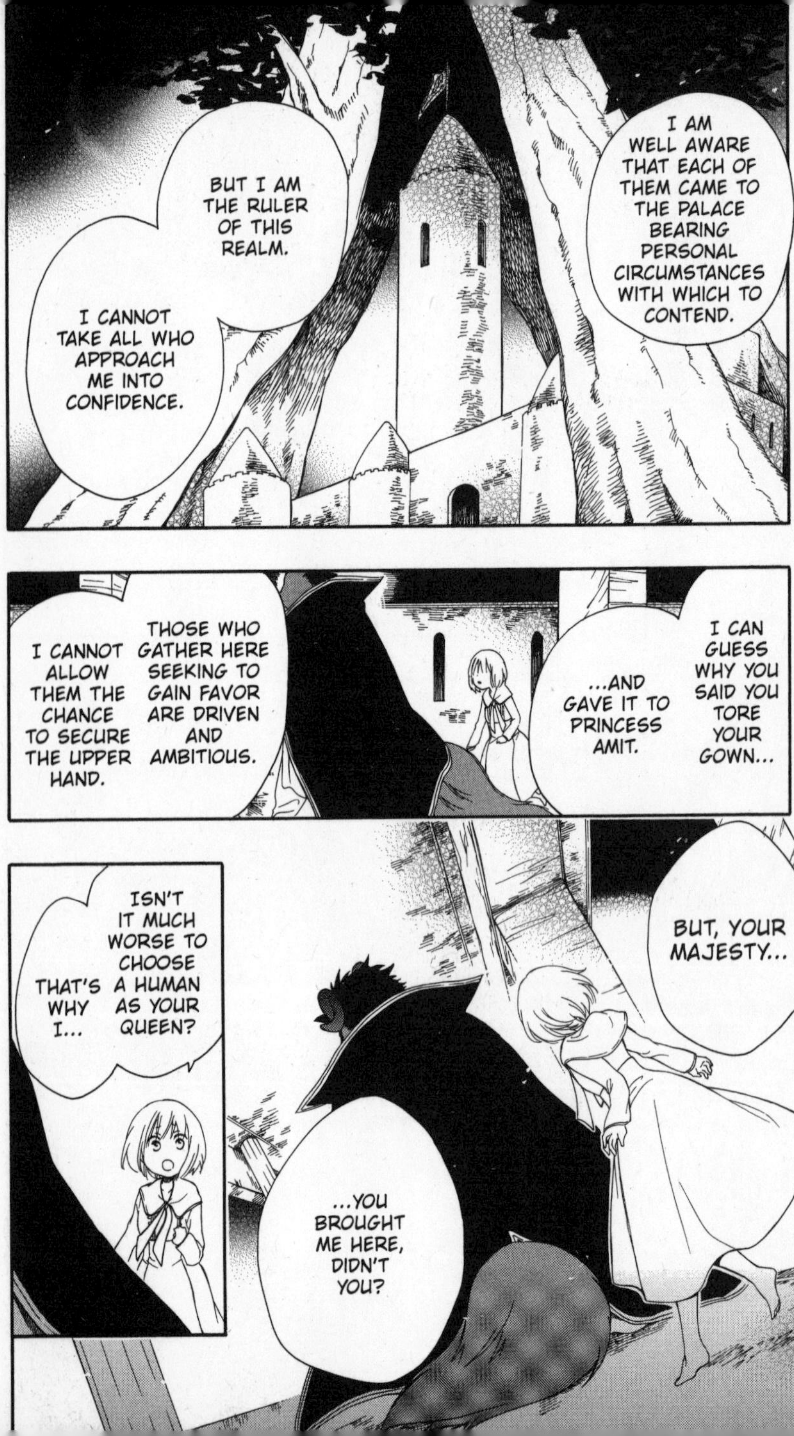
I AM WELL AWARE THAT EACH OF THEM CAME TO THE PALACE BEARING PERSONAL CIRCUMSTANCES WITH WHICH TO CONTEND.
BUT I AM THE RULER OF THIS REALM.
I CANNOT TAKE ALL WHO APPROACH ME INTO CONFIDENCE.
I CAN GUESS WHY YOU SAID YOU TORE YOUR GOWN...
...AND GAVE IT TO PRINCESS AMIT.
THOSE WHO GATHER HERE SEEKING TO GAIN FAVOR ARE DRIVEN AND AMBITIOUS.
I CANNOT ALLOW THEM THE CHANCE TO SECURE THE UPPER HAND.
BUT, YOUR MAJESTY...
...YOU BROUGHT ME HERE, DIDN'T YOU?
ISN'T IT MUCH WORSE TO CHOOSE A HUMAN AS YOUR QUEEN?
THAT'S WHY I...

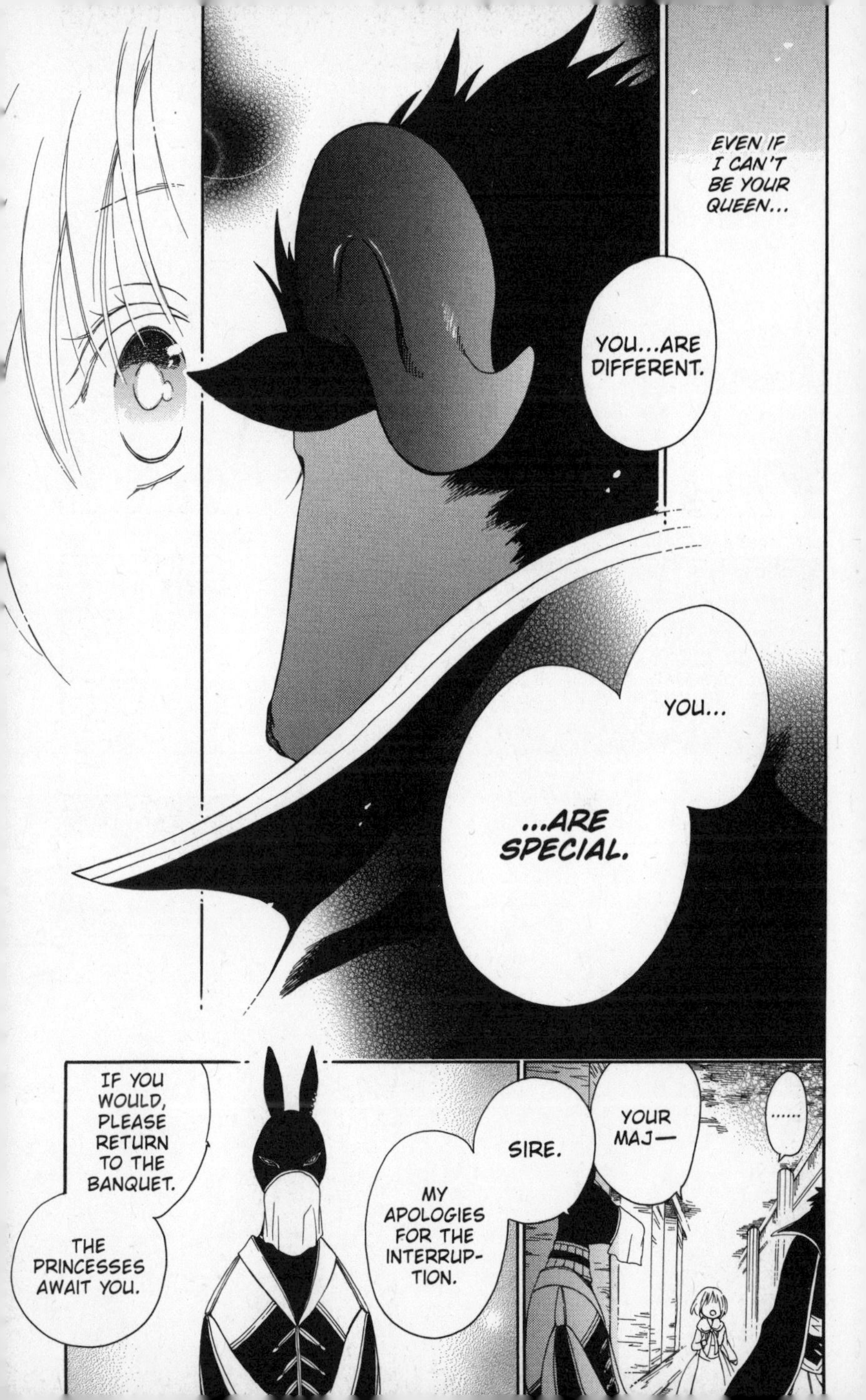
EVEN IF I CAN'T BE YOUR QUEEN...
YOU...ARE DIFFERENT.
YOU...
...ARE SPECIAL.
......
YOUR MAJ—
SIRE.
MY APOLOGIES FOR THE INTERRUP-TION.
IF YOU WOULD, PLEASE RETURN TO THE BANQUET.
THE PRINCESSES AWAIT YOU.

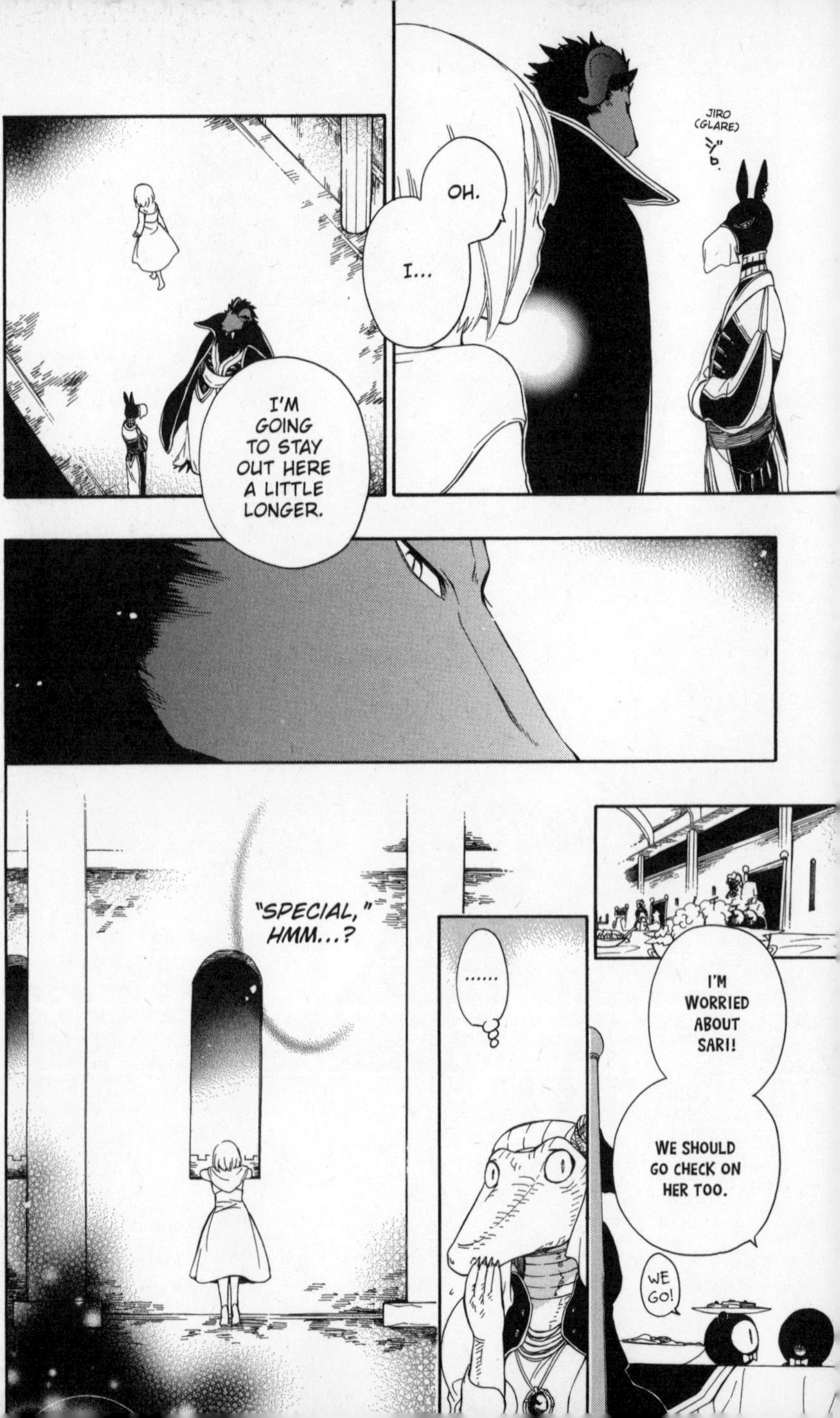
JIRO (GLARE)
OH.
I...
I'M GOING TO STAY OUT HERE A LITTLE LONGER.
I'M WORRIED ABOUT SARI!
WE SHOULD GO CHECK ON HER TOO.
WE GO!
......
"SPECIAL," HMM...?

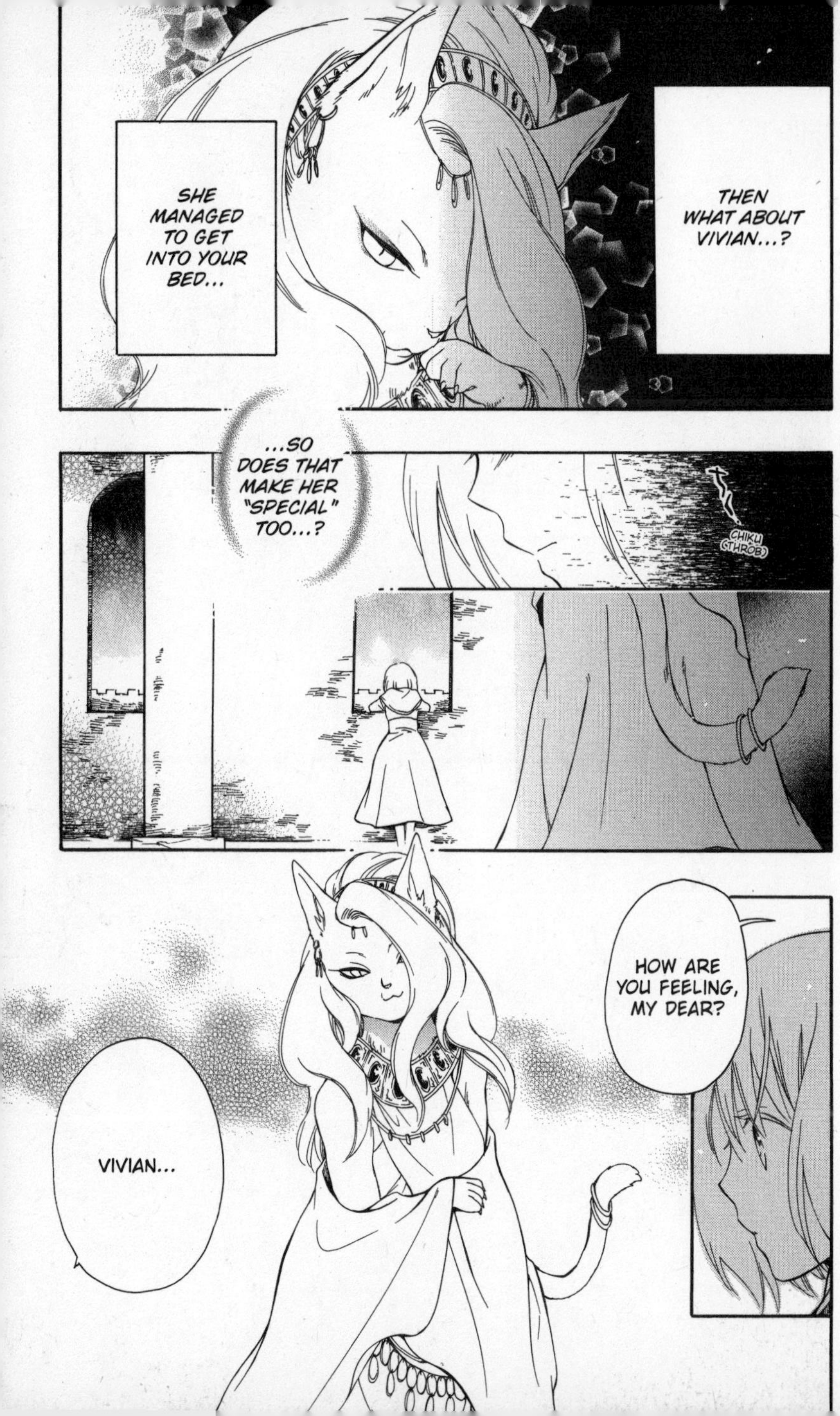
THEN WHAT ABOUT VIVIAN...?
SHE MANAGED TO GET INTO YOUR BED...
...SO DOES THAT MAKE HER "SPECIAL" TOO...?
CHIKU (THROB)
HOW ARE YOU FEELING, MY DEAR?
VIVIAN...

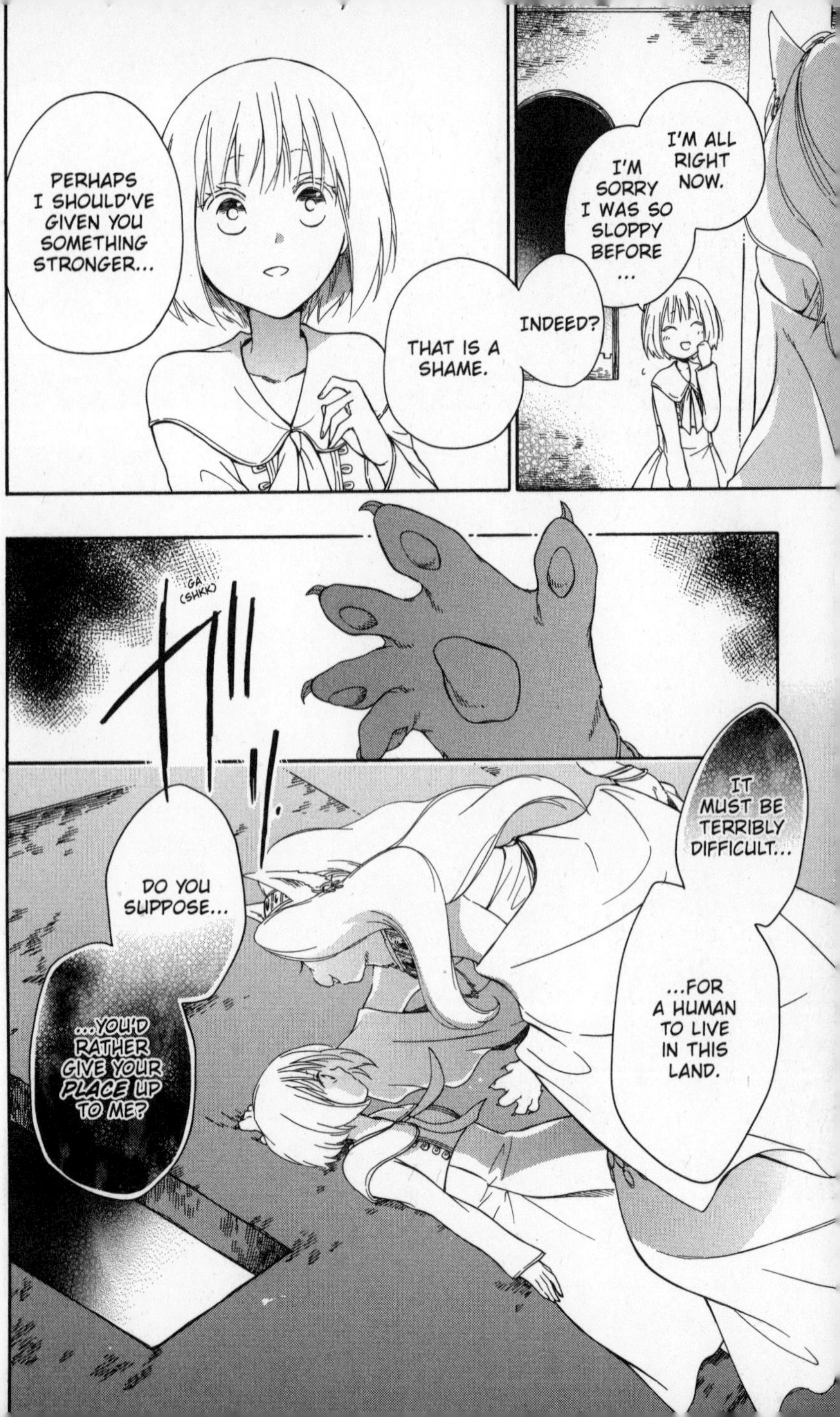
I'M ALL RIGHT NOW.
I'M SORRY I WAS SO SLOPPY BEFORE...
INDEED?
THAT IS A SHAME.
PERHAPS I SHOULD'VE GIVEN YOU SOMETHING STRONGER...
GA (SHKK)
IT MUST BE TERRIBLY DIFFICULT...
...FOR A HUMAN TO LIVE IN THIS LAND.
DO YOU SUPPOSE...
...YOU'D RATHER GIVE YOUR PLACE UP TO ME?

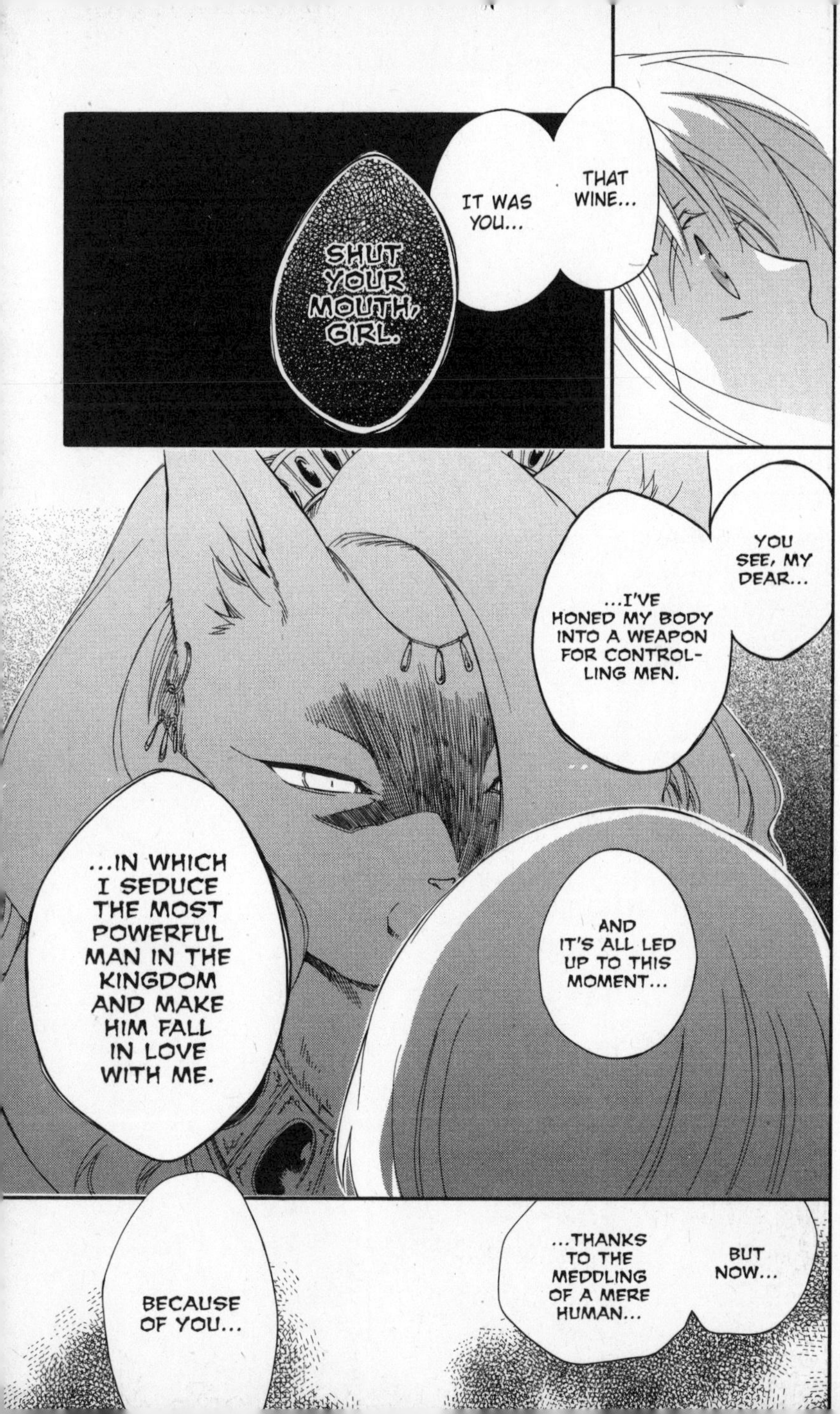
THAT WINE...
IT WAS YOU...
SHUT YOUR MOUTH, GIRL.
YOU SEE, MY DEAR...
...I'VE HONED MY BODY INTO A WEAPON FOR CONTROL-LING MEN.
AND IT'S ALL LED UP TO THIS MOMENT...
...IN WHICH I SEDUCE THE MOST POWERFUL MAN IN THE KINGDOM AND MAKE HIM FALL IN LOVE WITH ME.
BUT NOW...
...THANKS TO THE MEDDLING OF A MERE HUMAN...
BECAUSE OF YOU...

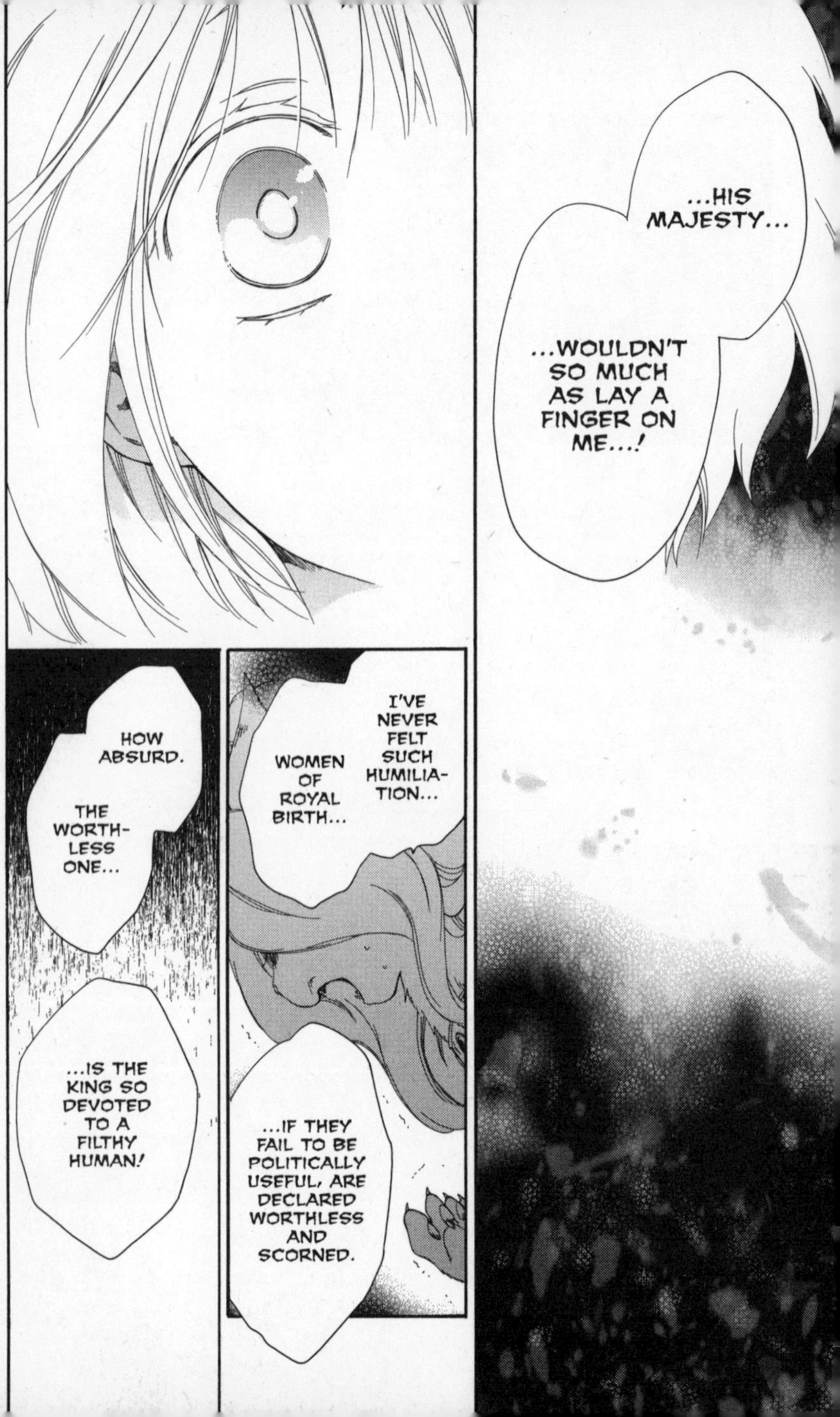
...HIS MAJESTY...
...WOULDN'T SO MUCH AS LAY A FINGER ON ME...!
I'VE NEVER FELT SUCH HUMILIATION...
WOMEN OF ROYAL BIRTH...
...IF THEY FAIL TO BE POLITICALLY USEFUL, ARE DECLARED WORTHLESS AND SCORNED.
HOW ABSURD.
THE WORTHLESS ONE...
...IS THE KING SO DEVOTED TO A FILTHY HUMAN!

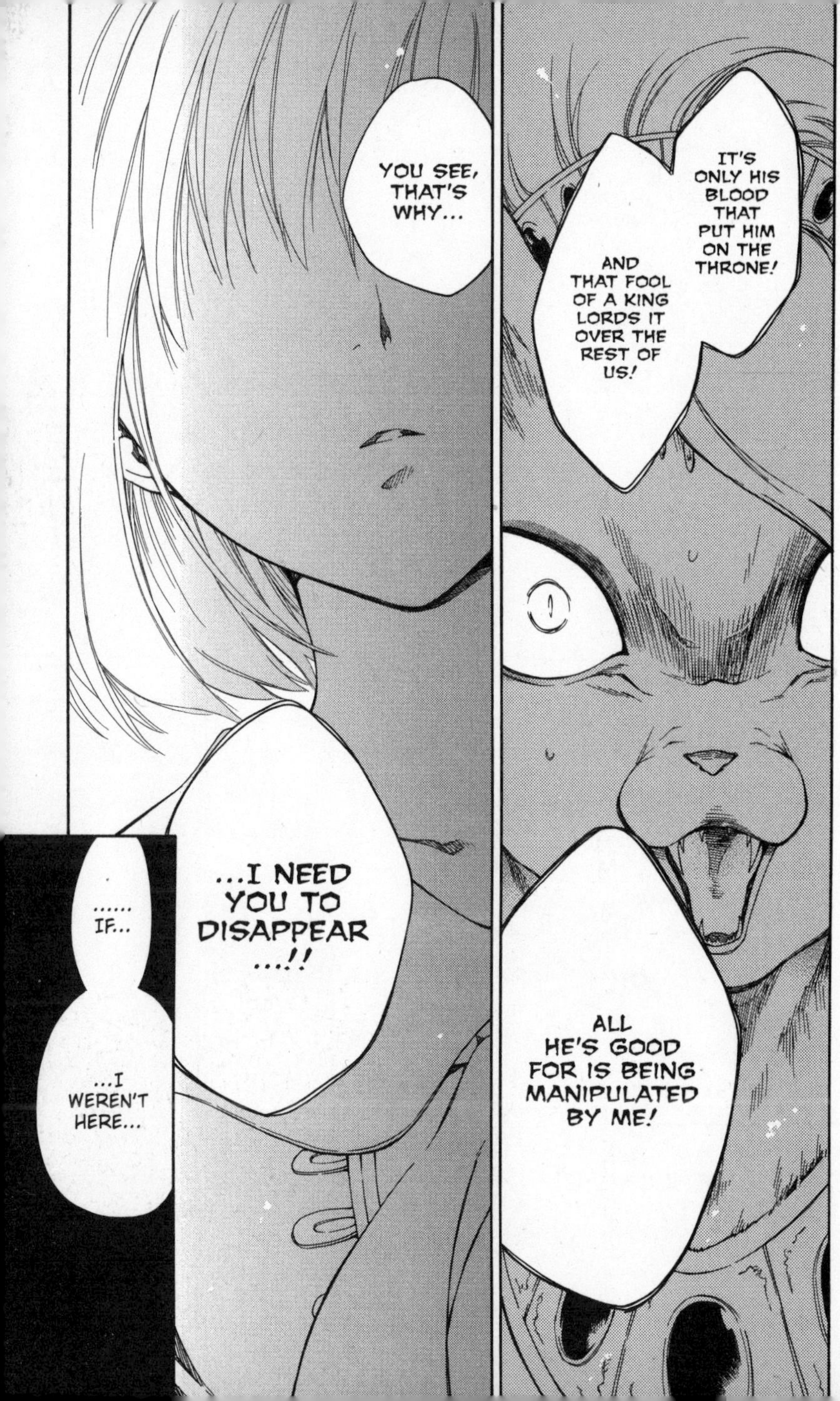
IT'S ONLY HIS BLOOD THAT PUT HIM ON THE THRONE!
AND THAT FOOL OF A KING LORDS IT OVER THE REST OF US!
ALL HE'S GOOD FOR IS BEING MANIPULATED BY ME!
YOU SEE, THAT'S WHY...
...I NEED YOU TO DISAPPEAR ...!!
...... IF...
...I WEREN'T HERE...

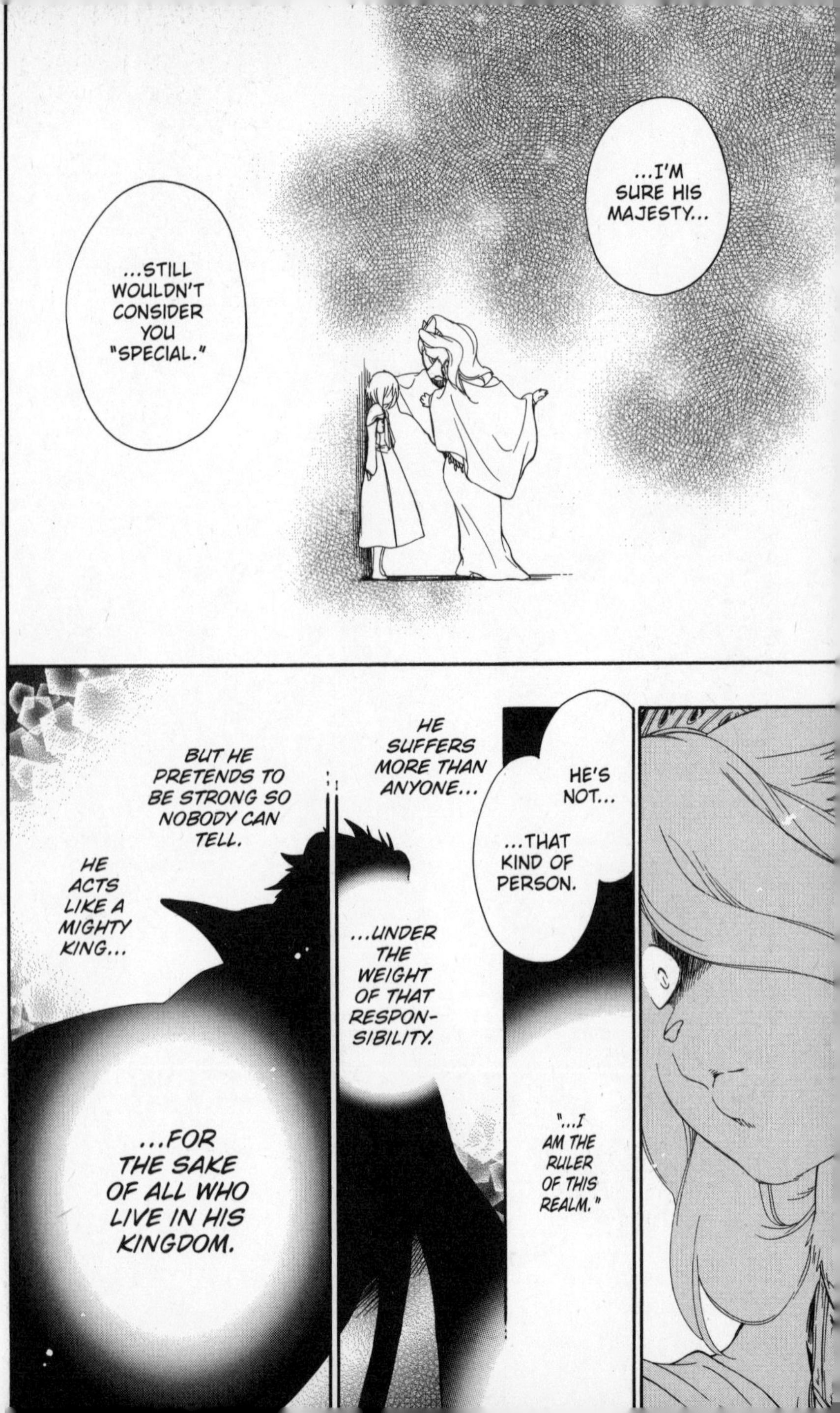
...I'M SURE HIS MAJESTY...
...STILL WOULDN'T CONSIDER YOU "SPECIAL."
HE'S NOT...
...THAT KIND OF PERSON.
"...I AM THE RULER OF THIS REALM."
HE SUFFERS MORE THAN ANYONE...
...UNDER THE WEIGHT OF THAT RESPONSIBILITY.
BUT HE PRETENDS TO BE STRONG SO NOBODY CAN TELL.
HE ACTS LIKE A MIGHTY KING...
...FOR THE SAKE OF ALL WHO LIVE IN HIS KINGDOM.

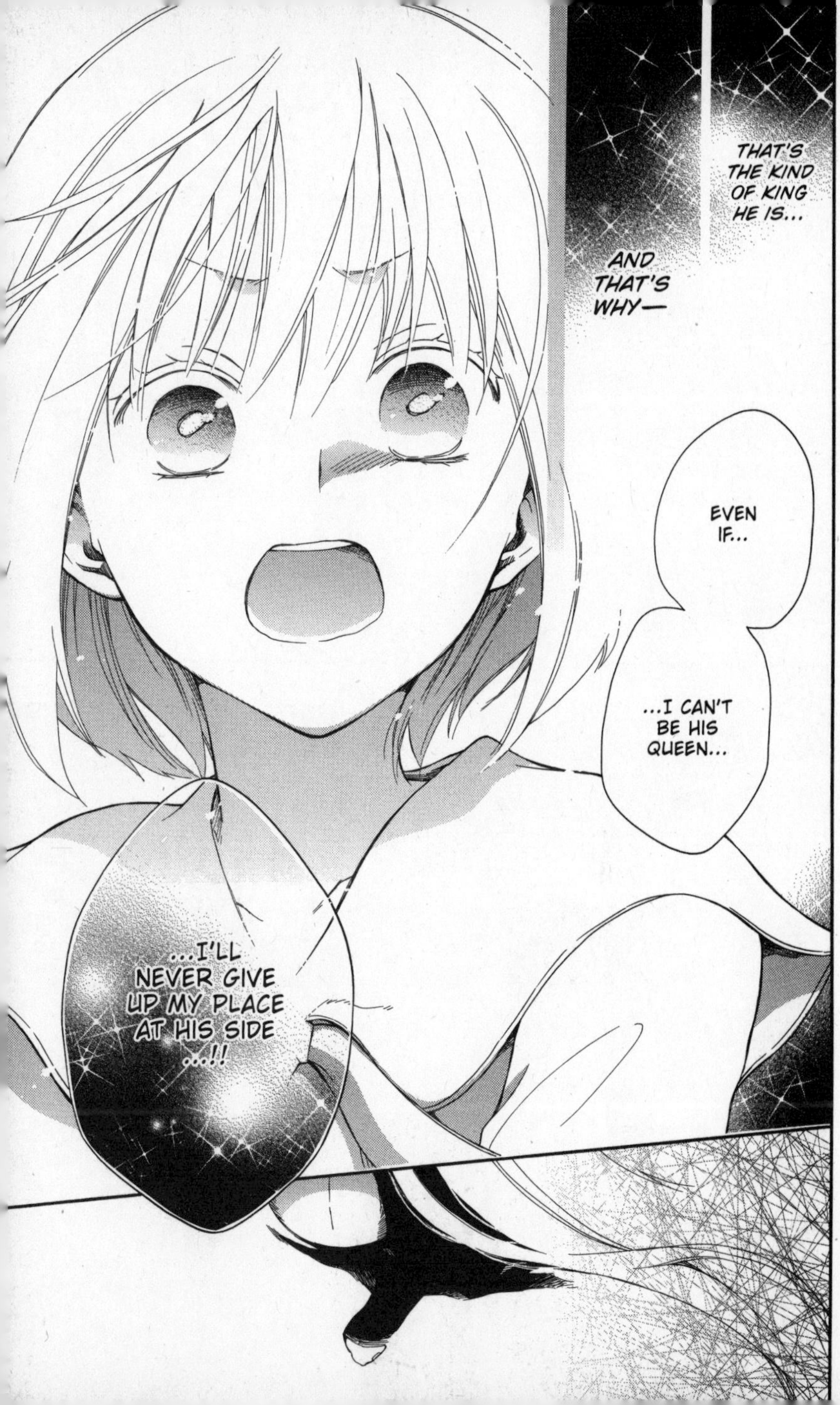
THAT'S THE KIND OF KING HE IS...
AND THAT'S WHY—
EVEN IF...
...I CAN'T BE HIS QUEEN...
...I'LL NEVER GIVE UP MY PLACE AT HIS SIDE ...!!

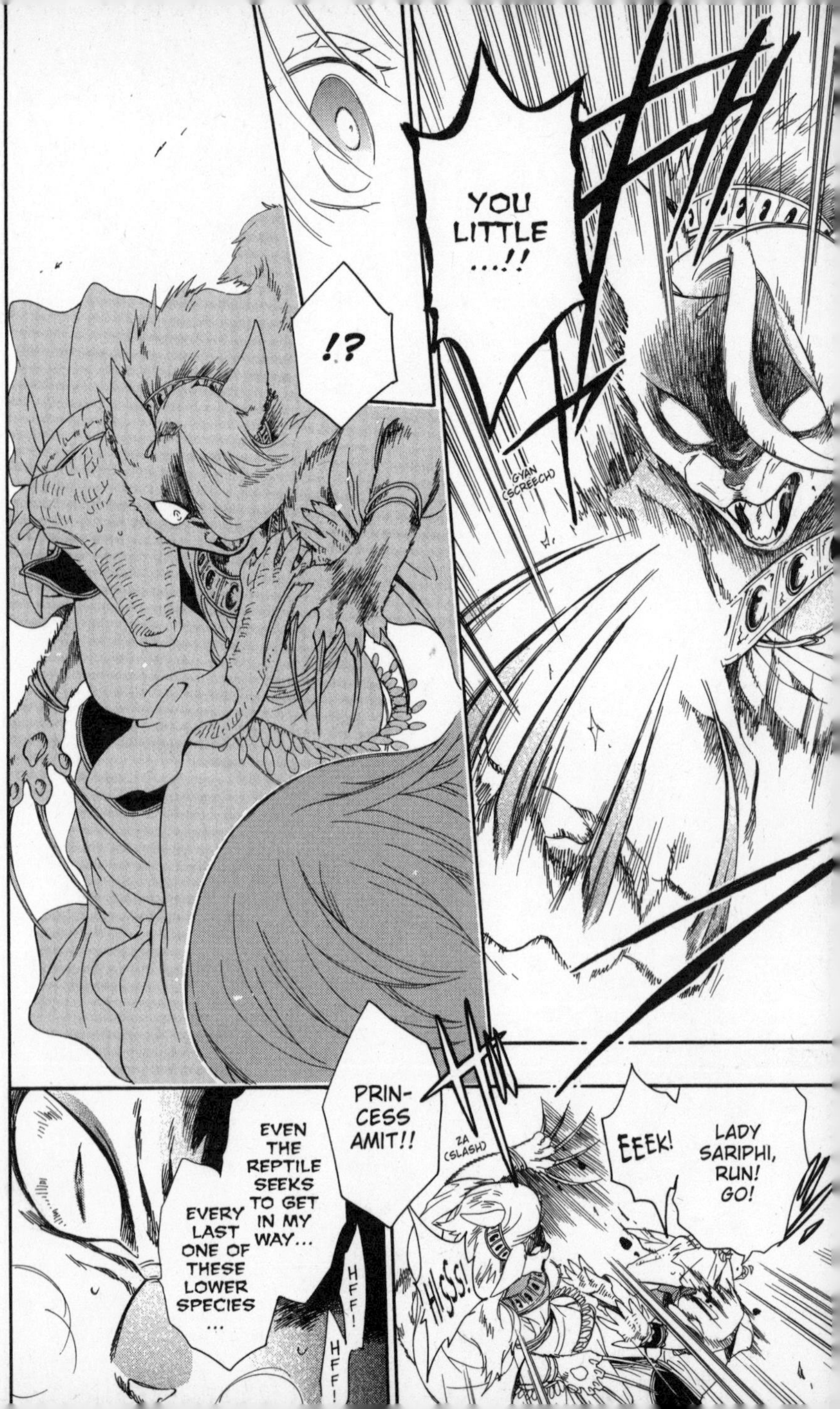
YOU LITTLE ...!!
GYAN (SCREECH)
!?
LADY SARIPHI, RUN! GO!
EEEK!
ZA (SLASH)
HISSS!
PRIN-CESS AMIT!!
EVEN THE REPTILE SEEKS TO GET IN MY WAY...
EVERY LAST ONE OF THESE LOWER SPECIES ...
HFF!
HFF!

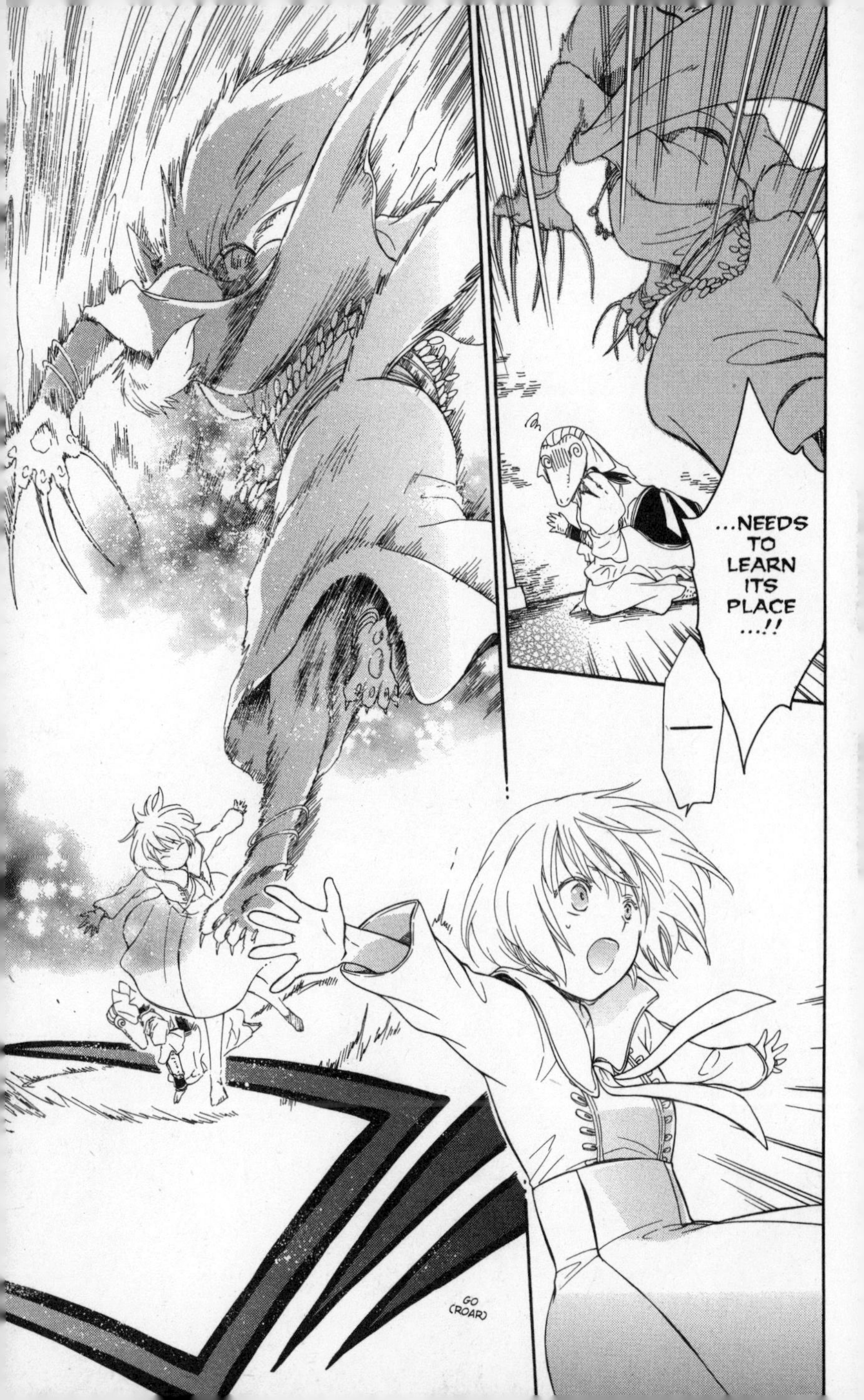
...NEEDS TO LEARN ITS PLACE ...!!
GO (ROAR)

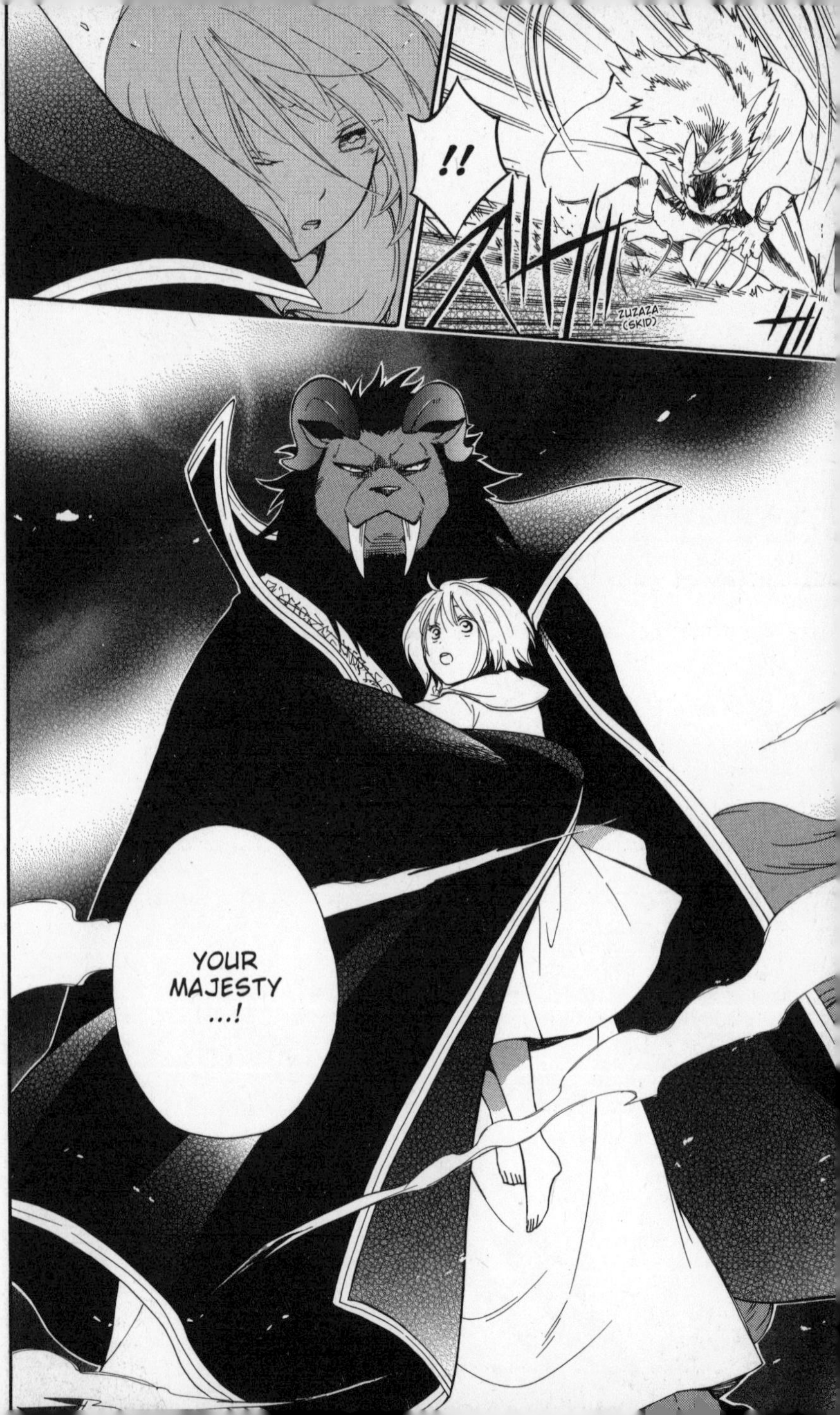
!!
ZUZAZA (SKID)
YOUR MAJESTY ...!

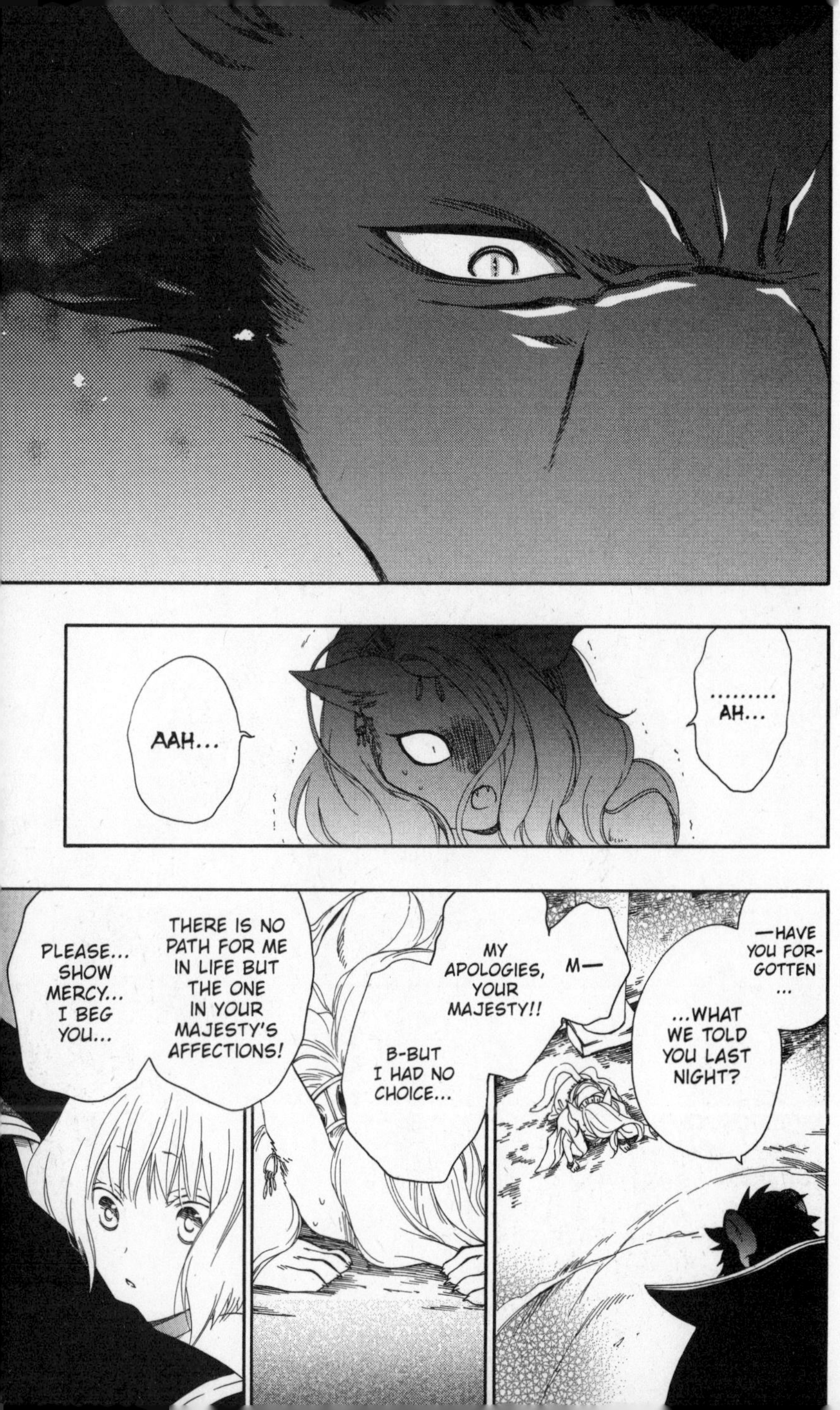
.........AH...
AAH...
—HAVE YOU FOR-GOTTEN...
...WHAT WE TOLD YOU LAST NIGHT?
M—
MY APOLOGIES, YOUR MAJESTY!!
B-BUT I HAD NO CHOICE...
THERE IS NO PATH FOR ME IN LIFE BUT THE ONE IN YOUR MAJESTY'S AFFECTIONS!
PLEASE... SHOW MERCY... I BEG YOU...

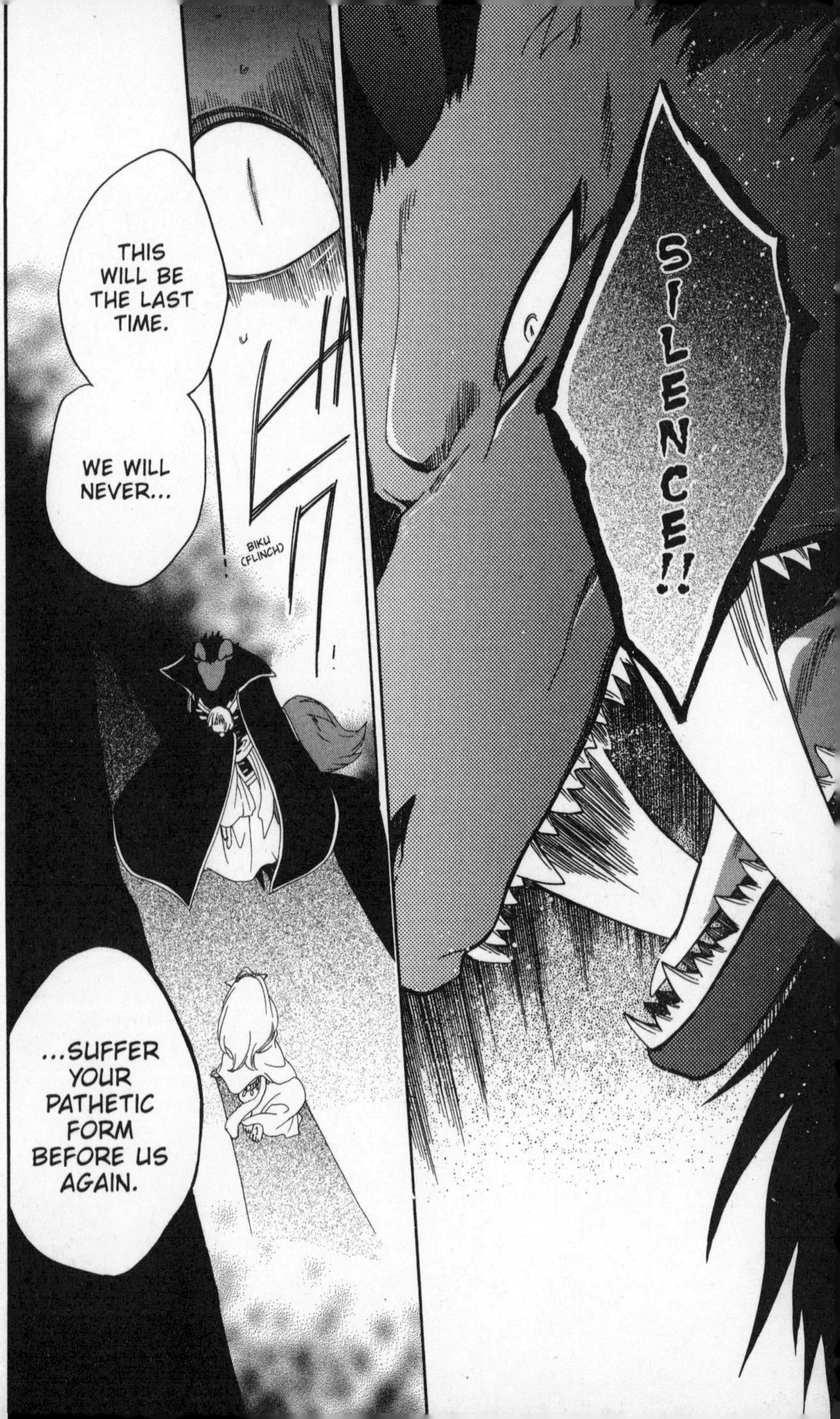
SILENCE!!
THIS WILL BE THE LAST TIME.
WE WILL NEVER...
BIKU (FLINCH)
...SUFFER YOUR PATHETIC FORM BEFORE US AGAIN.

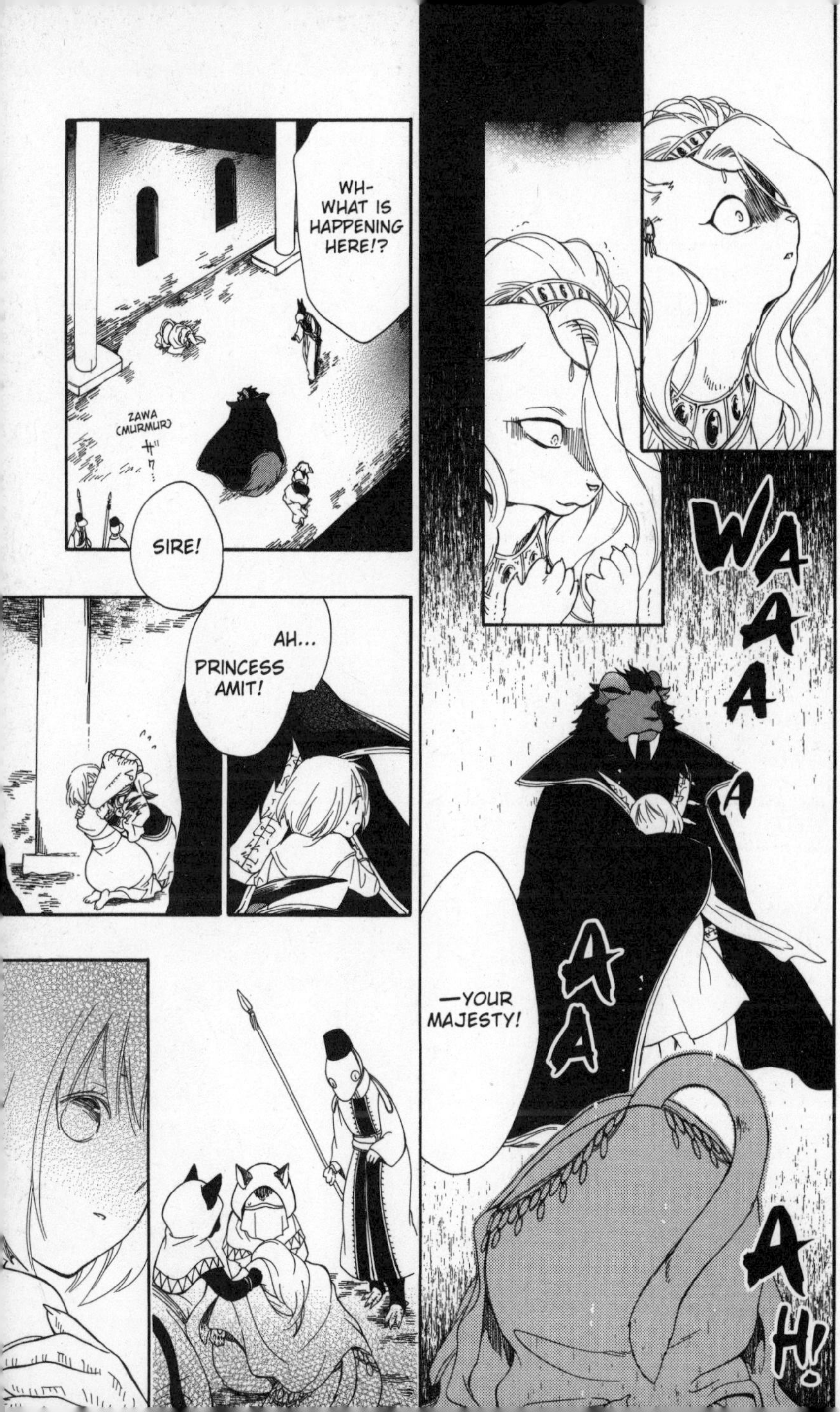
WAAAAAAAH!
—YOUR MAJESTY!
WH- WHAT IS HAPPENING HERE!?
ZAWA (MURMUR)
SIRE!
AH... PRINCESS AMIT!

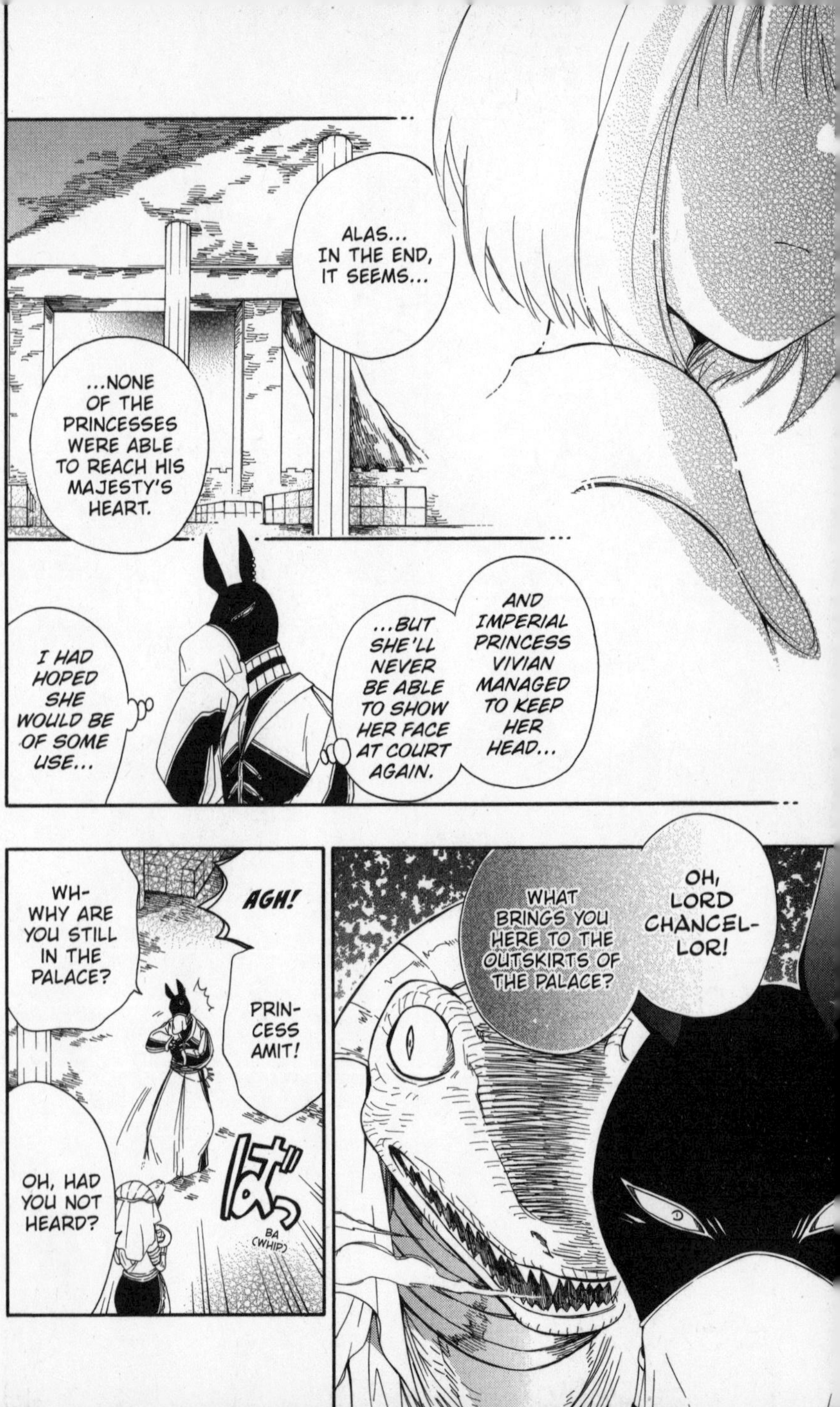
ALAS... IN THE END, IT SEEMS...
...NONE OF THE PRINCESSES WERE ABLE TO REACH HIS MAJESTY'S HEART.
AND IMPERIAL PRINCESS VIVIAN MANAGED TO KEEP HER HEAD...
...BUT SHE'LL NEVER BE ABLE TO SHOW HER FACE AT COURT AGAIN.
I HAD HOPED SHE WOULD BE OF SOME USE...
OH, LORD CHANCELLOR!
WHAT BRINGS YOU HERE TO THE OUTSKIRTS OF THE PALACE?
AGH!
PRINCESS AMIT!
WH-WHY ARE YOU STILL IN THE PALACE?
ばっ
BA (WHIP)
OH, HAD YOU NOT HEARD?

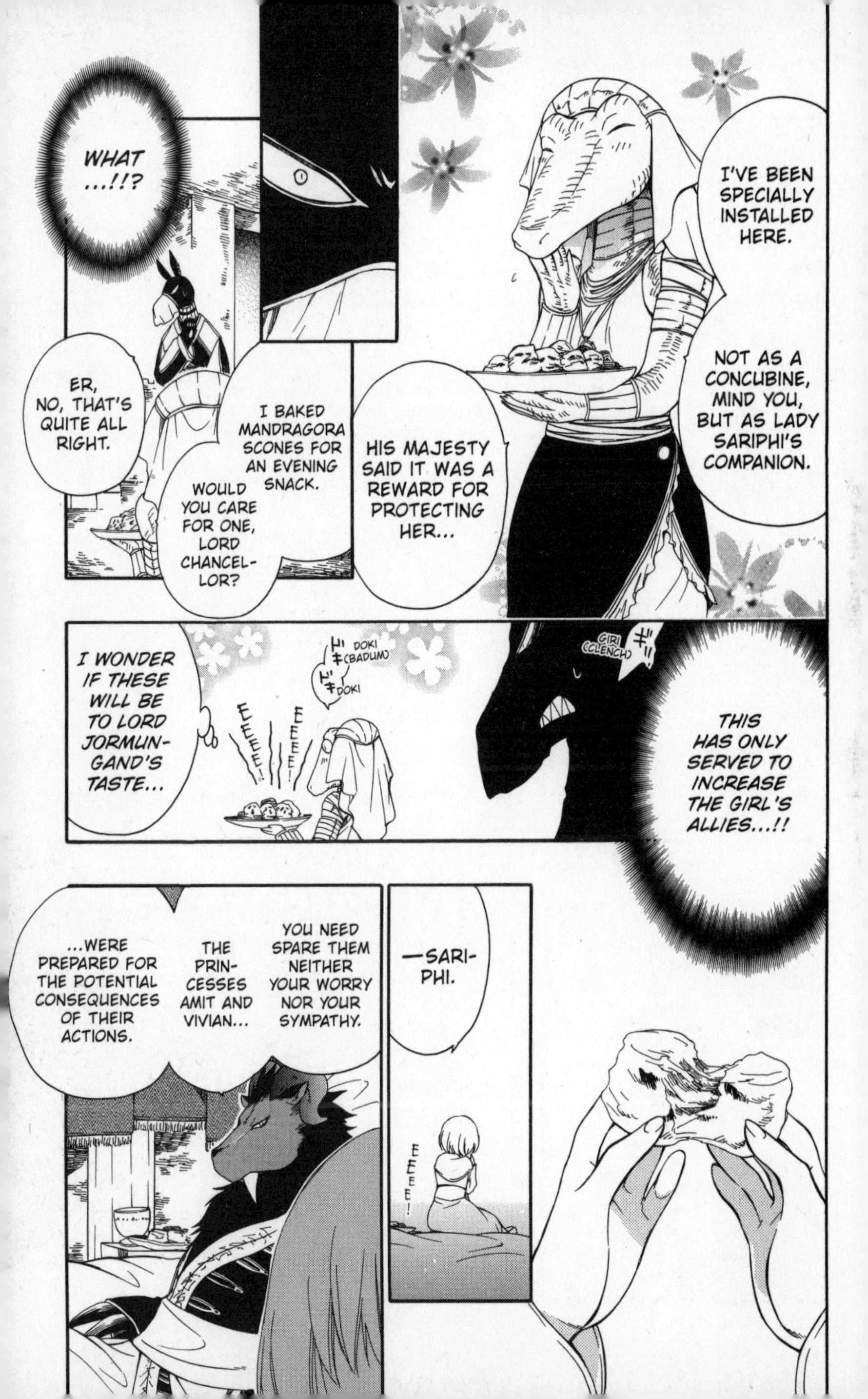
I'VE BEEN SPECIALLY INSTALLED HERE.
NOT AS A CONCUBINE, MIND YOU, BUT AS LADY SARIPHI'S COMPANION.
HIS MAJESTY SAID IT WAS A REWARD FOR PROTECTING HER...
WHAT...!!?
I BAKED MANDRAGORA SCONES FOR AN EVENING SNACK.
WOULD YOU CARE FOR ONE, LORD CHANCELLOR?
ER, NO, THAT'S QUITE ALL RIGHT.
GIRI (CLENCH)
THIS HAS ONLY SERVED TO INCREASE THE GIRL'S ALLIES...!!
DOKI (BADUM) DOKI
EEEE!
EEEE!
I WONDER IF THESE WILL BE TO LORD JORMUNGAND'S TASTE...
—SARIPHI.
EEEE!
YOU NEED SPARE THEM NEITHER YOUR WORRY NOR YOUR SYMPATHY.
THE PRINCESSES AMIT AND VIVIAN...
...WERE PREPARED FOR THE POTENTIAL CONSEQUENCES OF THEIR ACTIONS.

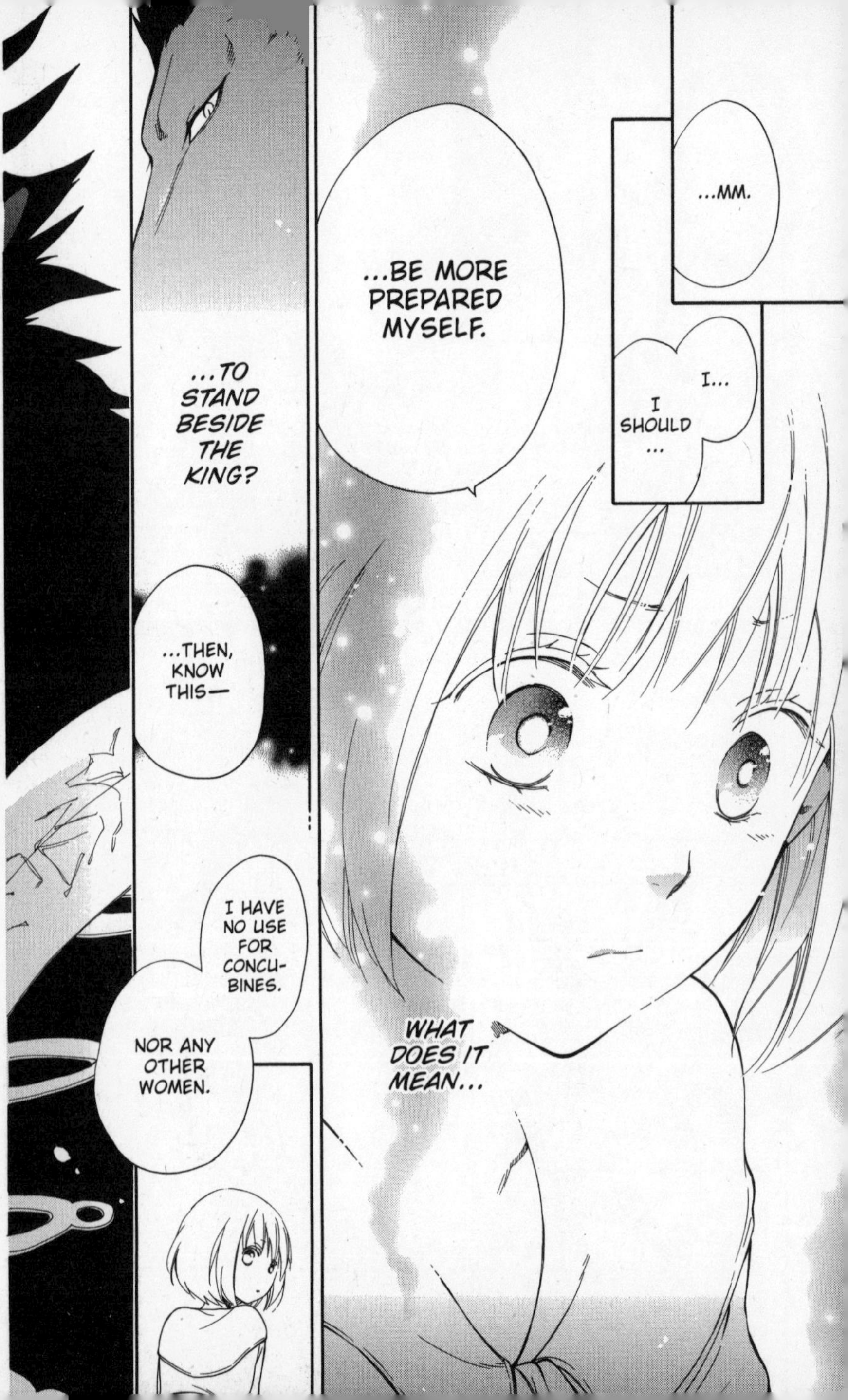
...MM.
I... I SHOULD ...
...BE MORE PREPARED MYSELF.
WHAT DOES IT MEAN...
...TO STAND BESIDE THE KING?
...THEN, KNOW THIS—
I HAVE NO USE FOR CONCUBINES.
NOR ANY OTHER WOMEN.

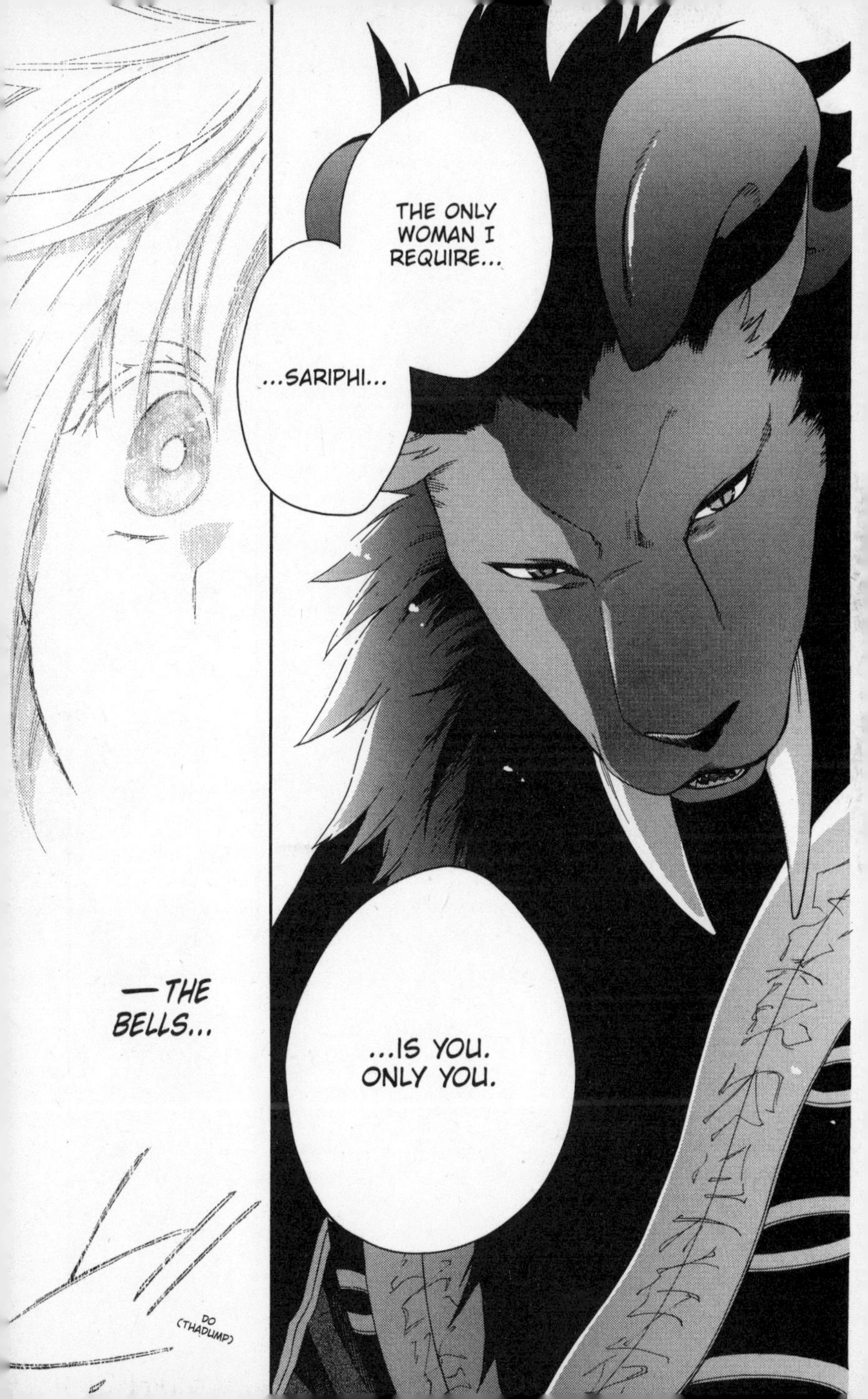
THE ONLY WOMAN I REQUIRE...
...SARIPHI...
...IS YOU. ONLY YOU.
—THE BELLS...
DO (THADUMP)

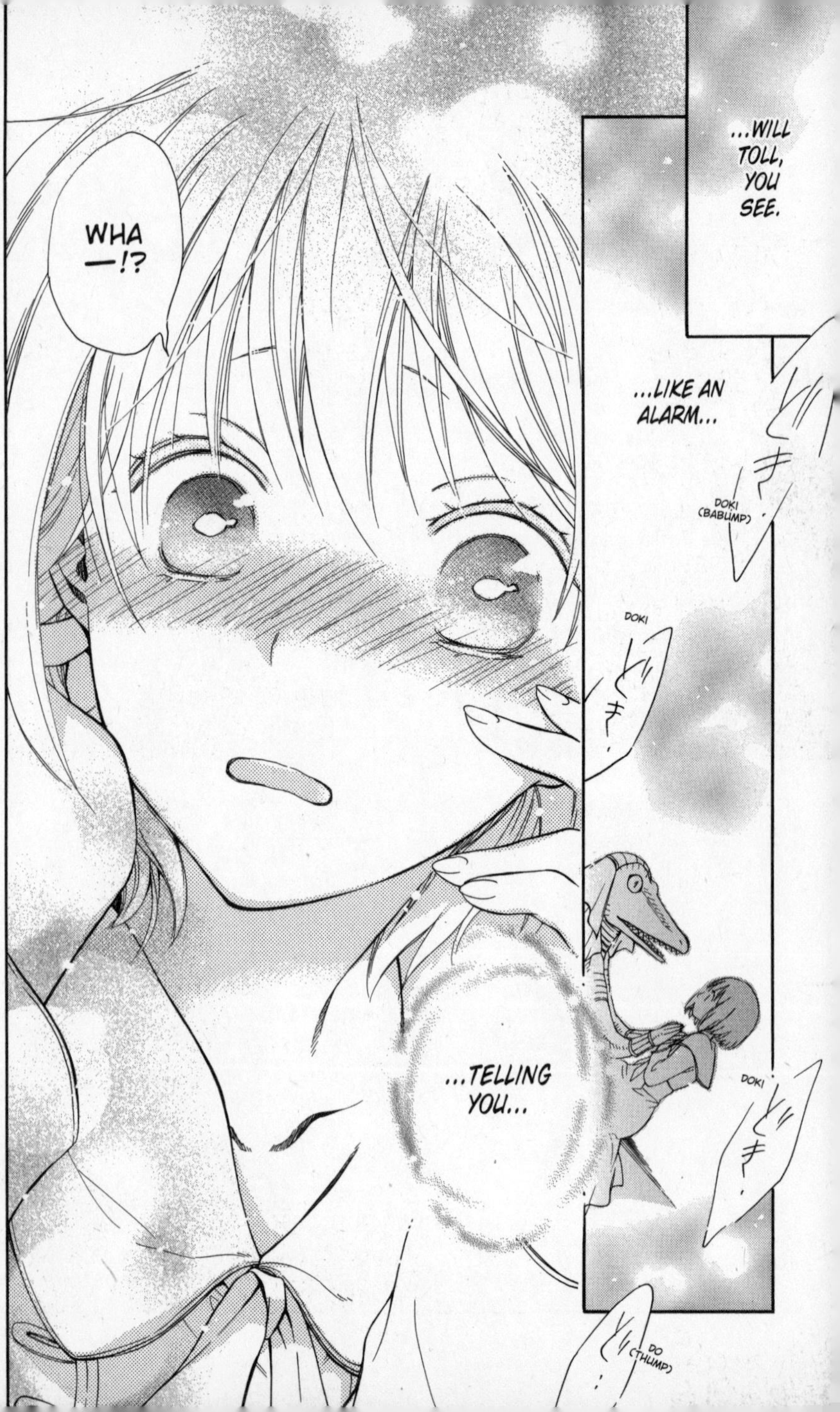
...WILL TOLL, YOU SEE.
...LIKE AN ALARM...
DOKI (BABUMP)
DOKI
DOKI
WHA—!?
...TELLING YOU...
DO (THUMP)

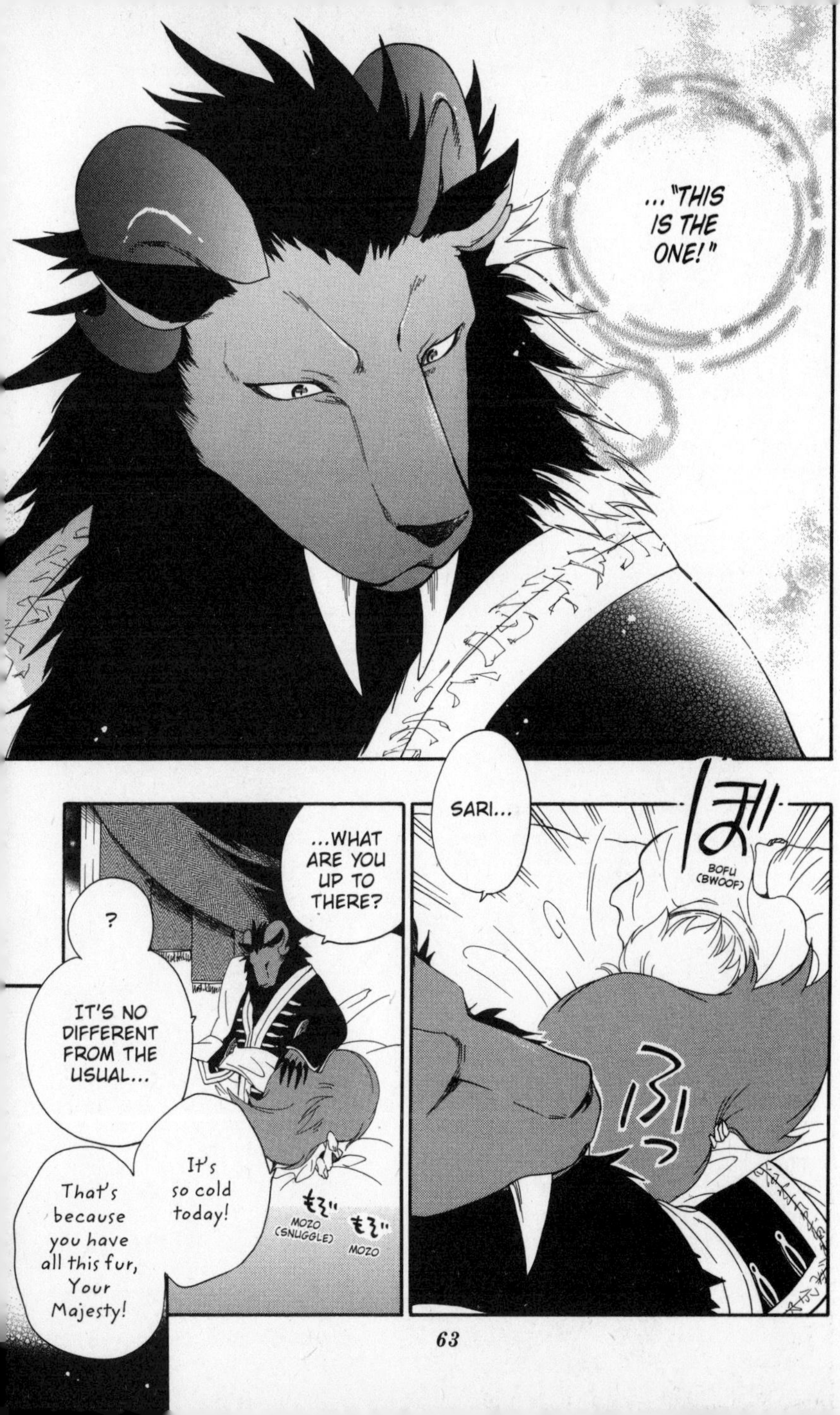
..."THIS IS THE ONE!"
SARI...
ぼ
BOFU (BWOOF)
ふっ
...WHAT ARE YOU UP TO THERE?
?
IT'S NO DIFFERENT FROM THE USUAL...
It's so cold today!
That's because you have all this fur, Your Majesty!
もぞ
MOZO (SNUGGLE)
もぞ
MOZO

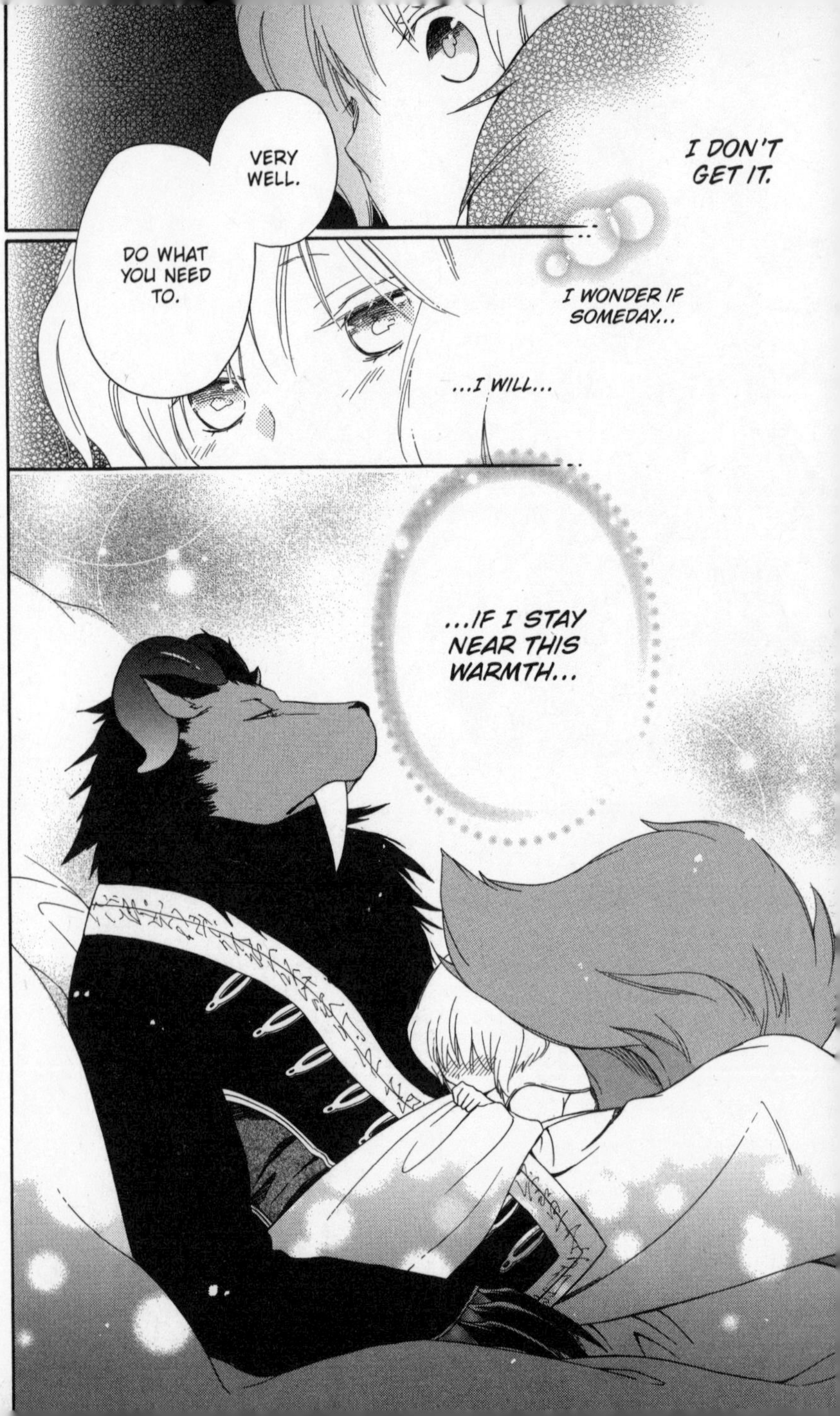
I DON'T GET IT.
VERY WELL.
DO WHAT YOU NEED TO.
I WONDER IF SOMEDAY...
...I WILL...
...IF I STAY NEAR THIS WARMTH...

episode.8

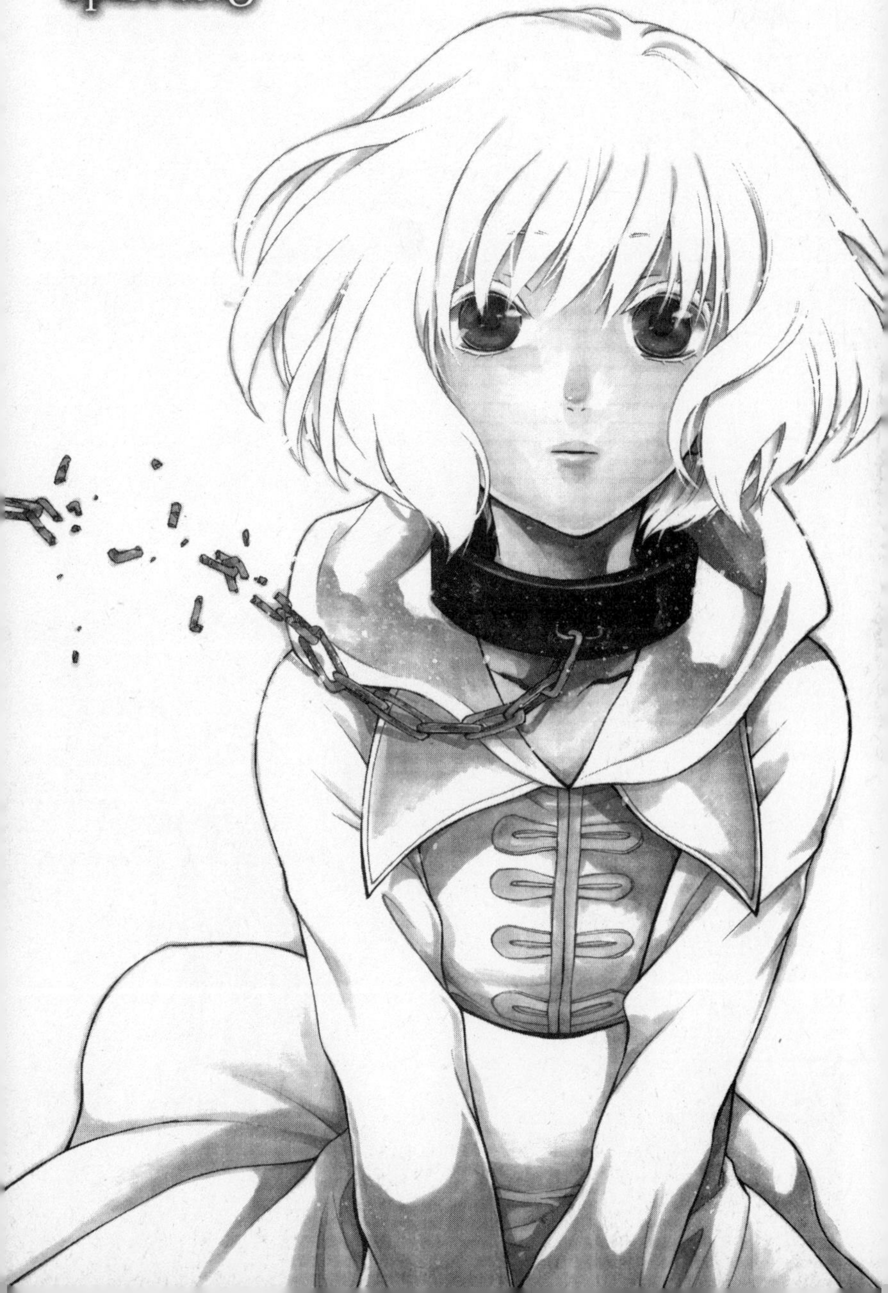

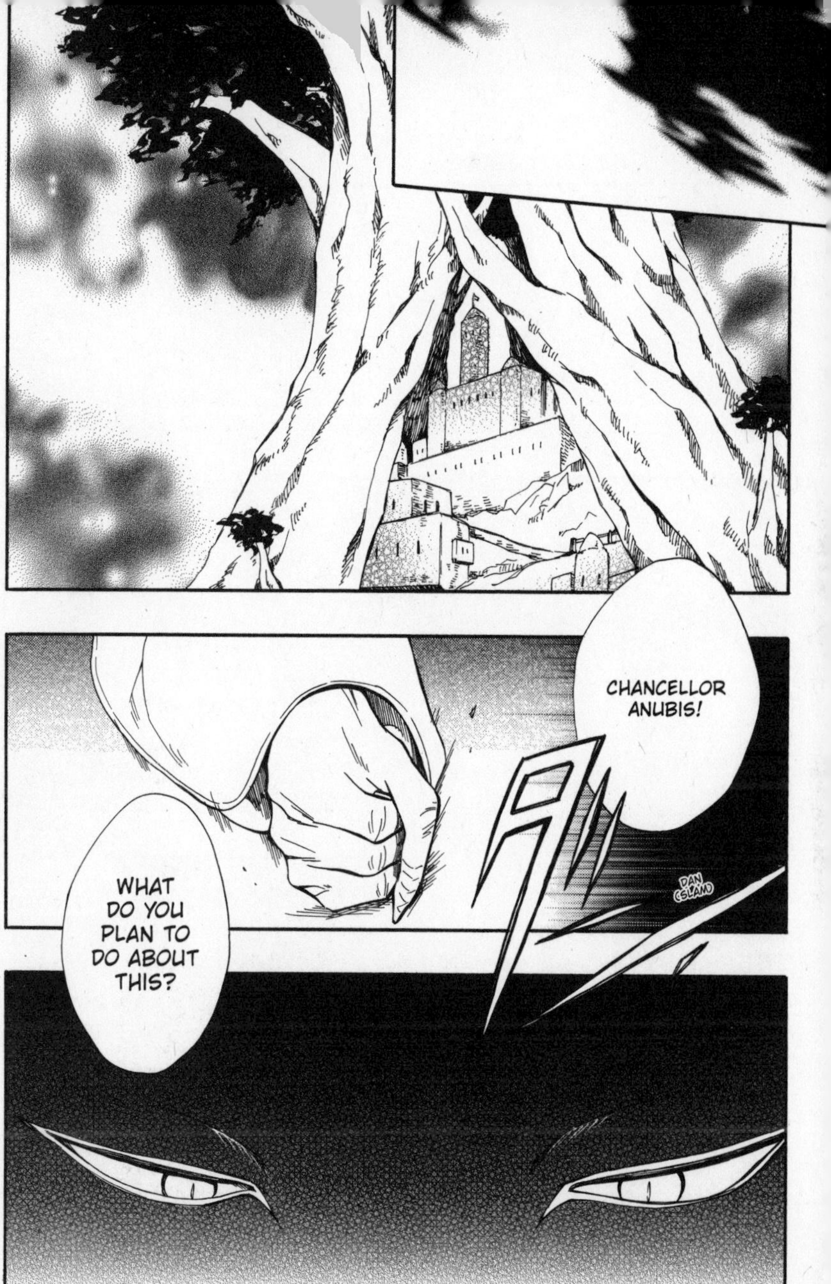
CHANCELLOR ANUBIS!
DAN (SLAM)
WHAT DO YOU PLAN TO DO ABOUT THIS?

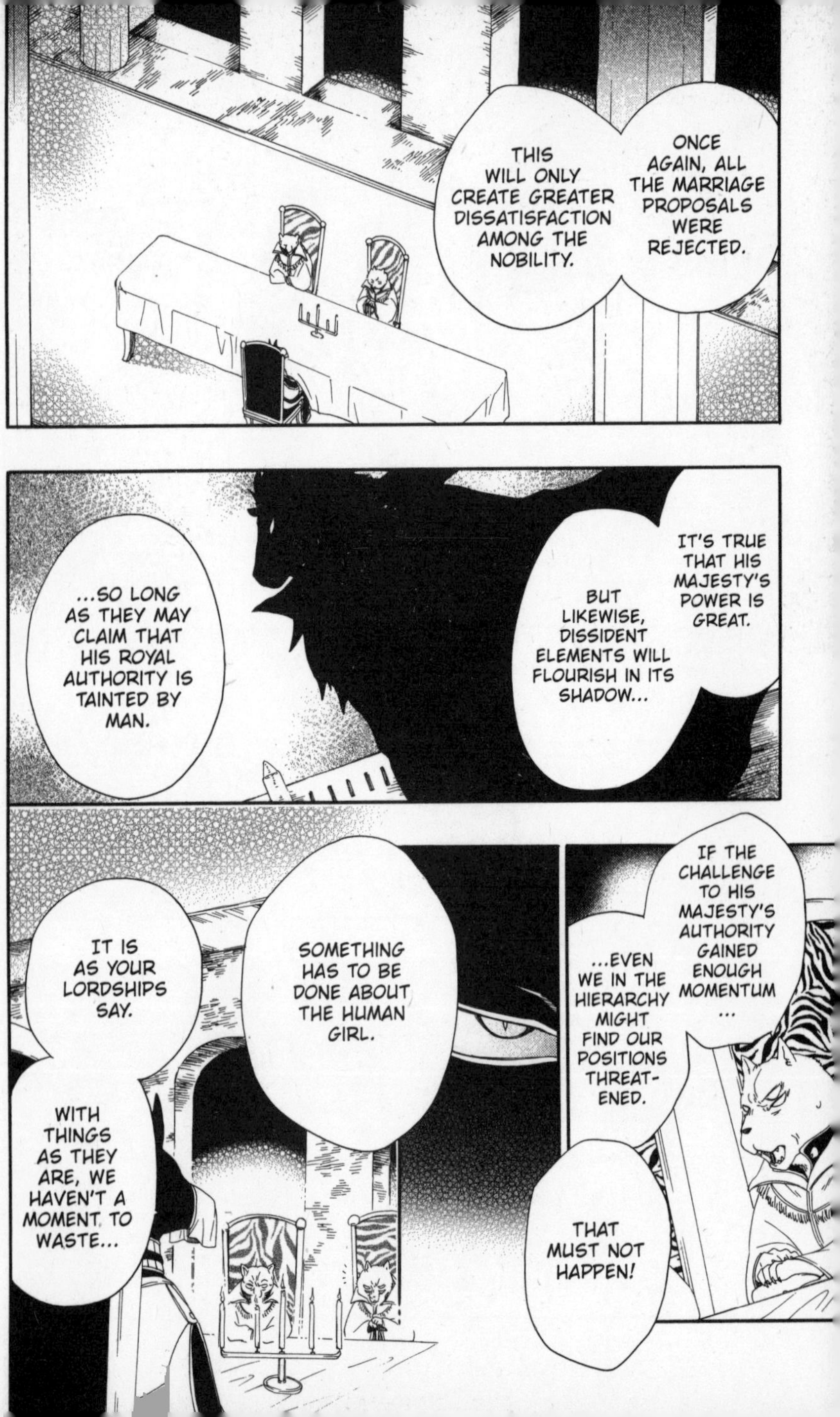
ONCE AGAIN, ALL THE MARRIAGE PROPOSALS WERE REJECTED.
THIS WILL ONLY CREATE GREATER DISSATISFACTION AMONG THE NOBILITY.
IT'S TRUE THAT HIS MAJESTY'S POWER IS GREAT.
BUT LIKEWISE, DISSIDENT ELEMENTS WILL FLOURISH IN ITS SHADOW...
...SO LONG AS THEY MAY CLAIM THAT HIS ROYAL AUTHORITY IS TAINTED BY MAN.
IF THE CHALLENGE TO HIS MAJESTY'S AUTHORITY GAINED ENOUGH MOMENTUM...
...EVEN WE IN THE HIERARCHY MIGHT FIND OUR POSITIONS THREAT-ENED.
THAT MUST NOT HAPPEN!
SOMETHING HAS TO BE DONE ABOUT THE HUMAN GIRL.
IT IS AS YOUR LORDSHIPS SAY.
WITH THINGS AS THEY ARE, WE HAVEN'T A MOMENT TO WASTE...

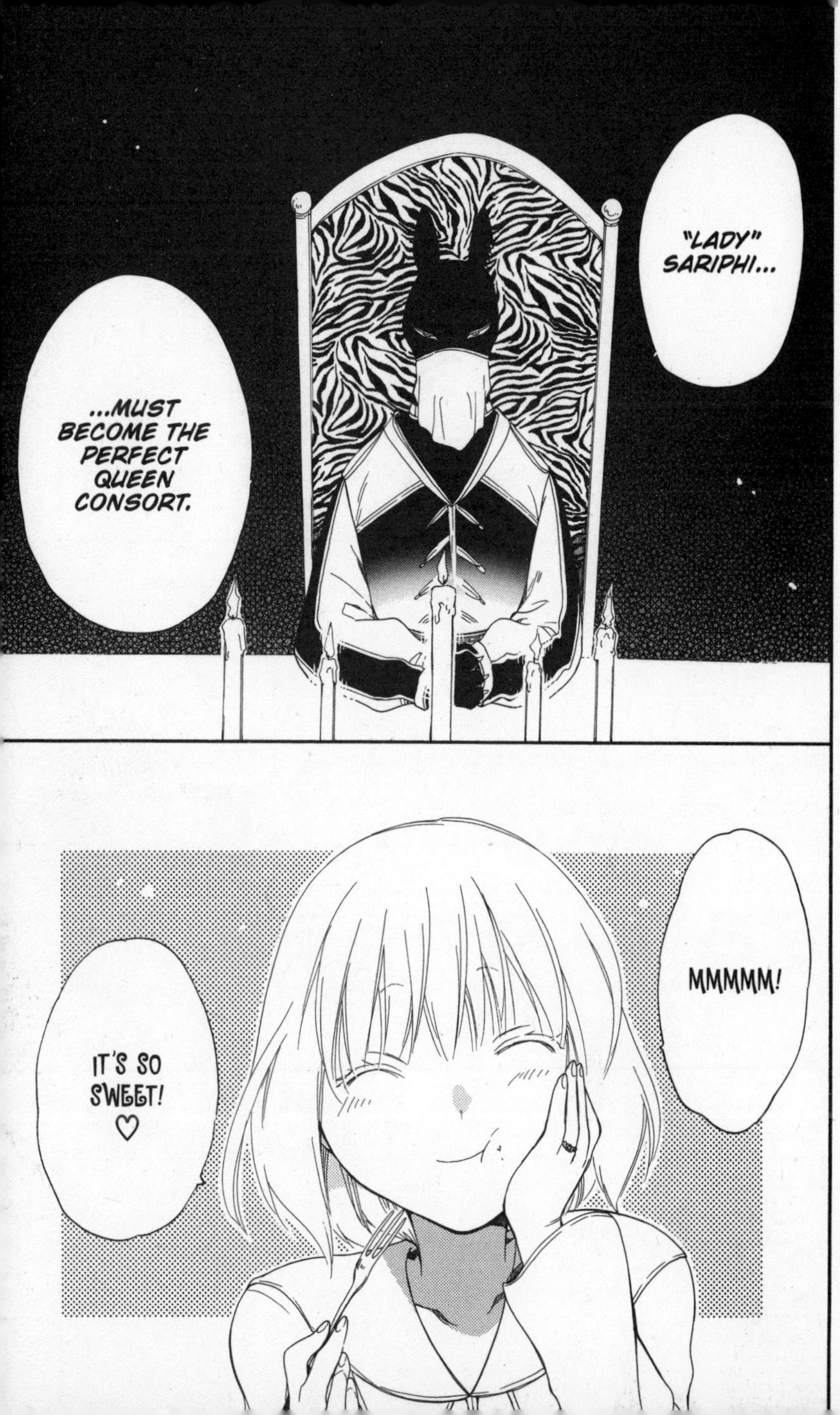
"LADY" SARIPHI...
...MUST BECOME THE PERFECT QUEEN CONSORT.
MMMMM!
IT'S SO SWEET! ♡

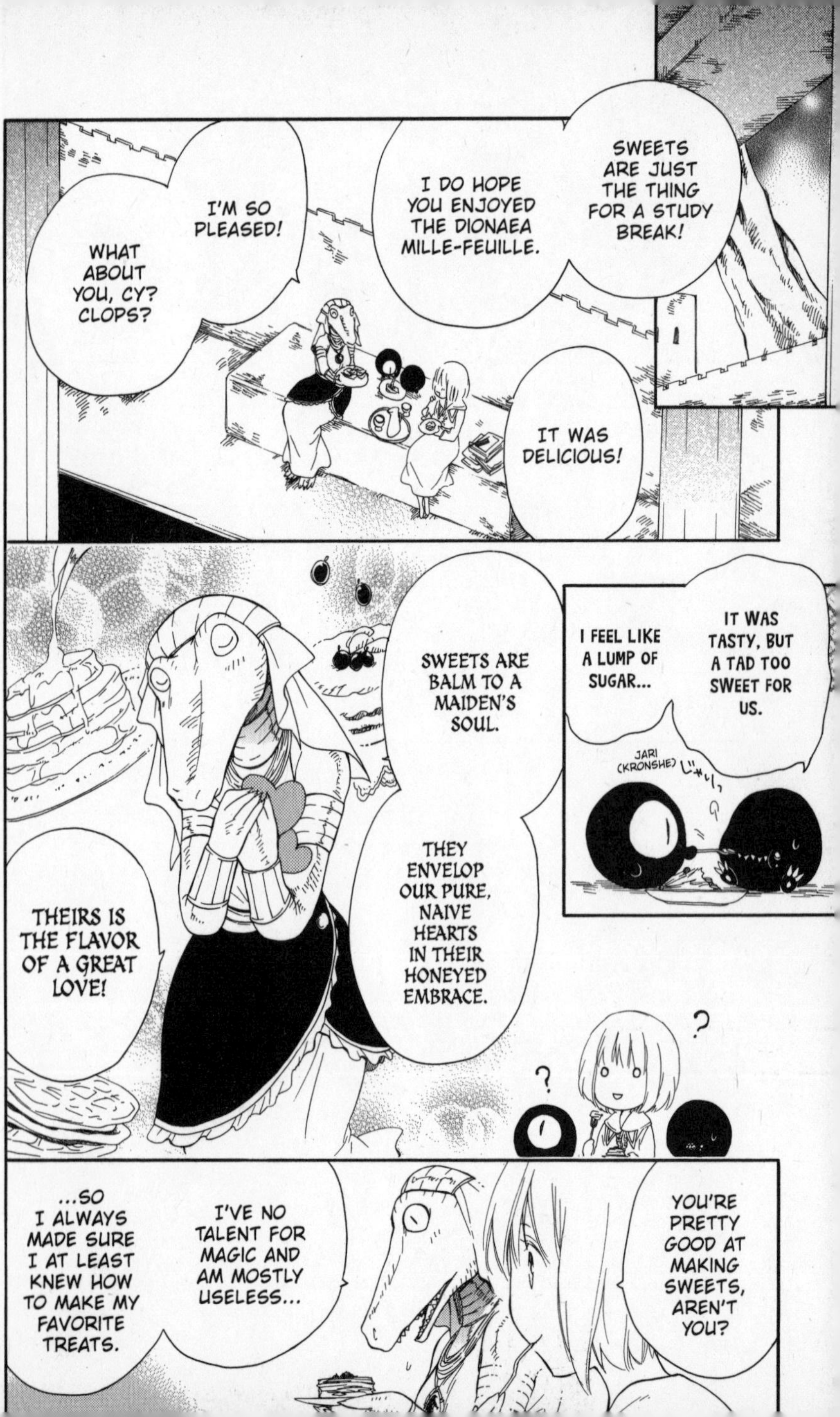
SWEETS ARE JUST THE THING FOR A STUDY BREAK!
I DO HOPE YOU ENJOYED THE DIONAEA MILLE-FEUILLE.
IT WAS DELICIOUS!
I'M SO PLEASED!
WHAT ABOUT YOU, CY? CLOPS?
IT WAS TASTY, BUT A TAD TOO SWEET FOR US.
I FEEL LIKE A LUMP OF SUGAR...
JARI (KRONSHE)
じゃり
SWEETS ARE BALM TO A MAIDEN'S SOUL.
THEY ENVELOP OUR PURE, NAIVE HEARTS IN THEIR HONEYED EMBRACE.
THEIRS IS THE FLAVOR OF A GREAT LOVE!
?
?
YOU'RE PRETTY GOOD AT MAKING SWEETS, AREN'T YOU?
I'VE NO TALENT FOR MAGIC AND AM MOSTLY USELESS...
...SO I ALWAYS MADE SURE I AT LEAST KNEW HOW TO MAKE MY FAVORITE TREATS.

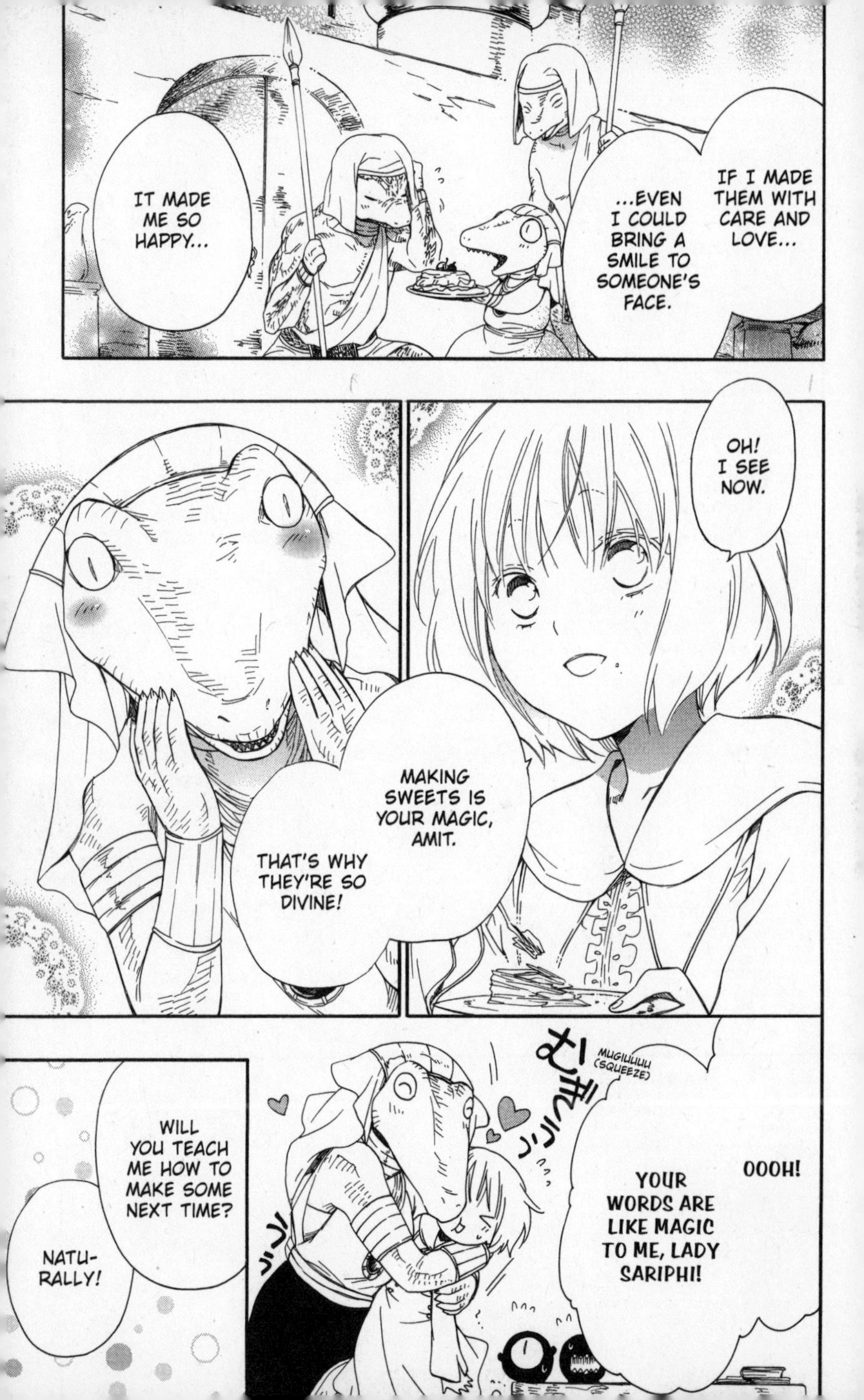
IF I MADE THEM WITH CARE AND LOVE...
...EVEN I COULD BRING A SMILE TO SOMEONE'S FACE.
IT MADE ME SO HAPPY...
OH! I SEE NOW.
MAKING SWEETS IS YOUR MAGIC, AMIT.
THAT'S WHY THEY'RE SO DIVINE!
MUGIUUUU (SQUEEZE)
OOOH!
YOUR WORDS ARE LIKE MAGIC TO ME, LADY SARIPHI!
WILL YOU TEACH ME HOW TO MAKE SOME NEXT TIME?
NATU-RALLY!

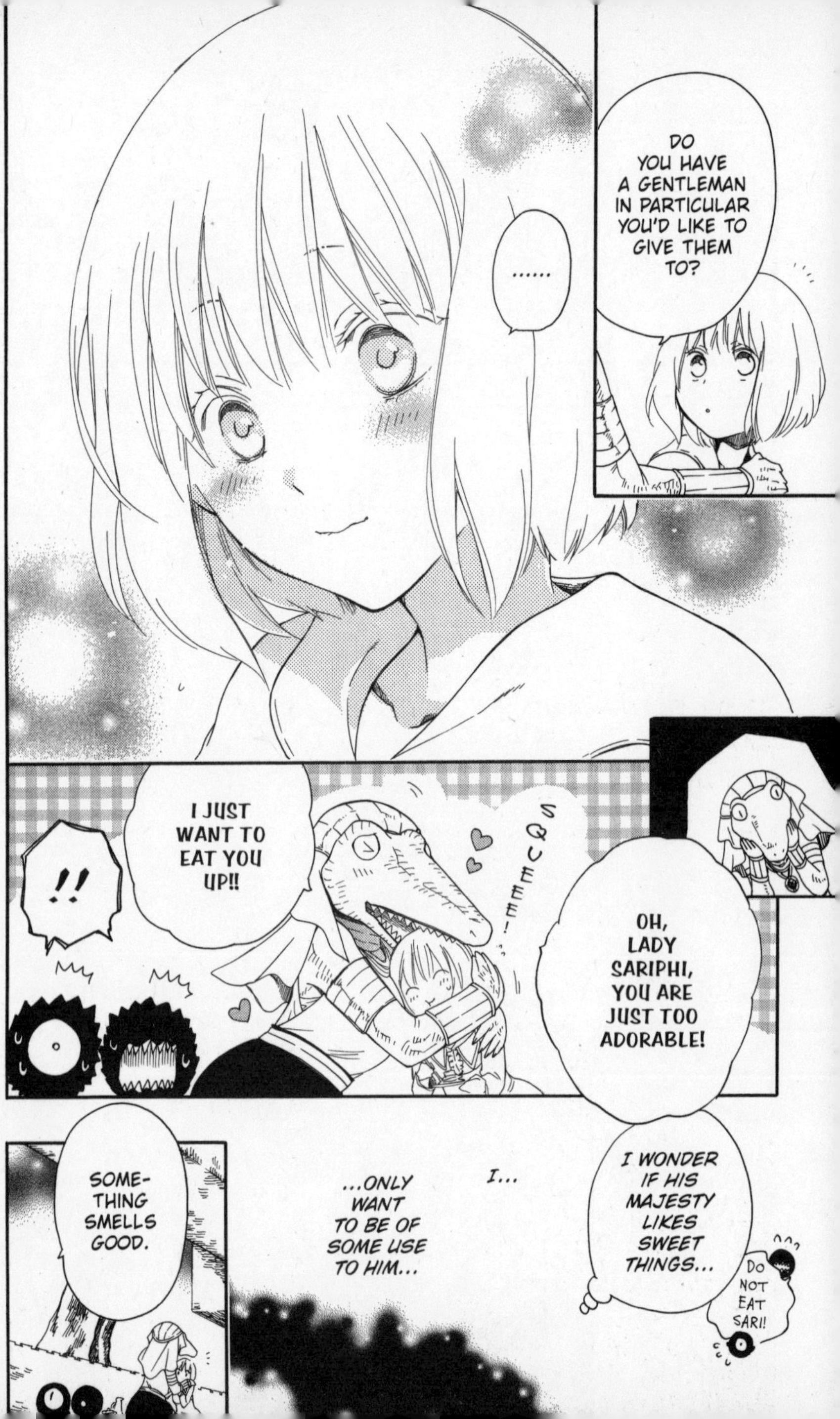

DO YOU HAVE A GENTLEMAN IN PARTICULAR YOU'D LIKE TO GIVE THEM TO?
......
OH, LADY SARIPHI, YOU ARE JUST TOO ADORABLE!
SQUEEE!
I JUST WANT TO EAT YOU UP!!
!!
I WONDER IF HIS MAJESTY LIKES SWEET THINGS...
DO NOT EAT SARI!
I...
...ONLY WANT TO BE OF SOME USE TO HIM...
SOME-THING SMELLS GOOD.

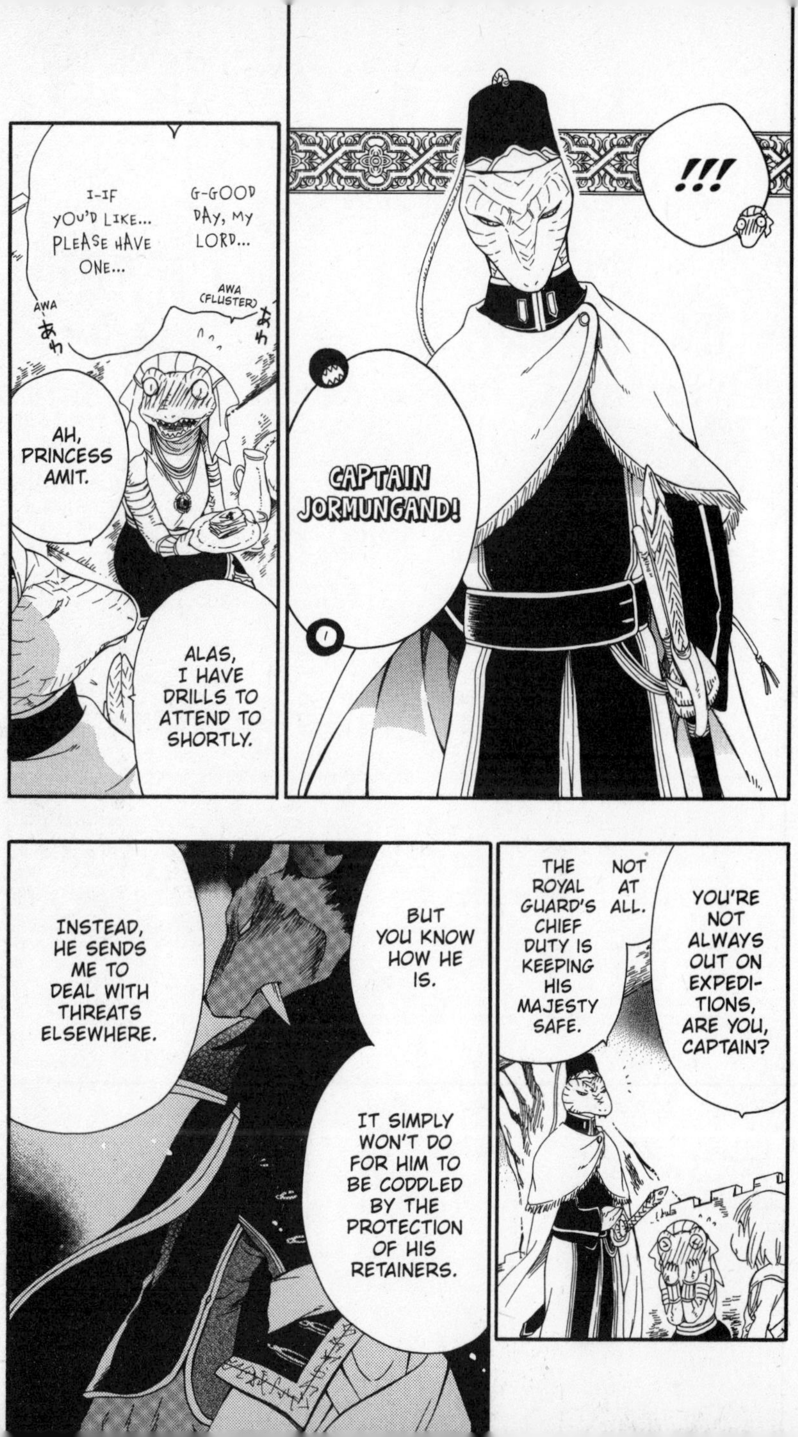
!!!
CAPTAIN JORMUNGAND!
G-GOOD DAY, MY LORD...
I-IF YOU'D LIKE... PLEASE HAVE ONE...
AWA (FLUSTER)
AWA
AH, PRINCESS AMIT.
ALAS, I HAVE DRILLS TO ATTEND TO SHORTLY.
YOU'RE NOT ALWAYS OUT ON EXPEDITIONS, ARE YOU, CAPTAIN?
NOT AT ALL.
THE ROYAL GUARD'S CHIEF DUTY IS KEEPING HIS MAJESTY SAFE.
BUT YOU KNOW HOW HE IS.
INSTEAD, HE SENDS ME TO DEAL WITH THREATS ELSEWHERE.
IT SIMPLY WON'T DO FOR HIM TO BE CODDLED BY THE PROTECTION OF HIS RETAINERS.

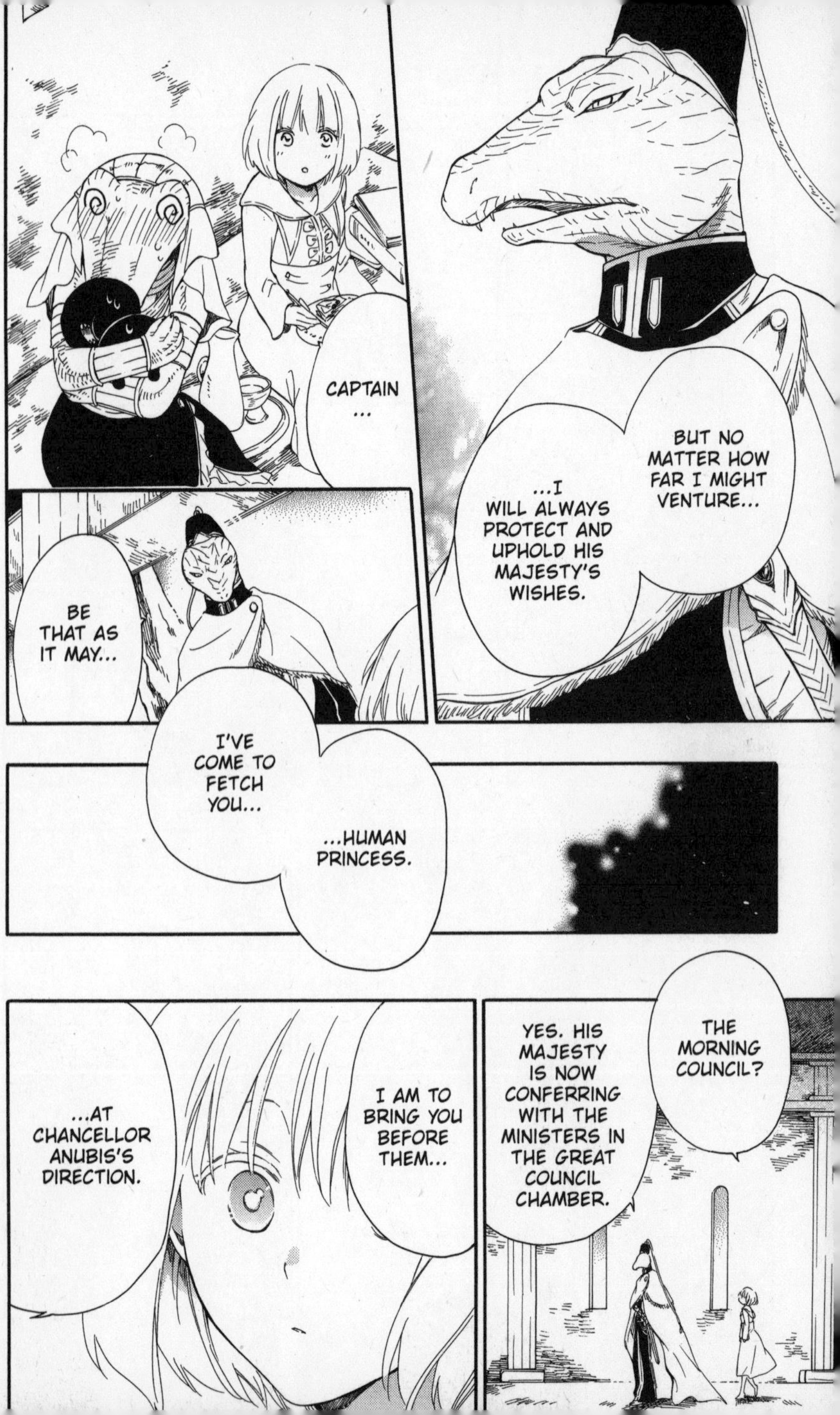
BUT NO MATTER HOW FAR I MIGHT VENTURE...
...I WILL ALWAYS PROTECT AND UPHOLD HIS MAJESTY'S WISHES.
CAPTAIN...
BE THAT AS IT MAY...
I'VE COME TO FETCH YOU...
...HUMAN PRINCESS.
THE MORNING COUNCIL?
YES. HIS MAJESTY IS NOW CONFERRING WITH THE MINISTERS IN THE GREAT COUNCIL CHAMBER.
I AM TO BRING YOU BEFORE THEM...
...AT CHANCELLOR ANUBIS'S DIRECTION.

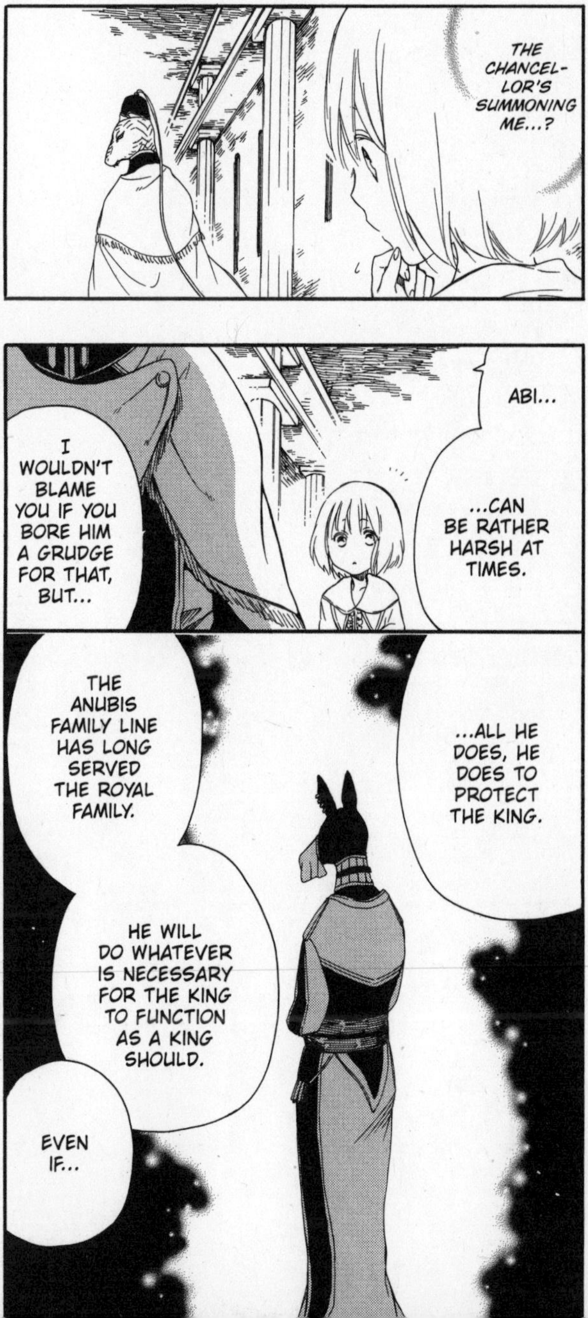
THE CHANCEL-LOR'S SUMMONING ME...?
ABI...
...CAN BE RATHER HARSH AT TIMES.
I WOULDN'T BLAME YOU IF YOU BORE HIM A GRUDGE FOR THAT, BUT...
...ALL HE DOES, HE DOES TO PROTECT THE KING.
THE ANUBIS FAMILY LINE HAS LONG SERVED THE ROYAL FAMILY.
HE WILL DO WHATEVER IS NECESSARY FOR THE KING TO FUNCTION AS A KING SHOULD.
EVEN IF...

AMIT

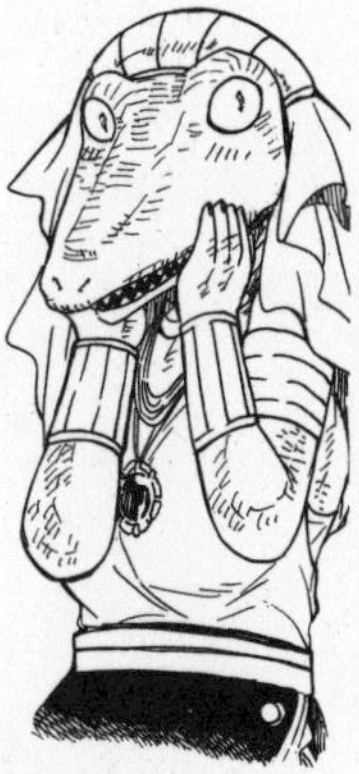

AMIT ORIGINALLY APPEARED IN A ONE-SHOT STORY CALLED "THE DEMON'S TAIL." HER SCARY FACE AND KINDHEARTED NATURE HAVEN'T CHANGED FROM THAT STORY, BUT AT MY EDITOR'S SUGGESTION, I ADDED HER MAIDENLY SENSE OF ROMANCE, WHICH TRANSFORMED HER INTO THE ADORABLE HEROINE SHE IS NOW. I THINK SHE'S THE MOST ROMANTICALLY INCLINED CHARACTER I'VE EVER DRAWN. SHE'S ALSO SOMEHOW TALLER THAN ANUBIS, WHICH CONCERNS ME... (IT CONCERNS ANUBIS TOO.)

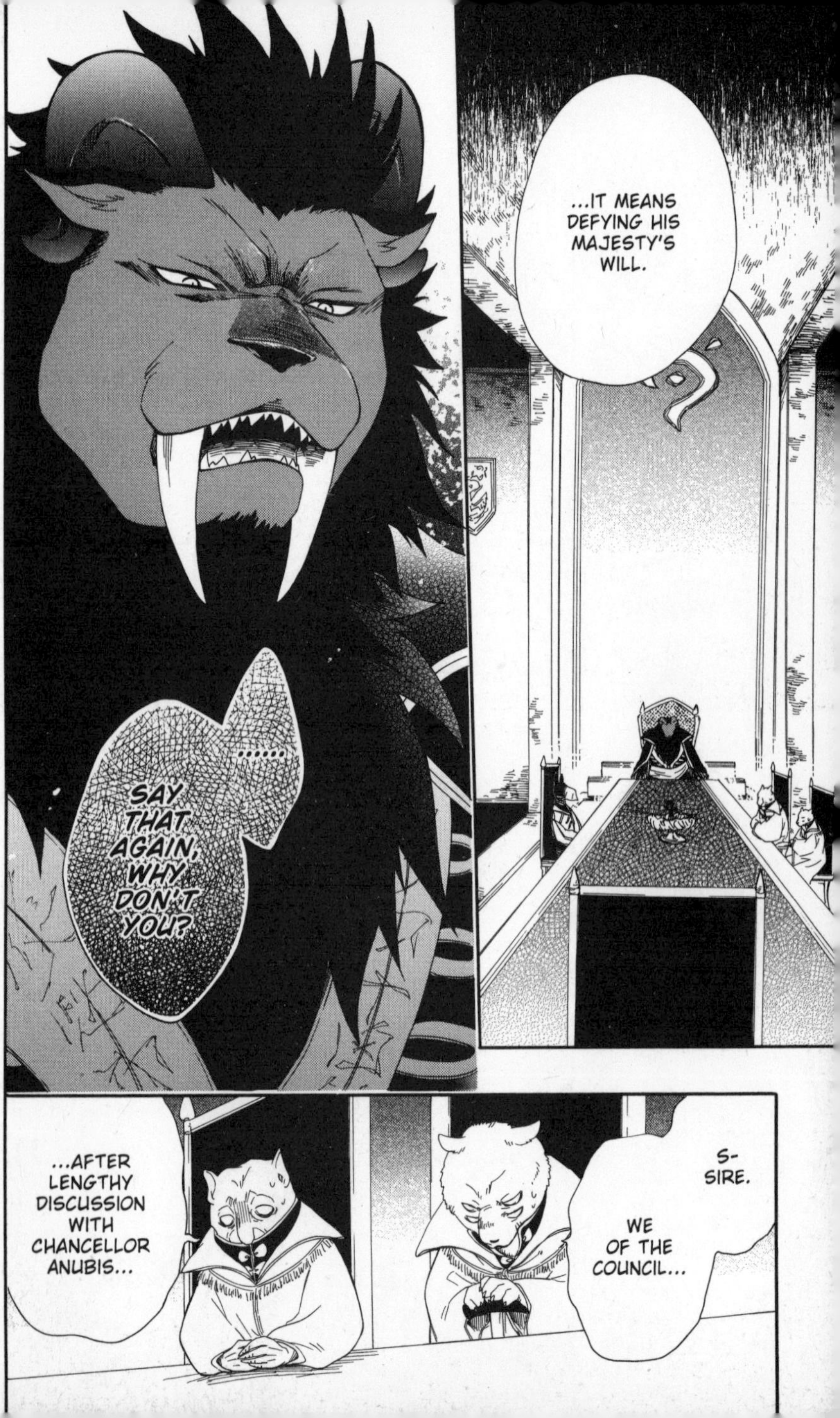
...IT MEANS DEFYING HIS MAJESTY'S WILL.
......
SAY THAT AGAIN, WHY DON'T YOU?
S-SIRE.
WE OF THE COUNCIL...
...AFTER LENGTHY DISCUSSION WITH CHANCELLOR ANUBIS...

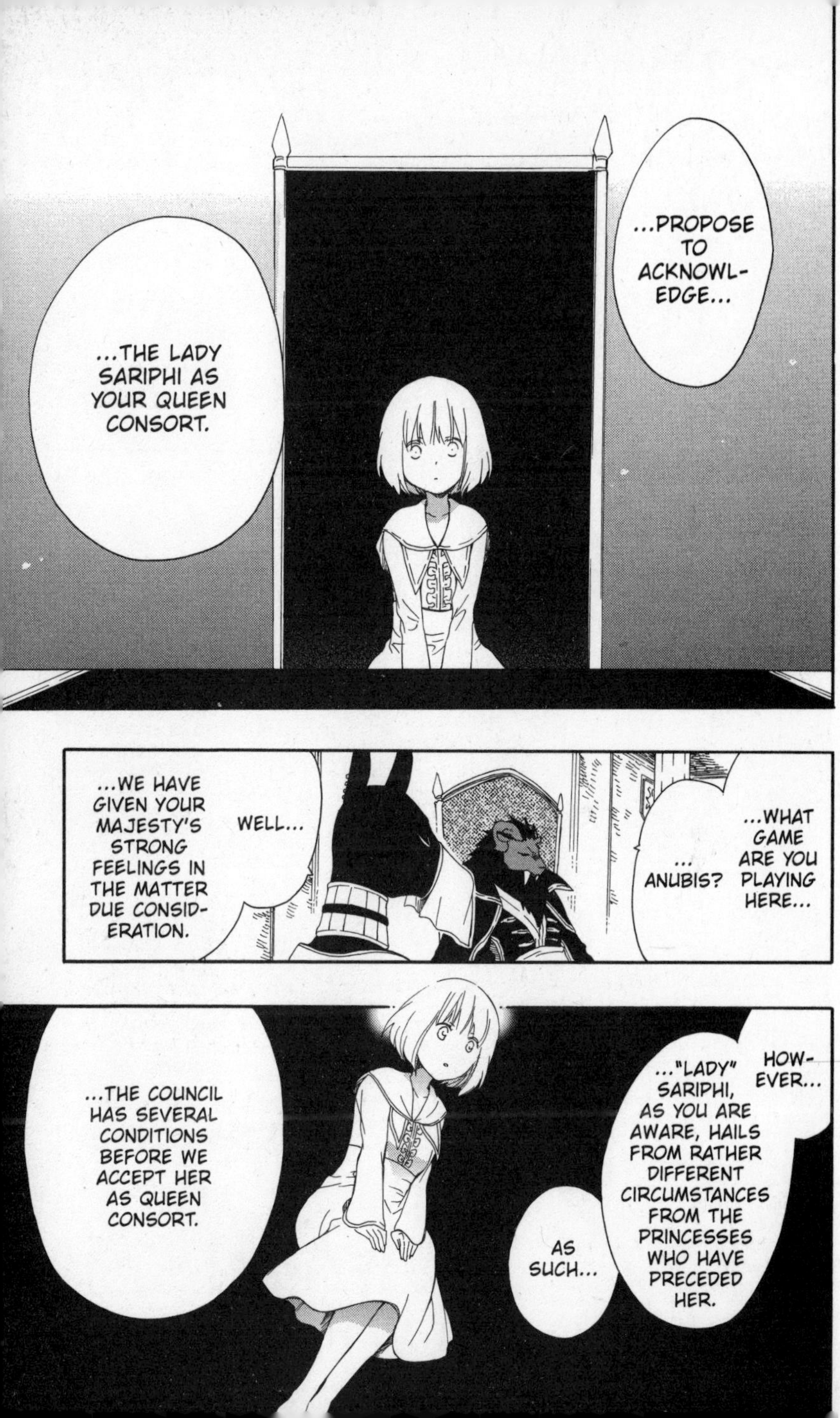
...PROPOSE TO ACKNOWL-EDGE...
...THE LADY SARIPHI AS YOUR QUEEN CONSORT.
...WHAT GAME ARE YOU PLAYING HERE...
...ANUBIS?
WELL...
...WE HAVE GIVEN YOUR MAJESTY'S STRONG FEELINGS IN THE MATTER DUE CONSID-ERATION.
HOW-EVER...
..."LADY" SARIPHI, AS YOU ARE AWARE, HAILS FROM RATHER DIFFERENT CIRCUMSTANCES FROM THE PRINCESSES WHO HAVE PRECEDED HER.
AS SUCH...
...THE COUNCIL HAS SEVERAL CONDITIONS BEFORE WE ACCEPT HER AS QUEEN CONSORT.

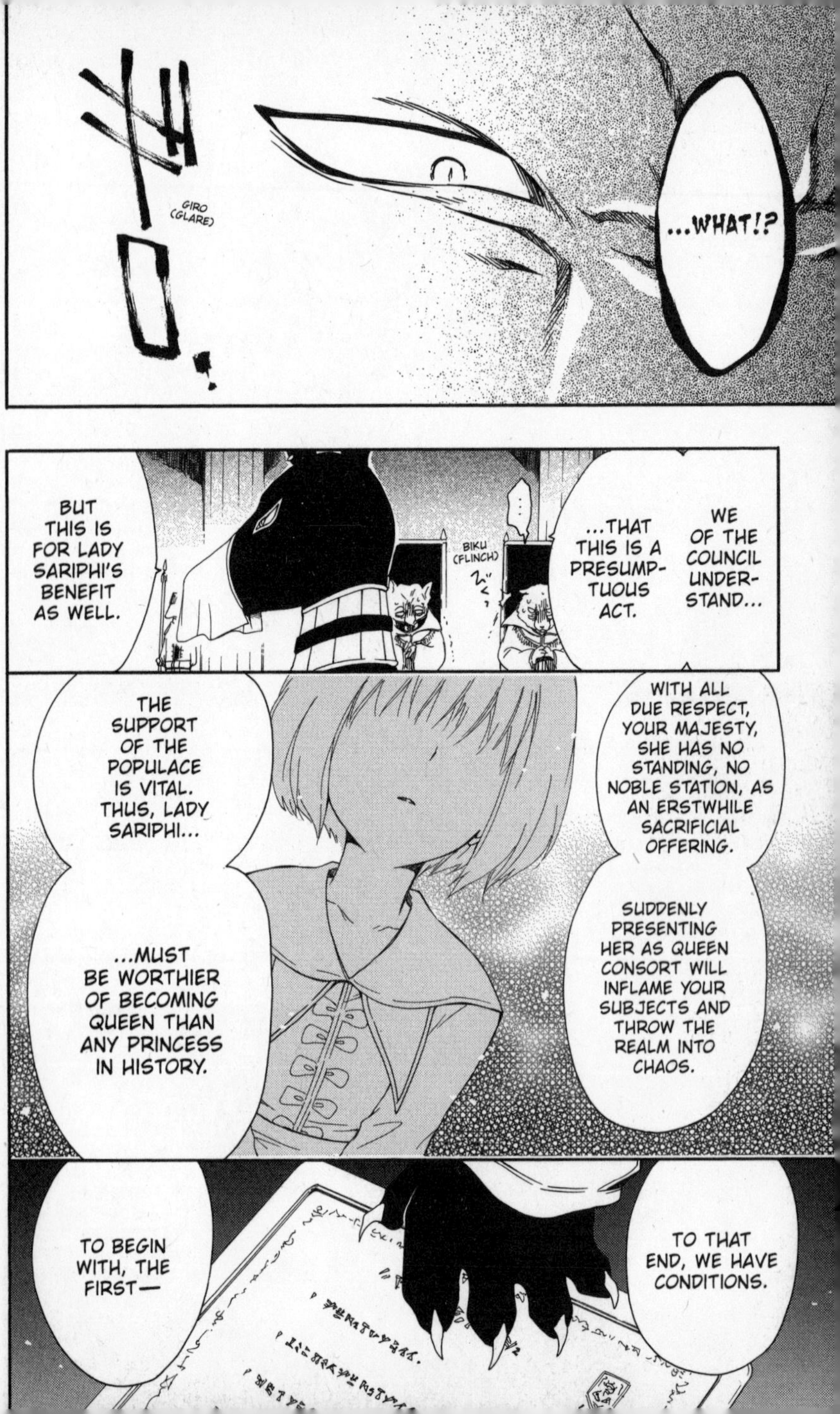
...WHAT!?
GIRO (GLARE)
WE OF THE COUNCIL UNDERSTAND...
...THAT THIS IS A PRESUMPTUOUS ACT.
BIKU (FLINCH)
BUT THIS IS FOR LADY SARIPHI'S BENEFIT AS WELL.
WITH ALL DUE RESPECT, YOUR MAJESTY, SHE HAS NO STANDING, NO NOBLE STATION, AS AN ERSTWHILE SACRIFICIAL OFFERING.
SUDDENLY PRESENTING HER AS QUEEN CONSORT WILL INFLAME YOUR SUBJECTS AND THROW THE REALM INTO CHAOS.
THE SUPPORT OF THE POPULACE IS VITAL. THUS, LADY SARIPHI...
...MUST BE WORTHIER OF BECOMING QUEEN THAN ANY PRINCESS IN HISTORY.
TO THAT END, WE HAVE CONDITIONS.
TO BEGIN WITH, THE FIRST—

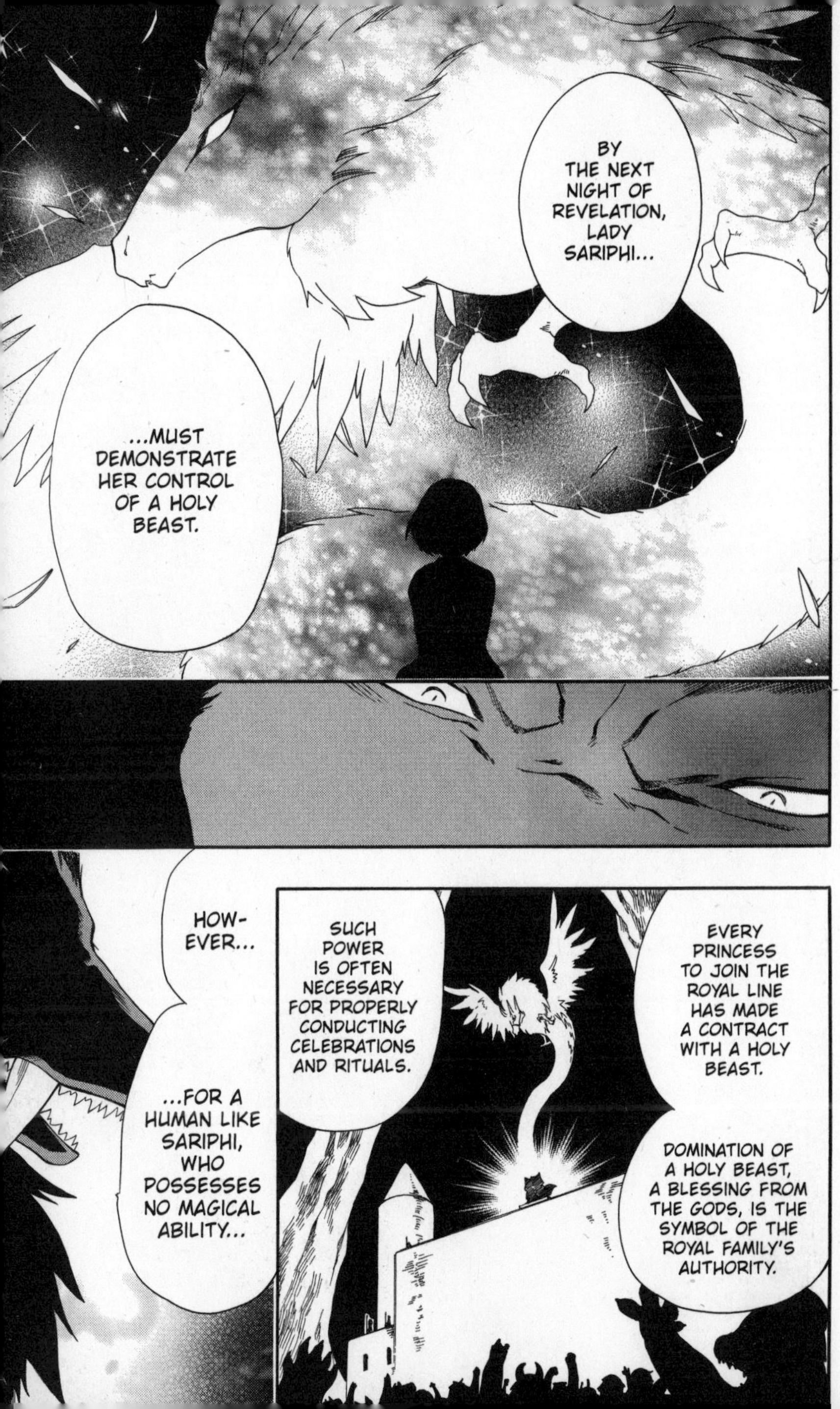
BY THE NEXT NIGHT OF REVELATION, LADY SARIPHI...
...MUST DEMONSTRATE HER CONTROL OF A HOLY BEAST.
EVERY PRINCESS TO JOIN THE ROYAL LINE HAS MADE A CONTRACT WITH A HOLY BEAST.
DOMINATION OF A HOLY BEAST, A BLESSING FROM THE GODS, IS THE SYMBOL OF THE ROYAL FAMILY'S AUTHORITY.
SUCH POWER IS OFTEN NECESSARY FOR PROPERLY CONDUCTING CELEBRATIONS AND RITUALS.
HOW-EVER...
...FOR A HUMAN LIKE SARIPHI, WHO POSSESSES NO MAGICAL ABILITY...

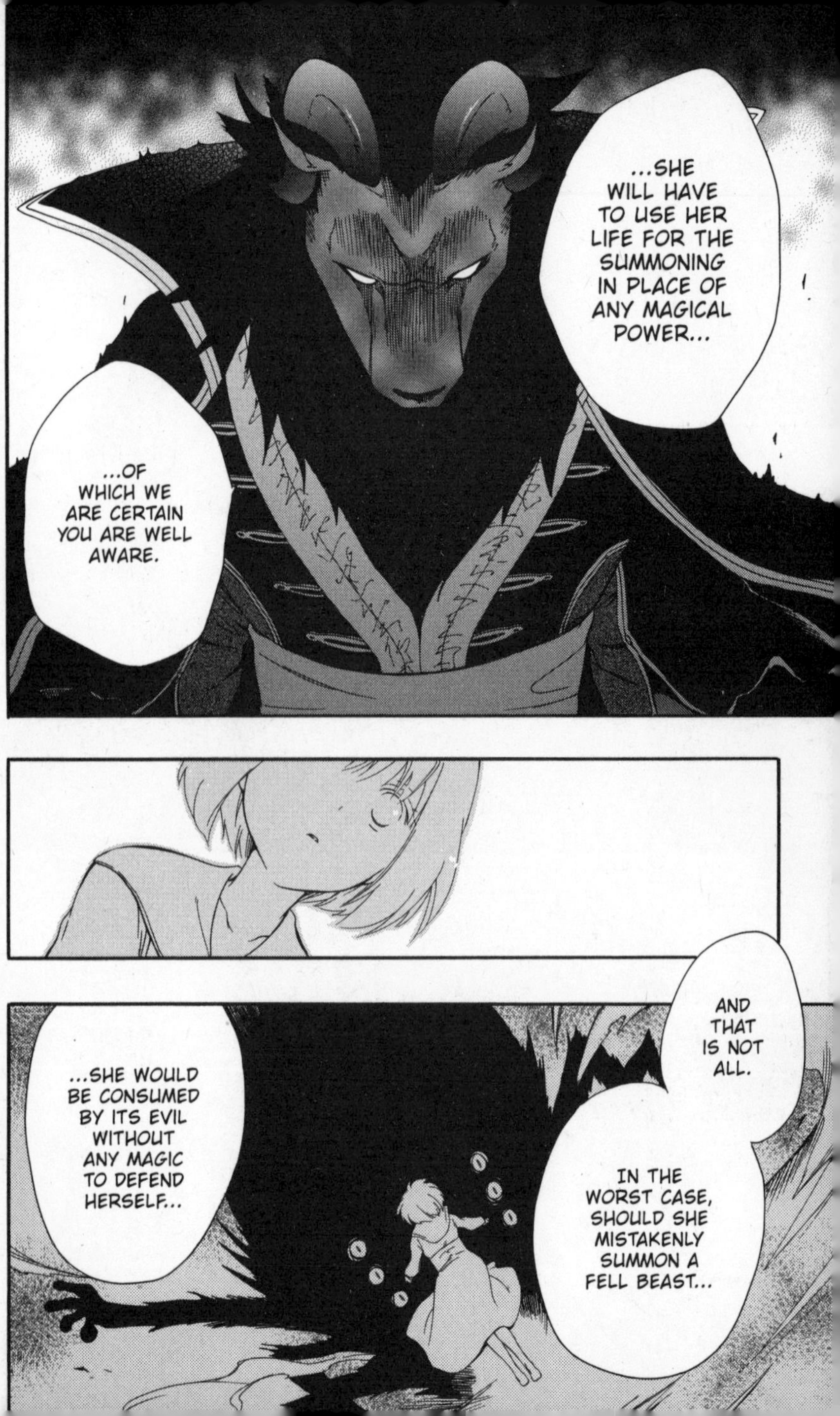
...SHE WILL HAVE TO USE HER LIFE FOR THE SUMMONING IN PLACE OF ANY MAGICAL POWER...
...OF WHICH WE ARE CERTAIN YOU ARE WELL AWARE.
AND THAT IS NOT ALL.
IN THE WORST CASE, SHOULD SHE MISTAKENLY SUMMON A FELL BEAST...
...SHE WOULD BE CONSUMED BY ITS EVIL WITHOUT ANY MAGIC TO DEFEND HERSELF...

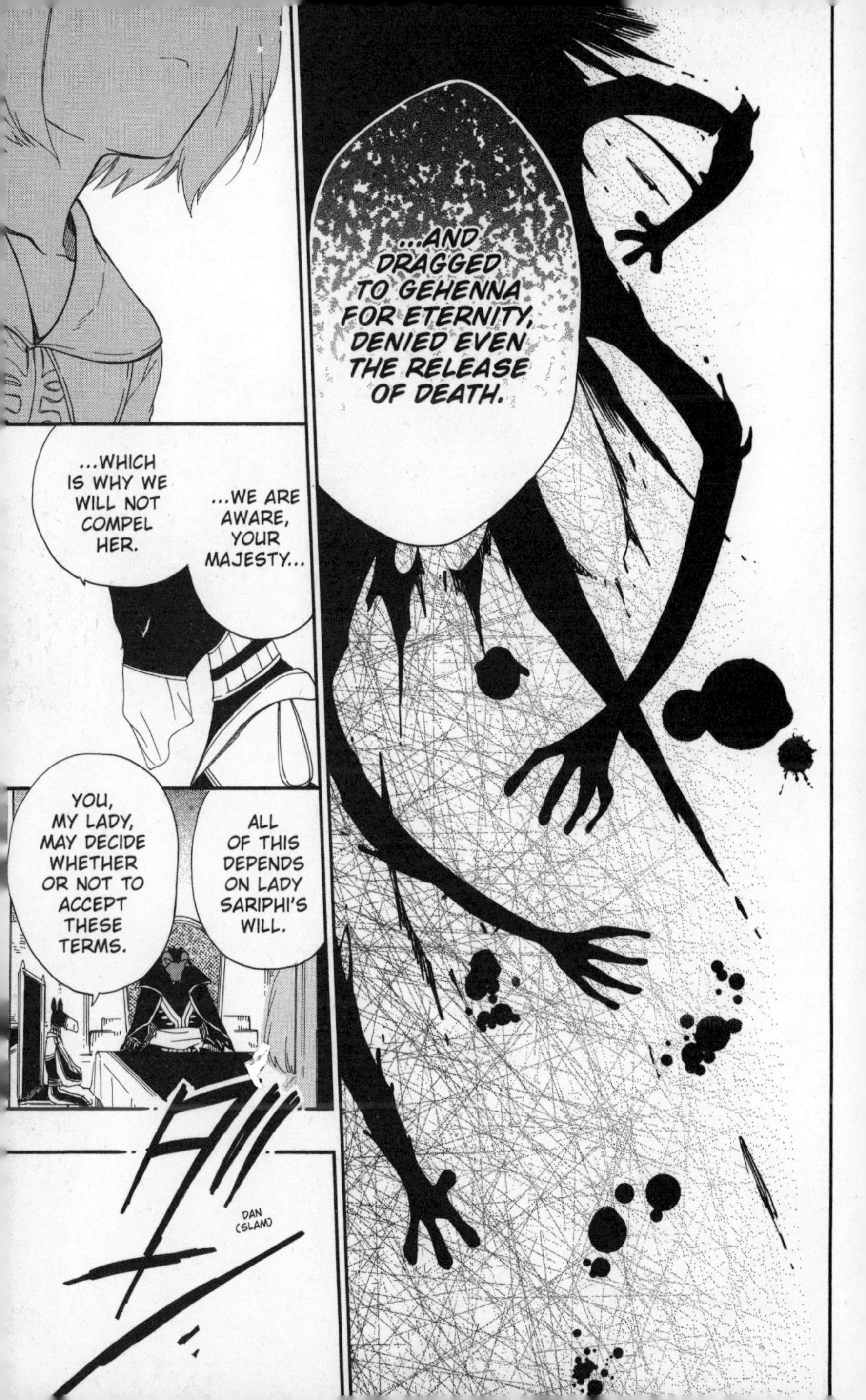
...AND DRAGGED TO GEHENNA FOR ETERNITY, DENIED EVEN THE RELEASE OF DEATH.
...WE ARE AWARE, YOUR MAJESTY...
...WHICH IS WHY WE WILL NOT COMPEL HER.
ALL OF THIS DEPENDS ON LADY SARIPHI'S WILL.
YOU, MY LADY, MAY DECIDE WHETHER OR NOT TO ACCEPT THESE TERMS.
DAN (SLAM)

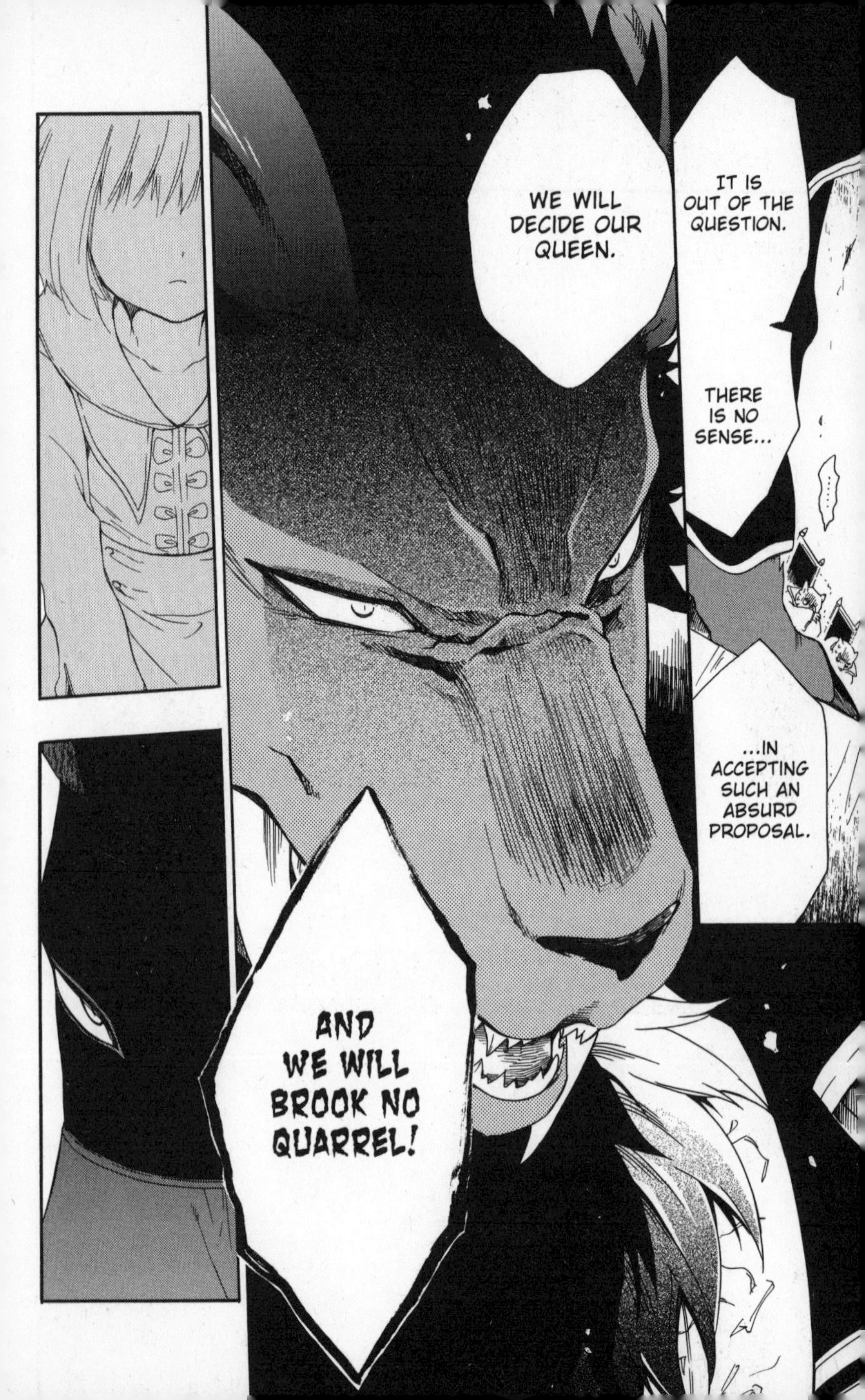
IT IS OUT OF THE QUESTION.
THERE IS NO SENSE...
...IN ACCEPTING SUCH AN ABSURD PROPOSAL.
WE WILL DECIDE OUR QUEEN.
AND WE WILL BROOK NO QUARREL!

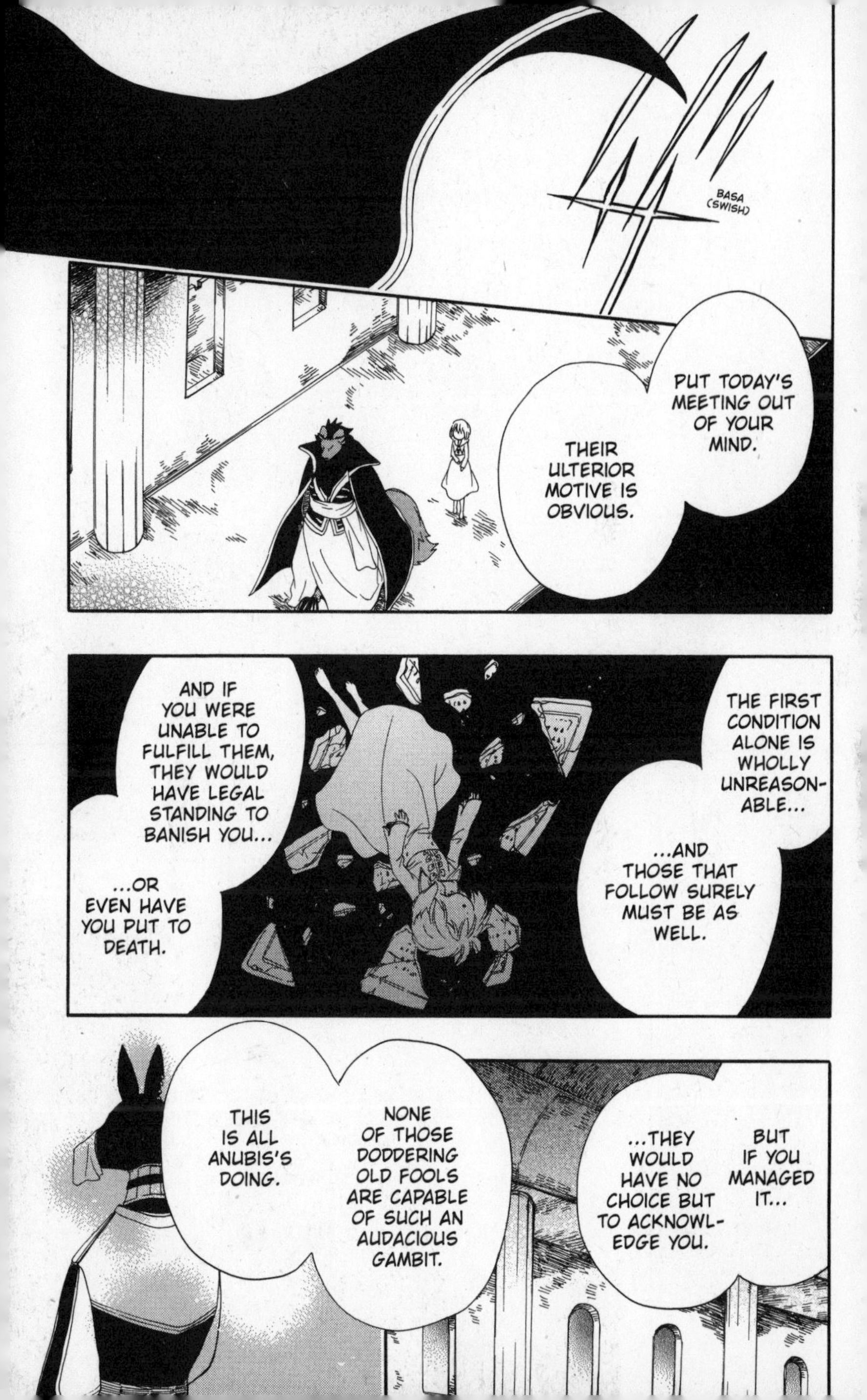
BASA (SWISH)
PUT TODAY'S MEETING OUT OF YOUR MIND.
THEIR ULTERIOR MOTIVE IS OBVIOUS.
THE FIRST CONDITION ALONE IS WHOLLY UNREASONABLE...
...AND THOSE THAT FOLLOW SURELY MUST BE AS WELL.
AND IF YOU WERE UNABLE TO FULFILL THEM, THEY WOULD HAVE LEGAL STANDING TO BANISH YOU...
...OR EVEN HAVE YOU PUT TO DEATH.
BUT IF YOU MANAGED IT...
...THEY WOULD HAVE NO CHOICE BUT TO ACKNOWLEDGE YOU.
NONE OF THOSE DODDERING OLD FOOLS ARE CAPABLE OF SUCH AN AUDACIOUS GAMBIT.
THIS IS ALL ANUBIS'S DOING.

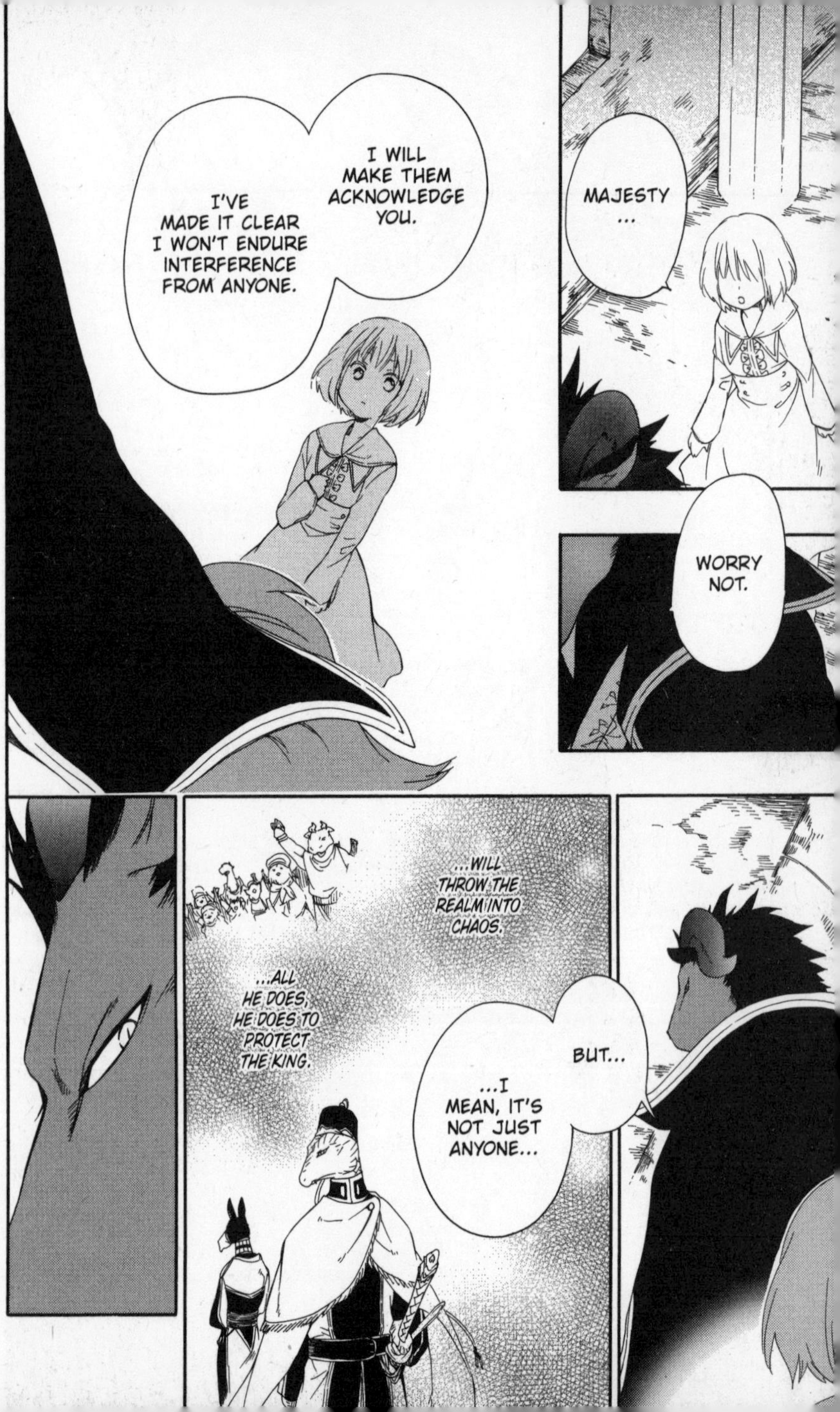
MAJESTY ...
WORRY NOT.
I WILL MAKE THEM ACKNOWLEDGE YOU.
I'VE MADE IT CLEAR I WON'T ENDURE INTERFERENCE FROM ANYONE.
BUT...
...I MEAN, IT'S NOT JUST ANYONE...
...WILL THROW THE REALM INTO CHAOS.
...ALL HE DOES, HE DOES TO PROTECT THE KING.

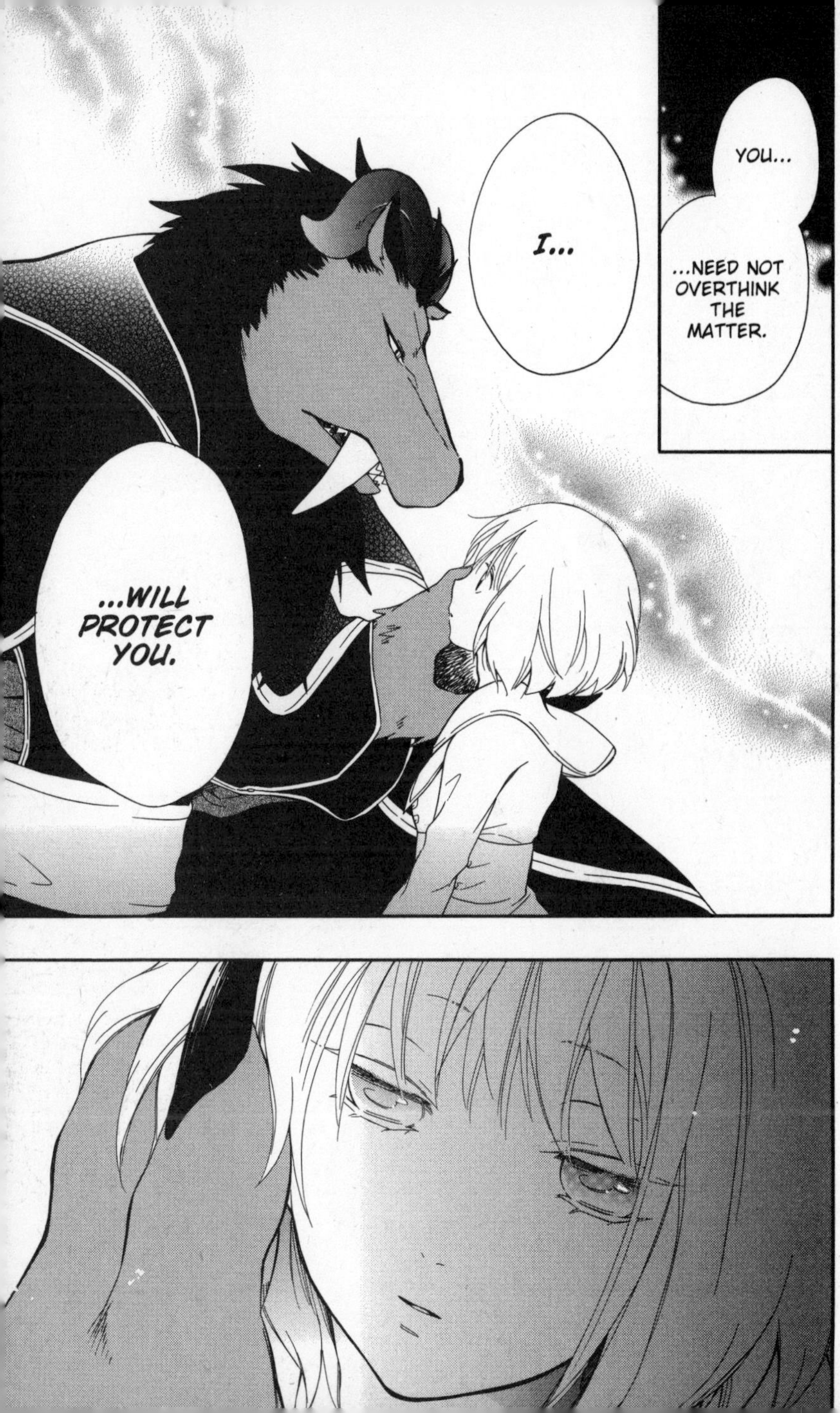
YOU...
...NEED NOT OVERTHINK THE MATTER.
I...
...WILL PROTECT YOU.

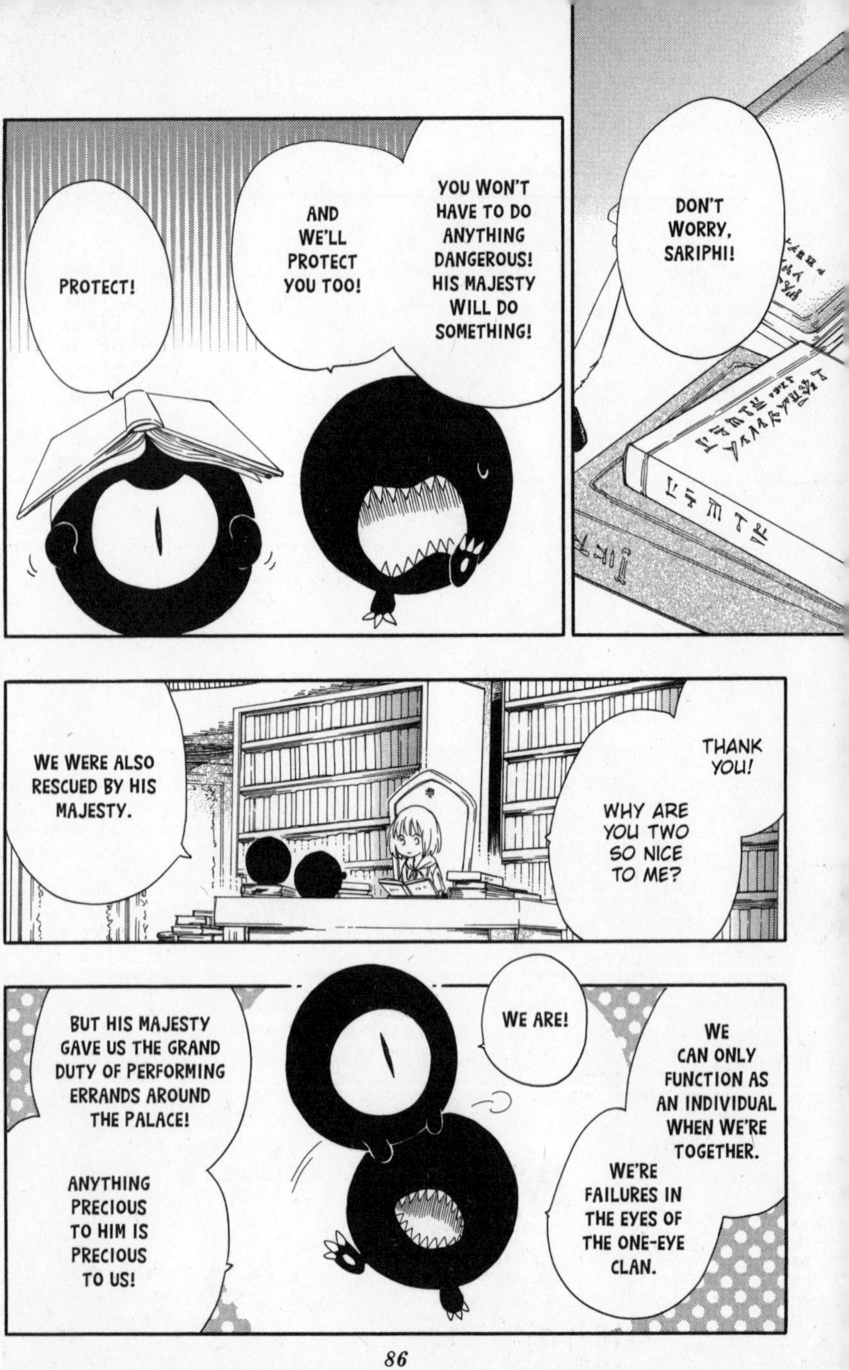
DON'T WORRY, SARIPHI!
YOU WON'T HAVE TO DO ANYTHING DANGEROUS! HIS MAJESTY WILL DO SOMETHING!
AND WE'LL PROTECT YOU TOO!
PROTECT!
THANK YOU!
WHY ARE YOU TWO SO NICE TO ME?
WE WERE ALSO RESCUED BY HIS MAJESTY.
WE ARE!
WE CAN ONLY FUNCTION AS AN INDIVIDUAL WHEN WE'RE TOGETHER.
WE'RE FAILURES IN THE EYES OF THE ONE-EYE CLAN.
BUT HIS MAJESTY GAVE US THE GRAND DUTY OF PERFORMING ERRANDS AROUND THE PALACE!
ANYTHING PRECIOUS TO HIM IS PRECIOUS TO US!

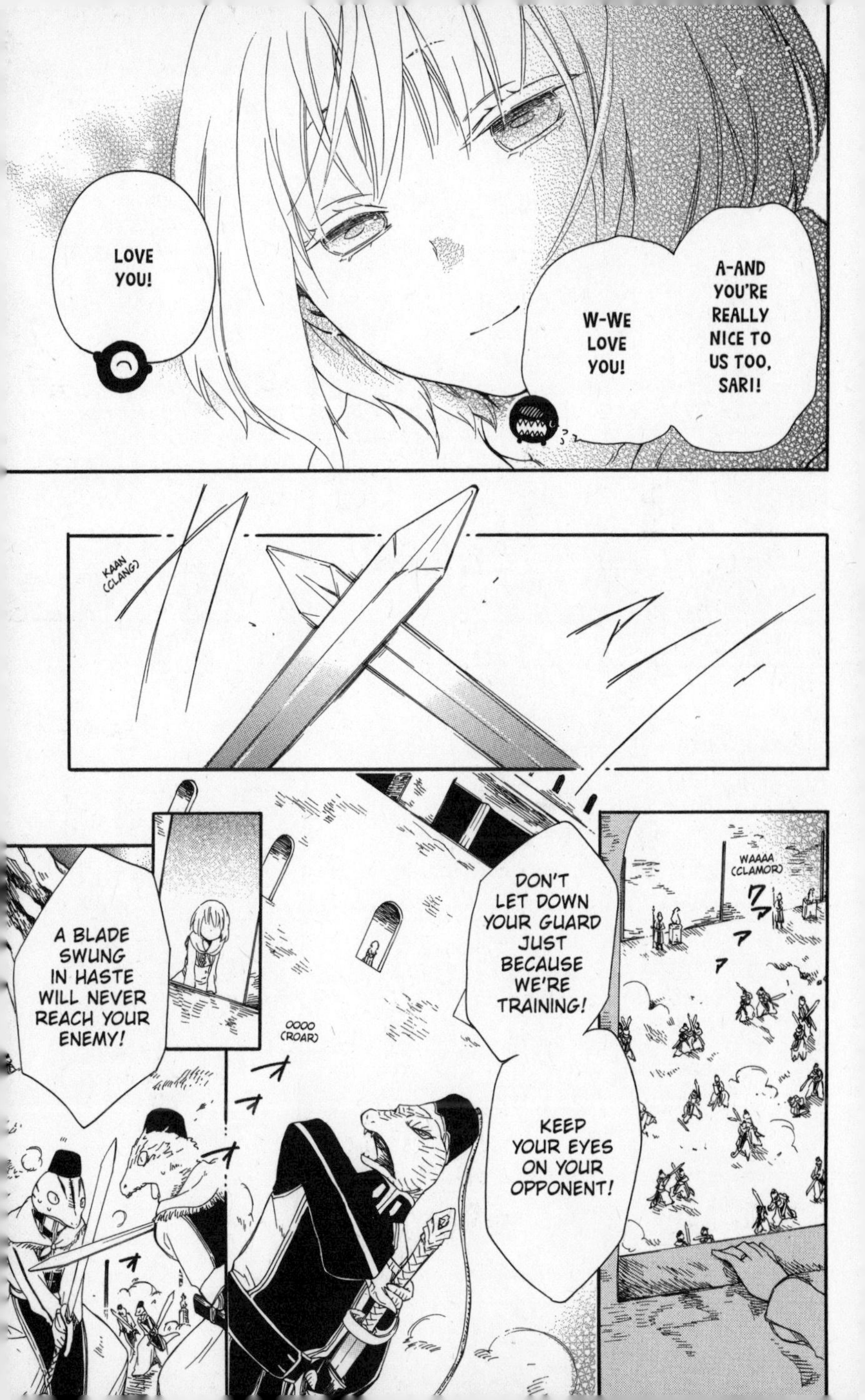

A-AND YOU'RE REALLY NICE TO US TOO, SARI!
W-WE LOVE YOU!
LOVE YOU!
KAAN (CLANG)
WAAAA (CLAMOR)
DON'T LET DOWN YOUR GUARD JUST BECAUSE WE'RE TRAINING!
KEEP YOUR EYES ON YOUR OPPONENT!
A BLADE SWUNG IN HASTE WILL NEVER REACH YOUR ENEMY!
OOOO (ROAR)

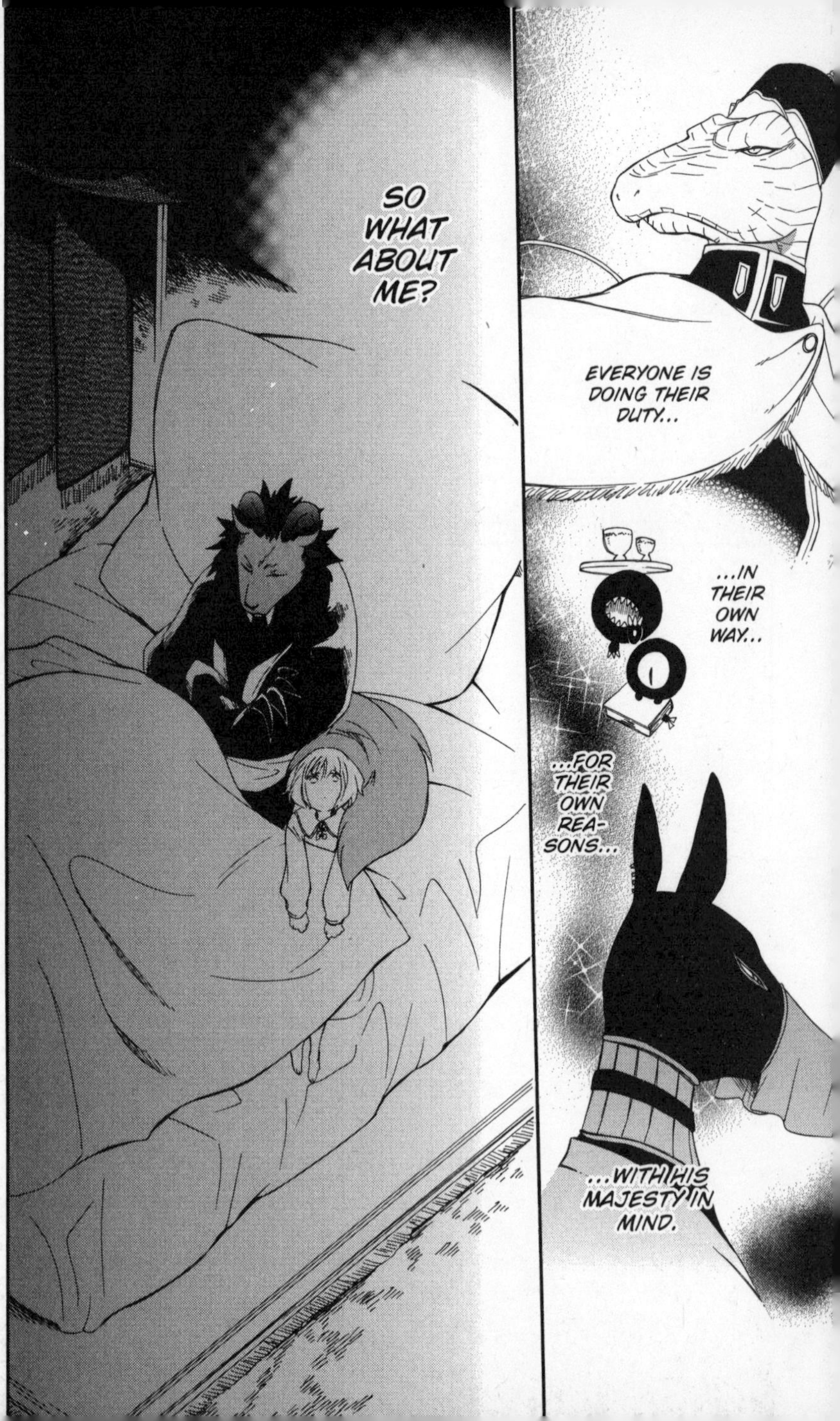
EVERYONE IS DOING THEIR DUTY...
...IN THEIR OWN WAY...
...FOR THEIR OWN REA-SONS...
...WITH HIS MAJESTY IN MIND.
SO WHAT ABOUT ME?

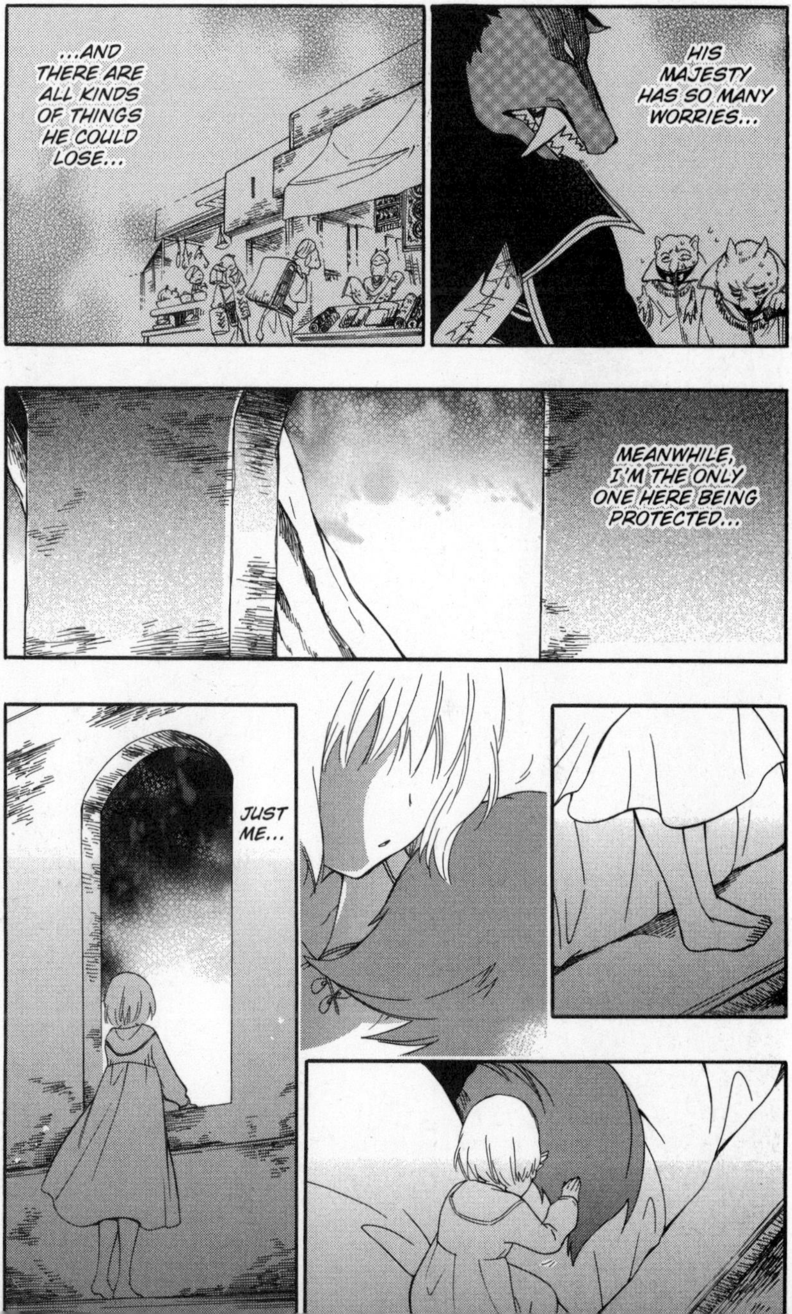
HIS MAJESTY HAS SO MANY WORRIES...
...AND THERE ARE ALL KINDS OF THINGS HE COULD LOSE...
MEANWHILE, I'M THE ONLY ONE HERE BEING PROTECTED...
JUST ME...

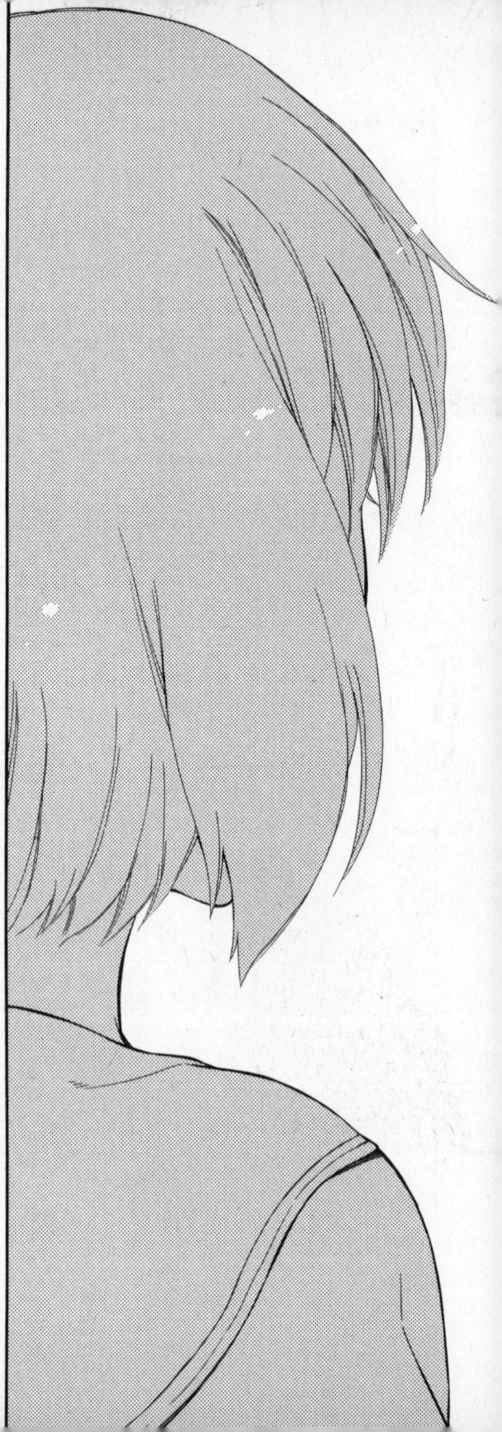

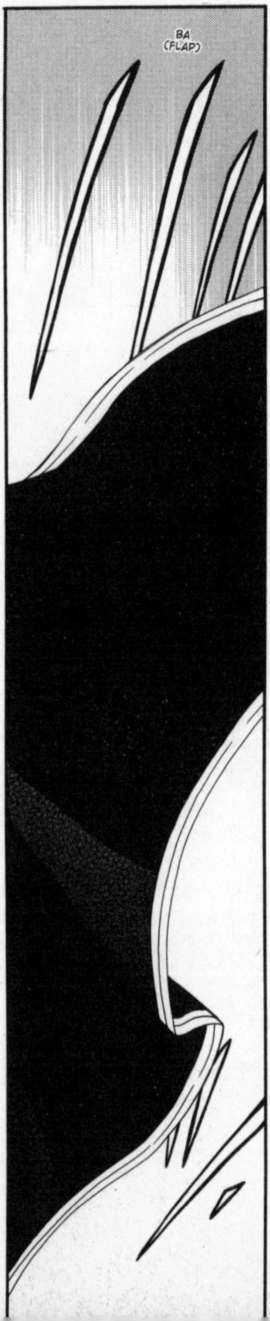
BA
(FLAP)

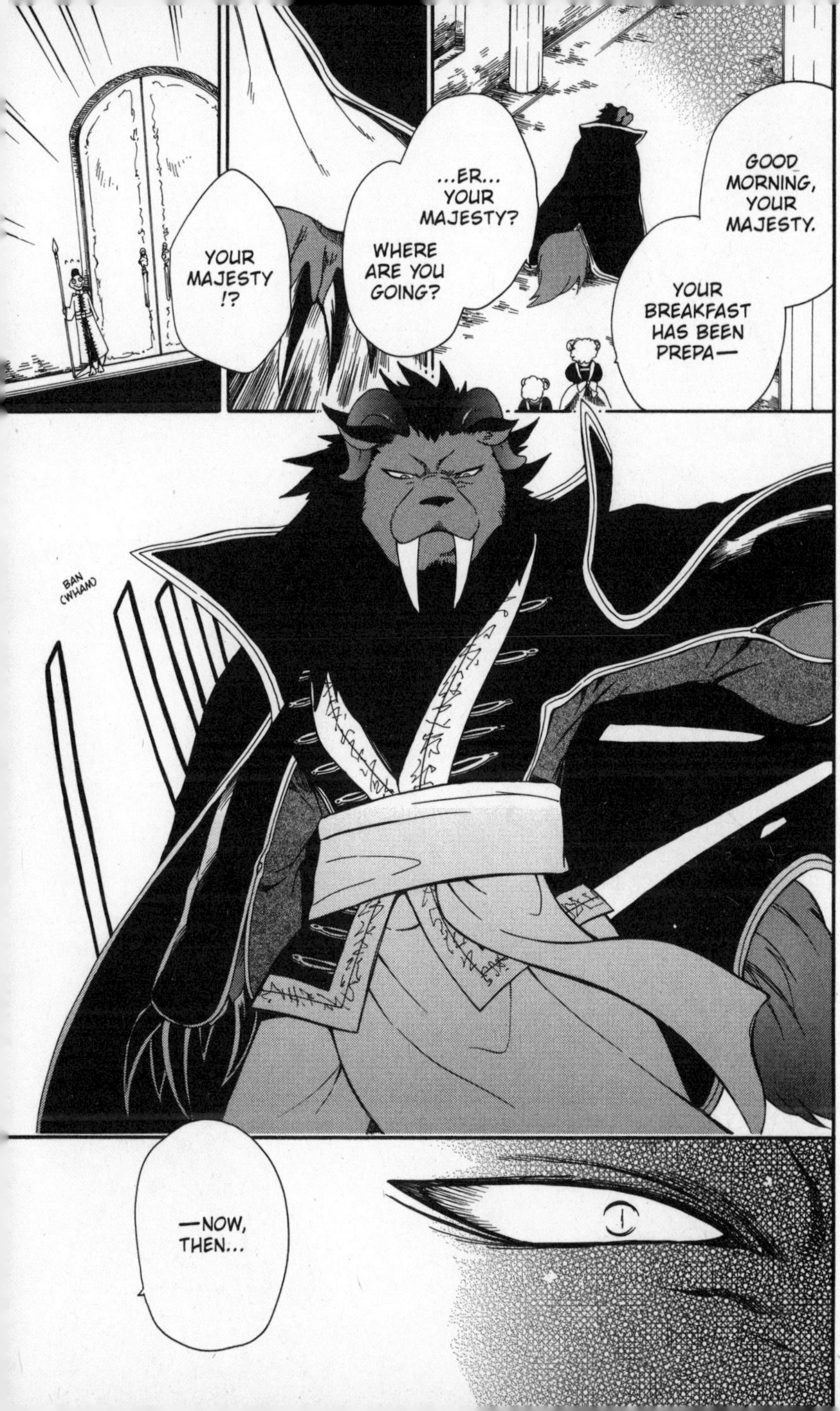
GOOD MORNING, YOUR MAJESTY.
YOUR BREAKFAST HAS BEEN PREPA—
...ER... YOUR MAJESTY?
WHERE ARE YOU GOING?
YOUR MAJESTY !?
BAN (WHAM)
—NOW, THEN...

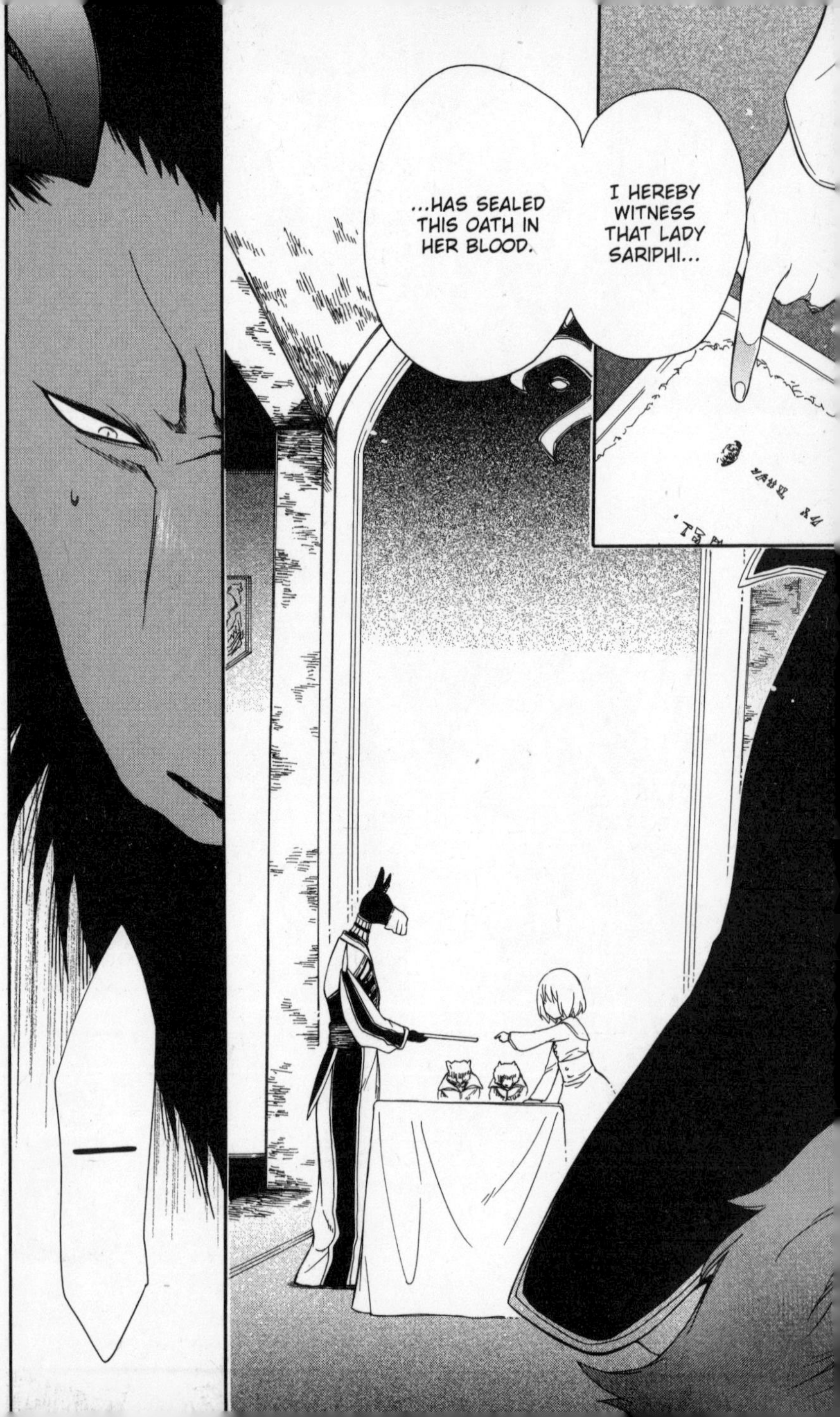
I HEREBY WITNESS THAT LADY SARIPHI...
...HAS SEALED THIS OATH IN HER BLOOD.

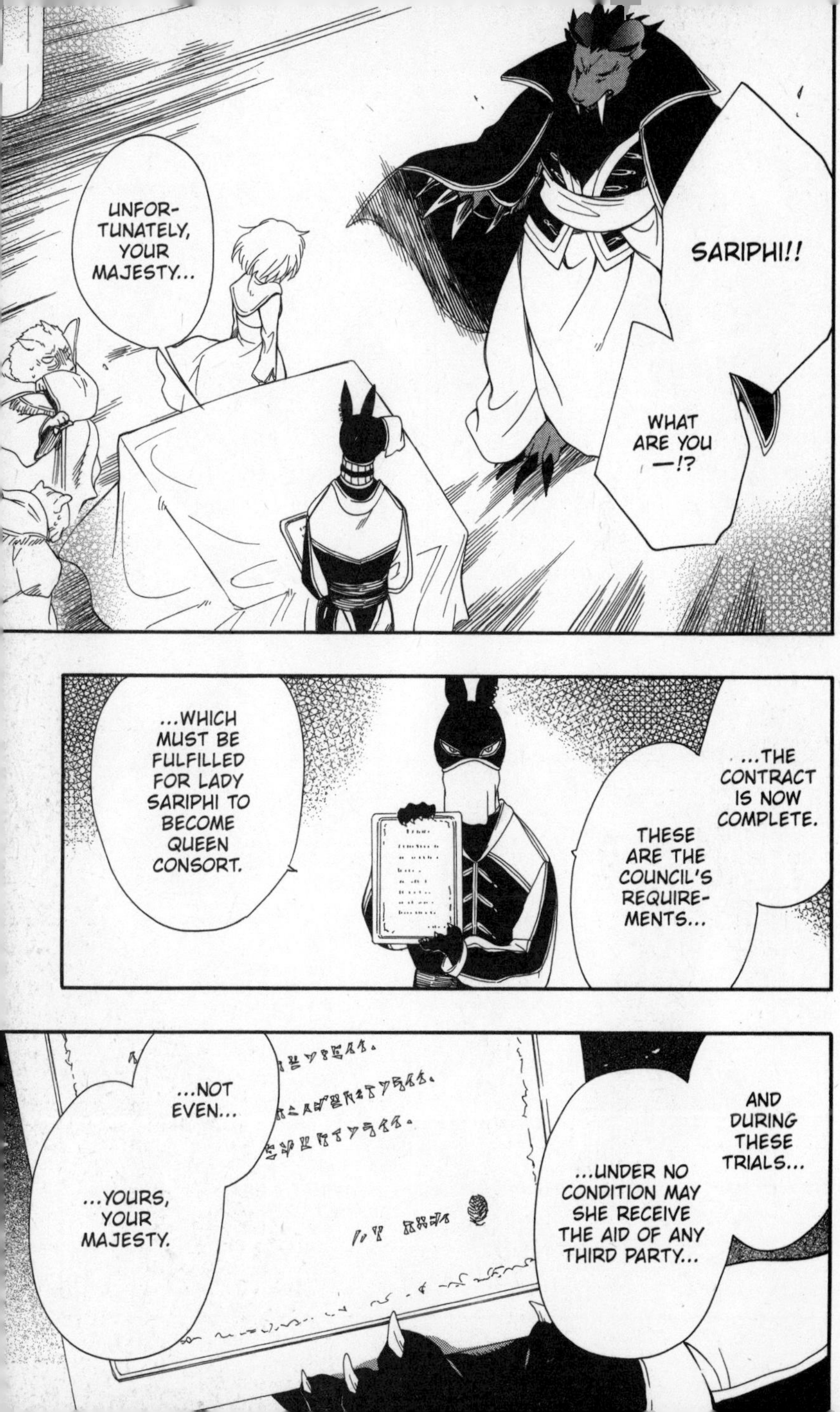
SARIPHI!!
WHAT ARE YOU —!?
UNFOR-TUNATELY, YOUR MAJESTY...
...THE CONTRACT IS NOW COMPLETE.
THESE ARE THE COUNCIL'S REQUIRE-MENTS...
...WHICH MUST BE FULFILLED FOR LADY SARIPHI TO BECOME QUEEN CONSORT.
AND DURING THESE TRIALS...
...UNDER NO CONDITION MAY SHE RECEIVE THE AID OF ANY THIRD PARTY...
...NOT EVEN...
...YOURS, YOUR MAJESTY.

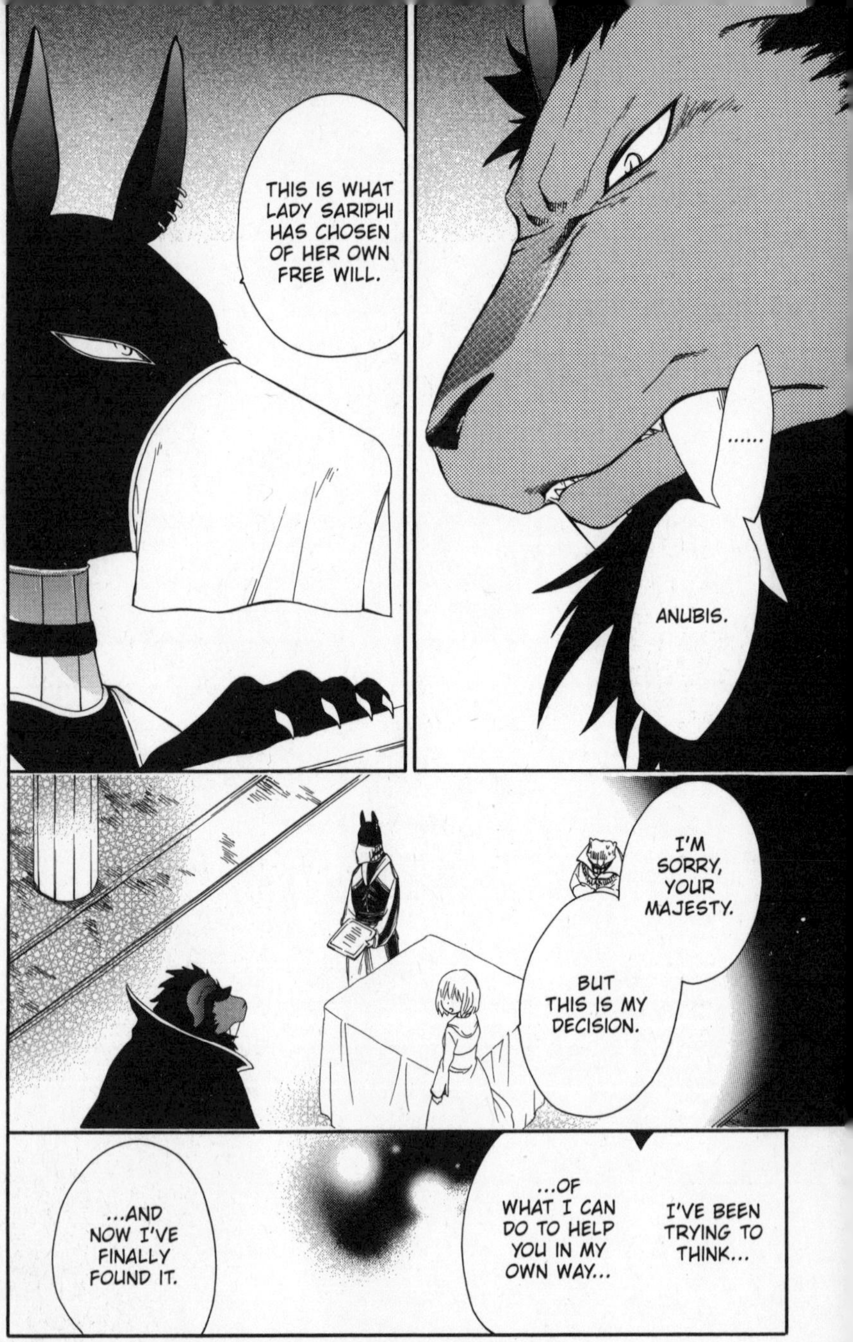
......
ANUBIS.
THIS IS WHAT LADY SARIPHI HAS CHOSEN OF HER OWN FREE WILL.
I'M SORRY, YOUR MAJESTY.
BUT THIS IS MY DECISION.
I'VE BEEN TRYING TO THINK...
...OF WHAT I CAN DO TO HELP YOU IN MY OWN WAY...
...AND NOW I'VE FINALLY FOUND IT.

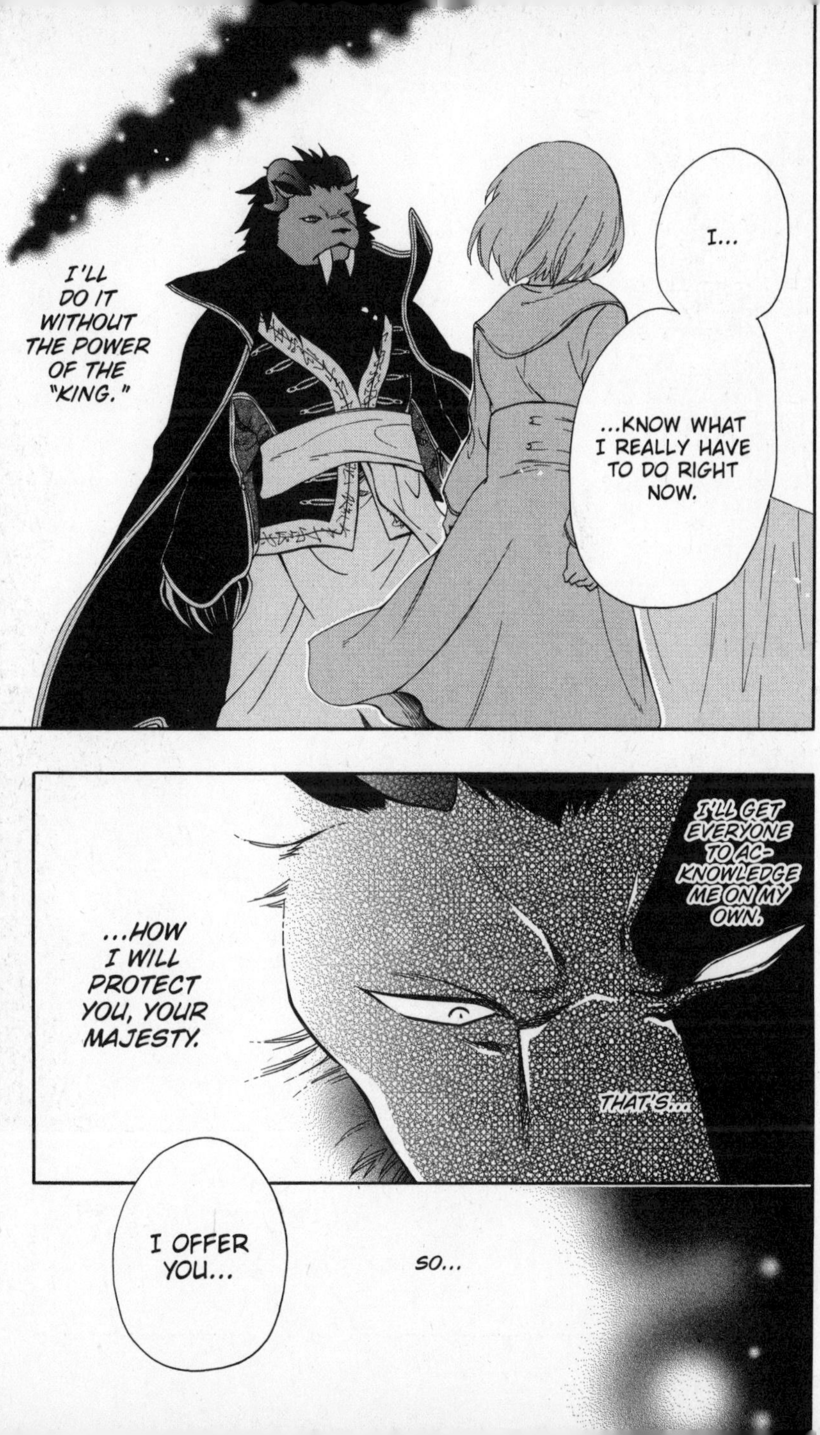
I...
...KNOW WHAT I REALLY HAVE TO DO RIGHT NOW.
I'LL DO IT WITHOUT THE POWER OF THE "KING."
I'LL GET EVERYONE TO AC-KNOWLEDGE ME ON MY OWN.
THAT'S...
...HOW I WILL PROTECT YOU, YOUR MAJESTY.
SO...
I OFFER YOU...

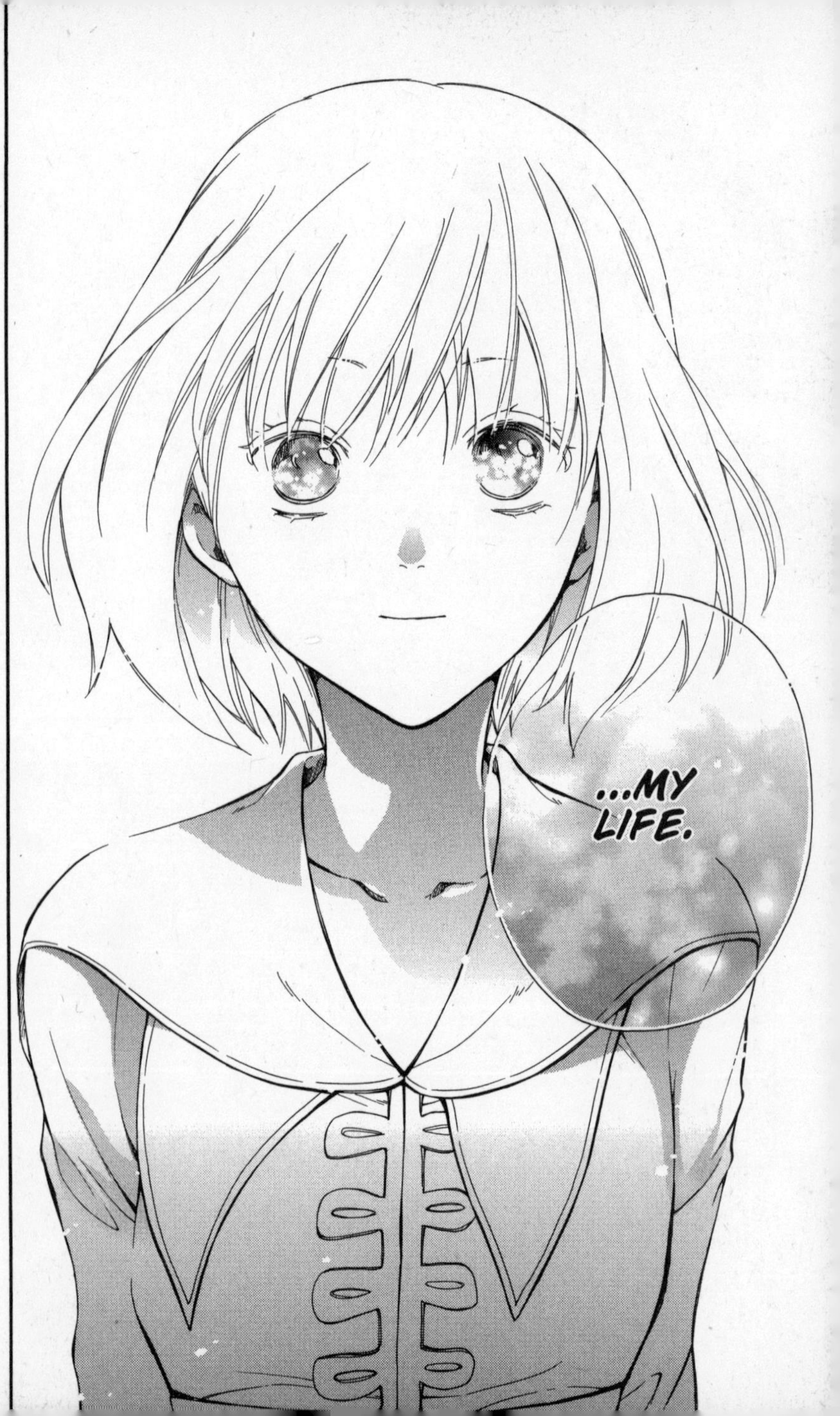
...MY
LIFE.

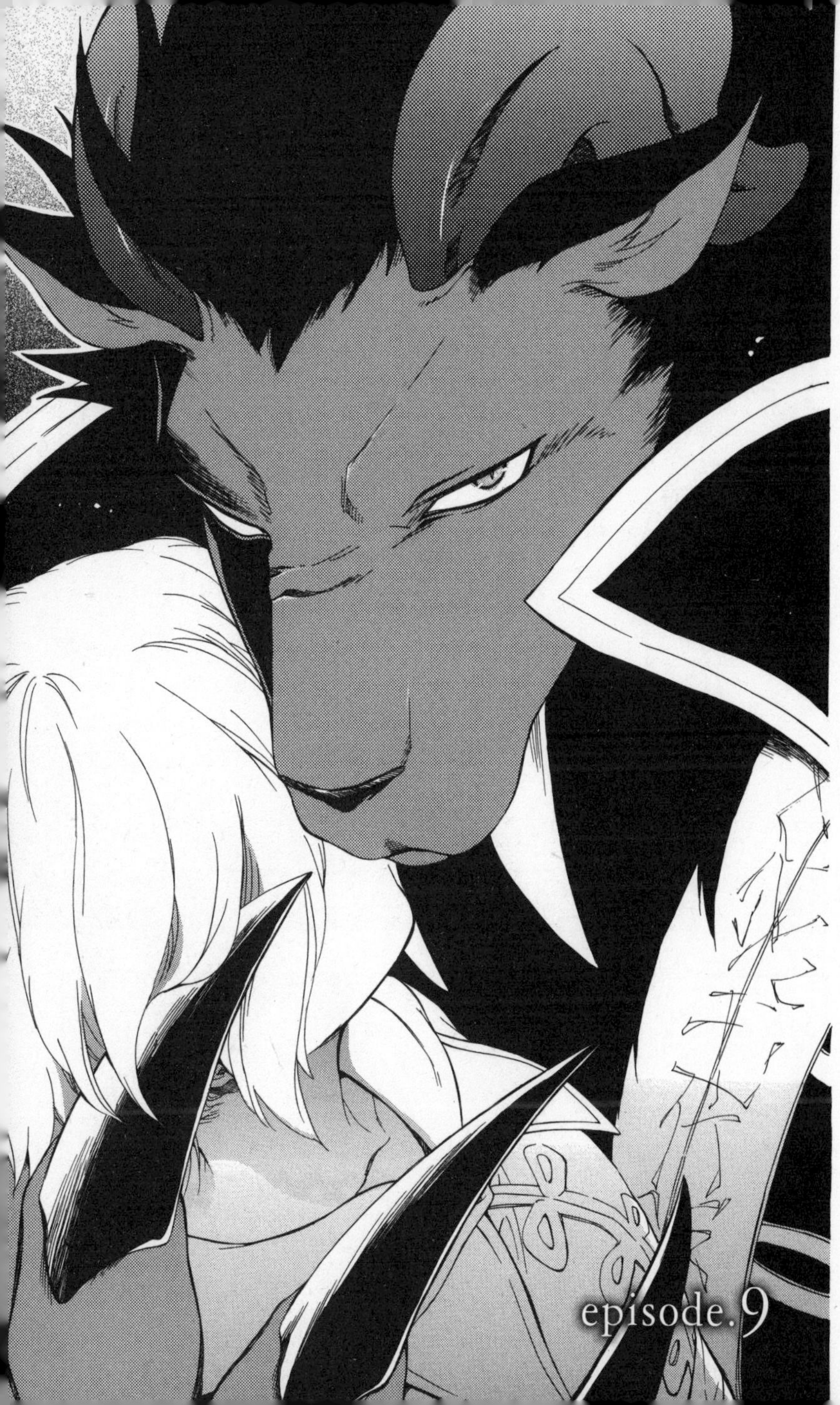
episode. 9

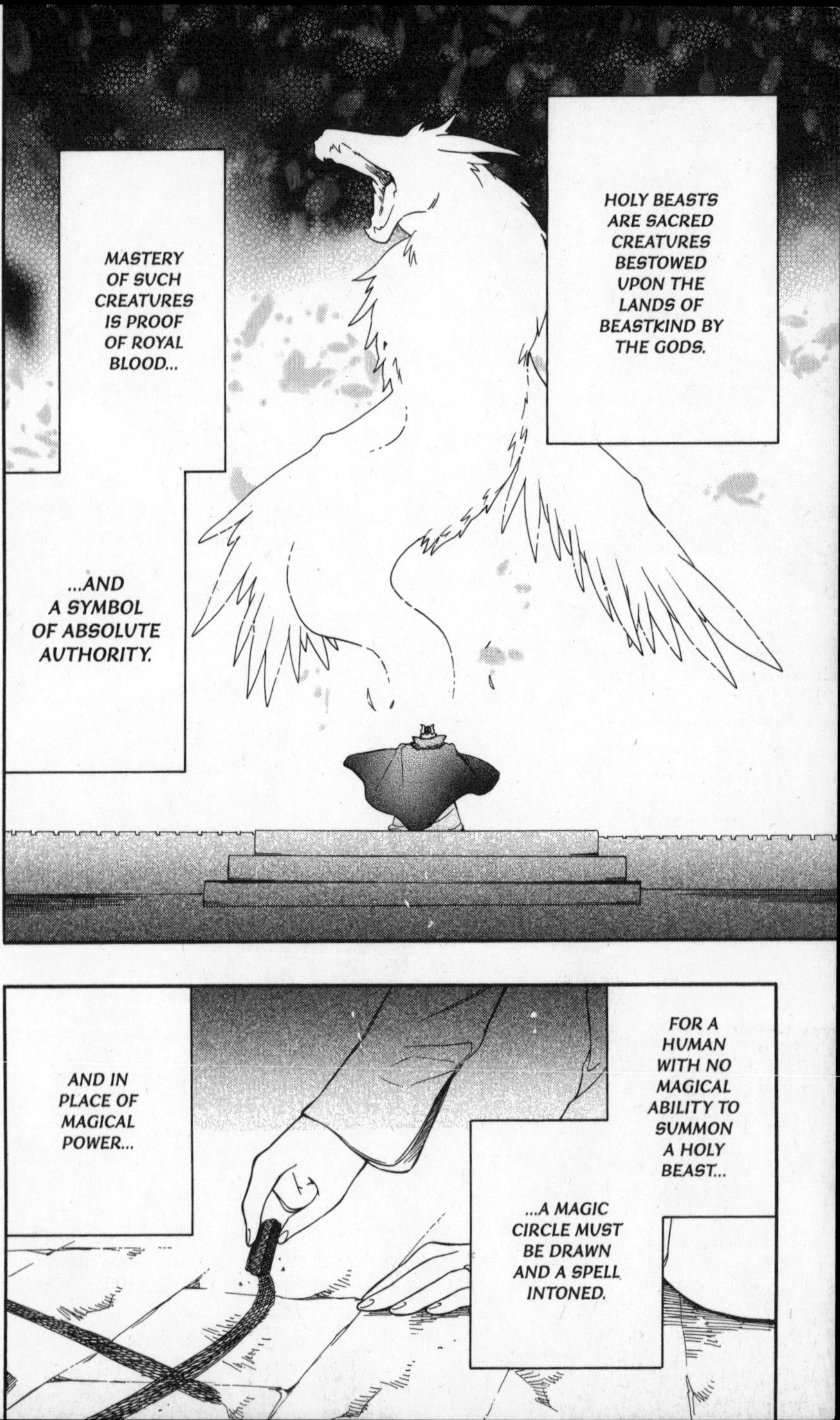
HOLY BEASTS ARE SACRED CREATURES BESTOWED UPON THE LANDS OF BEASTKIND BY THE GODS.
MASTERY OF SUCH CREATURES IS PROOF OF ROYAL BLOOD...
...AND A SYMBOL OF ABSOLUTE AUTHORITY.
FOR A HUMAN WITH NO MAGICAL ABILITY TO SUMMON A HOLY BEAST...
AND IN PLACE OF MAGICAL POWER...
...A MAGIC CIRCLE MUST BE DRAWN AND A SPELL INTONED.

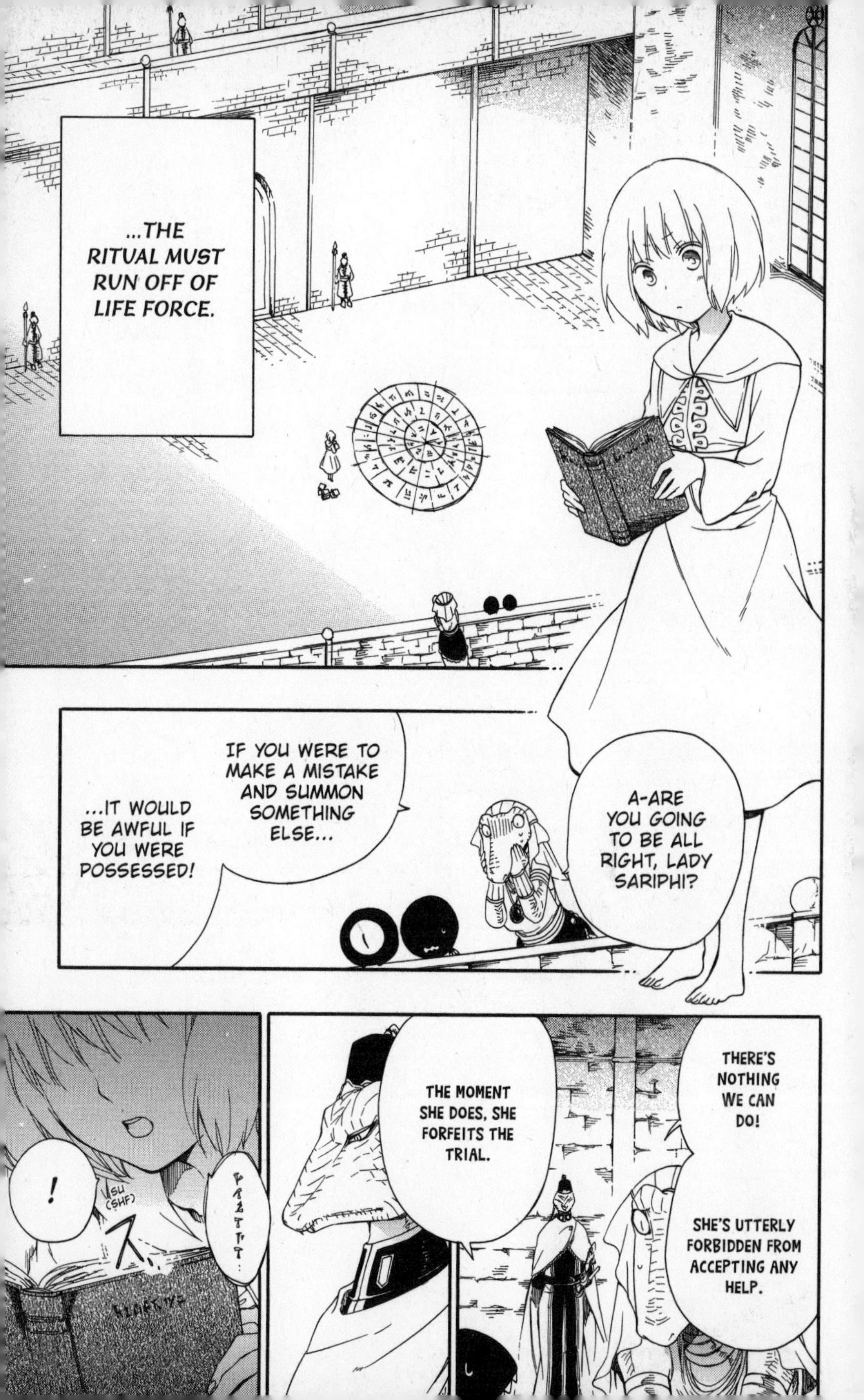
...THE RITUAL MUST RUN OFF OF LIFE FORCE.
A-ARE YOU GOING TO BE ALL RIGHT, LADY SARIPHI?
IF YOU WERE TO MAKE A MISTAKE AND SUMMON SOMETHING ELSE...
...IT WOULD BE AWFUL IF YOU WERE POSSESSED!
THERE'S NOTHING WE CAN DO!
SHE'S UTTERLY FORBIDDEN FROM ACCEPTING ANY HELP.
THE MOMENT SHE DOES, SHE FORFEITS THE TRIAL.
SU (SHF)
!

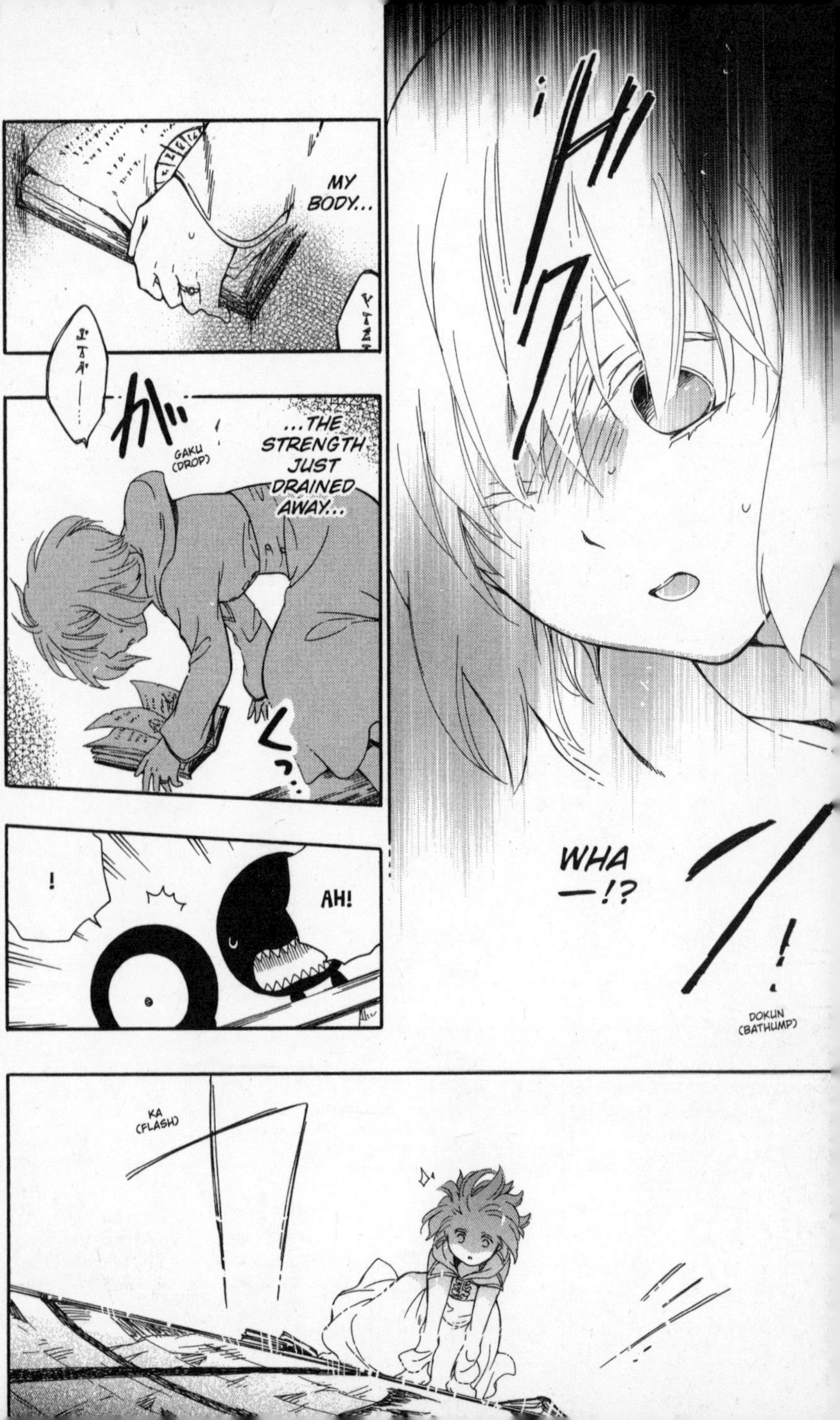
WHA—!?
DOKUN (BATHUMP)
MY BODY...
GAKU (DROP)
...THE STRENGTH JUST DRAINED AWAY...
!
AH!
KA (FLASH)

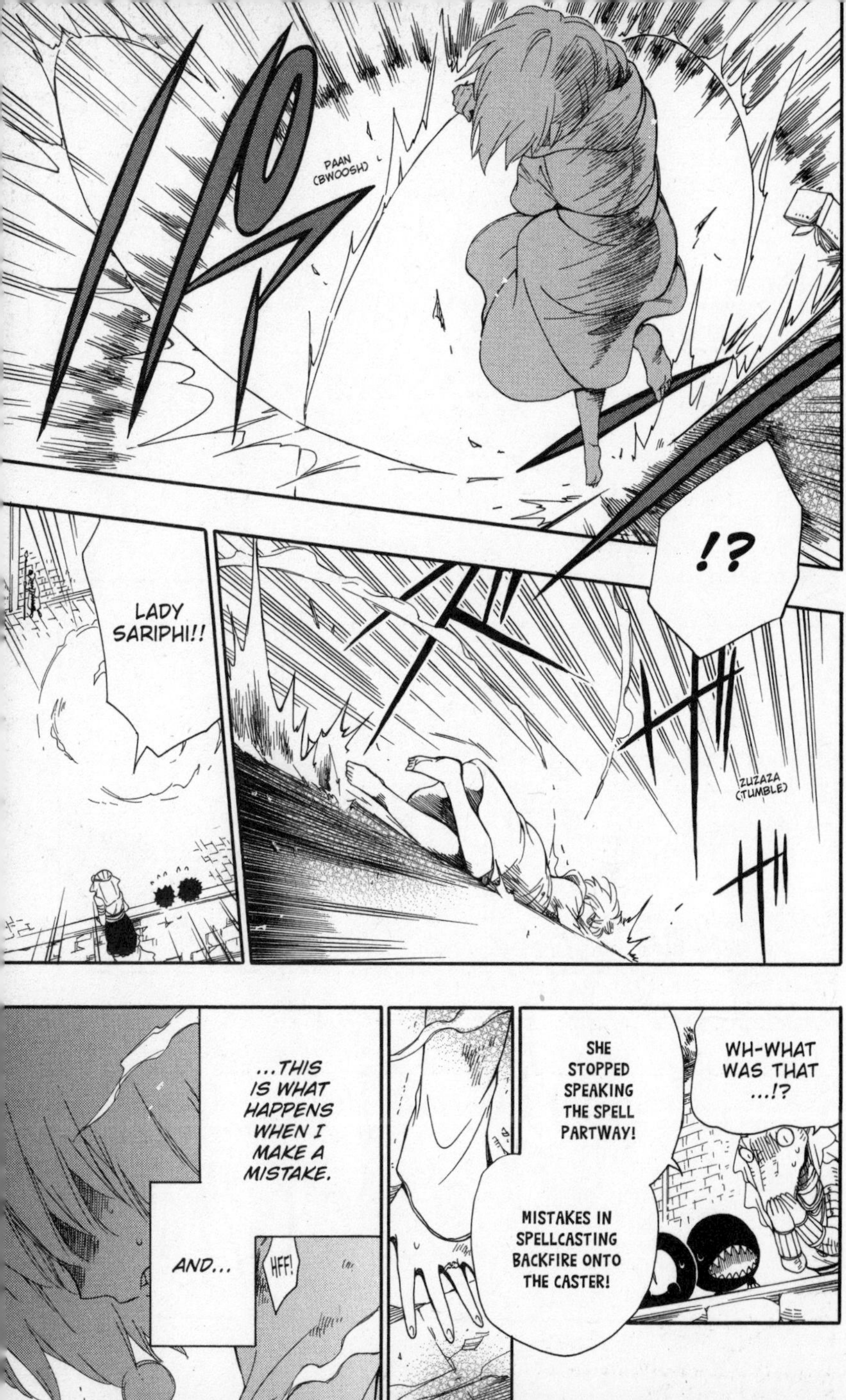
PAAN
(BWOOSH)
!?
ZUZAZA
(TUMBLE)
LADY SARIPHI!!
WH-WHAT WAS THAT ...!?
SHE STOPPED SPEAKING THE SPELL PARTWAY!
MISTAKES IN SPELLCASTING BACKFIRE ONTO THE CASTER!
...THIS IS WHAT HAPPENS WHEN I MAKE A MISTAKE.
AND...
HFF!

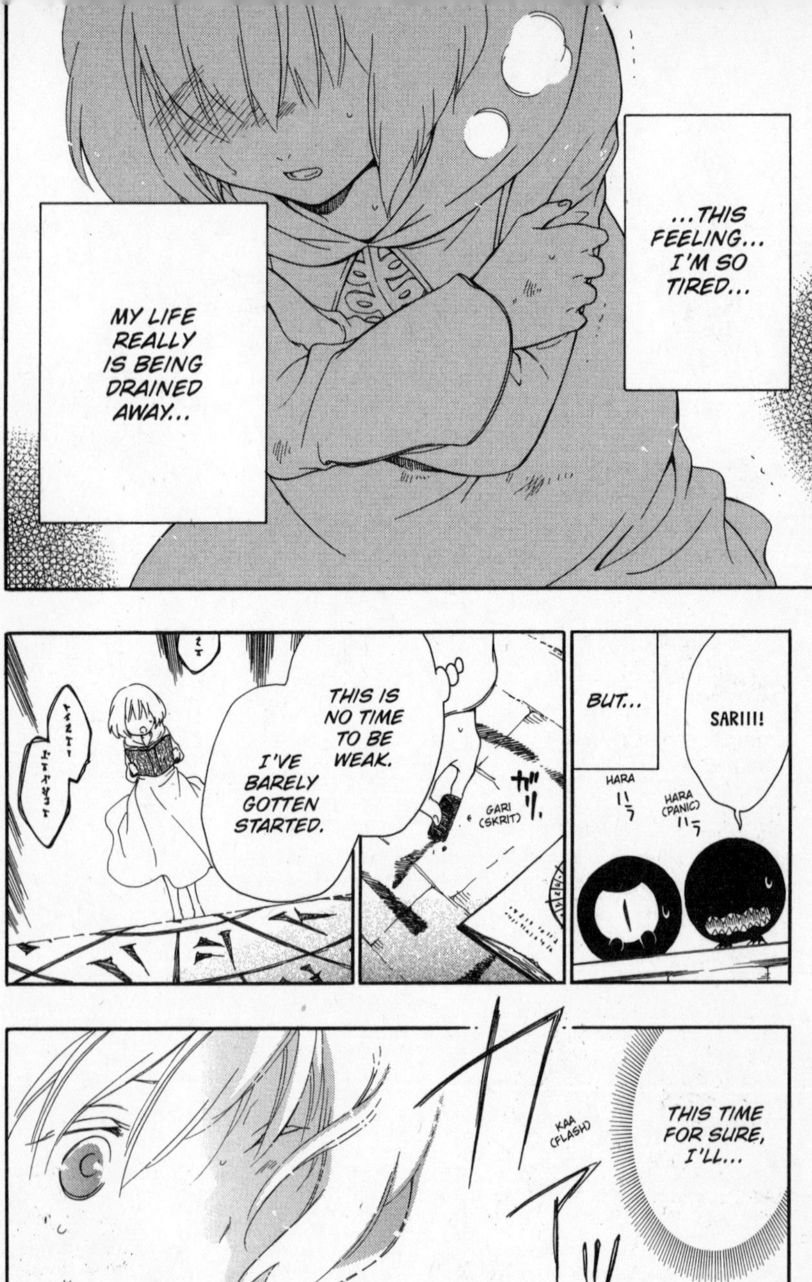

...THIS FEELING... I'M SO TIRED...
MY LIFE REALLY IS BEING DRAINED AWAY...
BUT...
SARIII!
HARA
HARA (PANIC)
GARI (SKRIT)
THIS IS NO TIME TO BE WEAK.
I'VE BARELY GOTTEN STARTED.
THIS TIME FOR SURE, I'LL...
KAA (FLASH)

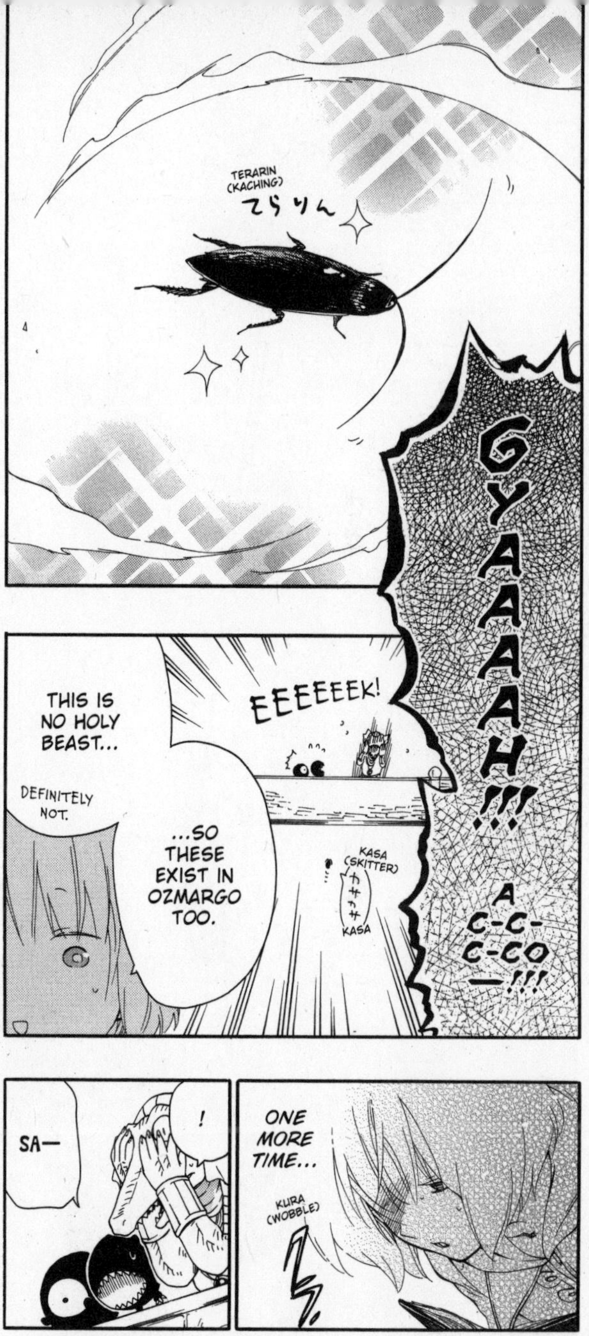
TERARIN (KACHING)
てらりん
GYAAAAAH!!!
A C-C-C-CO—!!!
EEEEEEK!
KASA (SKITTER) カサカサ KASA
THIS IS NO HOLY BEAST...
...SO THESE EXIST IN OZMARGO TOO.
DEFINITELY NOT.
ONE MORE TIME...
KURA (WOBBLE)
!
SA—

CAPTAIN JORMUNGAND

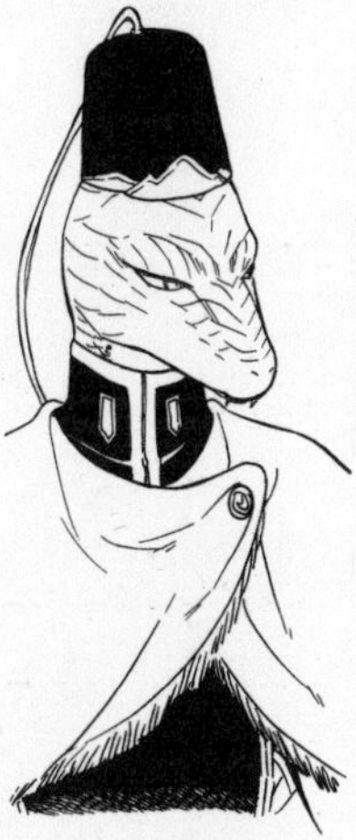

"STERN SOLDIER," "AMIT'S CRUSH," "ANUBIS'S PEER," "A COOL LIZARD CHARACTER"—I HAD ALL THESE DIFFERENT IDEAS FOR CHARACTERS I WANTED TO DO, AND I JUST WOUND UP MASHING THEM ALL TOGETHER. HE'S LESS "STERN" THAN SIMPLY NOBLE, AND HE'S MORE SNAKELIKE THAN LIZARDISH, BUT...ANYWAY, HE TURNED OUT COOL WHEN I DREW HIM! THAT WAS THE IMPORTANT THING. HE'S BEEN THROUGH A LOT.

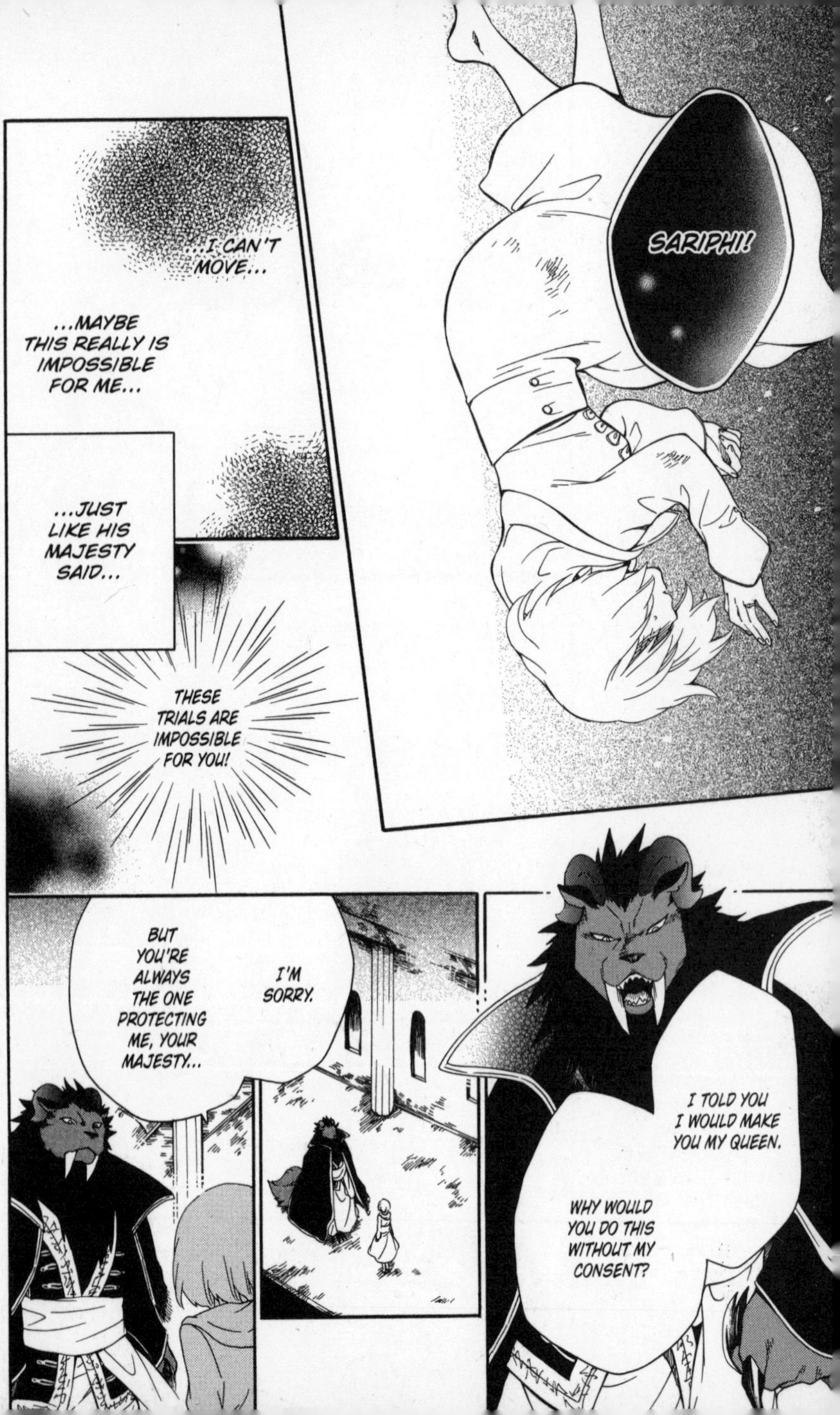
SARIPHI!
...I CAN'T MOVE...
...MAYBE THIS REALLY IS IMPOSSIBLE FOR ME...
...JUST LIKE HIS MAJESTY SAID...
THESE TRIALS ARE IMPOSSIBLE FOR YOU!
I TOLD YOU I WOULD MAKE YOU MY QUEEN.
WHY WOULD YOU DO THIS WITHOUT MY CONSENT?
I'M SORRY.
BUT YOU'RE ALWAYS THE ONE PROTECTING ME, YOUR MAJESTY...

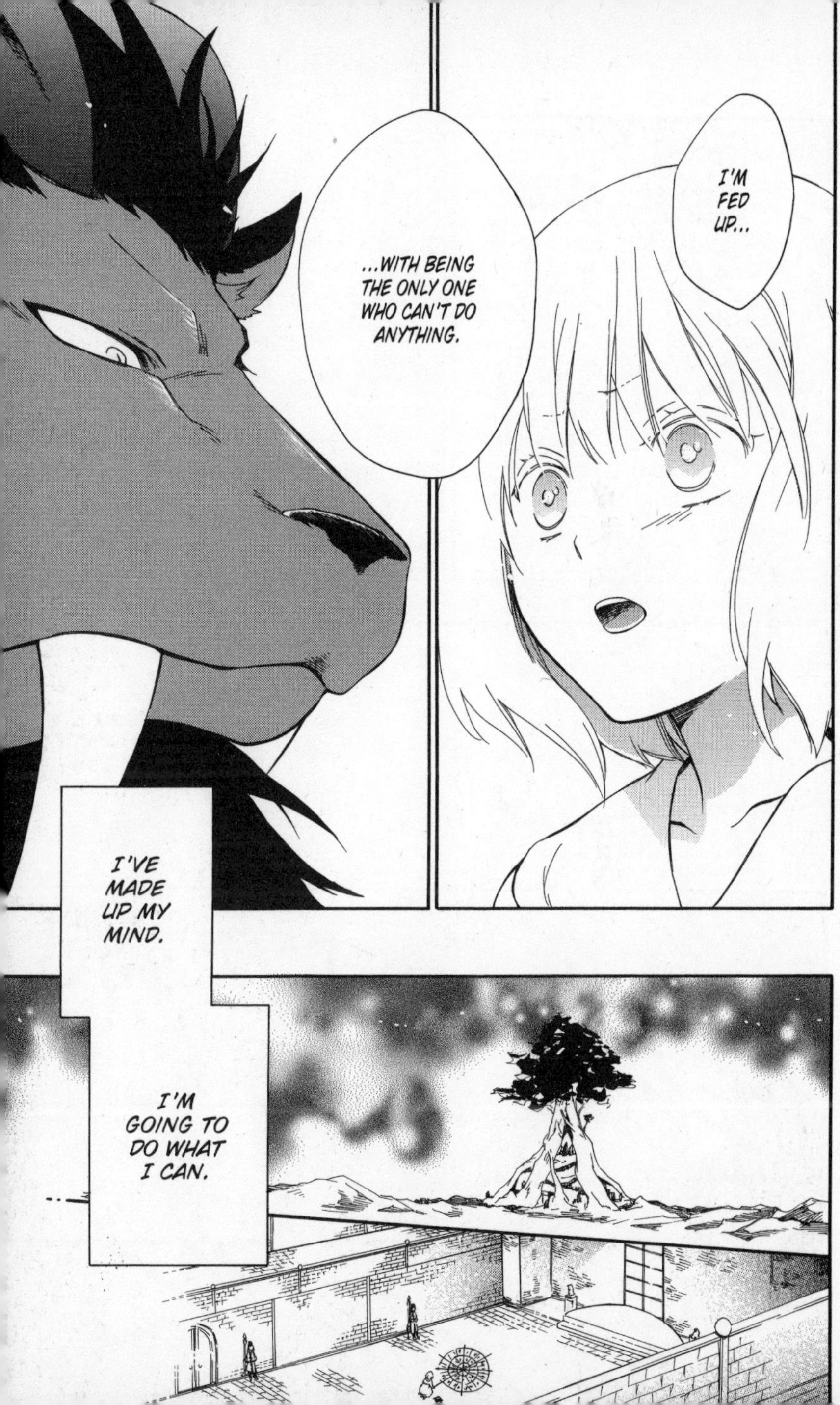
I'M FED UP...
...WITH BEING THE ONLY ONE WHO CAN'T DO ANYTHING.
I'VE MADE UP MY MIND.
I'M GOING TO DO WHAT I CAN.

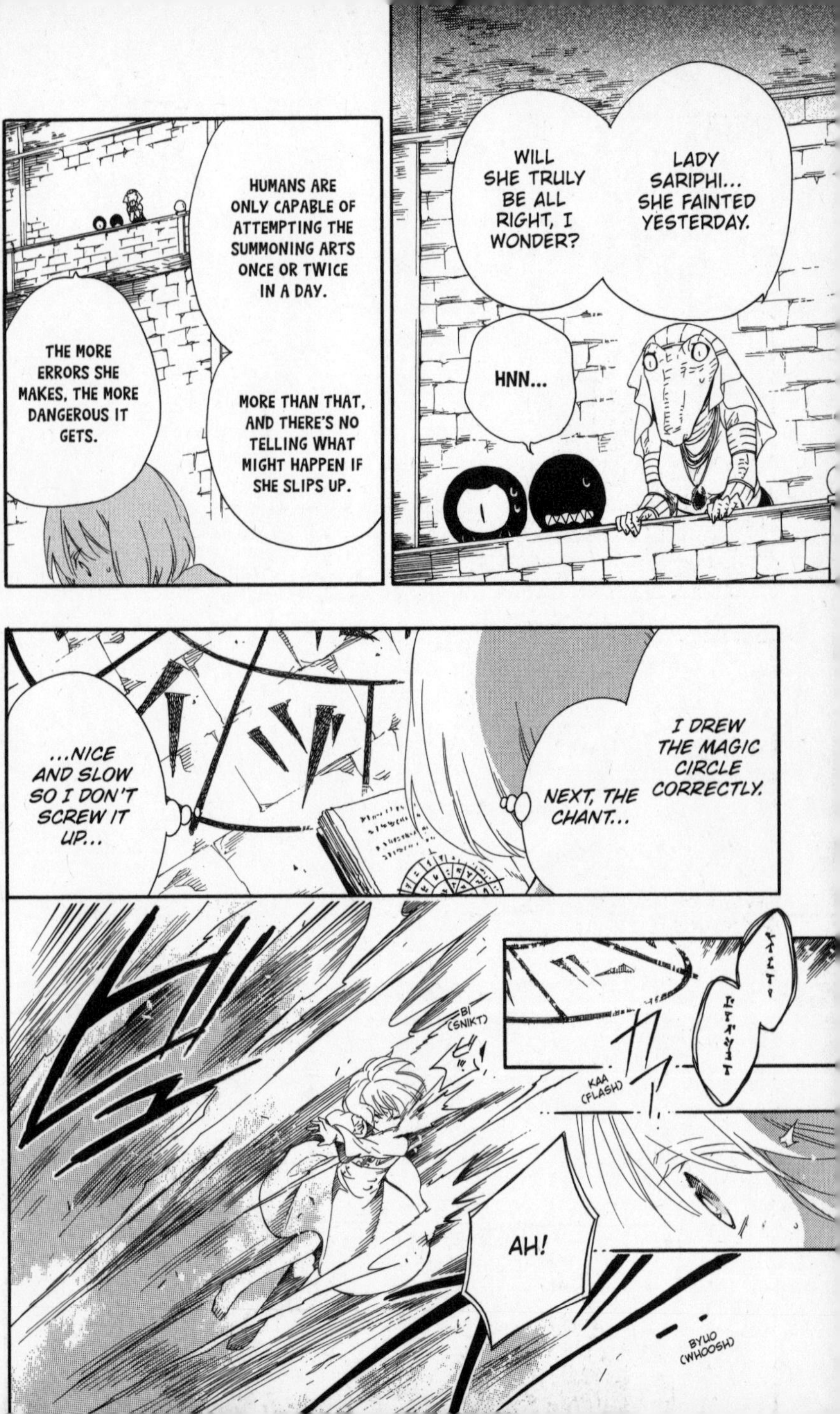

LADY SARIPHI... SHE FAINTED YESTERDAY.
WILL SHE TRULY BE ALL RIGHT, I WONDER?
HNN...
HUMANS ARE ONLY CAPABLE OF ATTEMPTING THE SUMMONING ARTS ONCE OR TWICE IN A DAY.
MORE THAN THAT, AND THERE'S NO TELLING WHAT MIGHT HAPPEN IF SHE SLIPS UP.
THE MORE ERRORS SHE MAKES, THE MORE DANGEROUS IT GETS.
I DREW THE MAGIC CIRCLE CORRECTLY.
NEXT, THE CHANT...
...NICE AND SLOW SO I DON'T SCREW IT UP...
KAA (FLASH)
BI (SNIKT)
AH!
BYUO (WHOOSH)

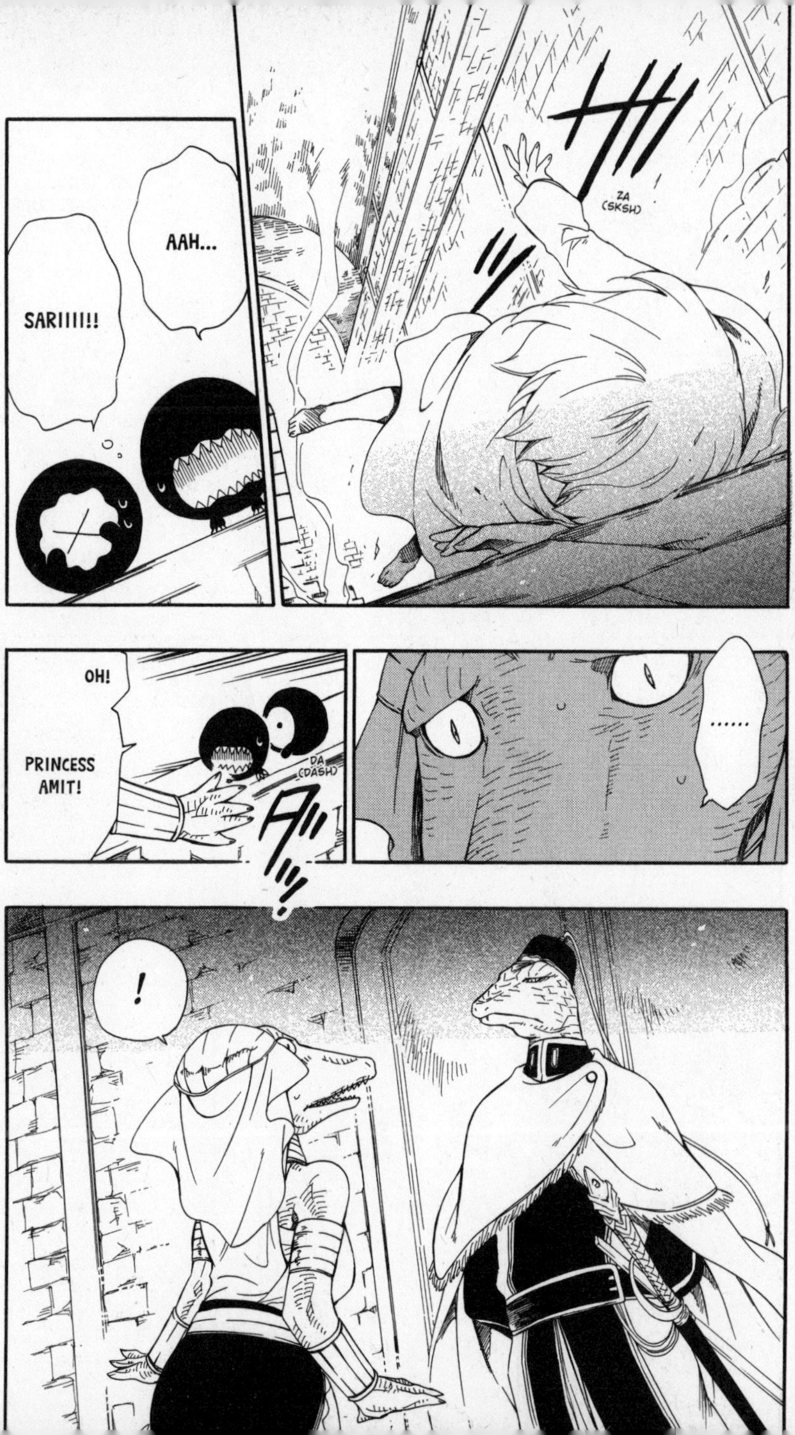
ZA (SKSH)
AAH...
SARIIIII!!
......
OH!
PRINCESS AMIT!
DA (DASH)
!

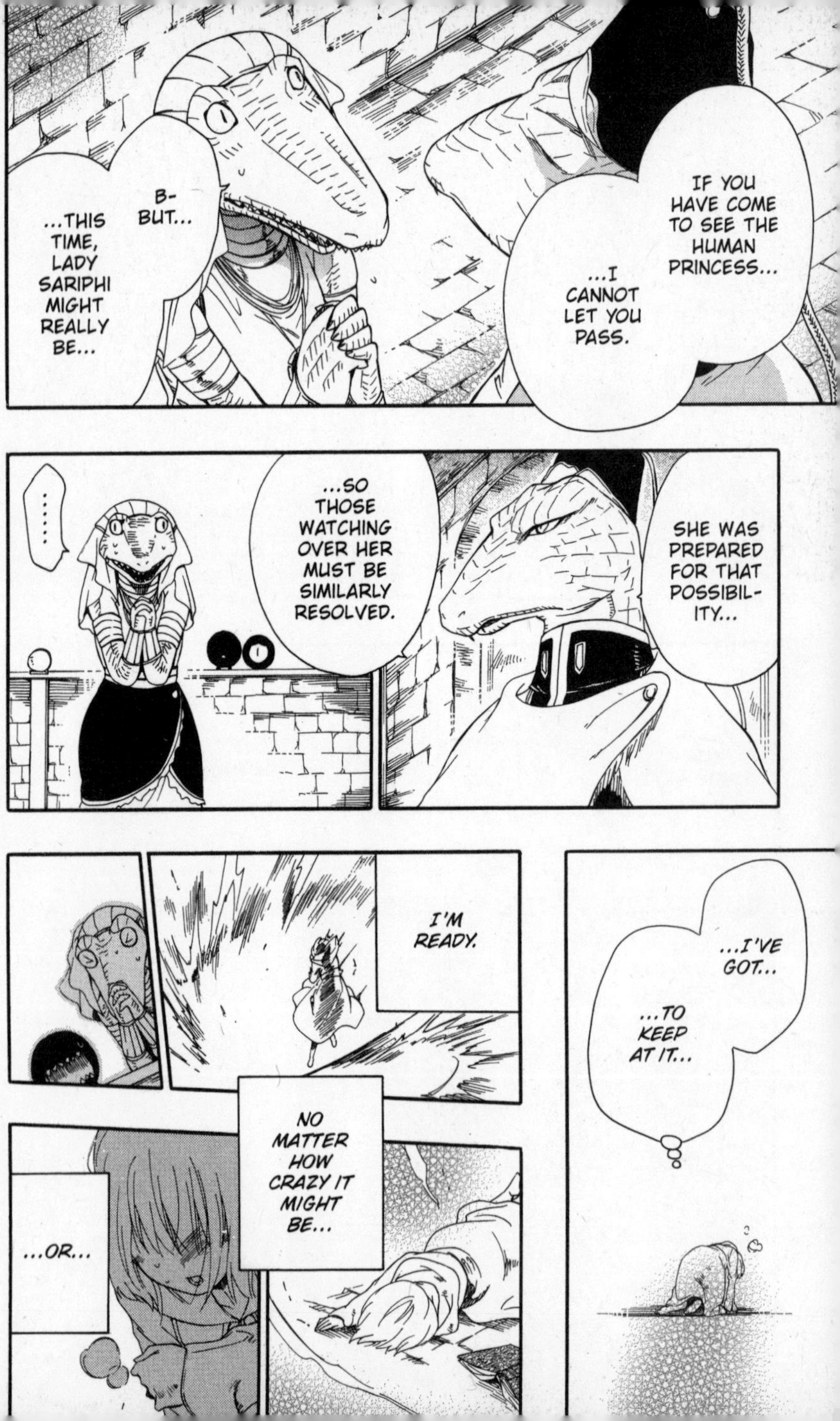
IF YOU HAVE COME TO SEE THE HUMAN PRINCESS...
...I CANNOT LET YOU PASS.
B-BUT...
...THIS TIME, LADY SARIPHI MIGHT REALLY BE...
SHE WAS PREPARED FOR THAT POSSIBIL-ITY...
...SO THOSE WATCHING OVER HER MUST BE SIMILARLY RESOLVED.
......
...I'VE GOT...
...TO KEEP AT IT...
I'M READY.
NO MATTER HOW CRAZY IT MIGHT BE...
...OR...

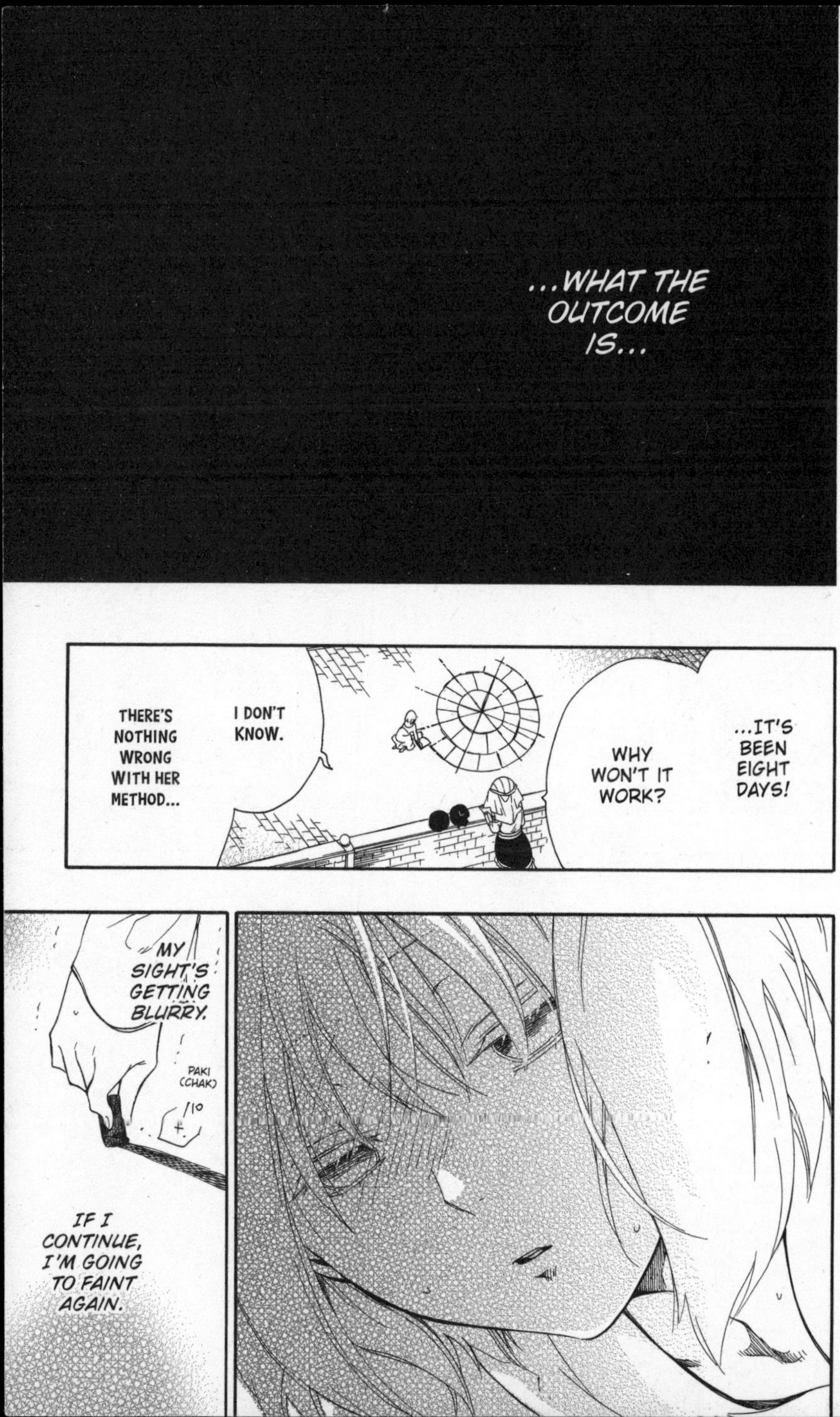
...WHAT THE OUTCOME IS...
...IT'S BEEN EIGHT DAYS!
WHY WON'T IT WORK?
I DON'T KNOW.
THERE'S NOTHING WRONG WITH HER METHOD...
MY SIGHT'S GETTING BLURRY.
PAKI (CHAK)
IF I CONTINUE, I'M GOING TO FAINT AGAIN.

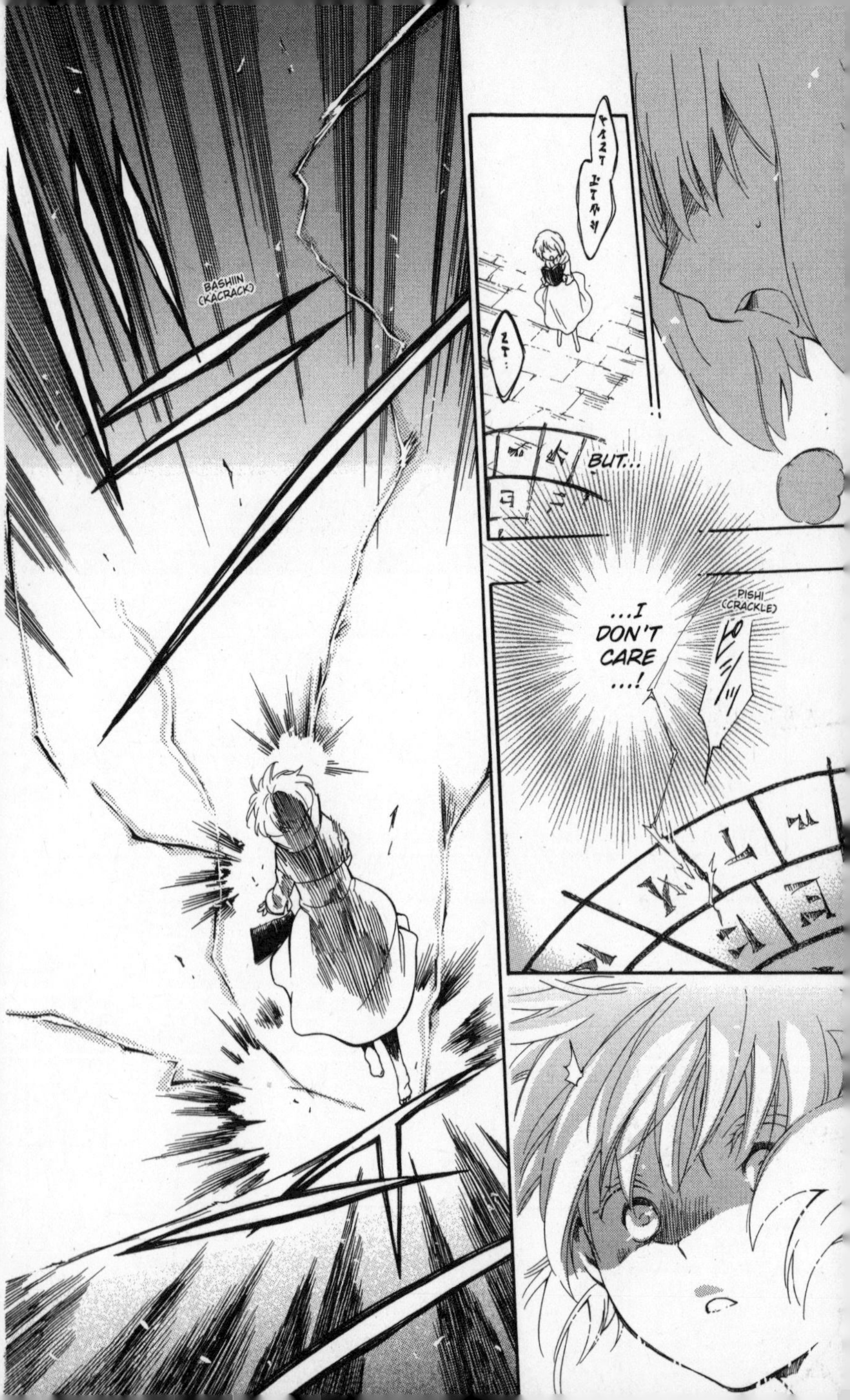
BUT...
...I DON'T CARE ...!
PISHI (CRACKLE)
BASHIIN (KACRACK)

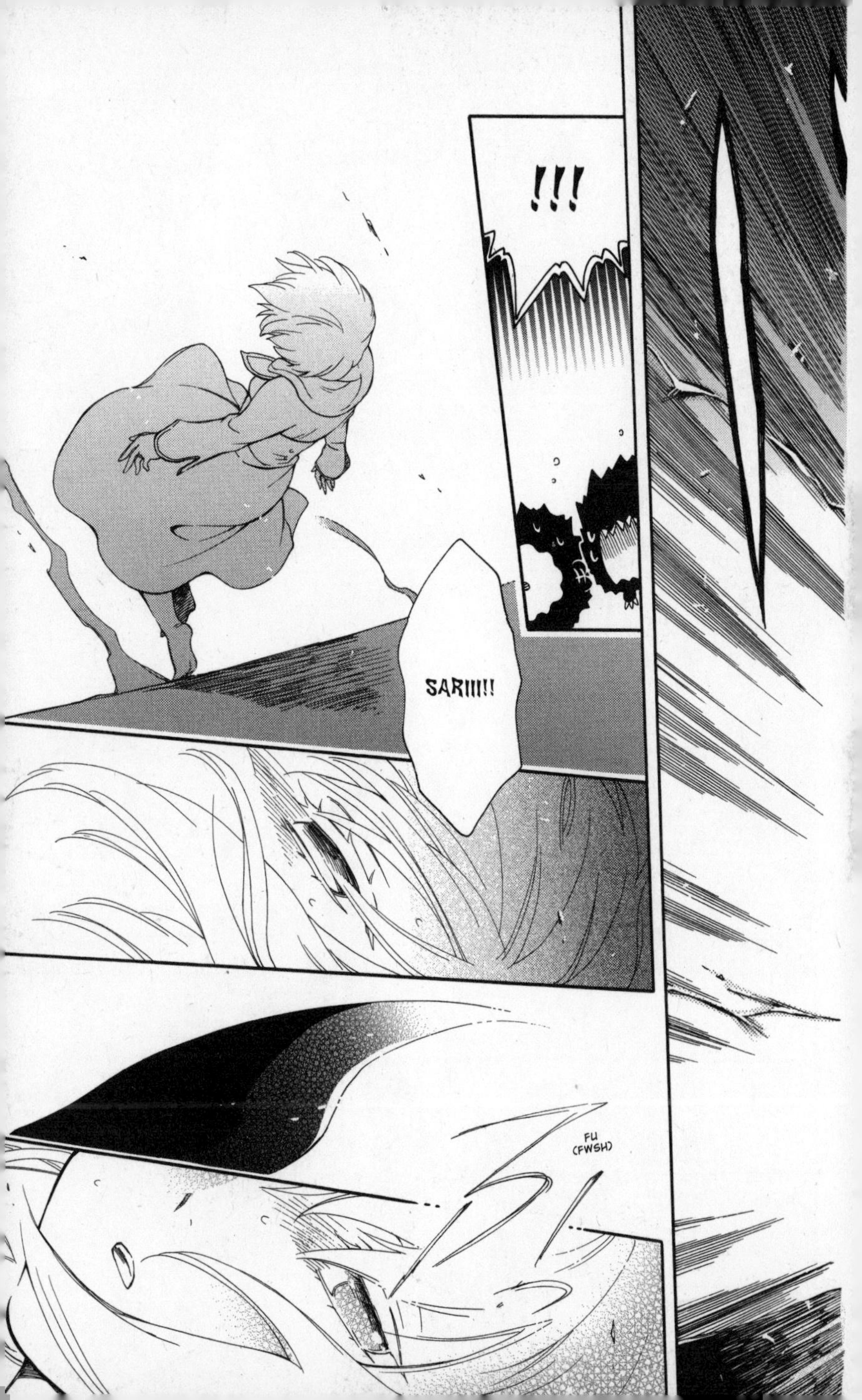
!!!
SARIIII!!
FU
(FWSH)

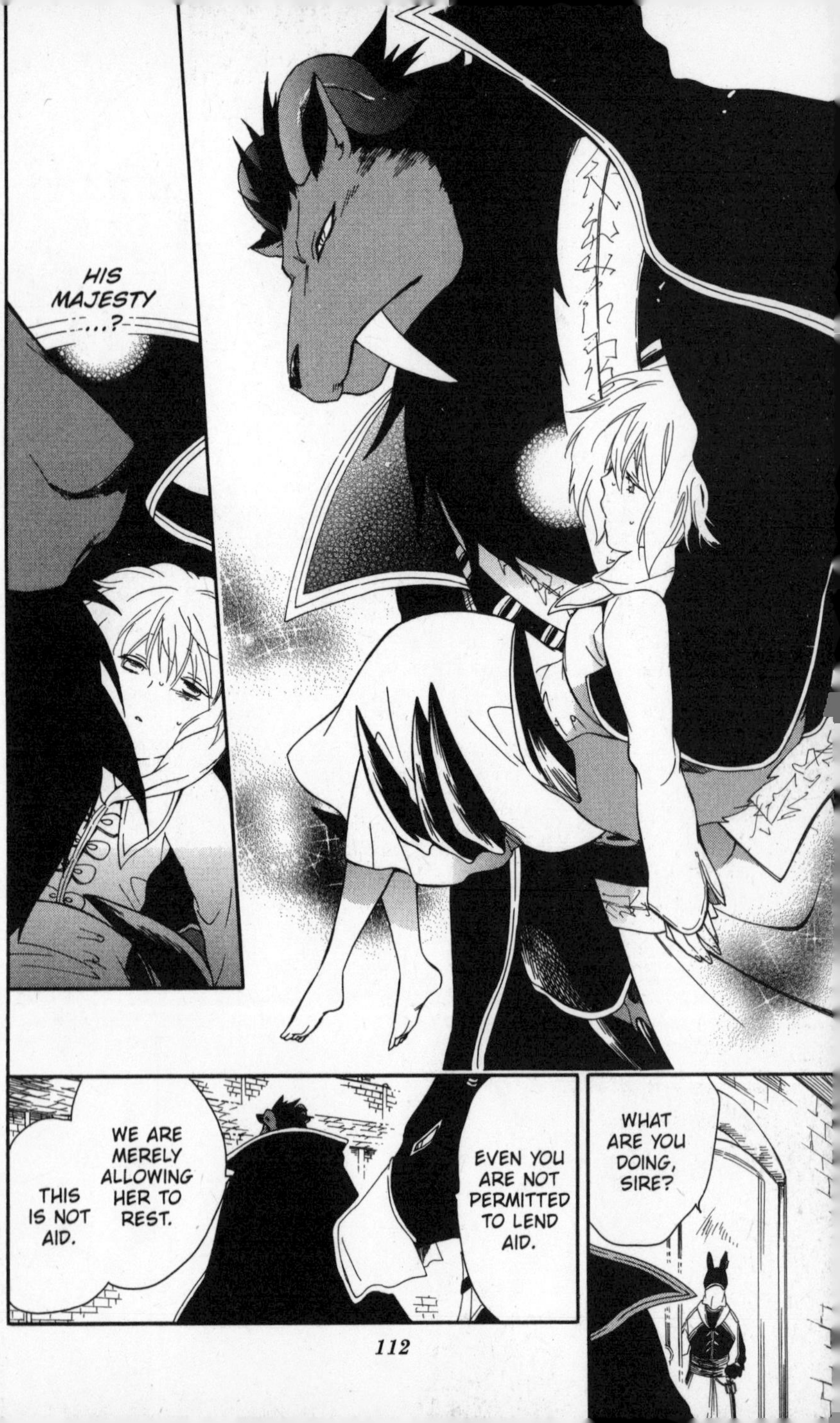
HIS MAJESTY ...?
WHAT ARE YOU DOING, SIRE?
EVEN YOU ARE NOT PERMITTED TO LEND AID.
WE ARE MERELY ALLOWING HER TO REST.
THIS IS NOT AID.

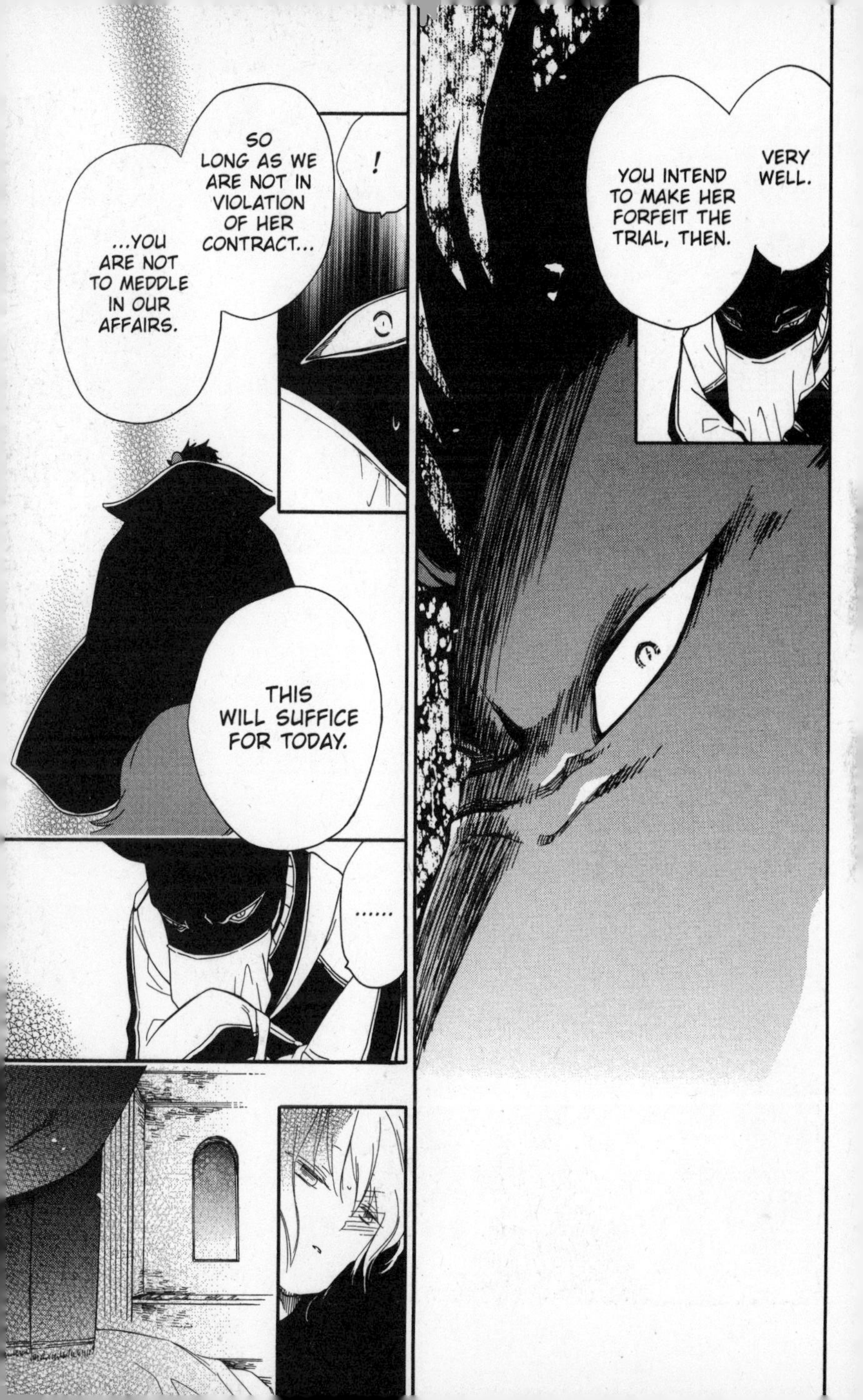
VERY WELL.
YOU INTEND TO MAKE HER FORFEIT THE TRIAL, THEN.
SO LONG AS WE ARE NOT IN VIOLATION OF HER CONTRACT...
!
...YOU ARE NOT TO MEDDLE IN OUR AFFAIRS.
THIS WILL SUFFICE FOR TODAY.
......

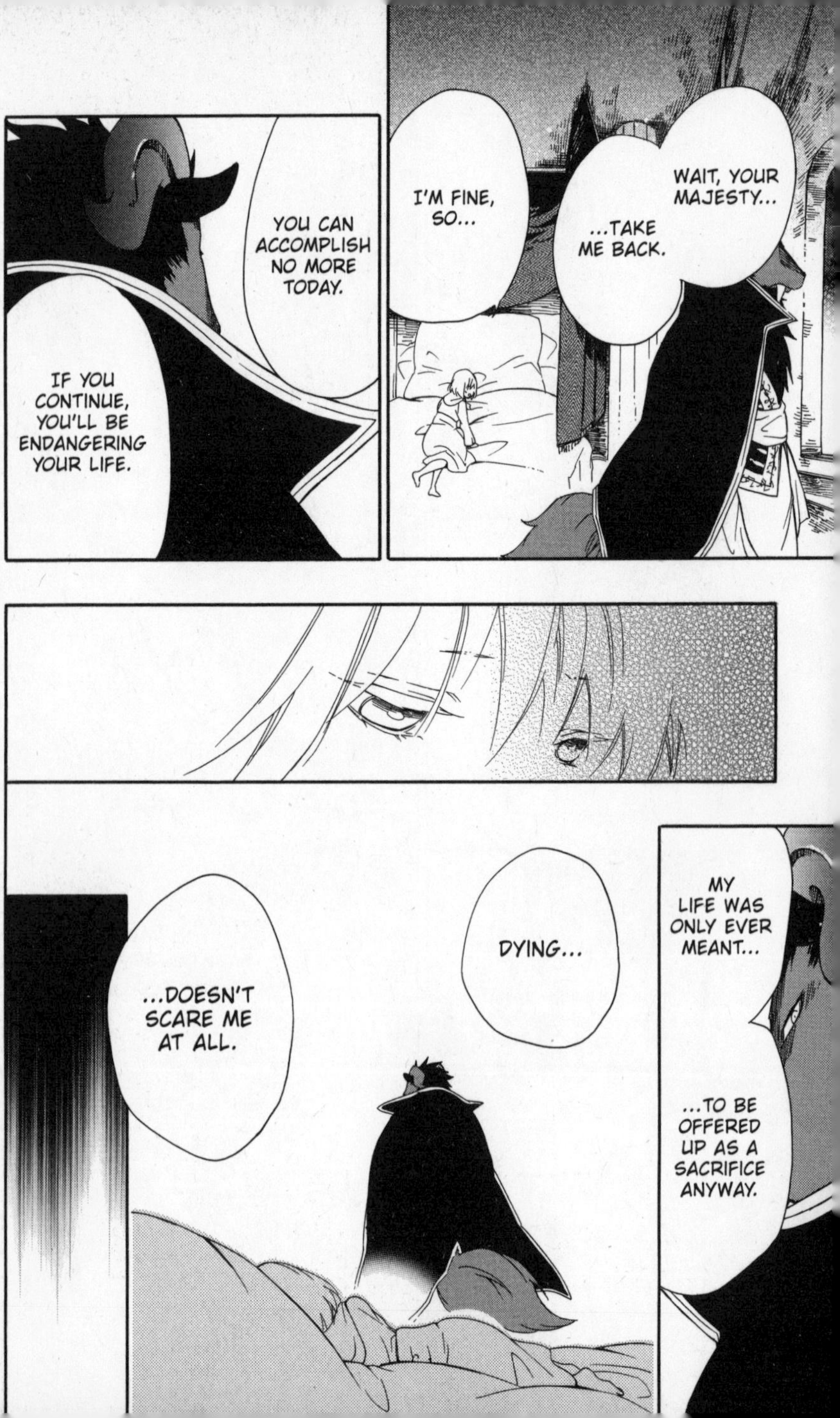
WAIT, YOUR MAJESTY...
...TAKE ME BACK.
I'M FINE, SO...
YOU CAN ACCOMPLISH NO MORE TODAY.
IF YOU CONTINUE, YOU'LL BE ENDANGERING YOUR LIFE.
MY LIFE WAS ONLY EVER MEANT...
...TO BE OFFERED UP AS A SACRIFICE ANYWAY.
DYING...
...DOESN'T SCARE ME AT ALL.

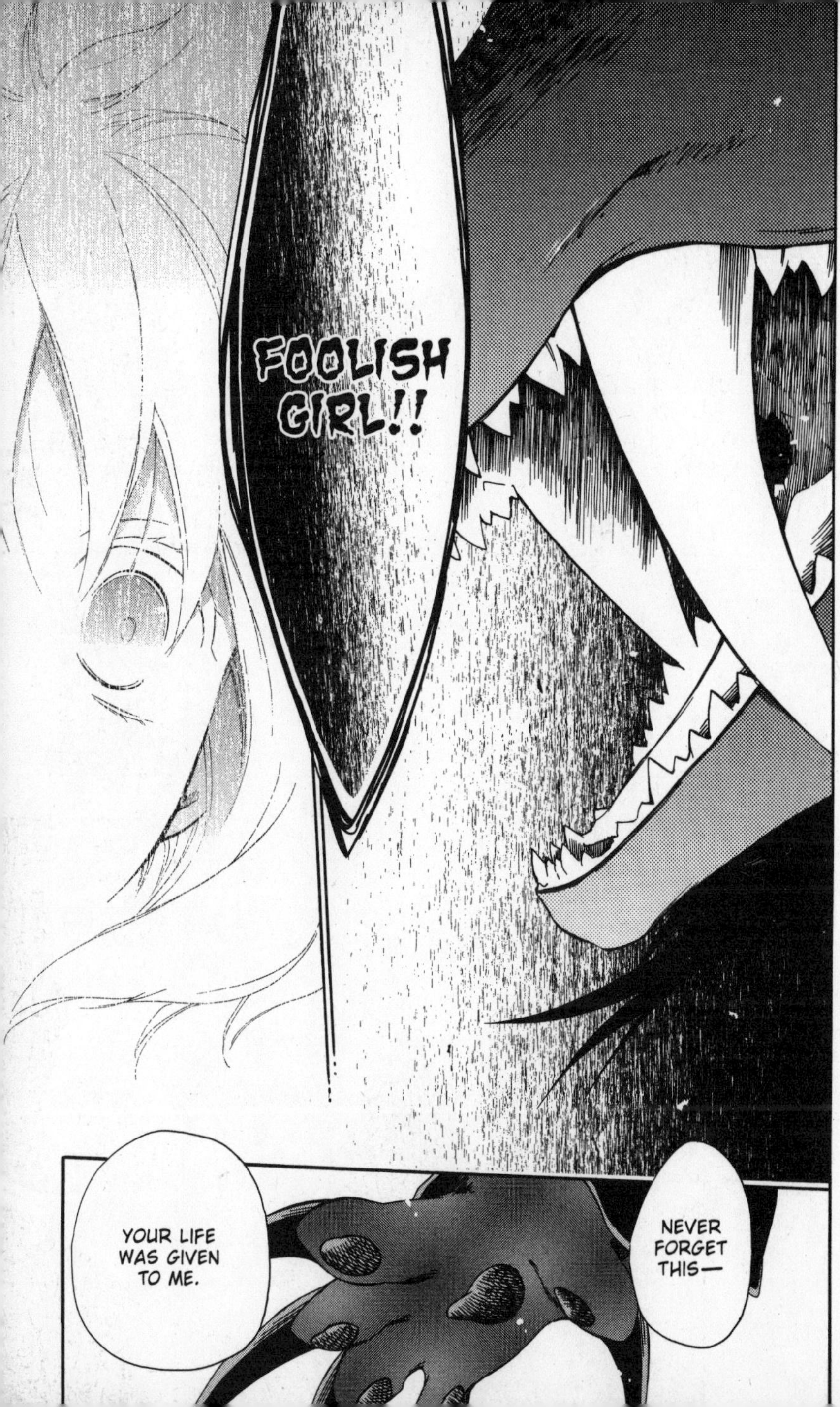
FOOLISH GIRL!!
NEVER FORGET THIS—
YOUR LIFE WAS GIVEN TO ME.

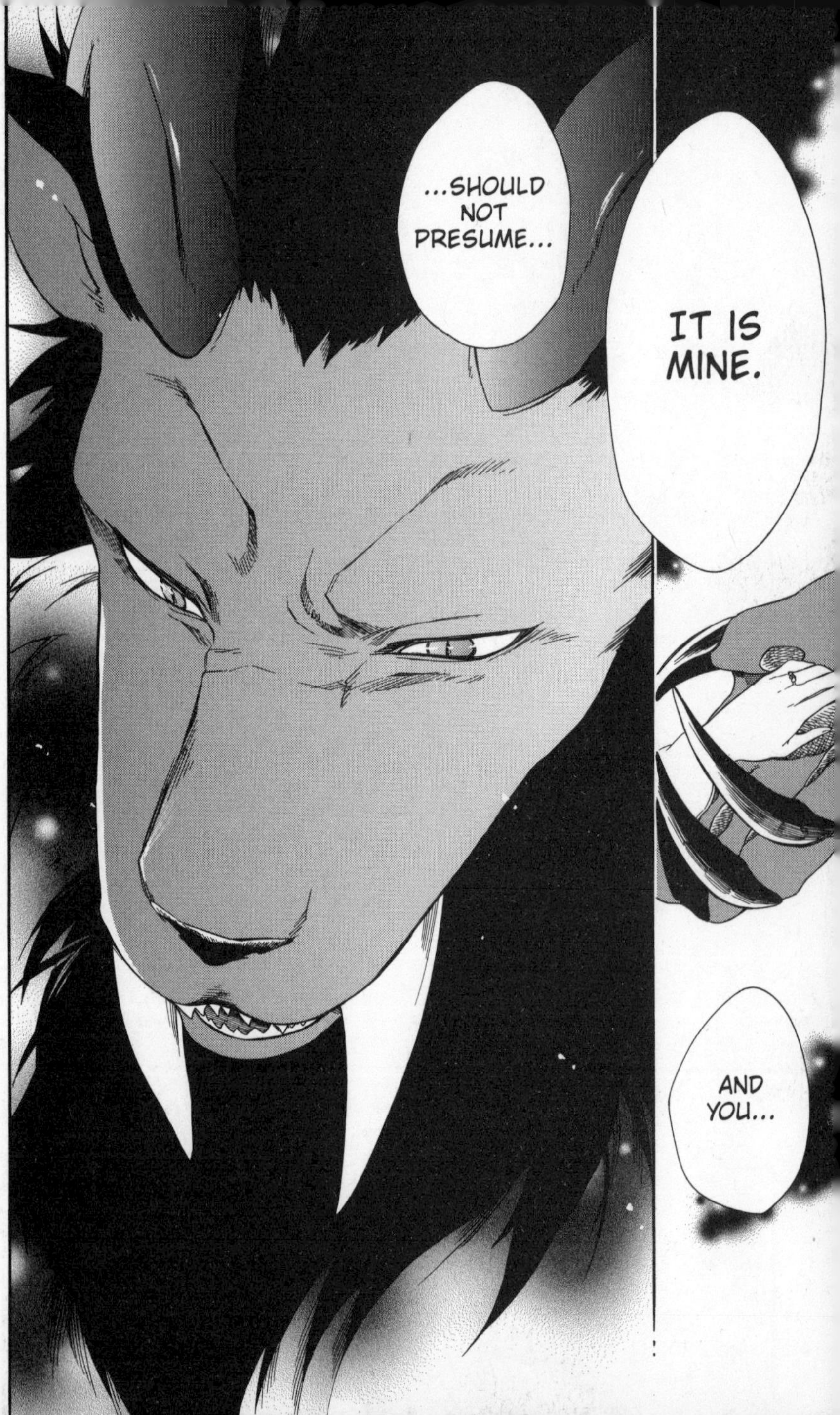
IT IS MINE.
AND YOU...
...SHOULD NOT PRESUME...

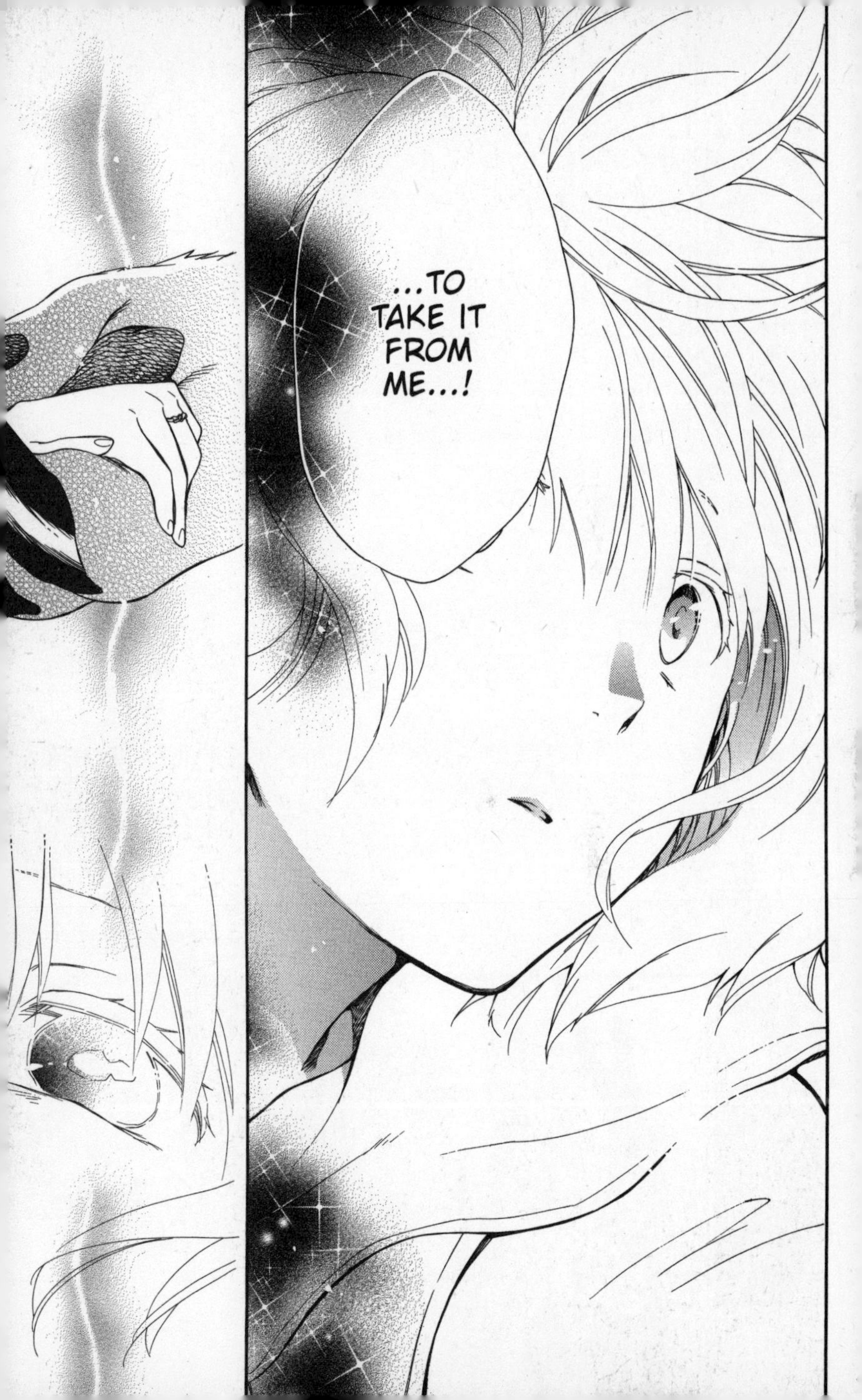
...TO TAKE IT FROM ME...!

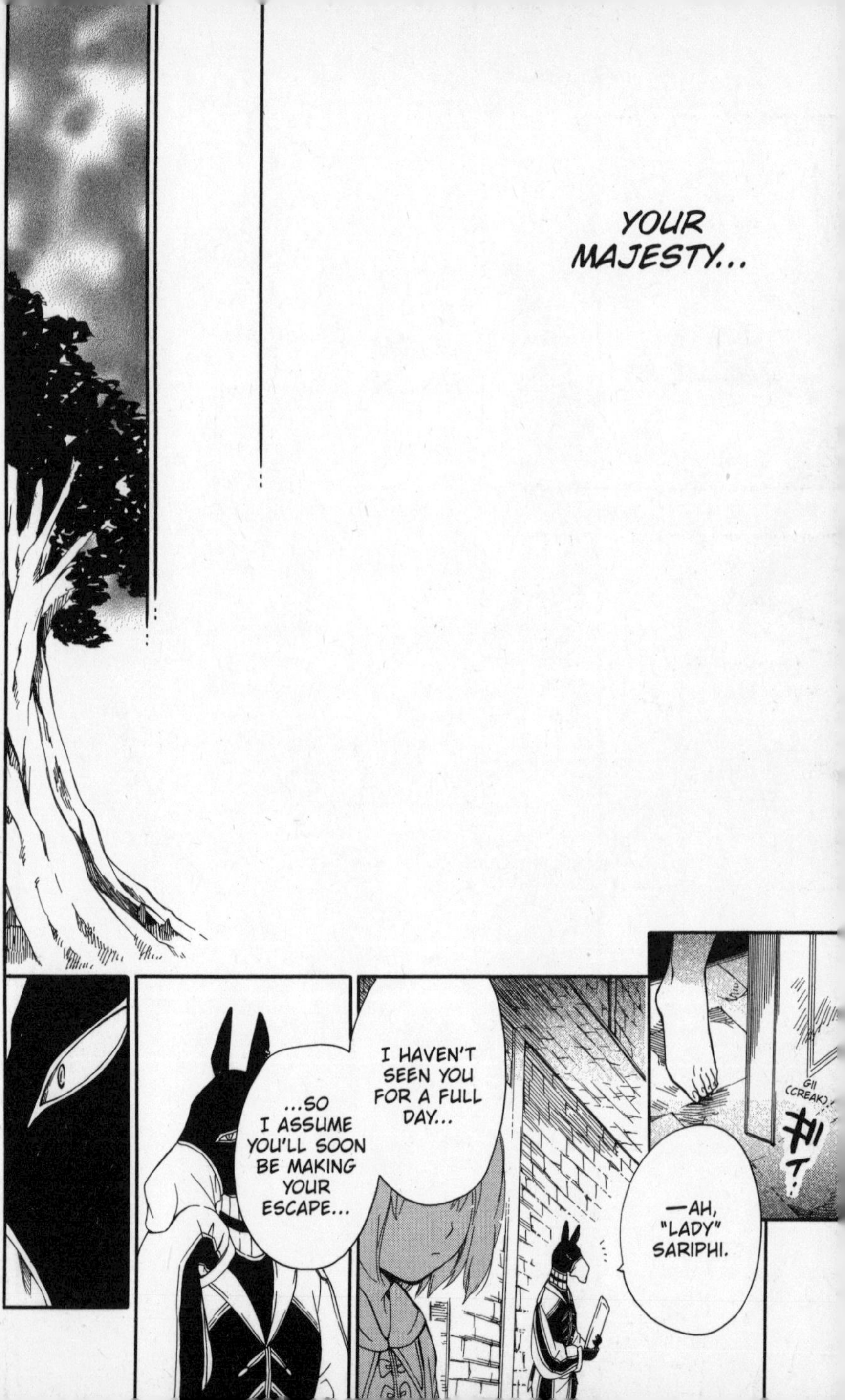
YOUR MAJESTY...
GII (CREAK)
—AH, "LADY" SARIPHI.
I HAVEN'T SEEN YOU FOR A FULL DAY...
...SO I ASSUME YOU'LL SOON BE MAKING YOUR ESCAPE...

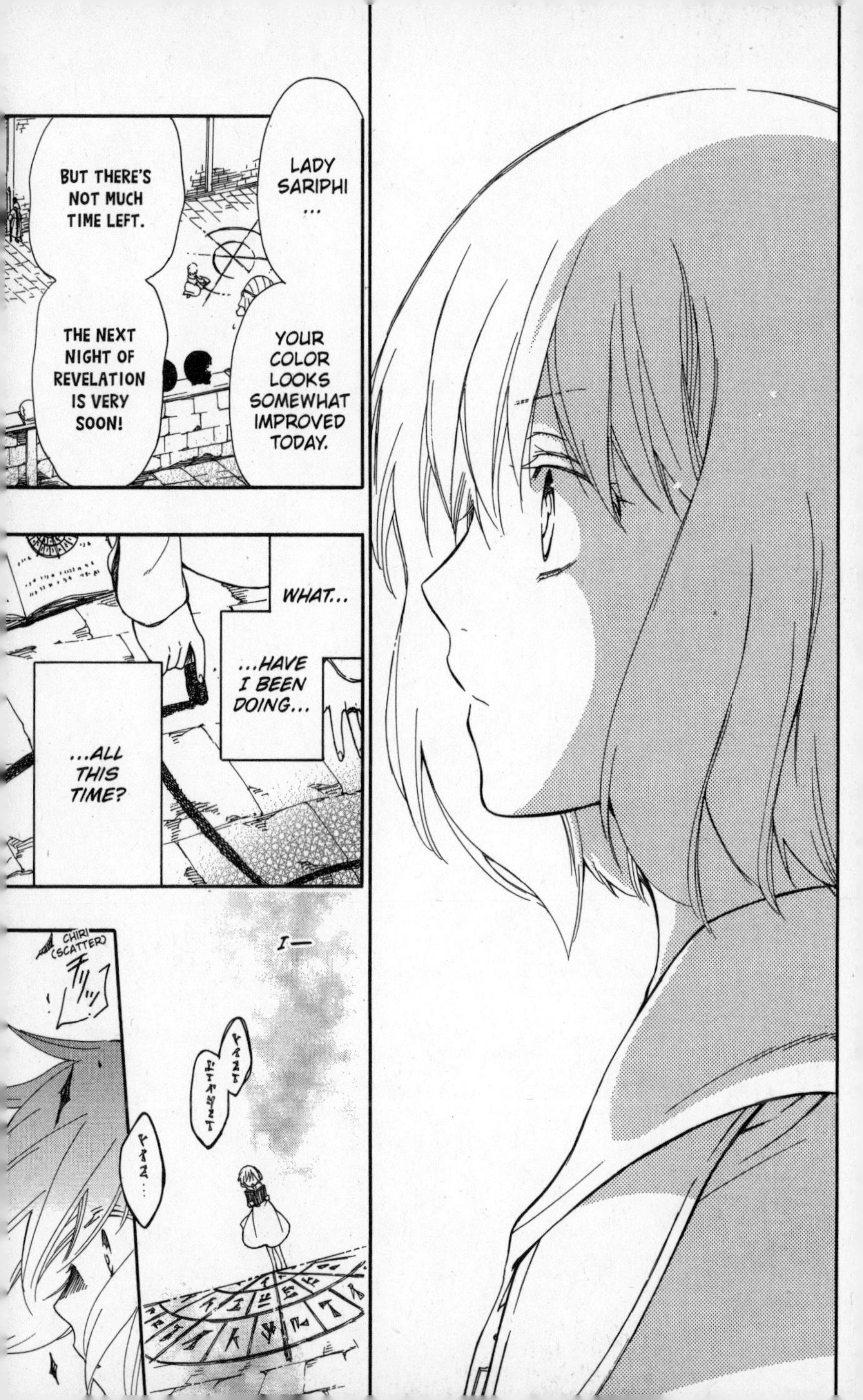
LADY SARIPHI...
YOUR COLOR LOOKS SOMEWHAT IMPROVED TODAY.
BUT THERE'S NOT MUCH TIME LEFT.
THE NEXT NIGHT OF REVELATION IS VERY SOON!
WHAT...
...HAVE I BEEN DOING...
...ALL THIS TIME?
I—
CHIRI (SCATTER)

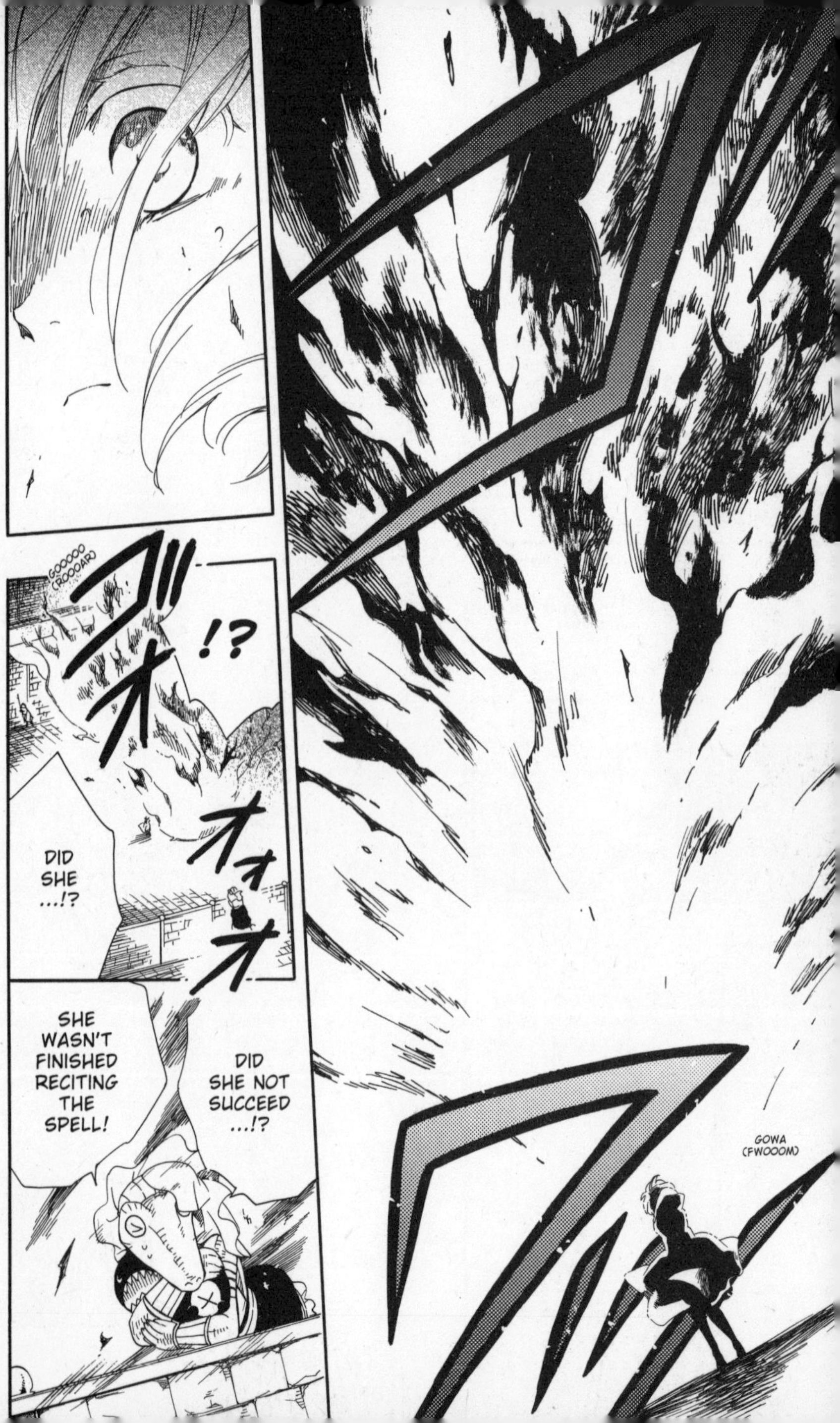
GOWA
(FWOOOM)
GOOOOO
(ROOOAR)
!?
DID SHE ...!?
DID SHE NOT SUCCEED ...!?
SHE WASN'T FINISHED RECITING THE SPELL!

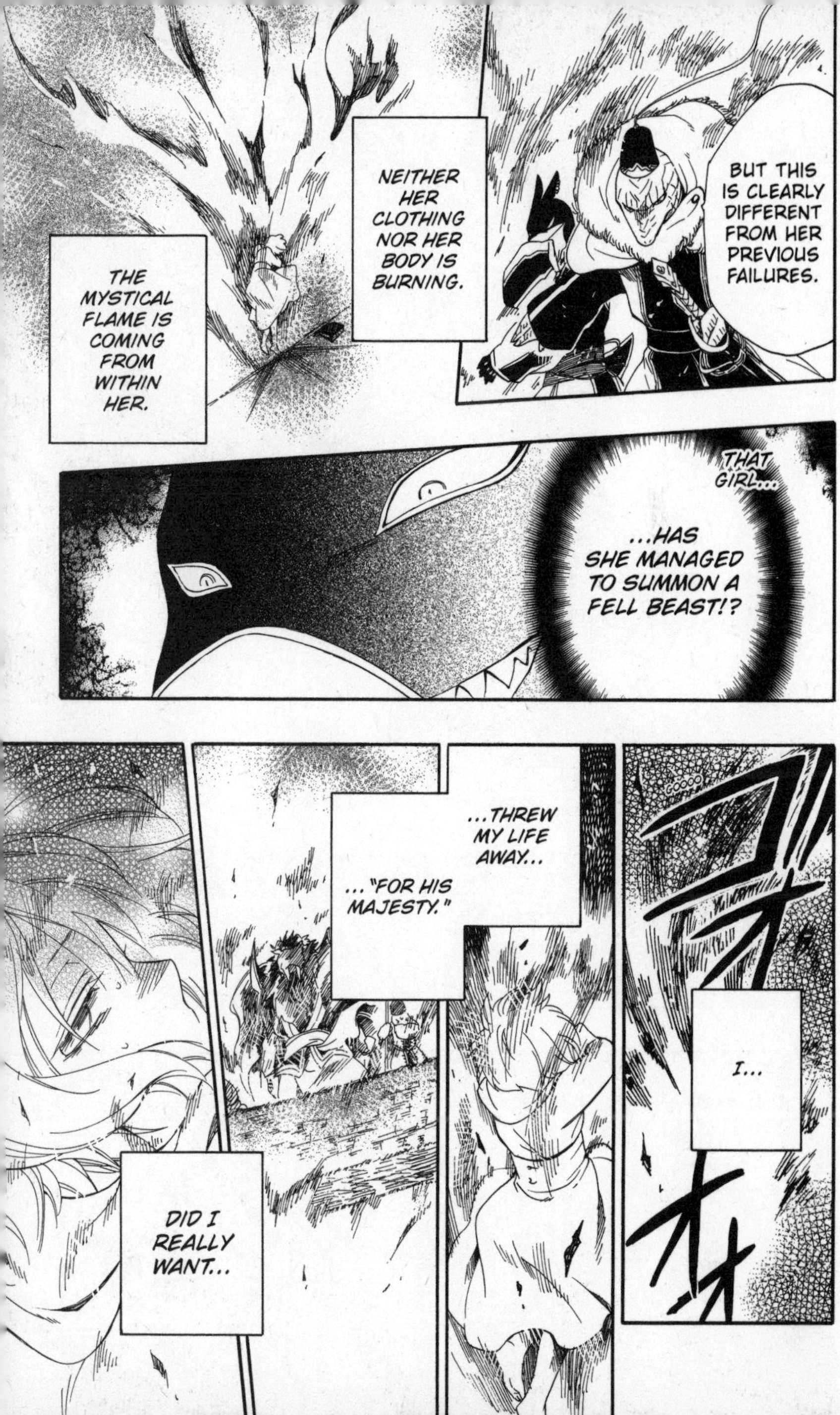
BUT THIS IS CLEARLY DIFFERENT FROM HER PREVIOUS FAILURES.
NEITHER HER CLOTHING NOR HER BODY IS BURNING.
THE MYSTICAL FLAME IS COMING FROM WITHIN HER.
THAT GIRL...
...HAS SHE MANAGED TO SUMMON A FELL BEAST!?
GOOOO
I...
...THREW MY LIFE AWAY...
..."FOR HIS MAJESTY."
DID I REALLY WANT...

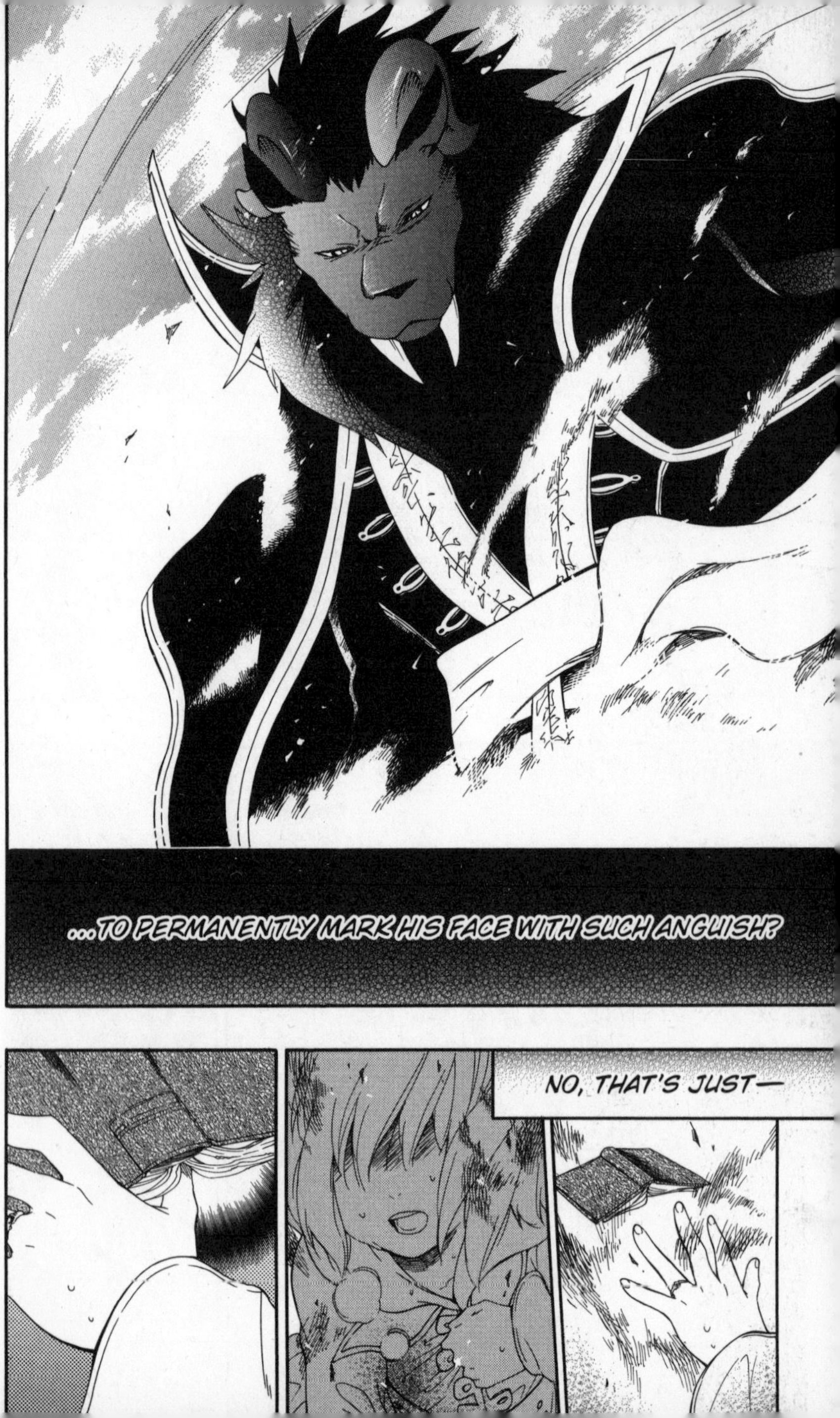
...TO PERMANENTLY MARK HIS FACE WITH SUCH ANGUISH?
NO, THAT'S JUST—

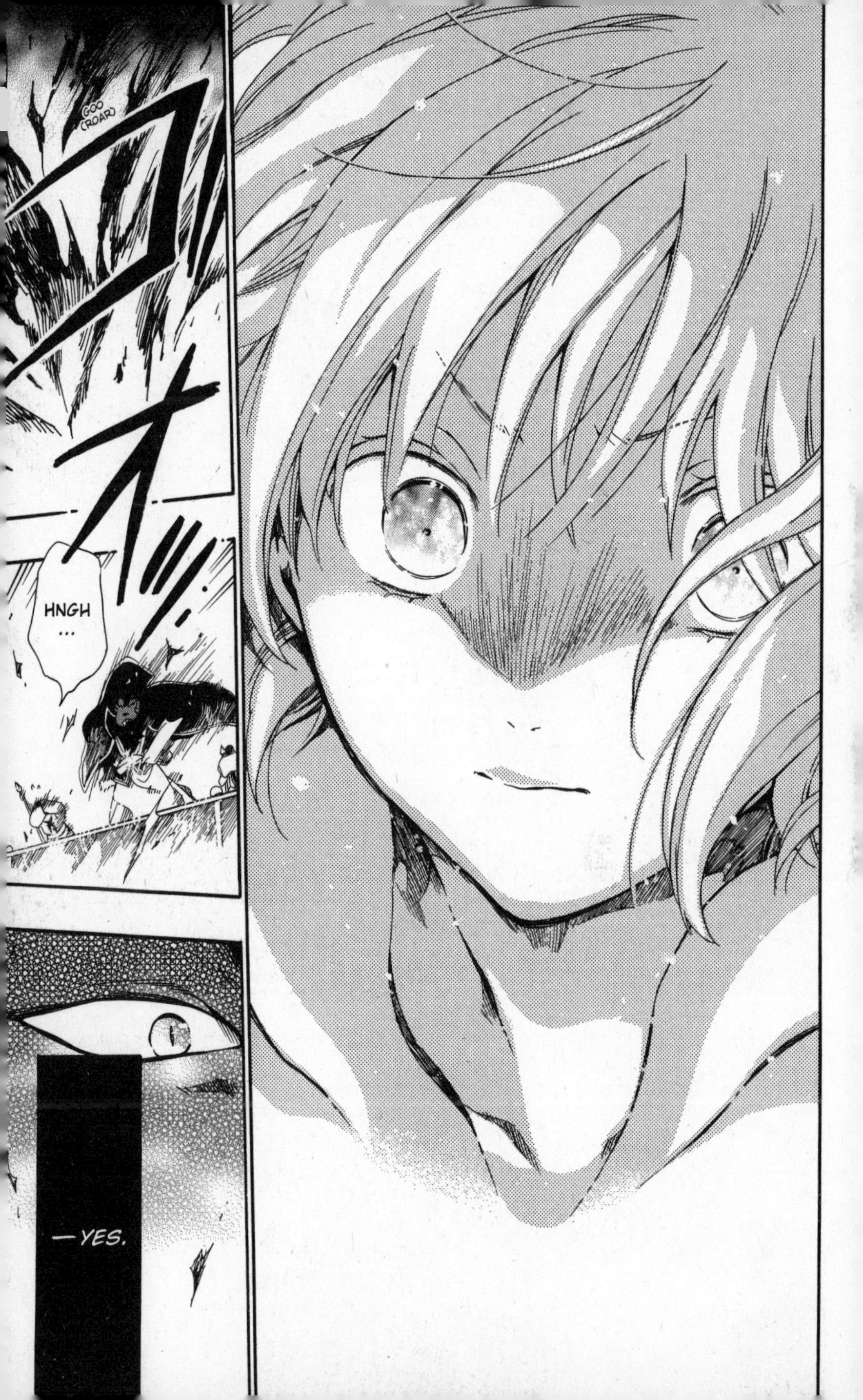
GOO (ROAR)
HNGH ...
—YES.

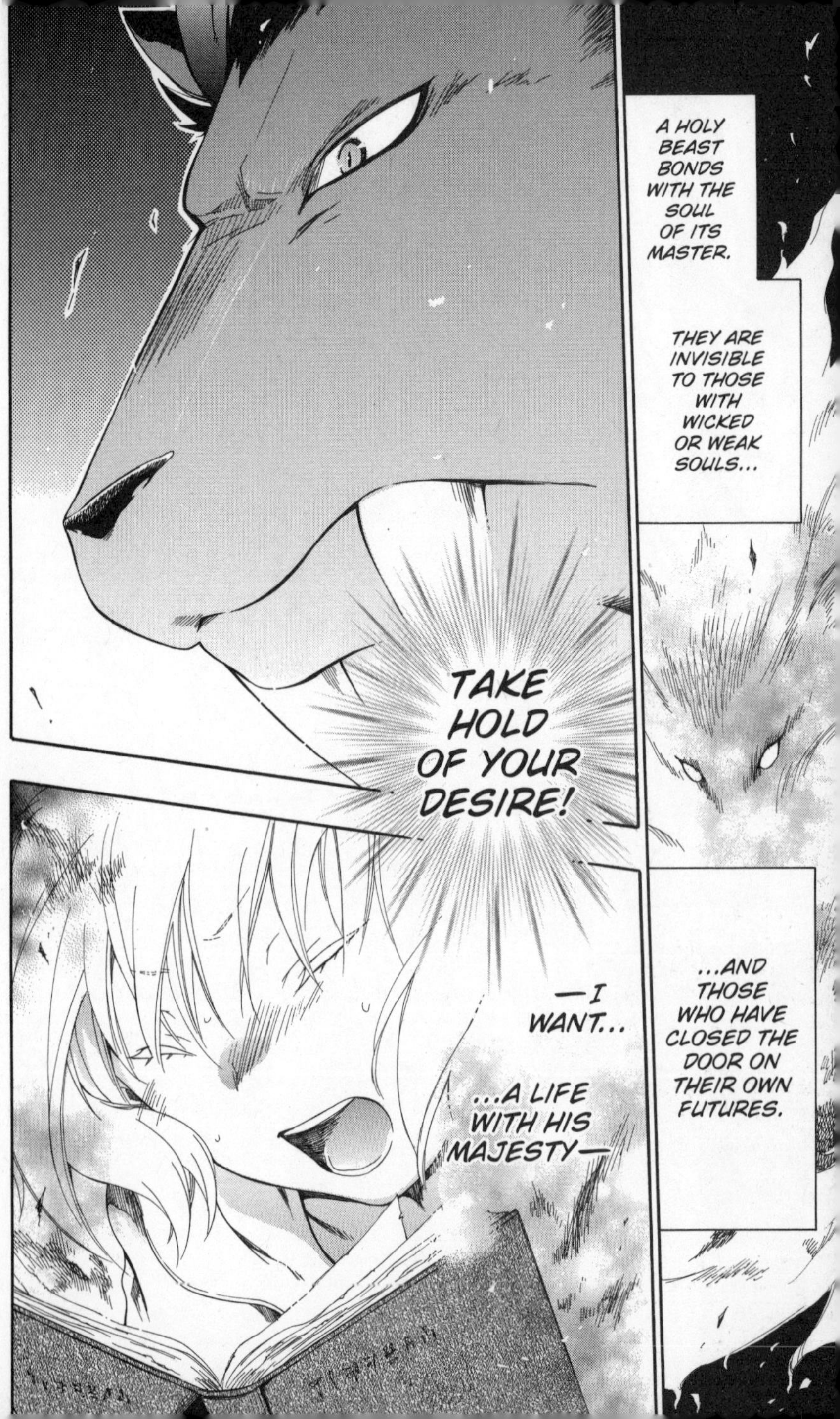
A HOLY BEAST BONDS WITH THE SOUL OF ITS MASTER.
THEY ARE INVISIBLE TO THOSE WITH WICKED OR WEAK SOULS...
...AND THOSE WHO HAVE CLOSED THE DOOR ON THEIR OWN FUTURES.
TAKE HOLD OF YOUR DESIRE!
—I WANT...
...A LIFE WITH HIS MAJESTY—

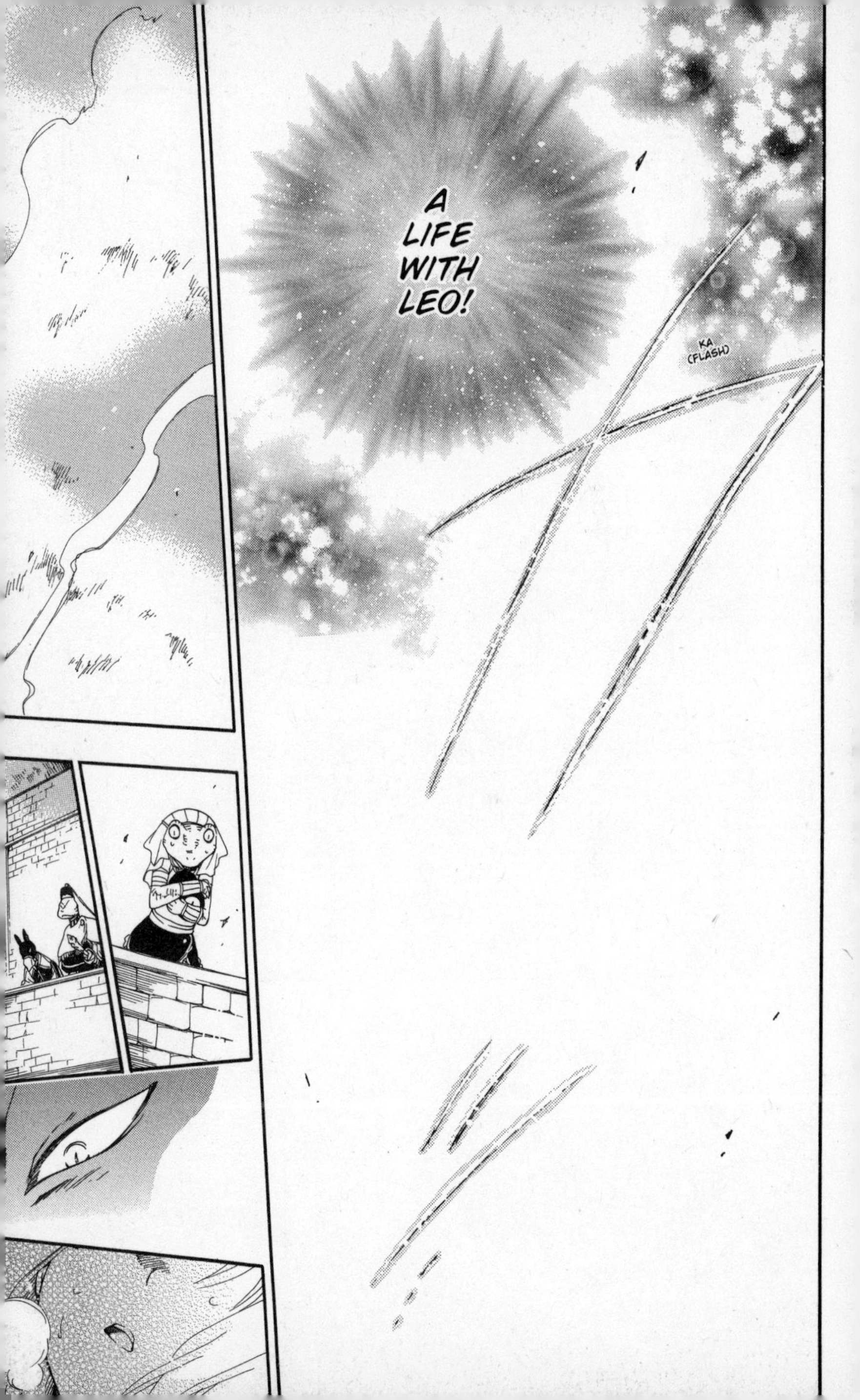
A LIFE WITH LEO!
KA
(FLASH)

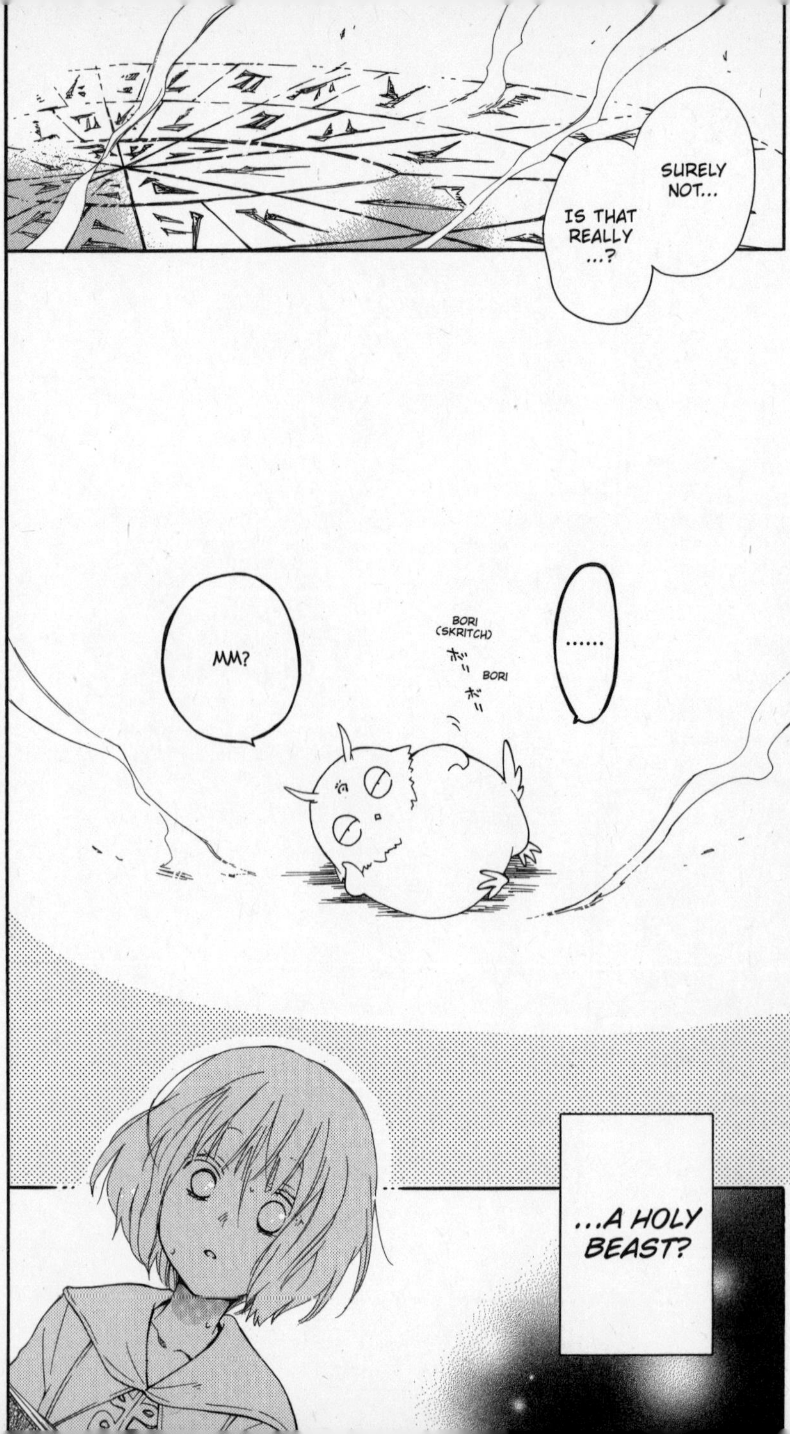
SURELY NOT...
IS THAT REALLY ...?
......
BORI (SKRITCH)
ボリ
BORI
ボリ
MM?
...A HOLY BEAST?

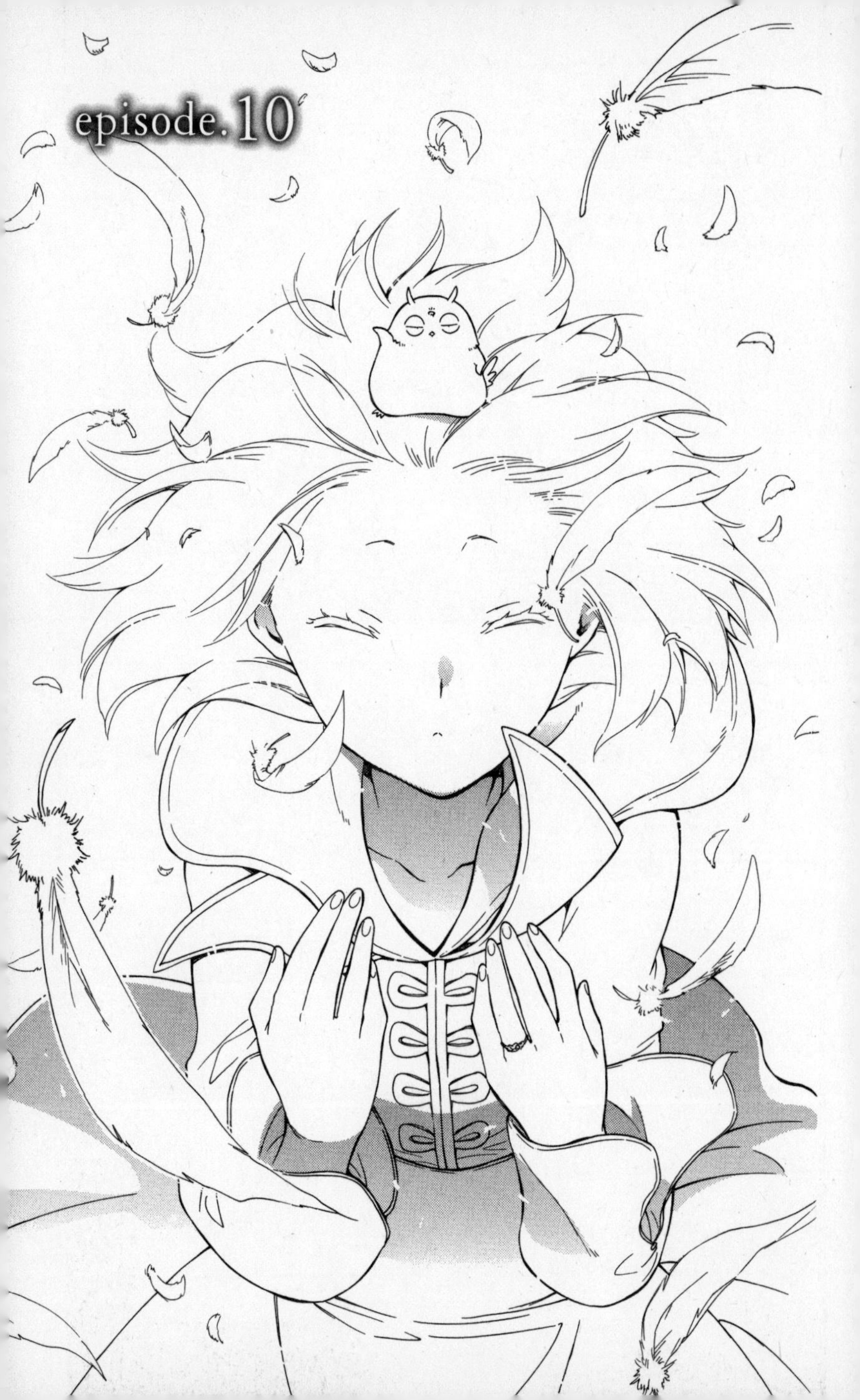
episode. 10

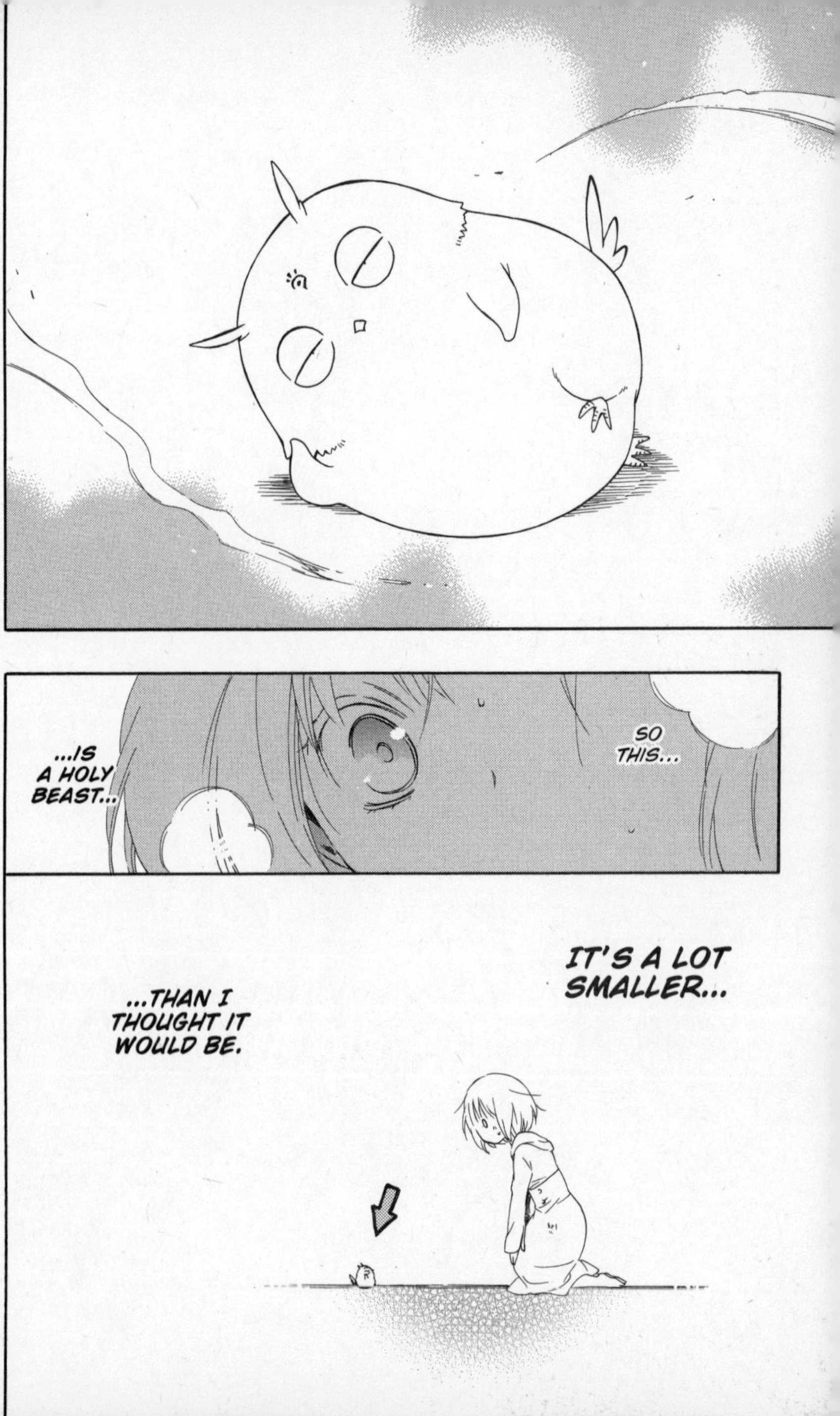
SO THIS...
...IS A HOLY BEAST...
IT'S A LOT SMALLER...
...THAN I THOUGHT IT WOULD BE.

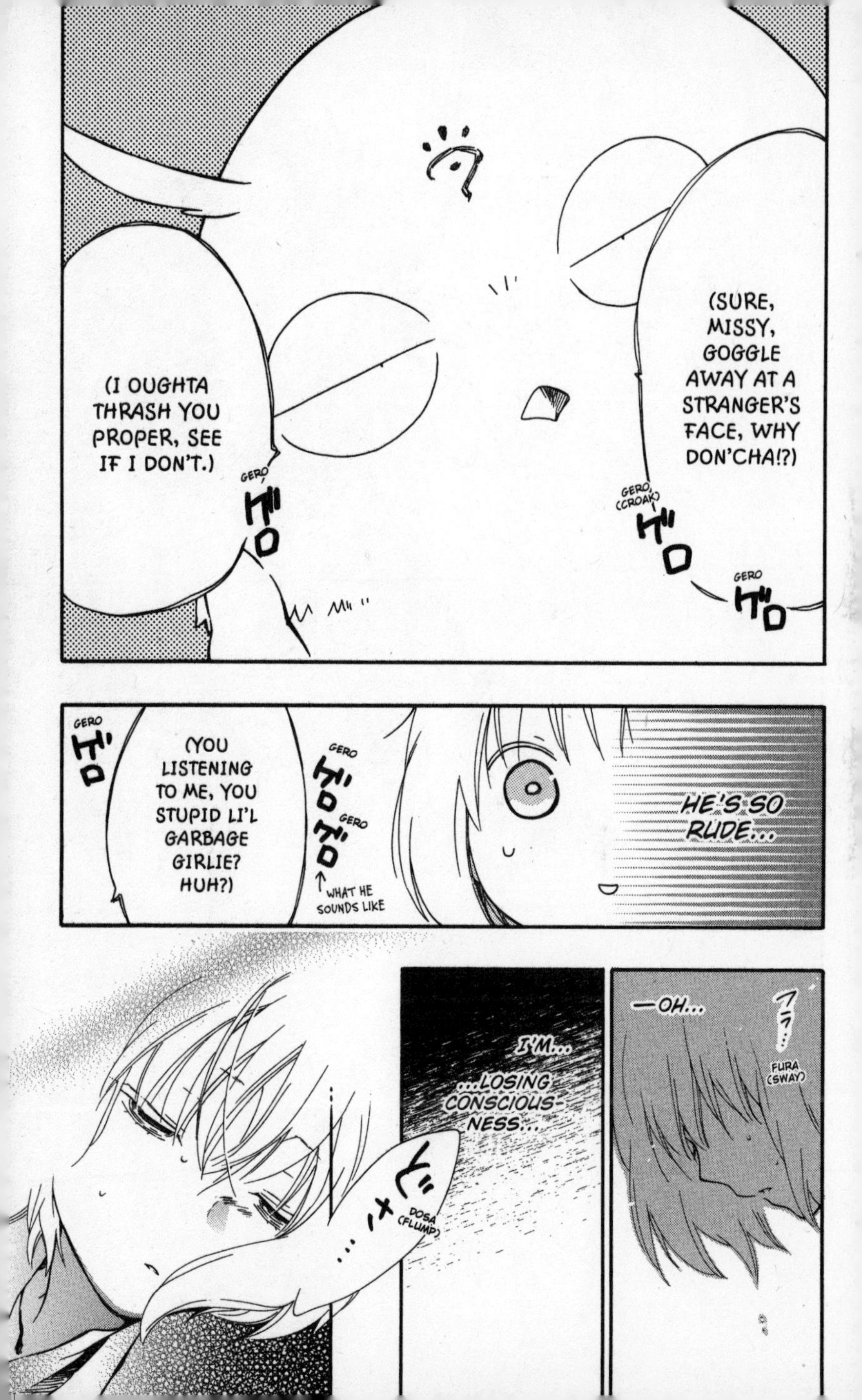
(SURE, MISSY, GOGGLE AWAY AT A STRANGER'S FACE, WHY DON'CHA!?)
GERO, (CROAK)
GERO
(I OUGHTA THRASH YOU PROPER, SEE IF I DON'T.)
GERO
HE'S SO RUDE...
GERO
GERO
↑WHAT HE SOUNDS LIKE
(YOU LISTENING TO ME, YOU STUPID LI'L GARBAGE GIRLIE? HUH?)
GERO
—OH...
FURA (SWAY)
I'M... ...LOSING CONSCIOUS-NESS...
DOSA (FLUMP)

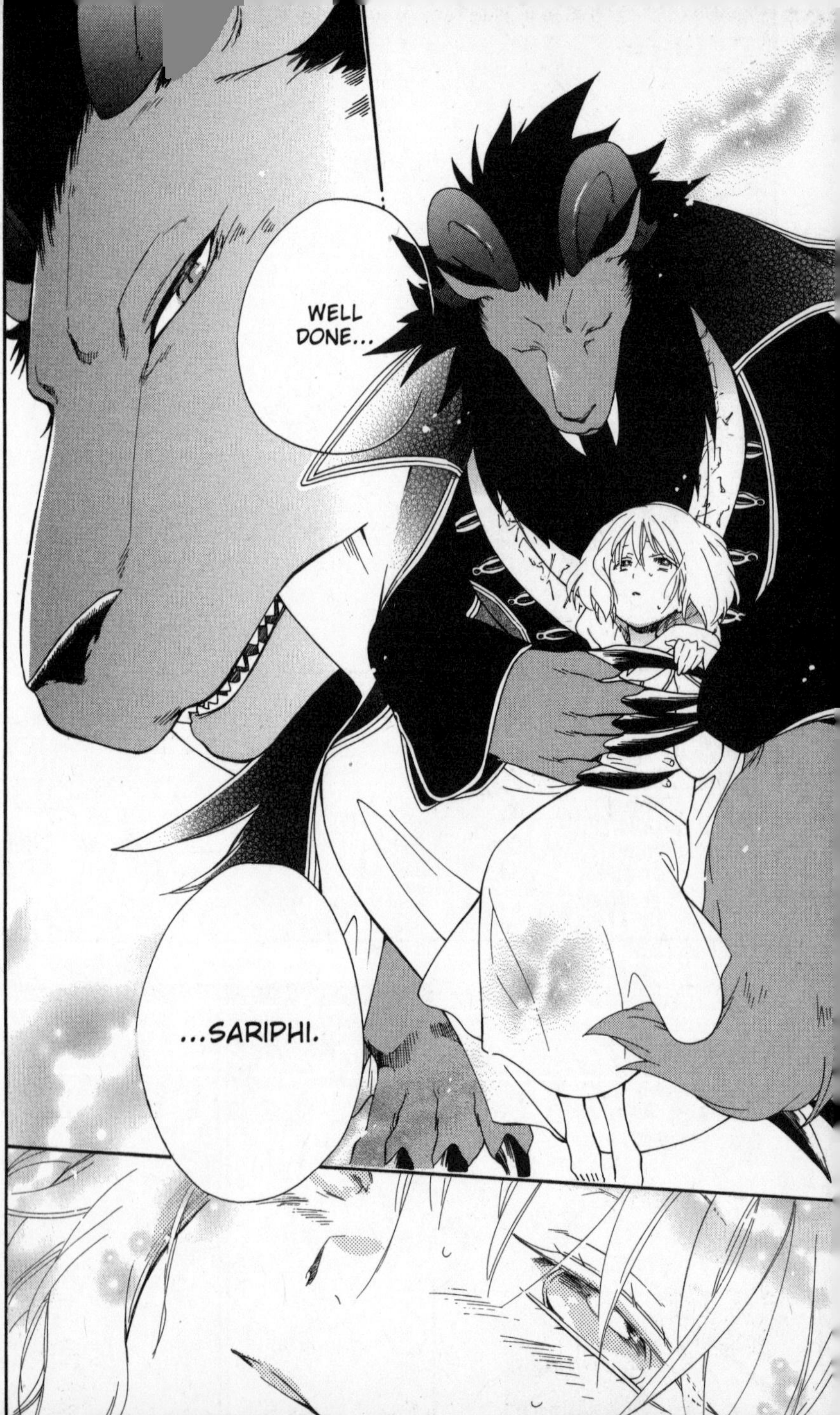
WELL DONE...
...SARIPHI.

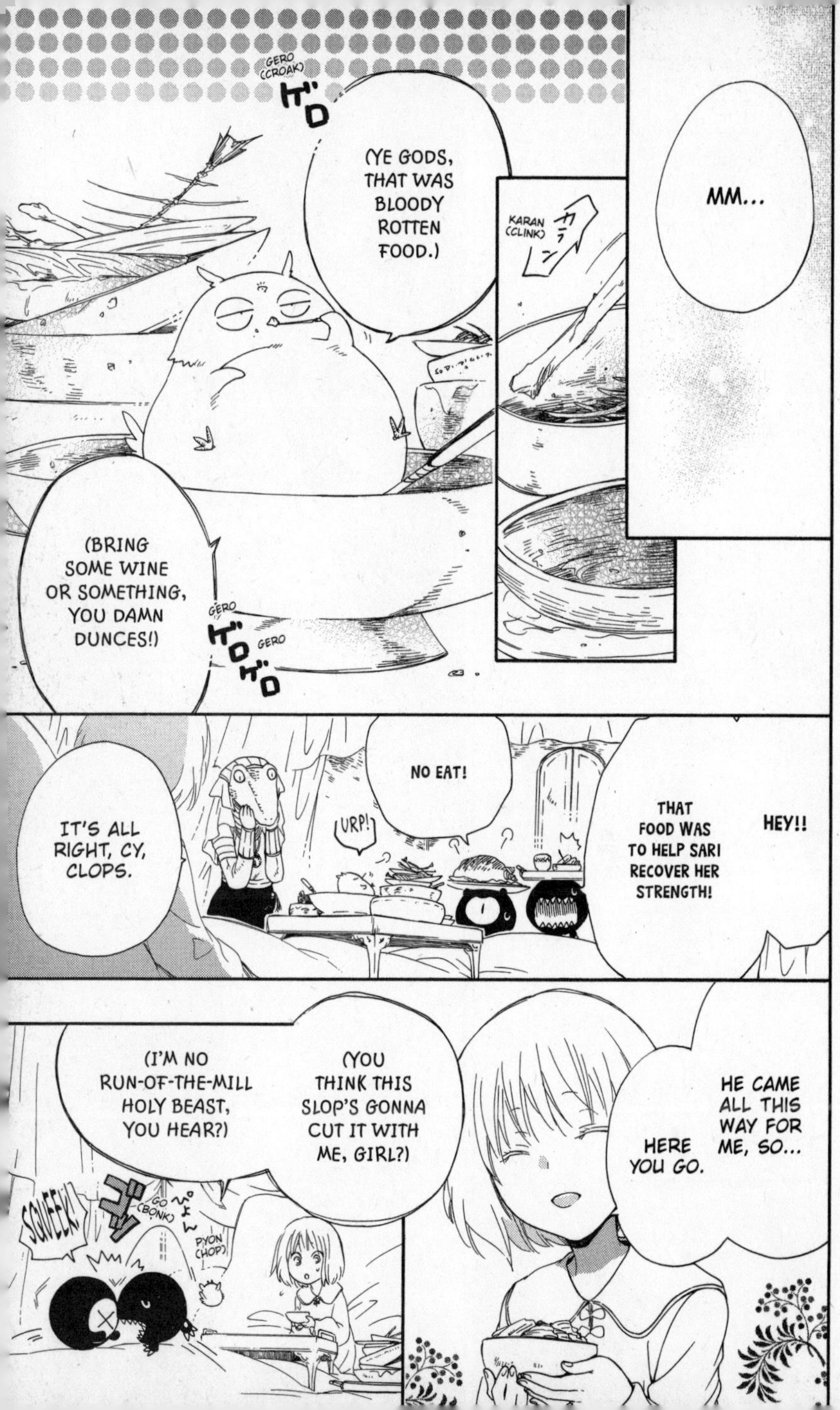
MM...
KARAN (CLINK)
GERO (CROAK)
(YE GODS, THAT WAS BLOODY ROTTEN FOOD.)
(BRING SOME WINE OR SOMETHING, YOU DAMN DUNCES!)
GERO GERO
HEY!!
THAT FOOD WAS TO HELP SARI RECOVER HER STRENGTH!
NO EAT!
URP!
IT'S ALL RIGHT, CY, CLOPS.
HE CAME ALL THIS WAY FOR ME, SO...
HERE YOU GO.
(YOU THINK THIS SLOP'S GONNA CUT IT WITH ME, GIRL?)
(I'M NO RUN-OF-THE-MILL HOLY BEAST, YOU HEAR?)
SQUEEK!
GO (BONK)
PYON (HOP)

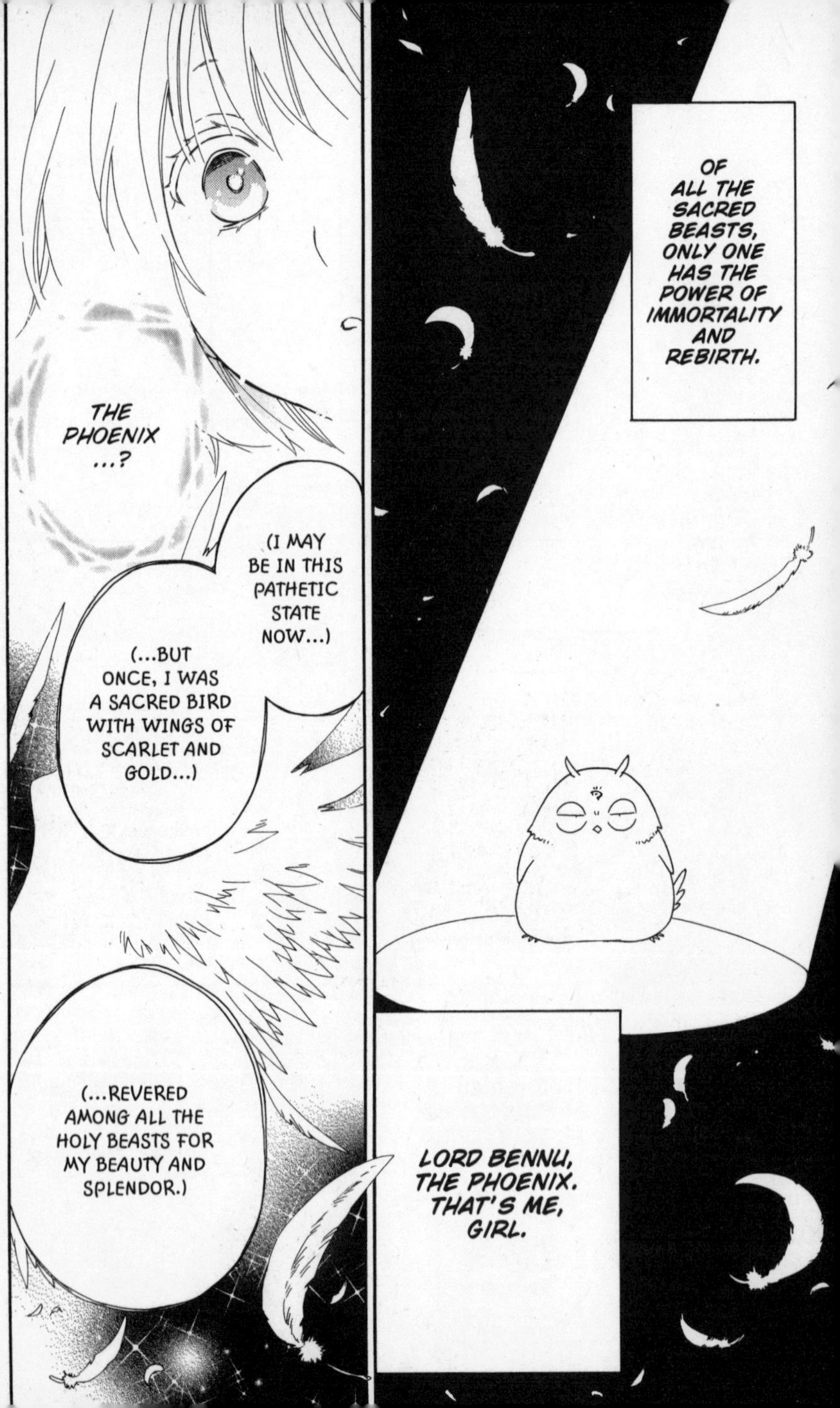

OF ALL THE SACRED BEASTS, ONLY ONE HAS THE POWER OF IMMORTALITY AND REBIRTH.
LORD BENNU, THE PHOENIX. THAT'S ME, GIRL.
THE PHOENIX ...?
(I MAY BE IN THIS PATHETIC STATE NOW...)
(...BUT ONCE, I WAS A SACRED BIRD WITH WINGS OF SCARLET AND GOLD...)
(...REVERED AMONG ALL THE HOLY BEASTS FOR MY BEAUTY AND SPLENDOR.)

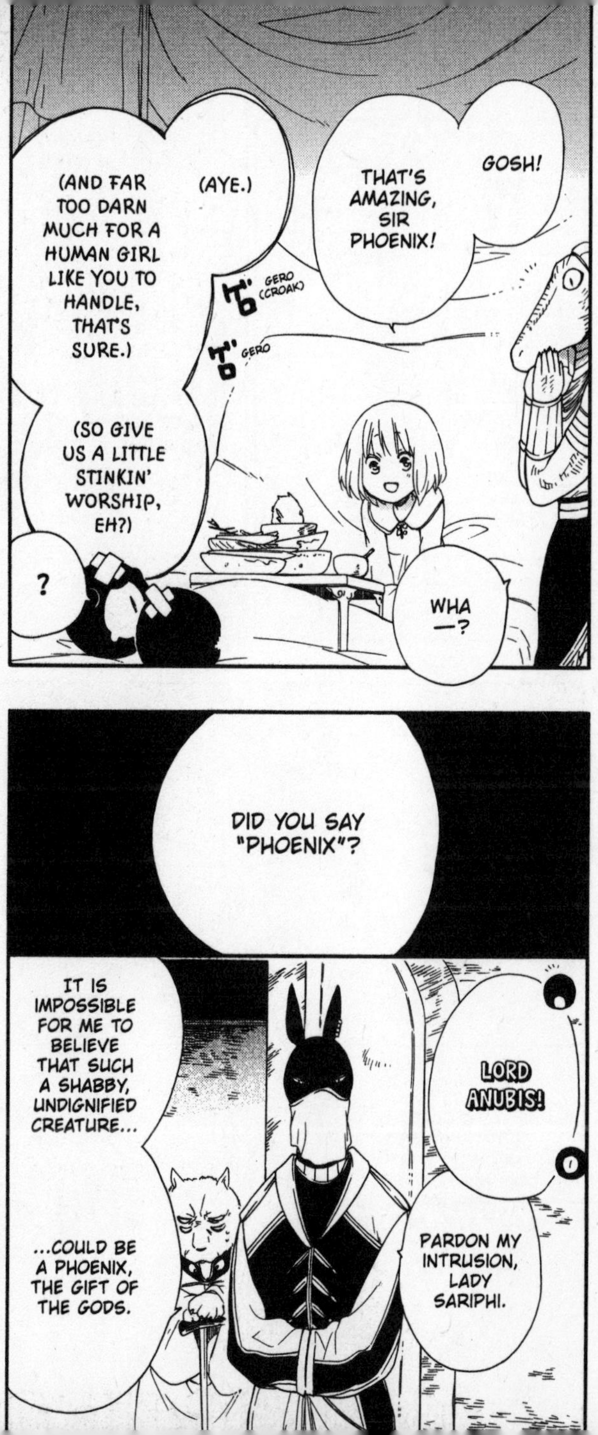
GOSH!
THAT'S AMAZING, SIR PHOENIX!
GERO (CROAK)
GERO
(AYE.)
(AND FAR TOO DARN MUCH FOR A HUMAN GIRL LIKE YOU TO HANDLE, THAT'S SURE.)
(SO GIVE US A LITTLE STINKIN' WORSHIP, EH?)
WHA—?
?
DID YOU SAY "PHOENIX"?
LORD ANUBIS!
PARDON MY INTRUSION, LADY SARIPHI.
IT IS IMPOSSIBLE FOR ME TO BELIEVE THAT SUCH A SHABBY, UNDIGNIFIED CREATURE...
...COULD BE A PHOENIX, THE GIFT OF THE GODS.

LITTLE BENNU, THE PHOENIX

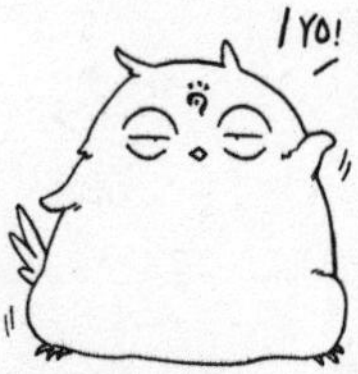
YO!

WHEN CREATING ANOTHER MASCOT CHARACTER, MY BIGGEST CONCERN WAS AVOIDING OVERLAP WITH CY AND CLOPS. SO I ENDED UP WITH THIS FOUL-MOUTHED OLD MAN. WHEN I FIRST DREW HIM, MY EDITOR GOT THE IMPRESSION HE WAS GOING TO BE A SILENT CHARACTER, BUT THE REALITY ENDED UP THE EXACT OPPOSITE. HE JUST SAYS WHATEVER'S ON HIS MIND, SO HE'S A FUN CHARACTER TO PLAY WITH. AND EVEN IN HIS BIG FORM, HE'S NOT THAT BIG.

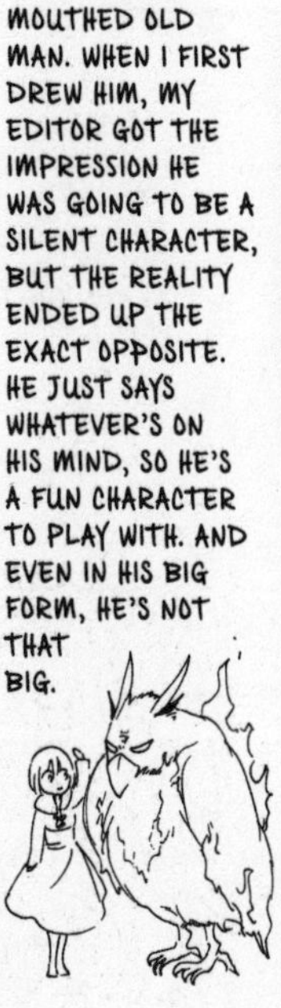

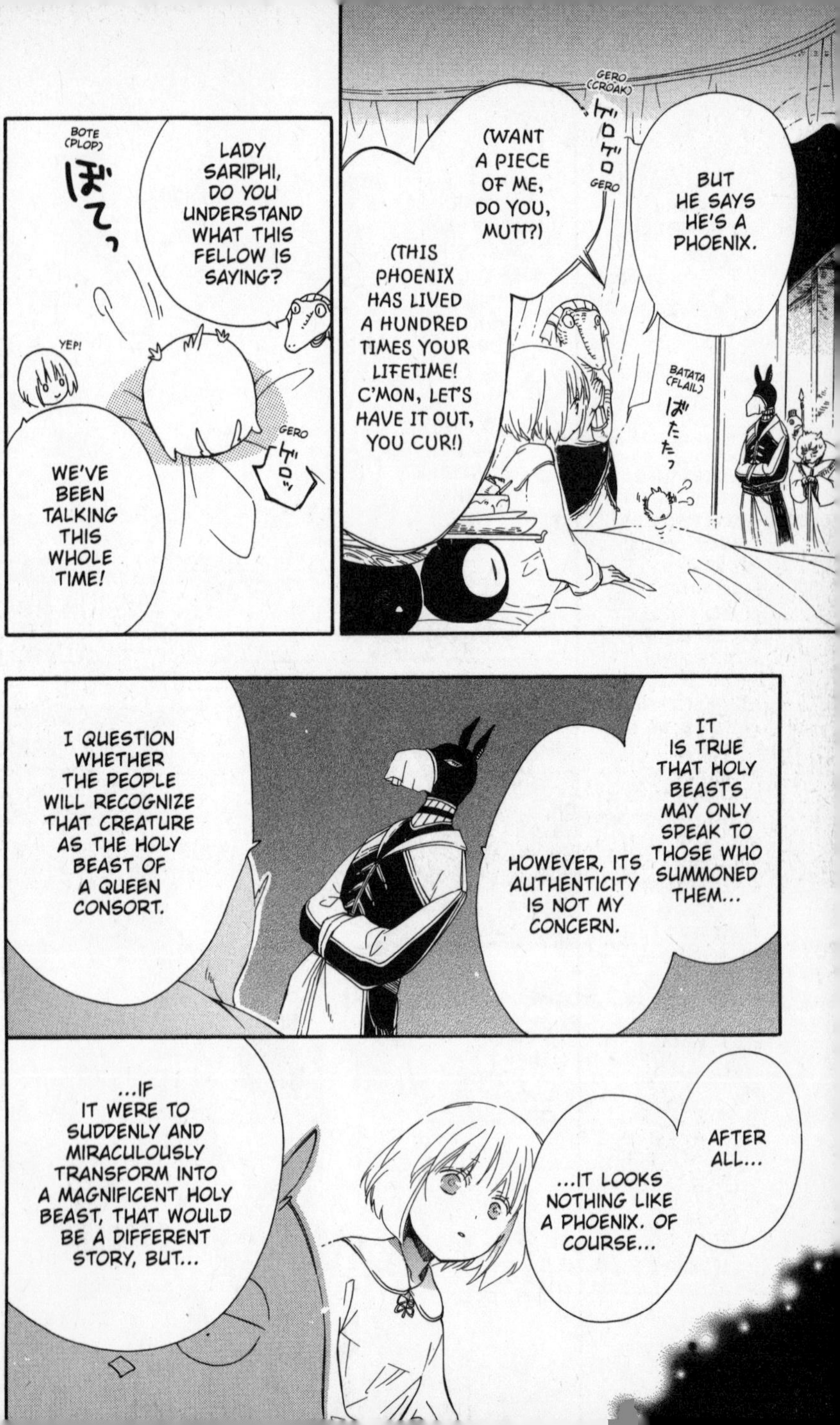
BUT HE SAYS HE'S A PHOENIX.
GERO (CROAK) ゲロゲロ GERO
(WANT A PIECE OF ME, DO YOU, MUTT?)
(THIS PHOENIX HAS LIVED A HUNDRED TIMES YOUR LIFETIME! C'MON, LET'S HAVE IT OUT, YOU CUR!)
BATATA (FLAIL) ばたたっ
BOTE (PLOP) ぼてっ
LADY SARIPHI, DO YOU UNDERSTAND WHAT THIS FELLOW IS SAYING?
GERO ゲロッ
YEP!
WE'VE BEEN TALKING THIS WHOLE TIME!
IT IS TRUE THAT HOLY BEASTS MAY ONLY SPEAK TO THOSE WHO SUMMONED THEM...
HOWEVER, ITS AUTHENTICITY IS NOT MY CONCERN.
I QUESTION WHETHER THE PEOPLE WILL RECOGNIZE THAT CREATURE AS THE HOLY BEAST OF A QUEEN CONSORT.
AFTER ALL...
...IT LOOKS NOTHING LIKE A PHOENIX. OF COURSE...
...IF IT WERE TO SUDDENLY AND MIRACULOUSLY TRANSFORM INTO A MAGNIFICENT HOLY BEAST, THAT WOULD BE A DIFFERENT STORY, BUT...

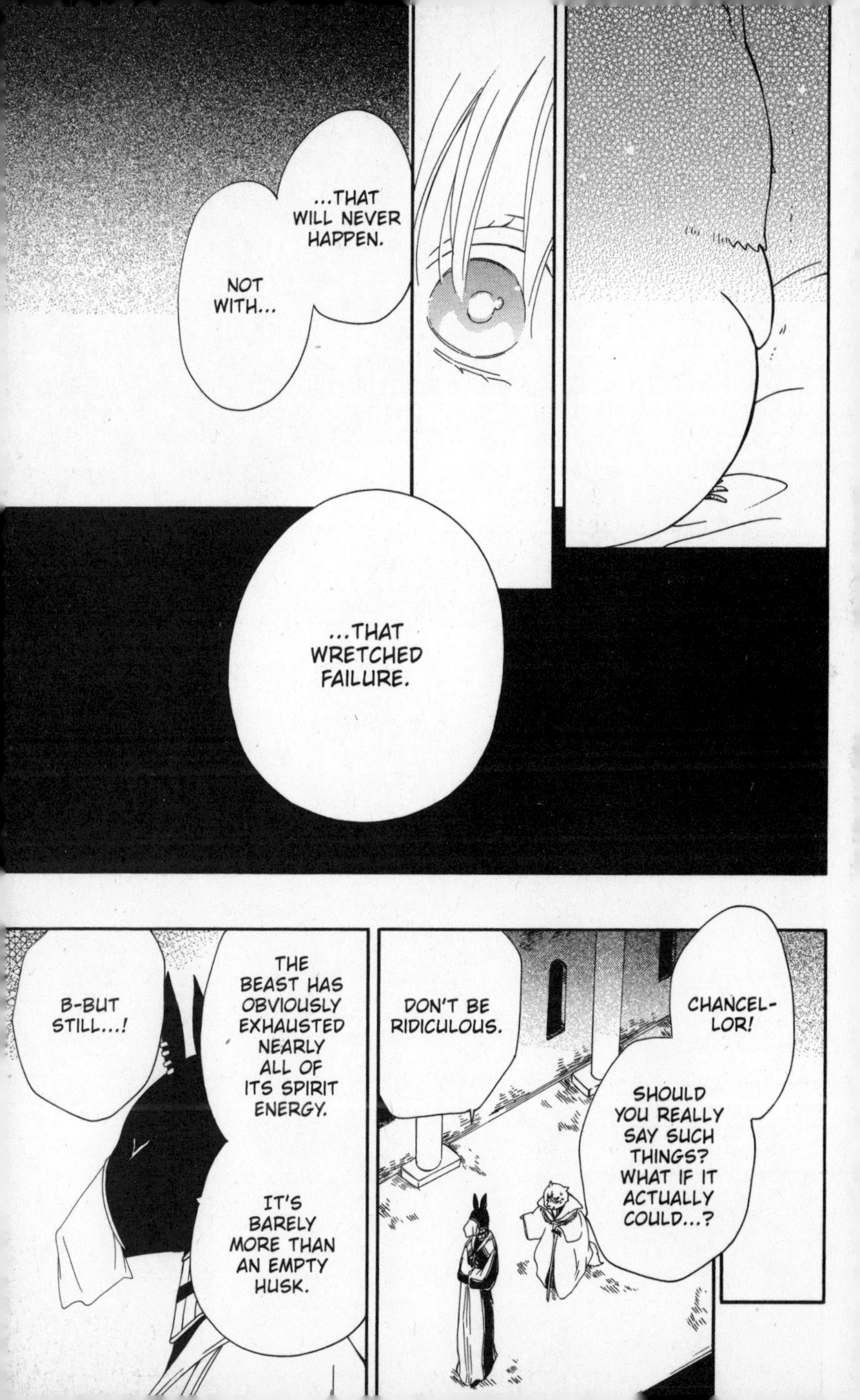
...THAT WILL NEVER HAPPEN.
NOT WITH...
...THAT WRETCHED FAILURE.
CHANCEL-LOR!
SHOULD YOU REALLY SAY SUCH THINGS? WHAT IF IT ACTUALLY COULD...?
DON'T BE RIDICULOUS.
THE BEAST HAS OBVIOUSLY EXHAUSTED NEARLY ALL OF ITS SPIRIT ENERGY.
IT'S BARELY MORE THAN AN EMPTY HUSK.
B-BUT STILL...!

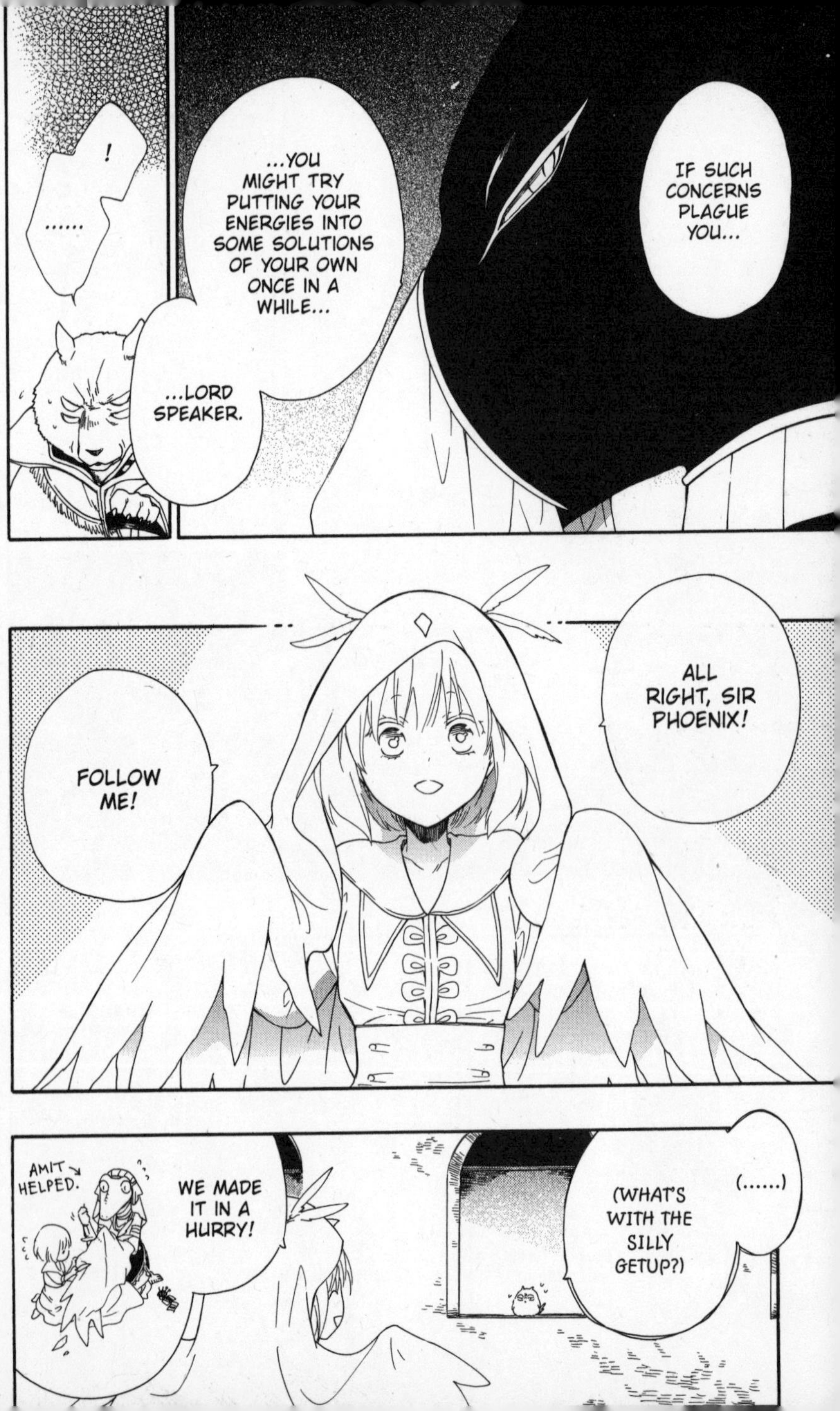
IF SUCH CONCERNS PLAGUE YOU...
...YOU MIGHT TRY PUTTING YOUR ENERGIES INTO SOME SOLUTIONS OF YOUR OWN ONCE IN A WHILE...
...LORD SPEAKER.
!
......
ALL RIGHT, SIR PHOENIX!
FOLLOW ME!
(......)
(WHAT'S WITH THE SILLY GETUP?)
WE MADE IT IN A HURRY!
AMIT HELPED.

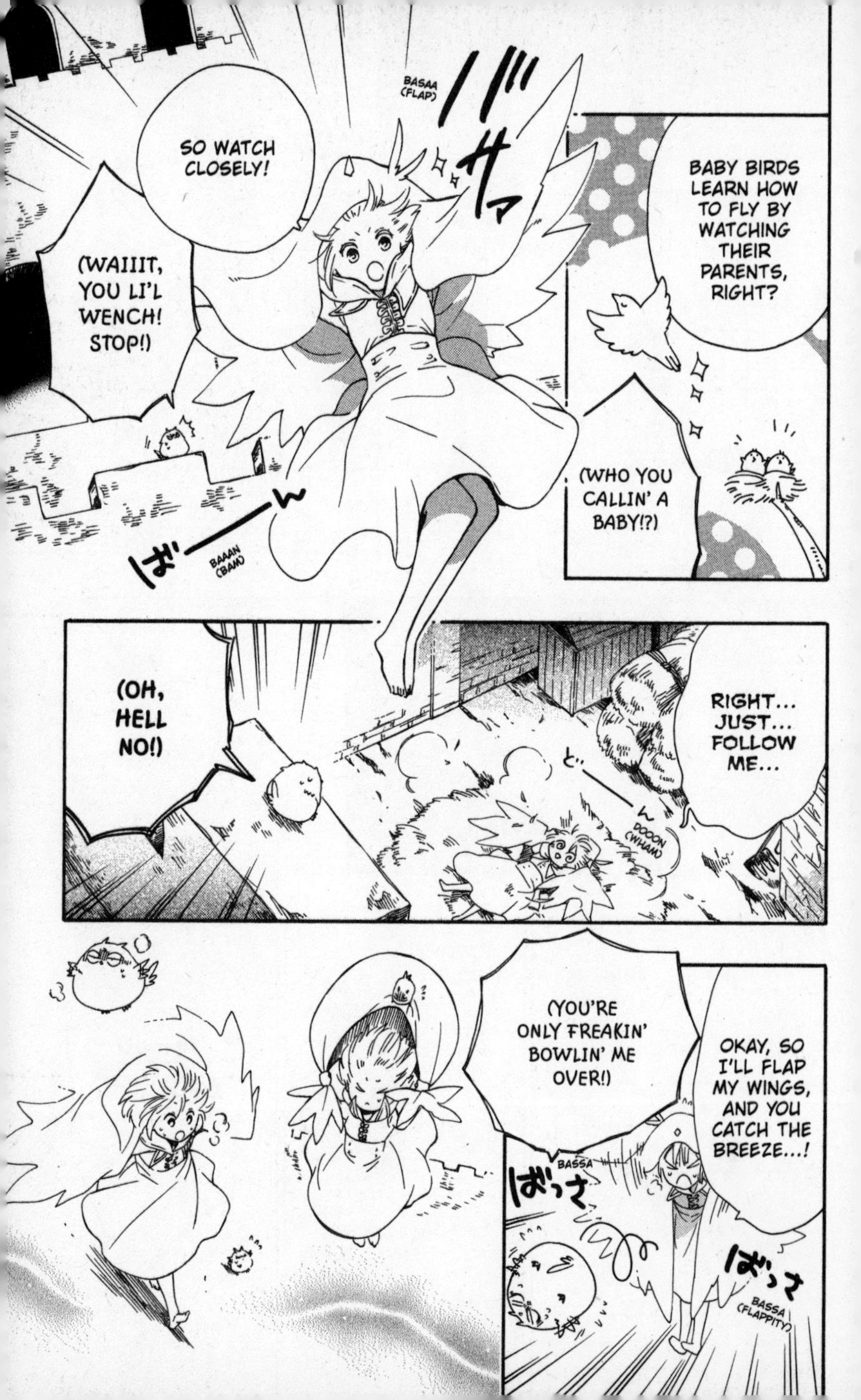
BABY BIRDS LEARN HOW TO FLY BY WATCHING THEIR PARENTS, RIGHT?
(WHO YOU CALLIN' A BABY!?)
バサァ
BASAA (FLAP)
SO WATCH CLOSELY!
(WAIIIT, YOU LI'L WENCH! STOP!)
ばーーん
BAAAN (BAM)
RIGHT... JUST... FOLLOW ME...
どーーん
DOOON (WHAM)
(OH, HELL NO!)
OKAY, SO I'LL FLAP MY WINGS, AND YOU CATCH THE BREEZE...!
ばっさ
BASSA (FLAPPITY)
(YOU'RE ONLY FREAKIN' BOWLIN' ME OVER!)
ばっさ
BASSA

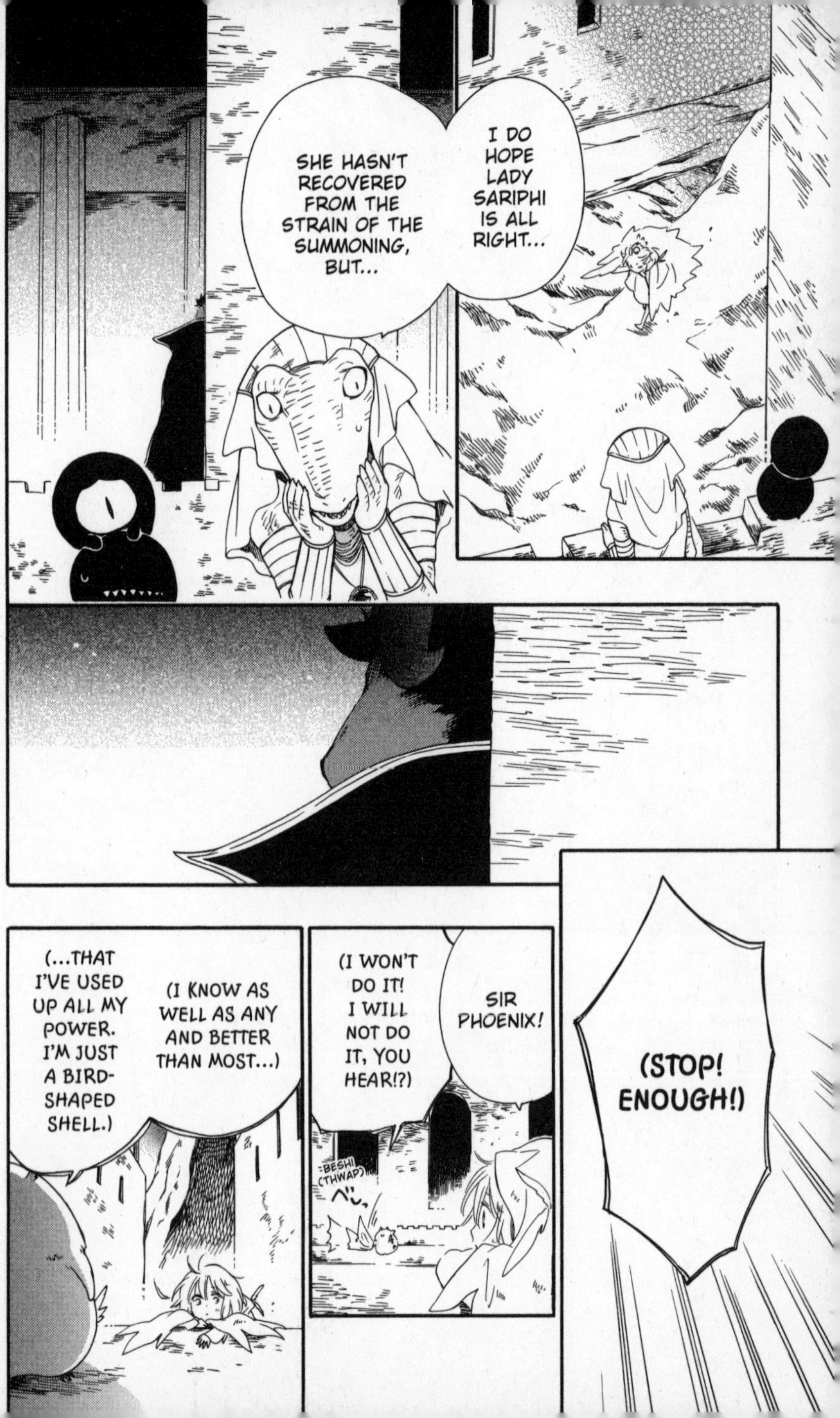
I DO HOPE LADY SARIPHI IS ALL RIGHT...
SHE HASN'T RECOVERED FROM THE STRAIN OF THE SUMMONING, BUT...
(STOP! ENOUGH!)
SIR PHOENIX!
(I WON'T DO IT! I WILL NOT DO IT, YOU HEAR!?)
=BESHI (THWAP)
べし
(I KNOW AS WELL AS ANY AND BETTER THAN MOST...)
(...THAT I'VE USED UP ALL MY POWER. I'M JUST A BIRD-SHAPED SHELL.)

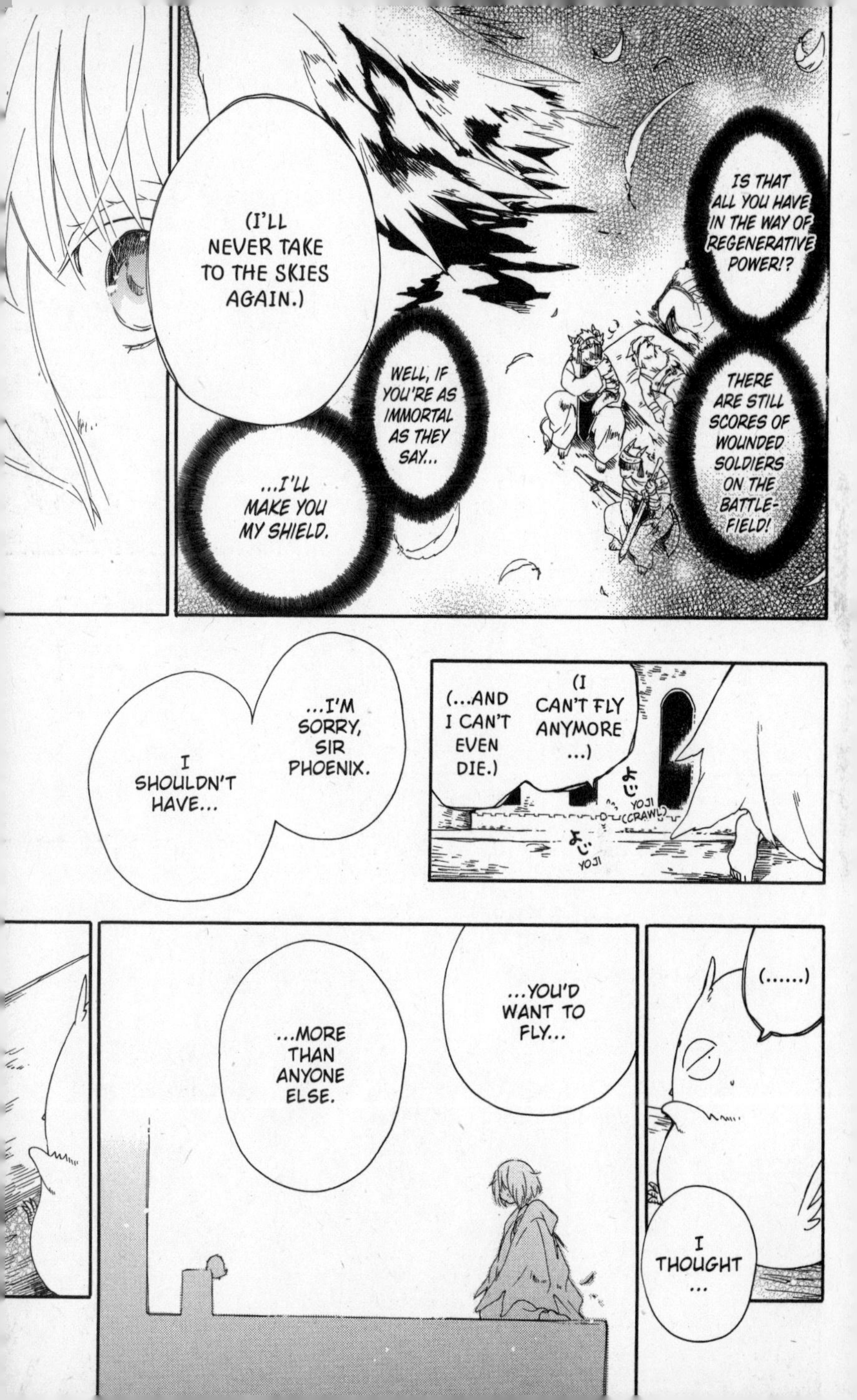
IS THAT ALL YOU HAVE IN THE WAY OF REGENERATIVE POWER!?
THERE ARE STILL SCORES OF WOUNDED SOLDIERS ON THE BATTLE-FIELD!
WELL, IF YOU'RE AS IMMORTAL AS THEY SAY...
...I'LL MAKE YOU MY SHIELD.
(I'LL NEVER TAKE TO THE SKIES AGAIN.)
(I CAN'T FLY ANYMORE ...)
(...AND I CAN'T EVEN DIE.)
よじ YOJI (CRAWL)
よじ YOJI
...I'M SORRY, SIR PHOENIX.
I SHOULDN'T HAVE...
(......)
I THOUGHT ...
...YOU'D WANT TO FLY...
...MORE THAN ANYONE ELSE.

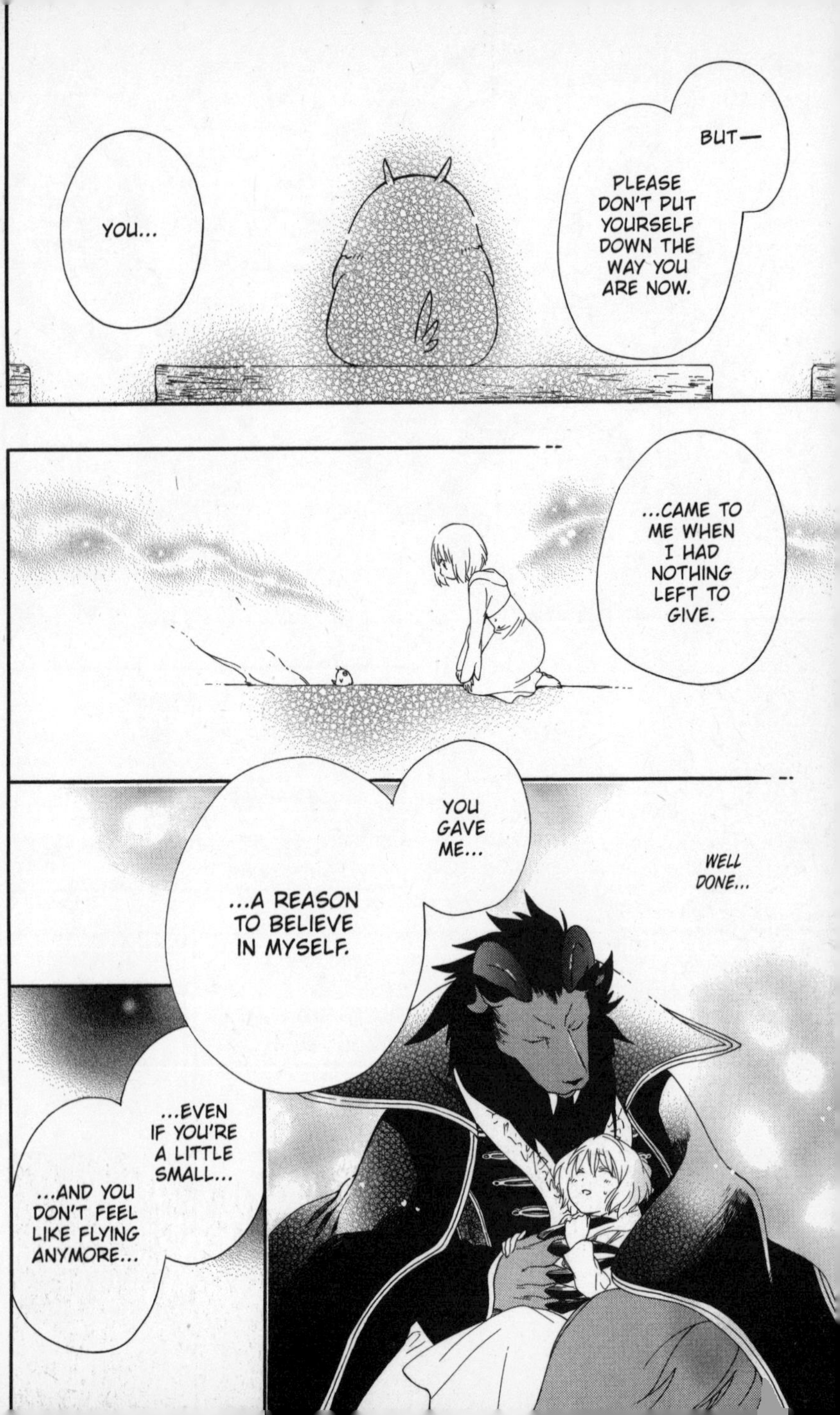
BUT— PLEASE DON'T PUT YOURSELF DOWN THE WAY YOU ARE NOW.
YOU...
...CAME TO ME WHEN I HAD NOTHING LEFT TO GIVE.
YOU GAVE ME...
...A REASON TO BELIEVE IN MYSELF.
WELL DONE...
...EVEN IF YOU'RE A LITTLE SMALL...
...AND YOU DON'T FEEL LIKE FLYING ANYMORE...

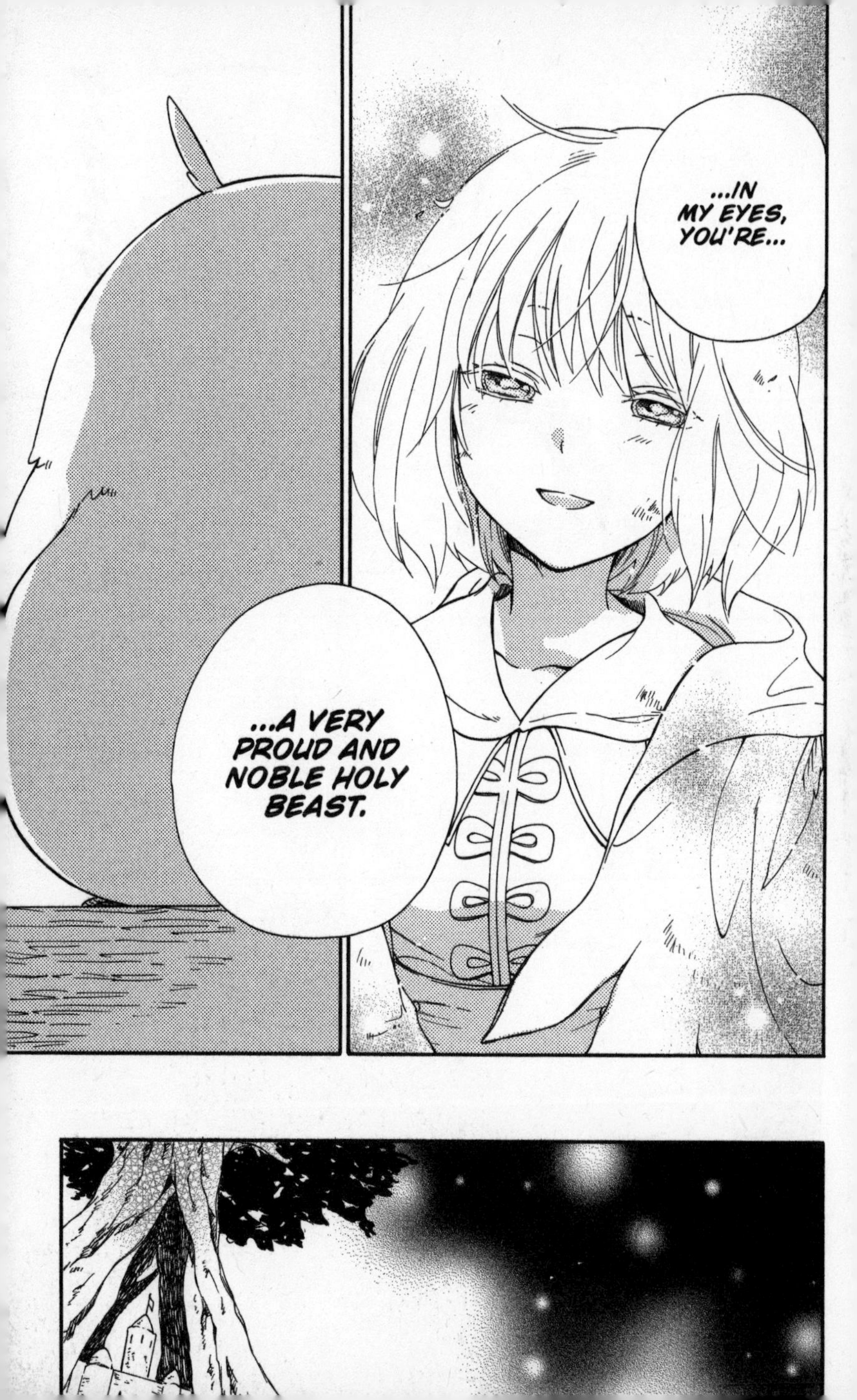
...IN MY EYES, YOU'RE...
...A VERY PROUD AND NOBLE HOLY BEAST.

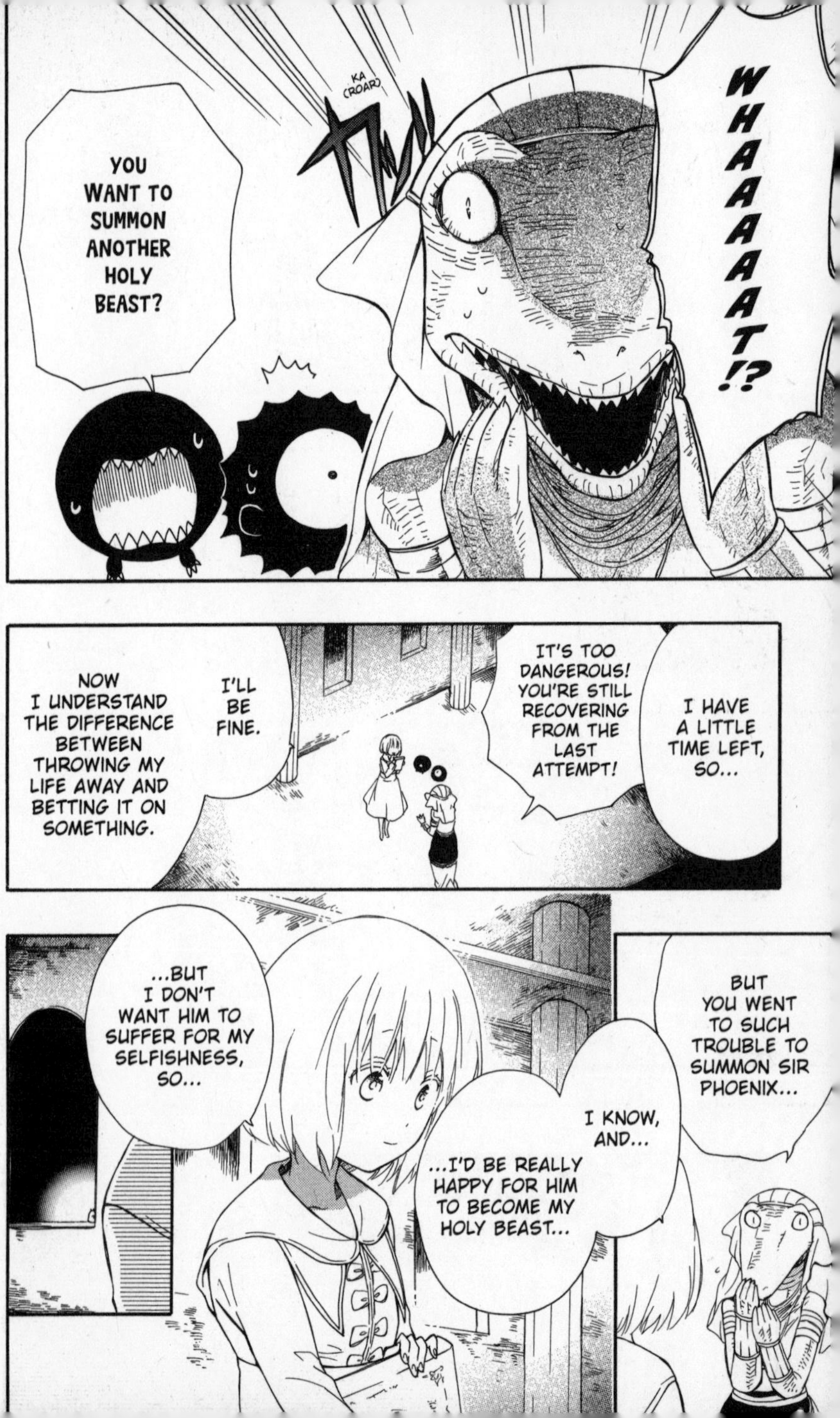
WHAAAAAT!?
KA (ROAR)
YOU WANT TO SUMMON ANOTHER HOLY BEAST?
I HAVE A LITTLE TIME LEFT, SO...
IT'S TOO DANGEROUS! YOU'RE STILL RECOVERING FROM THE LAST ATTEMPT!
I'LL BE FINE.
NOW I UNDERSTAND THE DIFFERENCE BETWEEN THROWING MY LIFE AWAY AND BETTING IT ON SOMETHING.
BUT YOU WENT TO SUCH TROUBLE TO SUMMON SIR PHOENIX...
I KNOW, AND...
...I'D BE REALLY HAPPY FOR HIM TO BECOME MY HOLY BEAST...
...BUT I DON'T WANT HIM TO SUFFER FOR MY SELFISHNESS, SO...

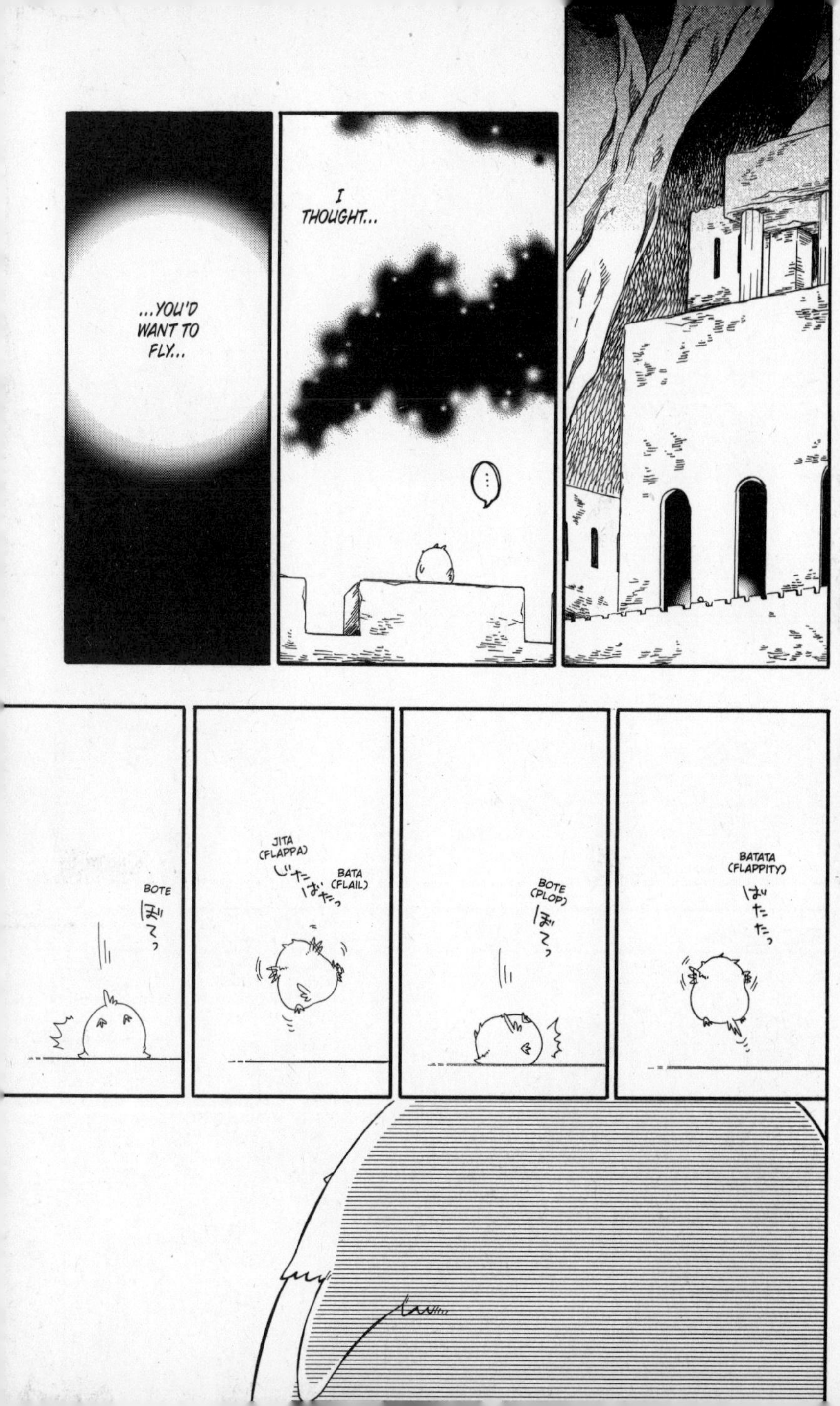
I THOUGHT...
...
...YOU'D WANT TO FLY...
BATATA (FLAPPITY)
ばたたっ
BOTE (PLOP)
ぼてっ
JITA (FLAPPA)
じた
BATA (FLAIL)
ばたっ
BOTE
ぼてっ

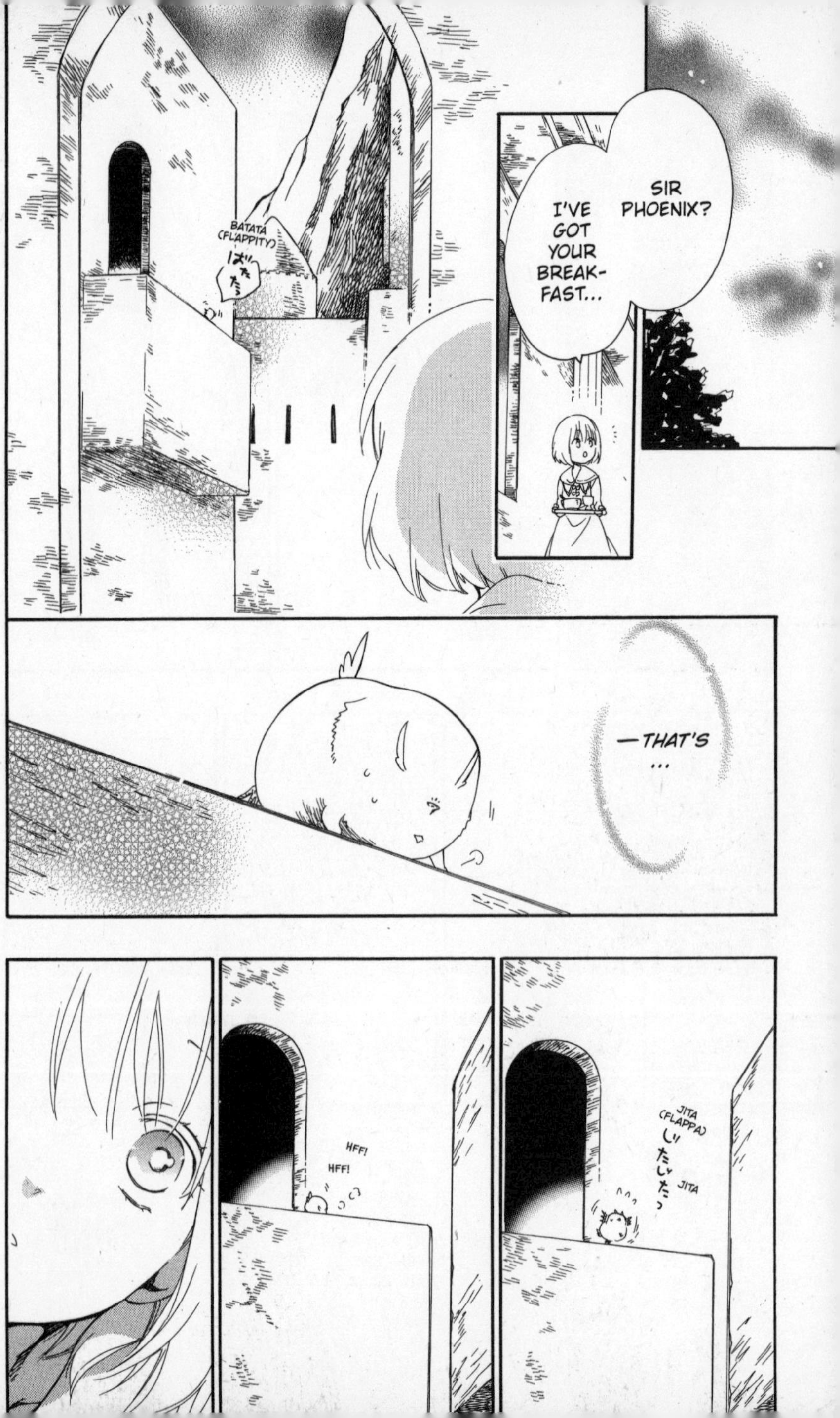
SIR PHOENIX?
I'VE GOT YOUR BREAK-FAST...
BATATA (FLAPPITY)
ばたた
—THAT'S ...
JITA (FLAPPA)
じたじた
JITA
HFF!
HFF!

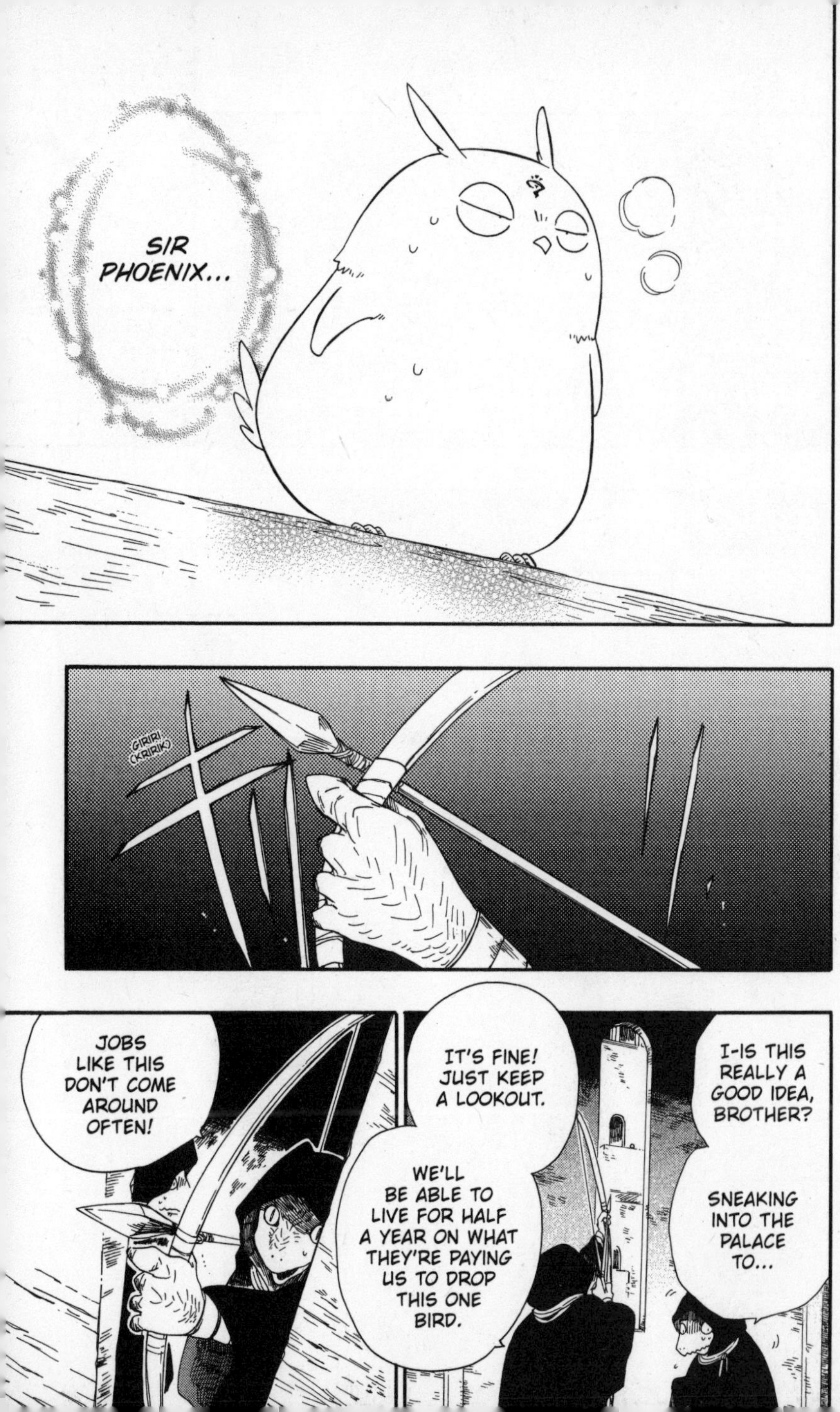
SIR PHOENIX...
GIRIRI (KRIRIK)
I-IS THIS REALLY A GOOD IDEA, BROTHER?
SNEAKING INTO THE PALACE TO...
IT'S FINE! JUST KEEP A LOOKOUT.
WE'LL BE ABLE TO LIVE FOR HALF A YEAR ON WHAT THEY'RE PAYING US TO DROP THIS ONE BIRD.
JOBS LIKE THIS DON'T COME AROUND OFTEN!

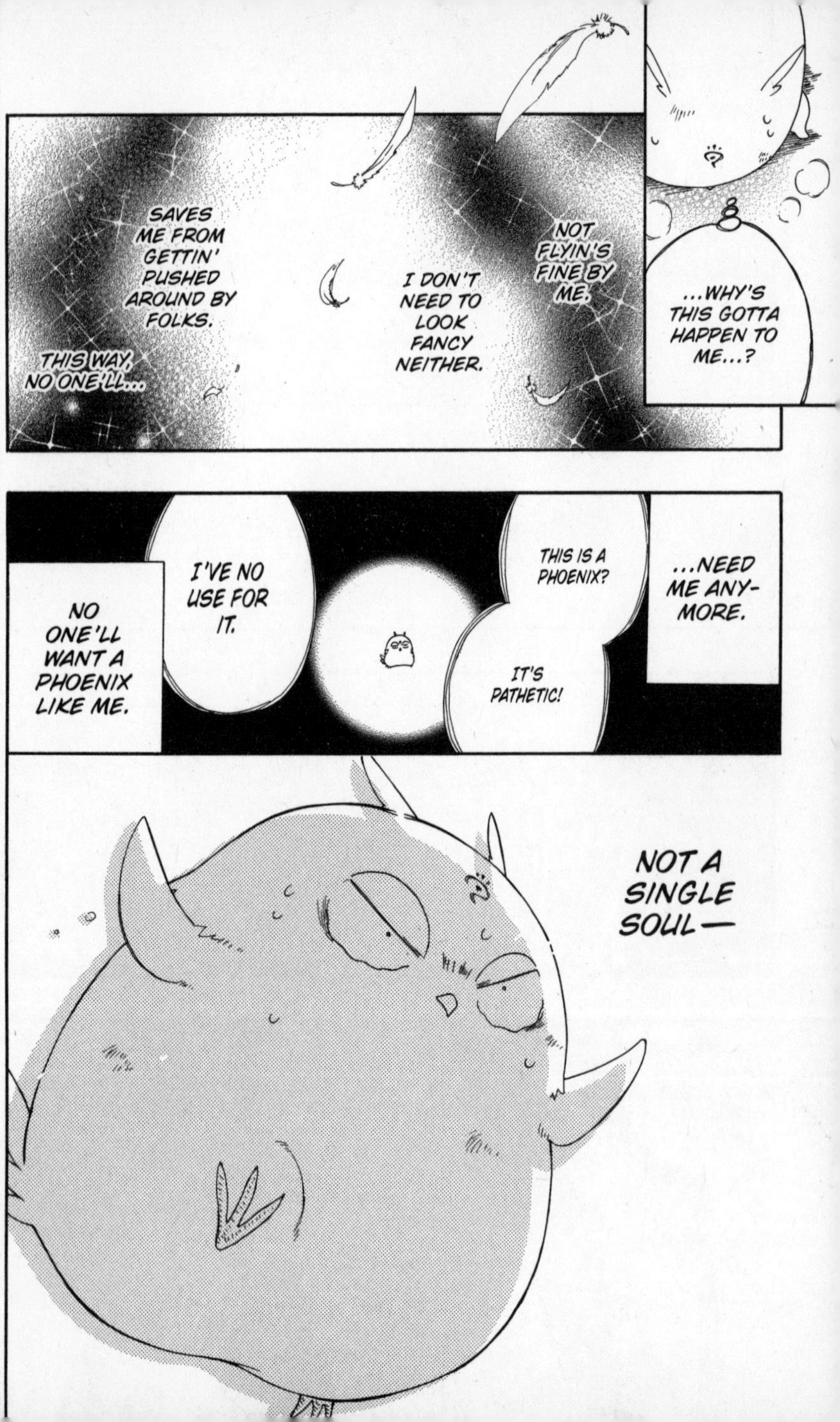
...WHY'S THIS GOTTA HAPPEN TO ME...?
NOT FLYIN'S FINE BY ME.
I DON'T NEED TO LOOK FANCY NEITHER.
SAVES ME FROM GETTIN' PUSHED AROUND BY FOLKS.
THIS WAY, NO ONE'LL...
...NEED ME ANY-MORE.
THIS IS A PHOENIX?
IT'S PATHETIC!
I'VE NO USE FOR IT.
NO ONE'LL WANT A PHOENIX LIKE ME.
NOT A SINGLE SOUL—

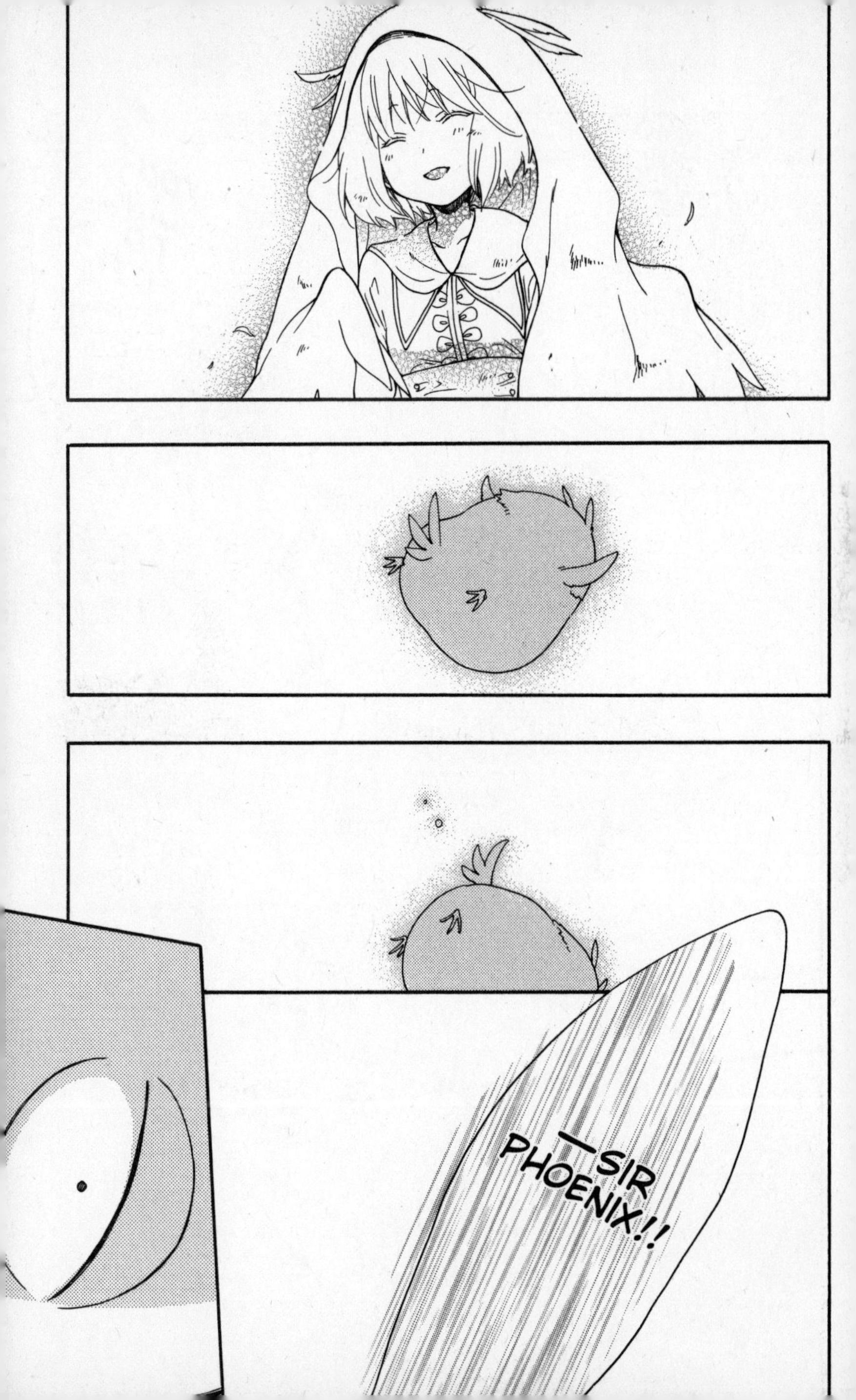
—SIR PHOENIX!!

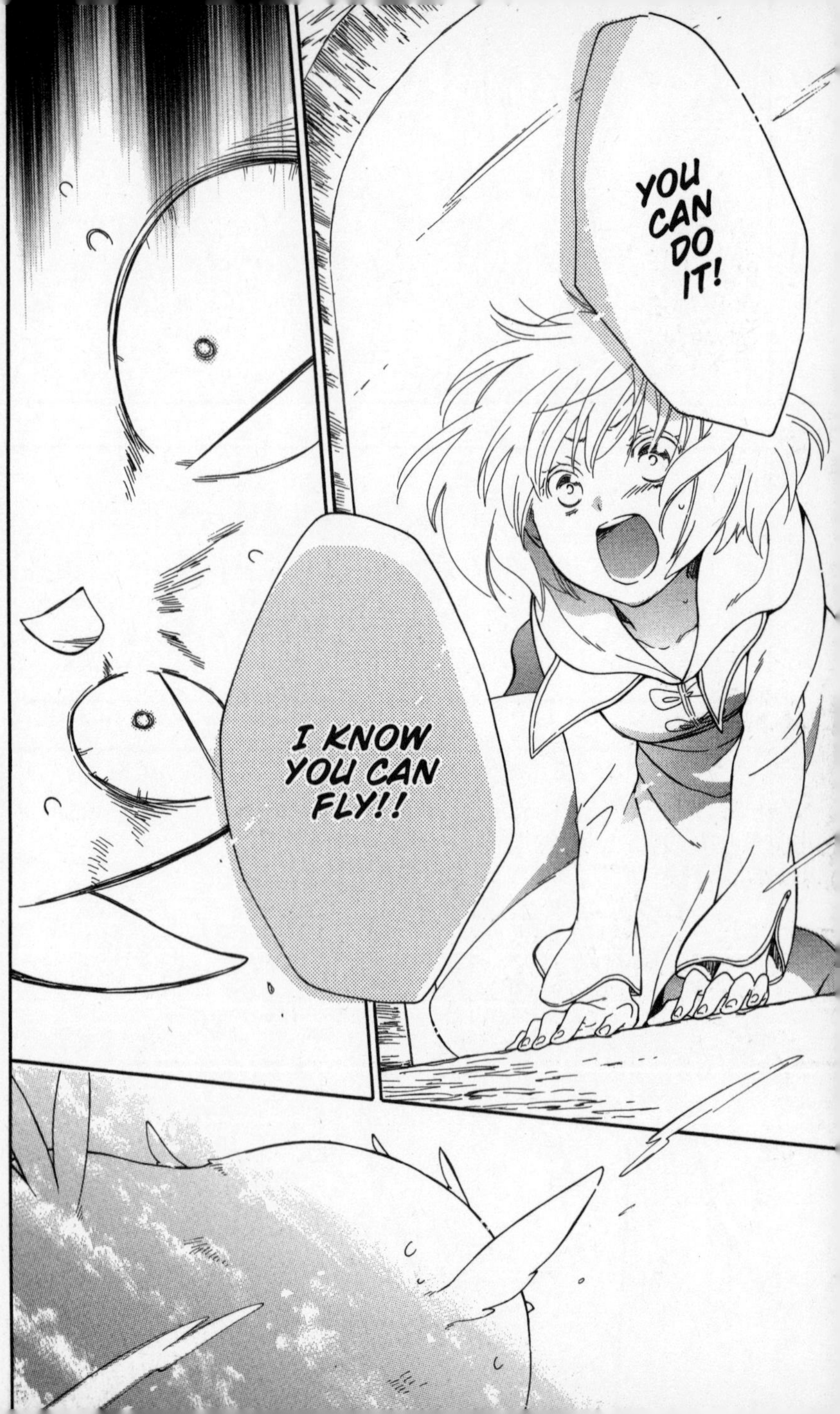
YOU CAN DO IT!
I KNOW YOU CAN FLY!!

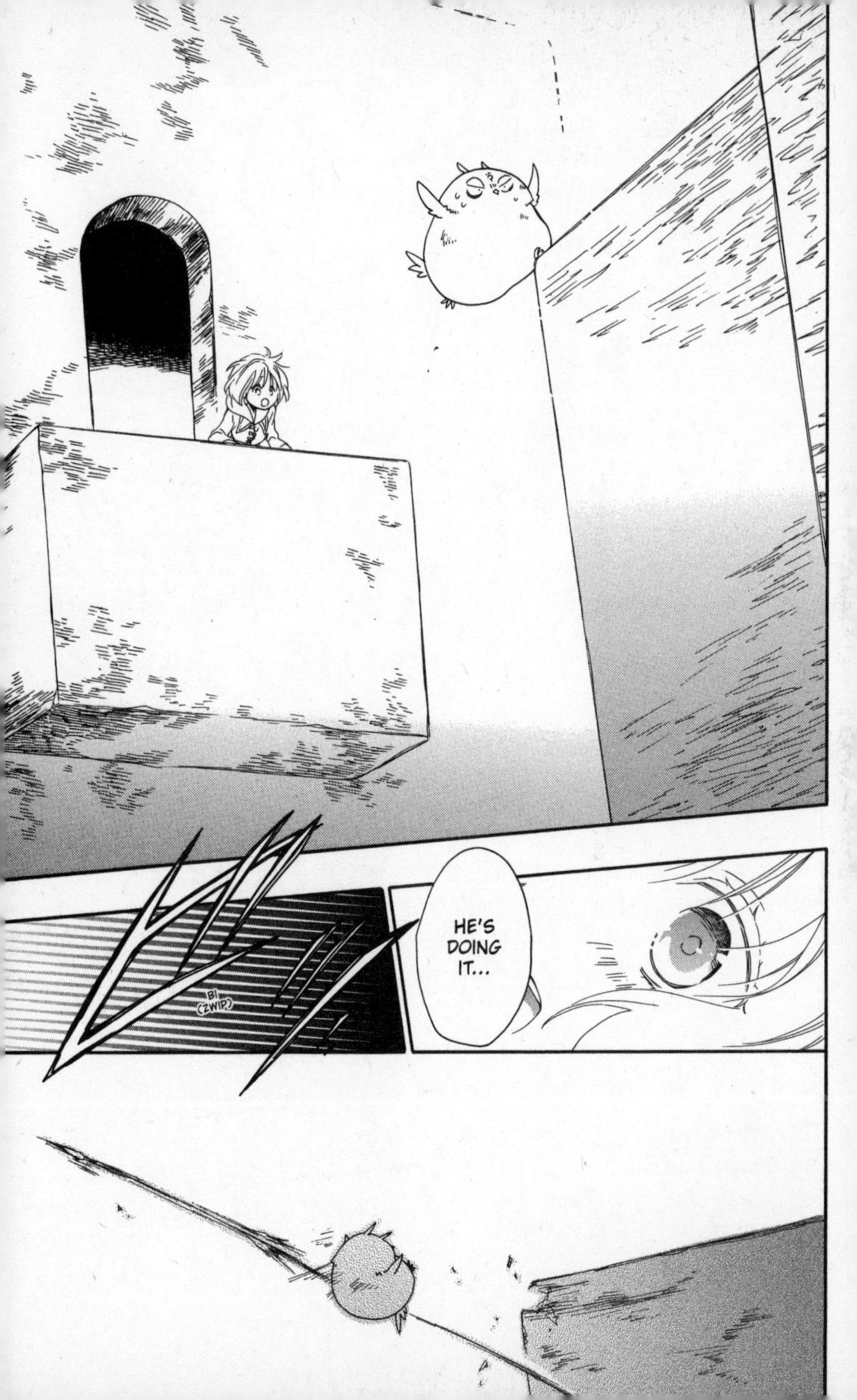
HE'S DOING IT...
BI (ZWIP)

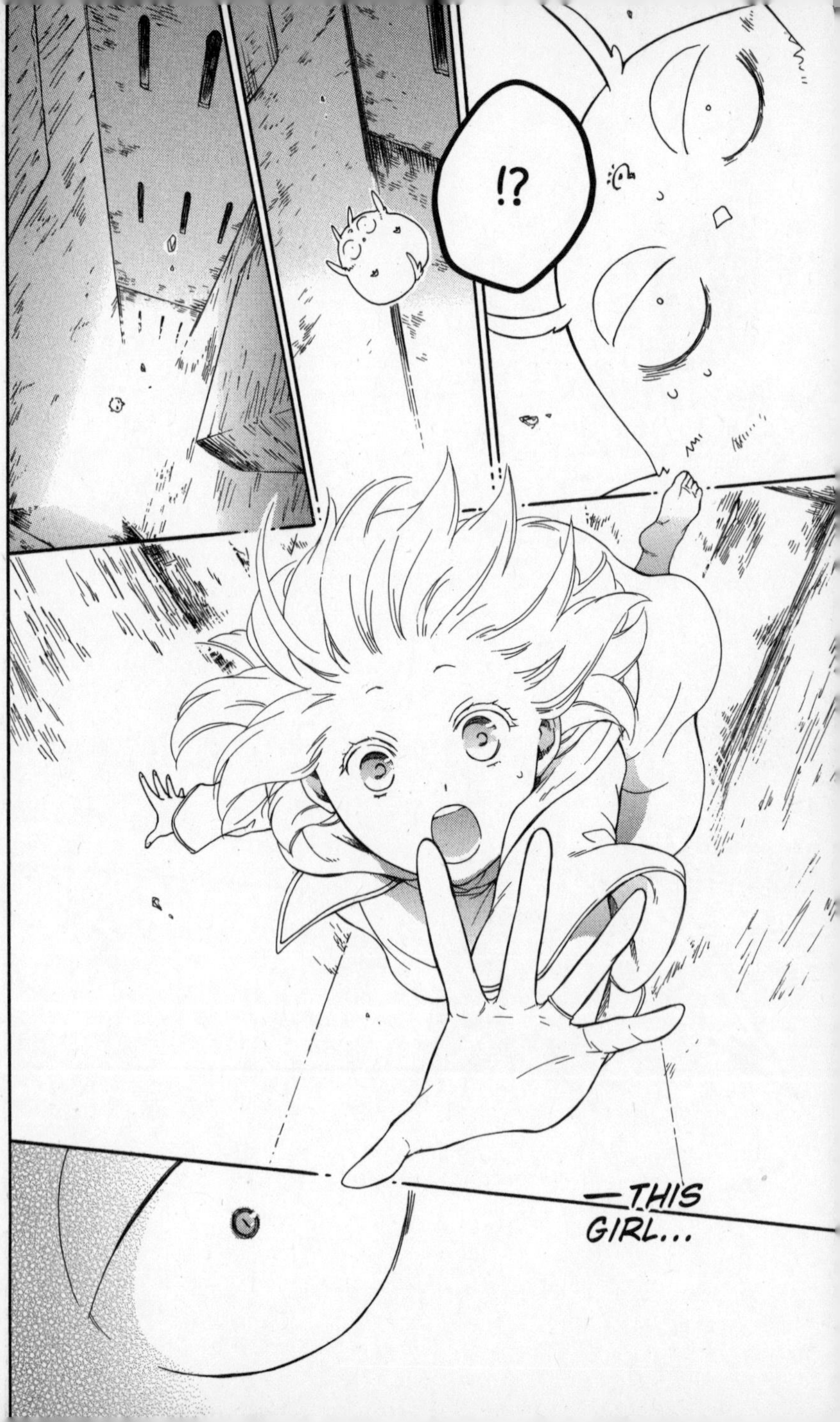
!?
—THIS GIRL...

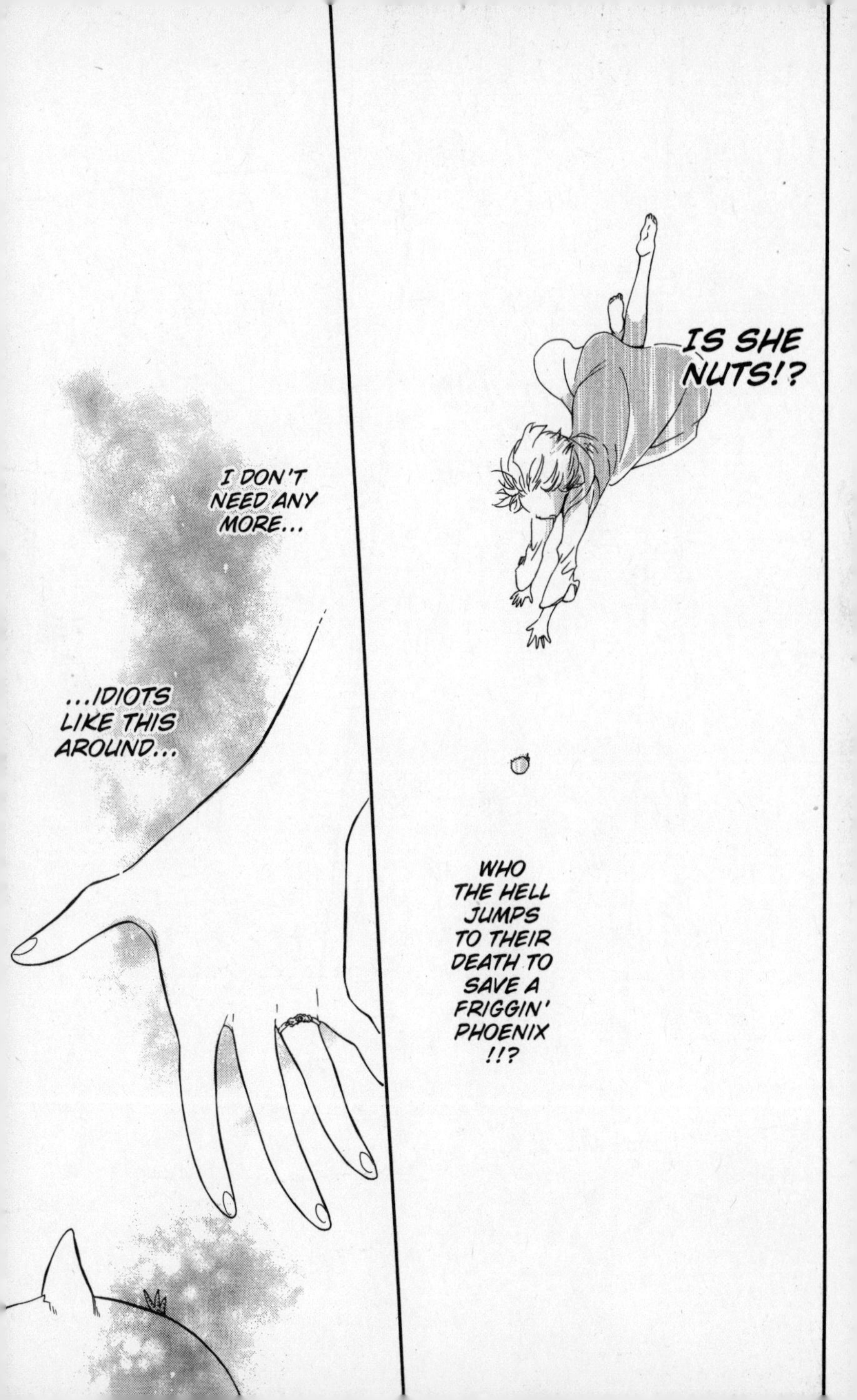
IS SHE NUTS!?
WHO THE HELL JUMPS TO THEIR DEATH TO SAVE A FRIGGIN' PHOENIX!!?
I DON'T NEED ANY MORE...
...IDIOTS LIKE THIS AROUND...

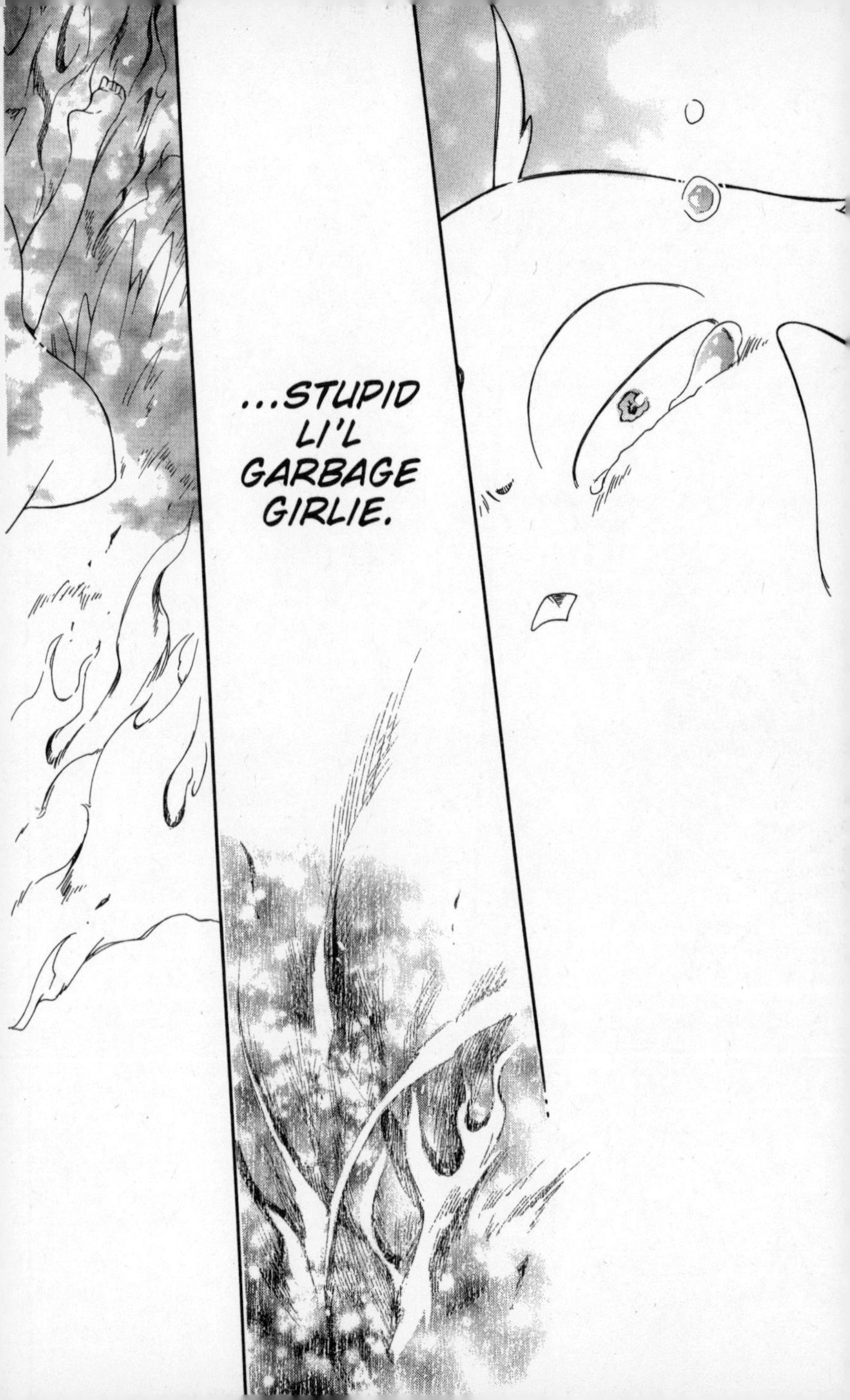
...STUPID LI'L GARBAGE GIRLIE.

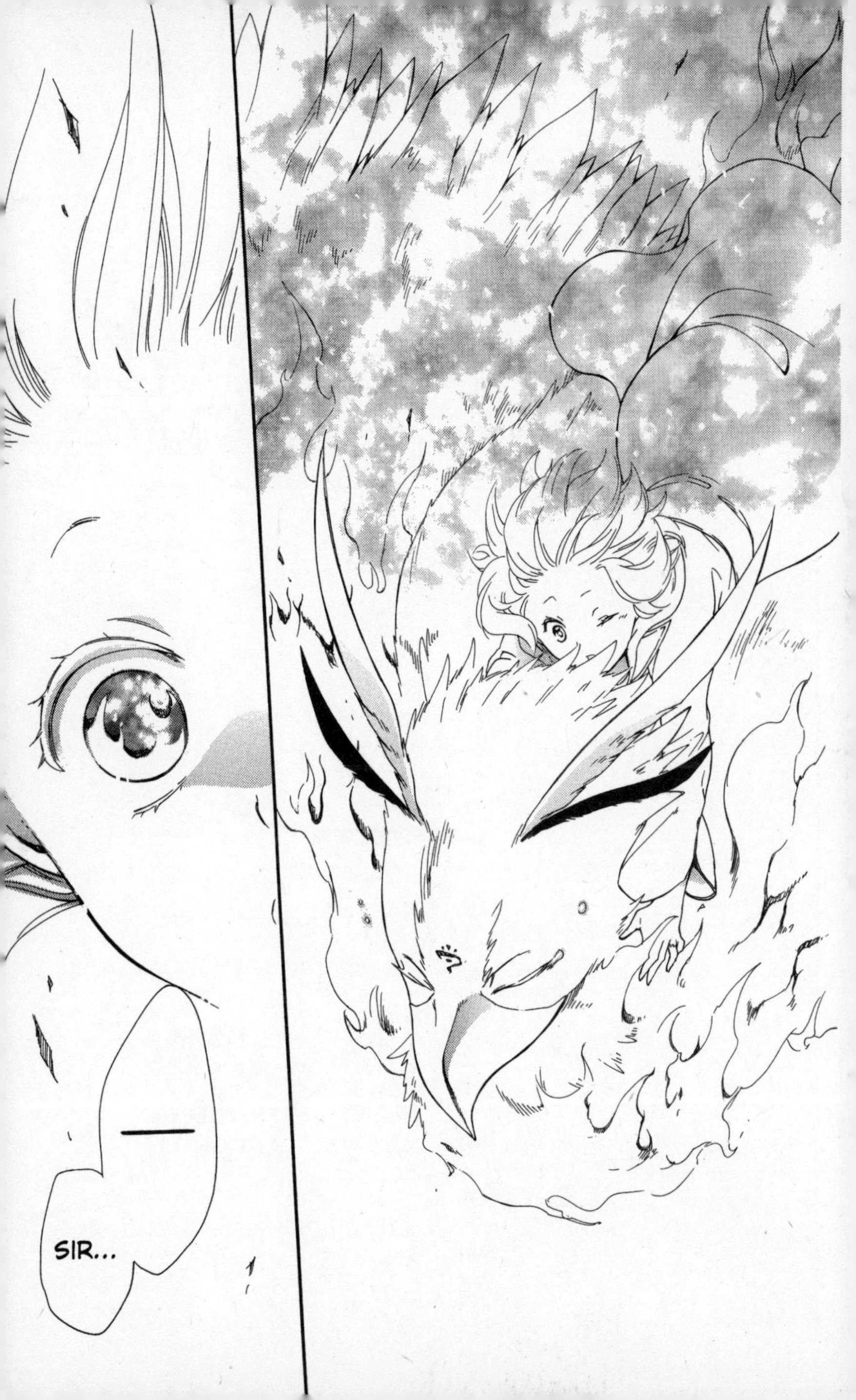
—
SIR...

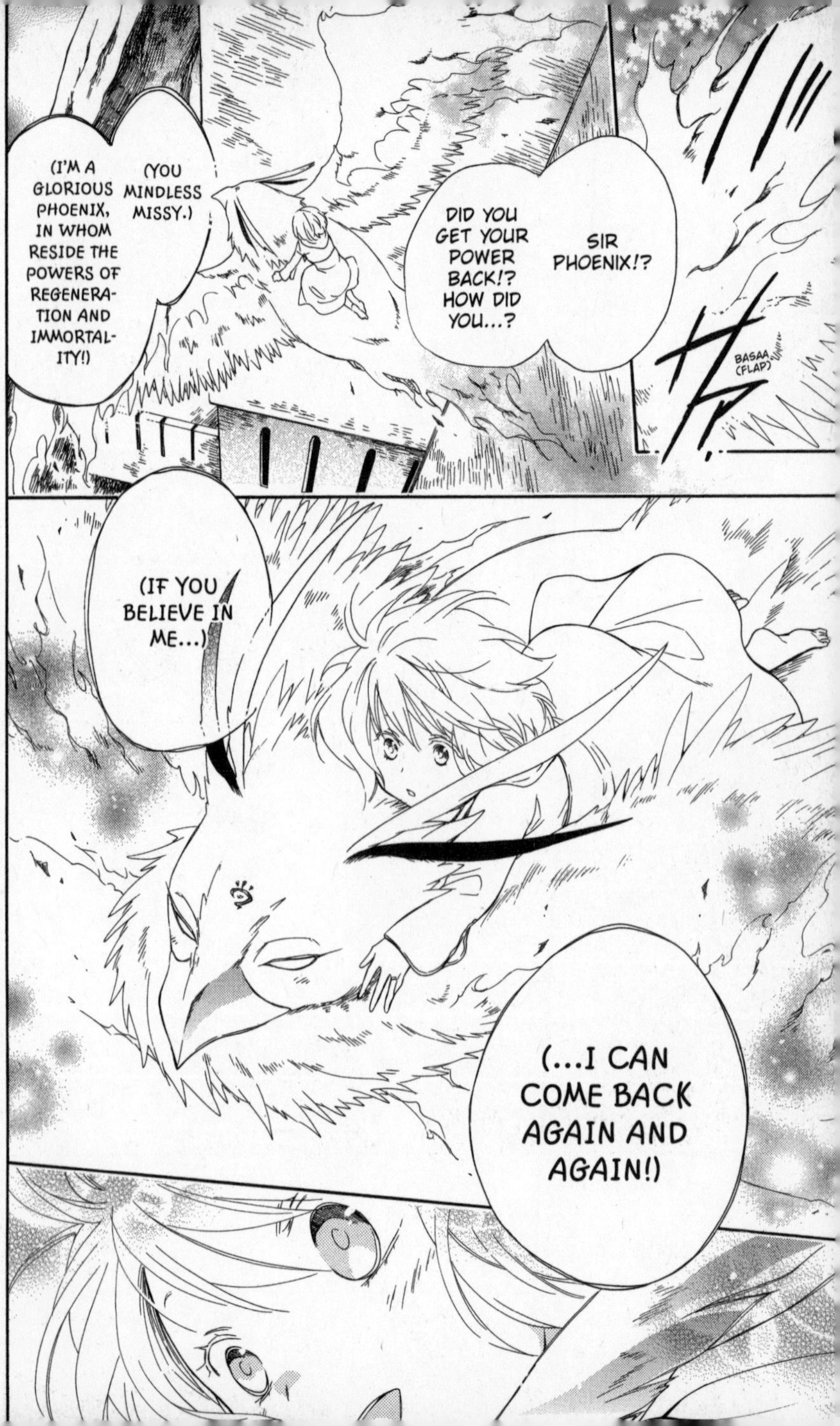
SIR PHOENIX!?
DID YOU GET YOUR POWER BACK!? HOW DID YOU...?
BASAA (FLAP)
(YOU MINDLESS MISSY.)
(I'M A GLORIOUS PHOENIX, IN WHOM RESIDE THE POWERS OF REGENERATION AND IMMORTALITY!)
(IF YOU BELIEVE IN ME...)
(...I CAN COME BACK AGAIN AND AGAIN!)

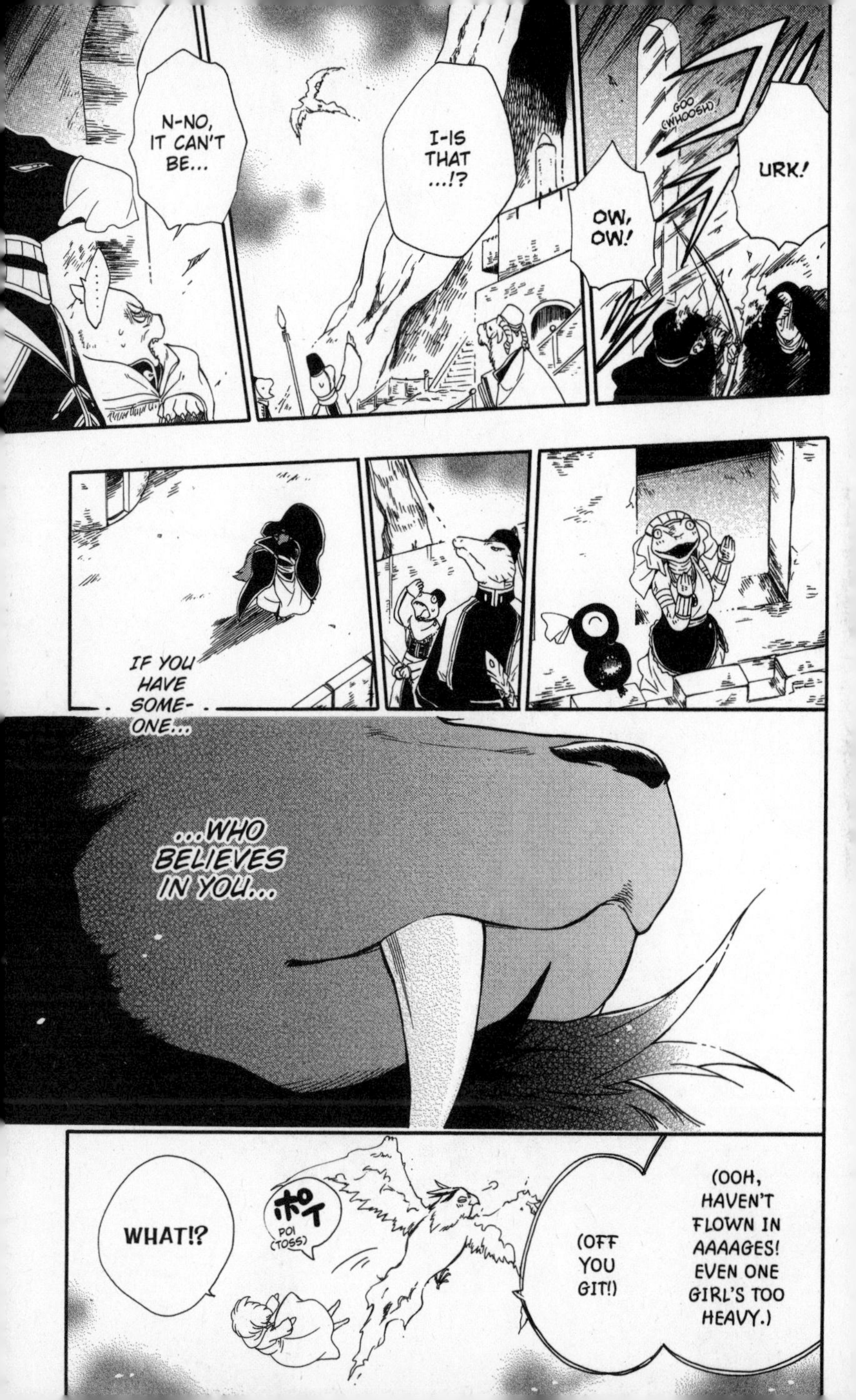
GOO (WHOOSH)
URK!
OW, OW!
I-IS THAT ...!?
N-NO, IT CAN'T BE...
...
IF YOU HAVE SOME-ONE...
...WHO BELIEVES IN YOU...
(OOH, HAVEN'T FLOWN IN AAAAGES! EVEN ONE GIRL'S TOO HEAVY.)
(OFF YOU GIT!)
ポイ
POI (TOSS)
WHAT!?

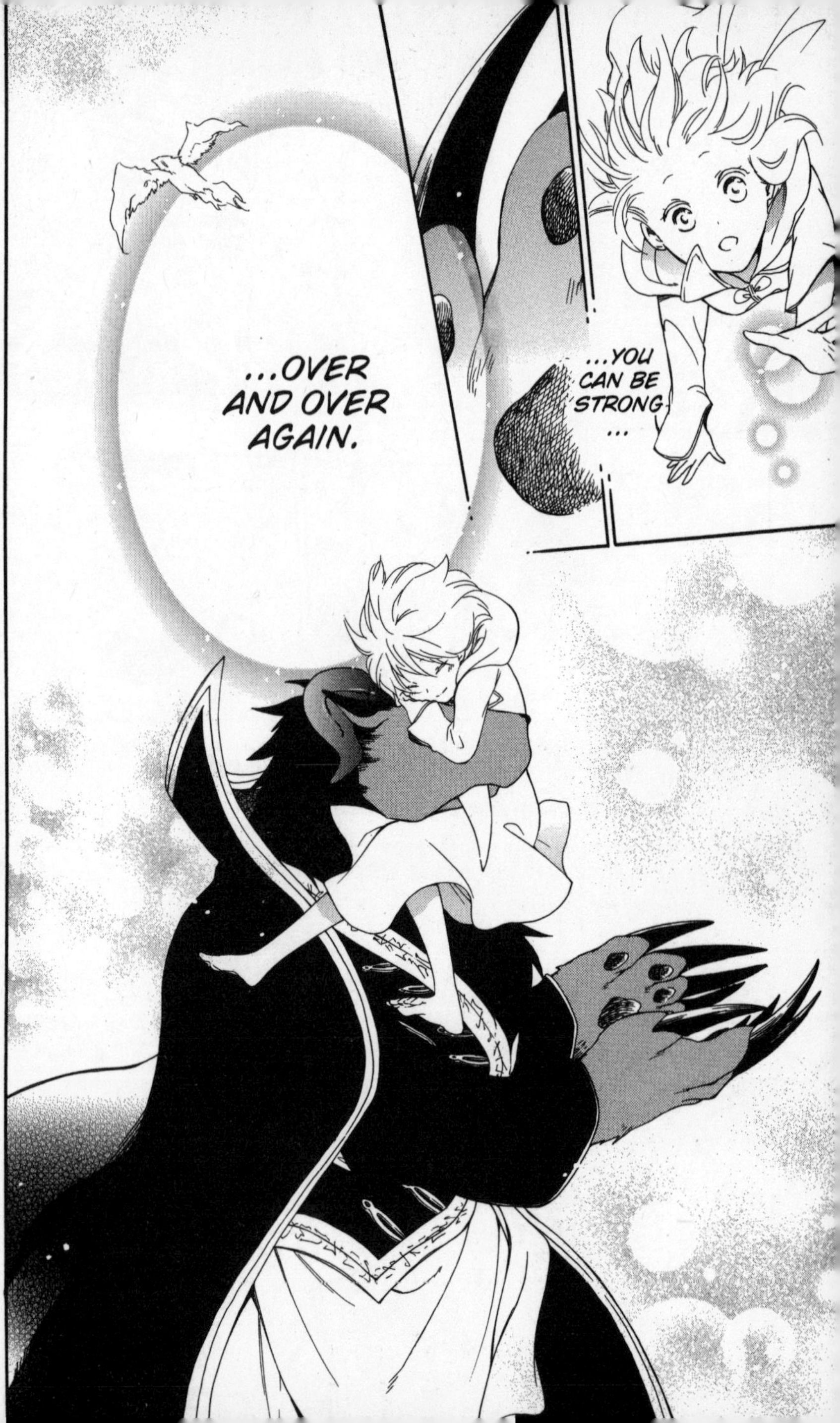
...YOU CAN BE STRONG...
...OVER AND OVER AGAIN.

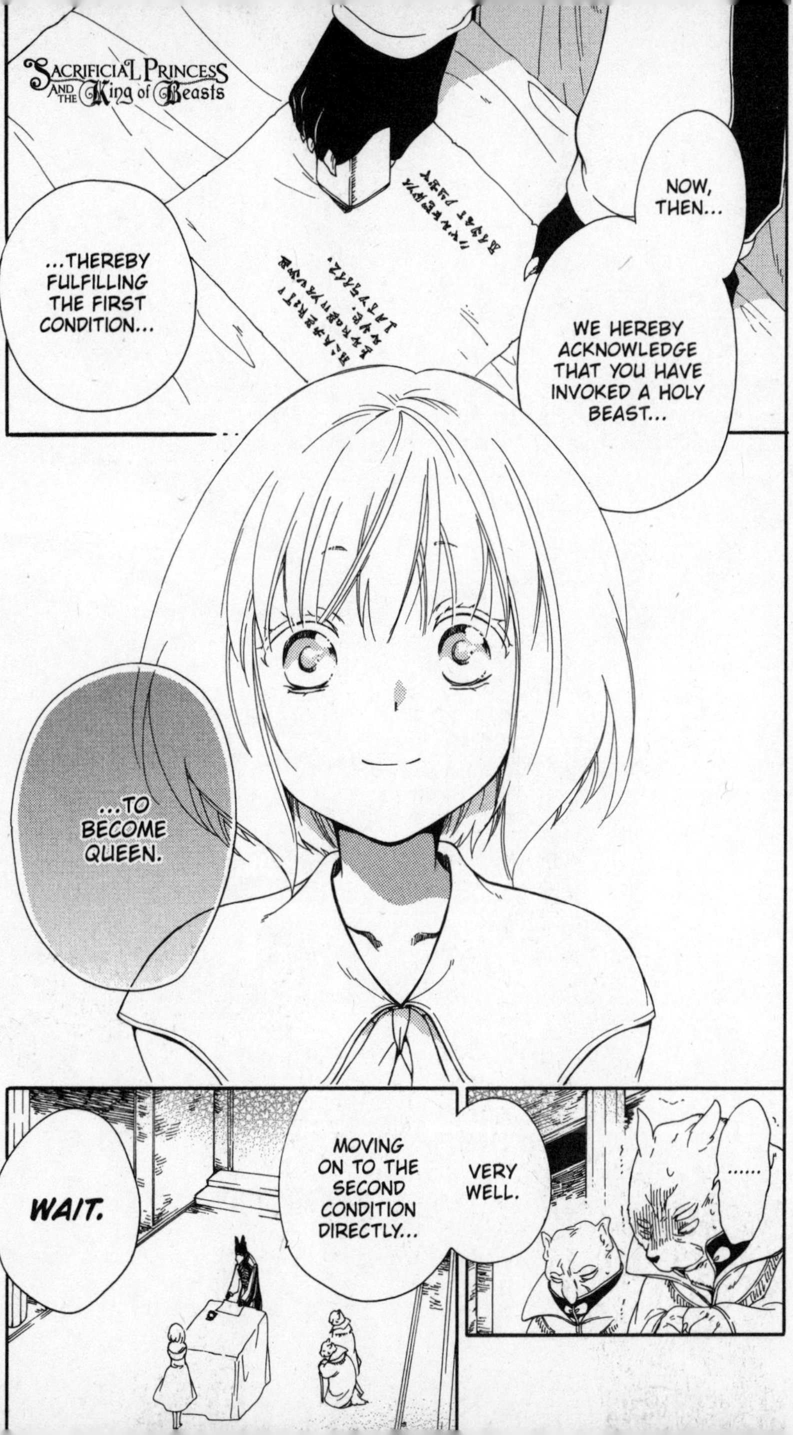

Sacrificial Princess and the King of Beasts
NOW, THEN...
WE HEREBY ACKNOWLEDGE THAT YOU HAVE INVOKED A HOLY BEAST...
...THEREBY FULFILLING THE FIRST CONDITION...
...TO BECOME QUEEN.
......
VERY WELL.
MOVING ON TO THE SECOND CONDITION DIRECTLY...
WAIT.

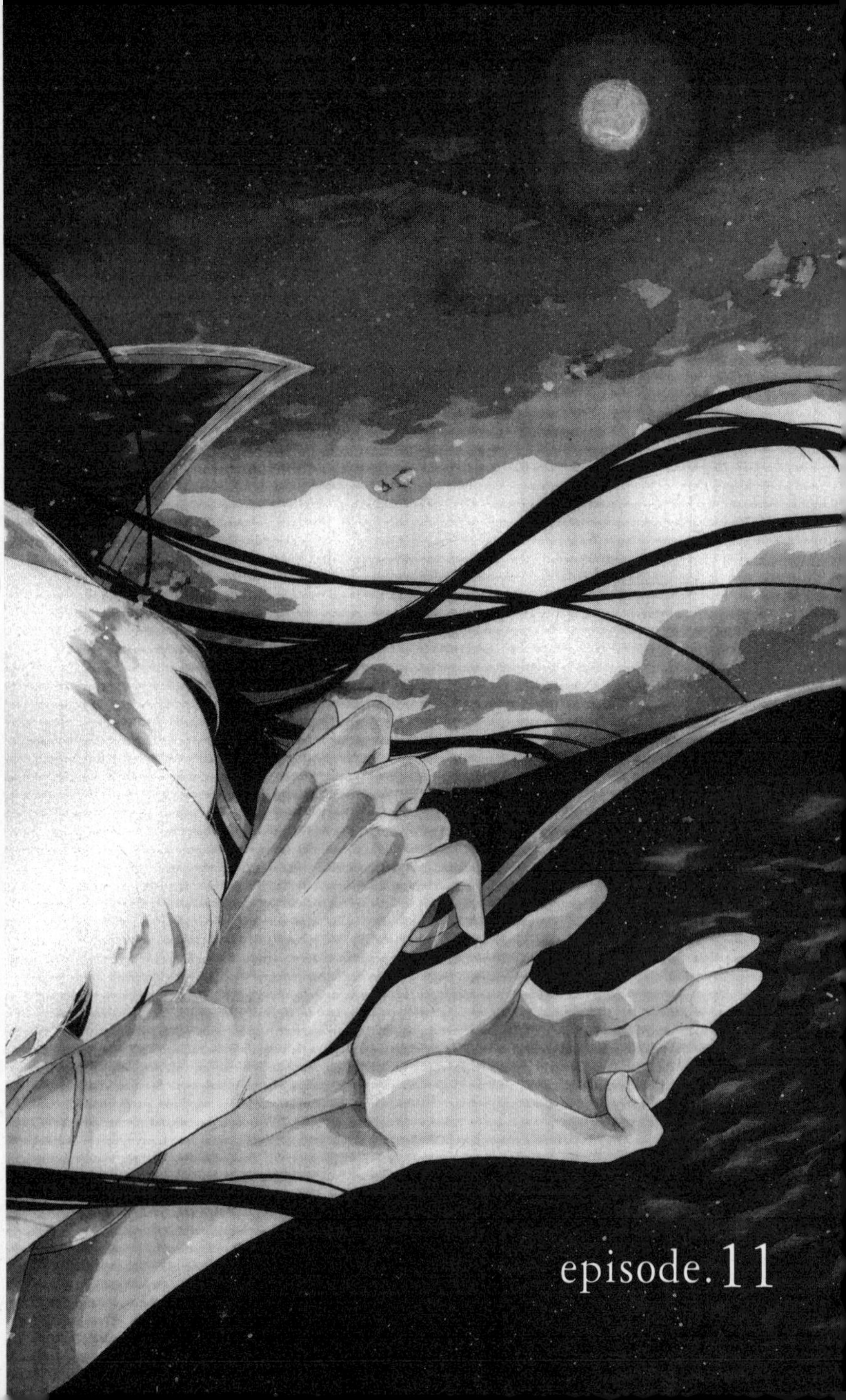
episode.11

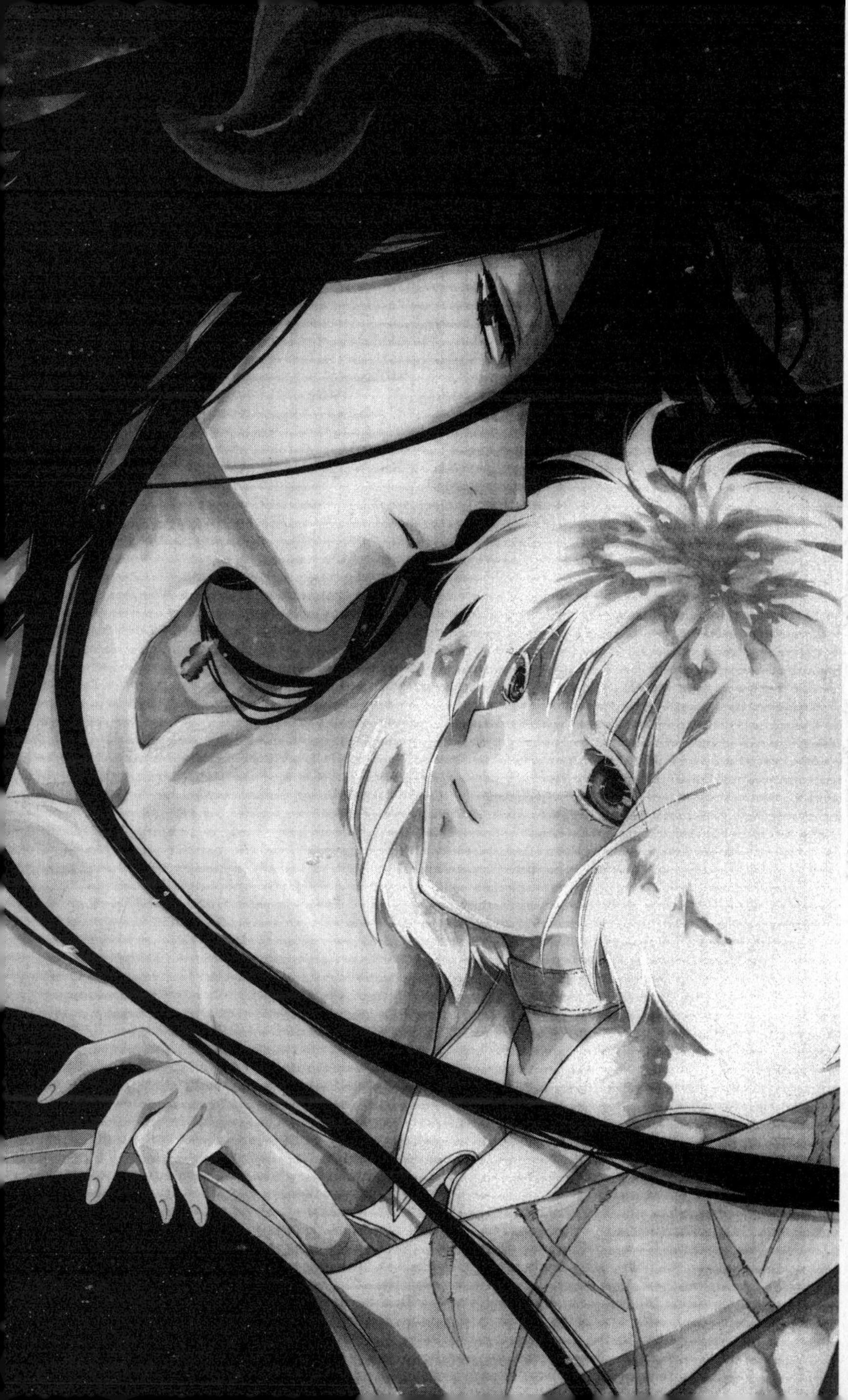

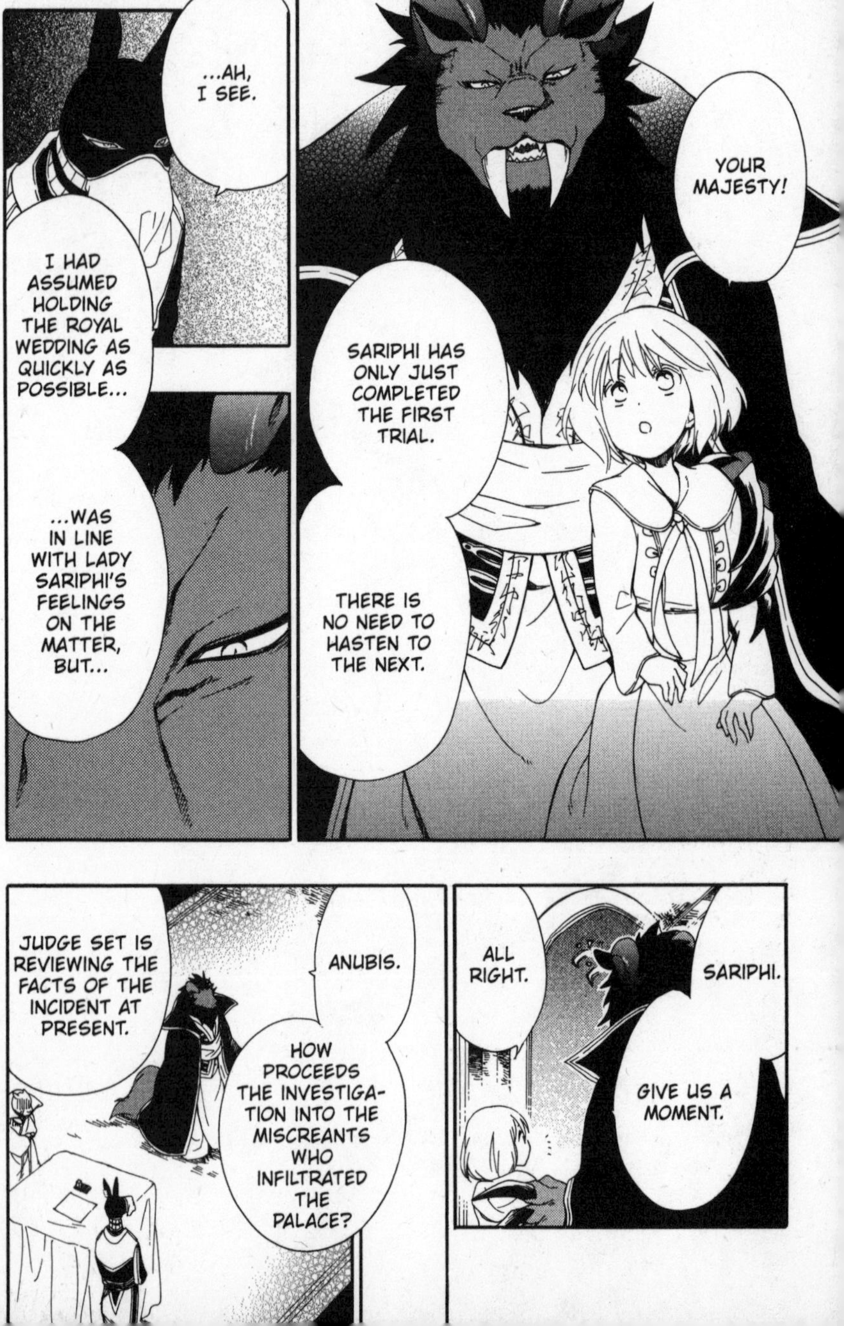
YOUR MAJESTY!
SARIPHI HAS ONLY JUST COMPLETED THE FIRST TRIAL.
THERE IS NO NEED TO HASTEN TO THE NEXT.
...AH, I SEE.
I HAD ASSUMED HOLDING THE ROYAL WEDDING AS QUICKLY AS POSSIBLE...
...WAS IN LINE WITH LADY SARIPHI'S FEELINGS ON THE MATTER, BUT...
SARIPHI.
GIVE US A MOMENT.
ALL RIGHT.
ANUBIS.
HOW PROCEEDS THE INVESTIGA-TION INTO THE MISCREANTS WHO INFILTRATED THE PALACE?
JUDGE SET IS REVIEWING THE FACTS OF THE INCIDENT AT PRESENT.

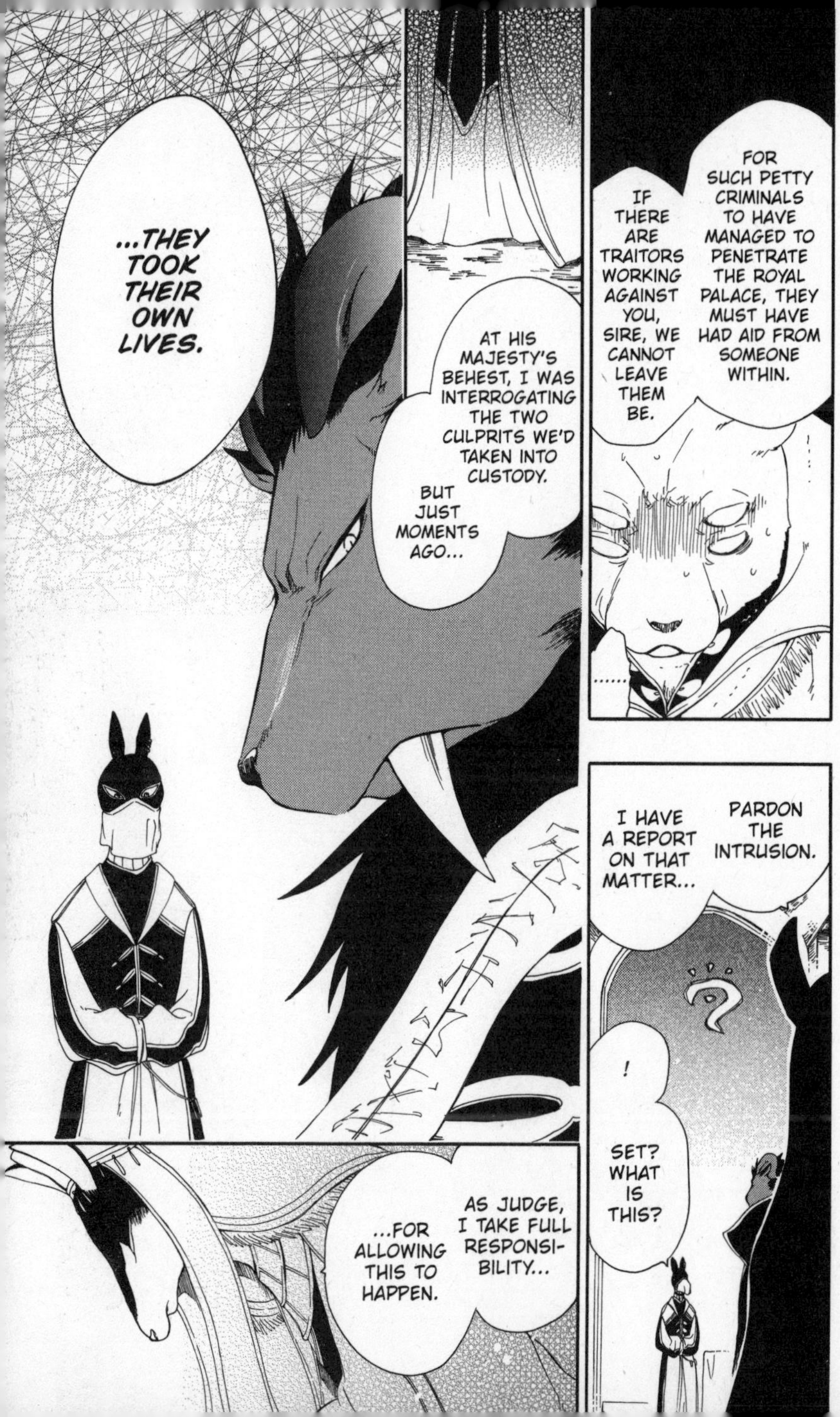
FOR SUCH PETTY CRIMINALS TO HAVE MANAGED TO PENETRATE THE ROYAL PALACE, THEY MUST HAVE HAD AID FROM SOMEONE WITHIN.
IF THERE ARE TRAITORS WORKING AGAINST YOU, SIRE, WE CANNOT LEAVE THEM BE.
......
AT HIS MAJESTY'S BEHEST, I WAS INTERROGATING THE TWO CULPRITS WE'D TAKEN INTO CUSTODY.
BUT JUST MOMENTS AGO...
...THEY TOOK THEIR OWN LIVES.
PARDON THE INTRUSION.
I HAVE A REPORT ON THAT MATTER...
?
!
SET? WHAT IS THIS?
AS JUDGE, I TAKE FULL RESPONSI-BILITY...
...FOR ALLOWING THIS TO HAPPEN.

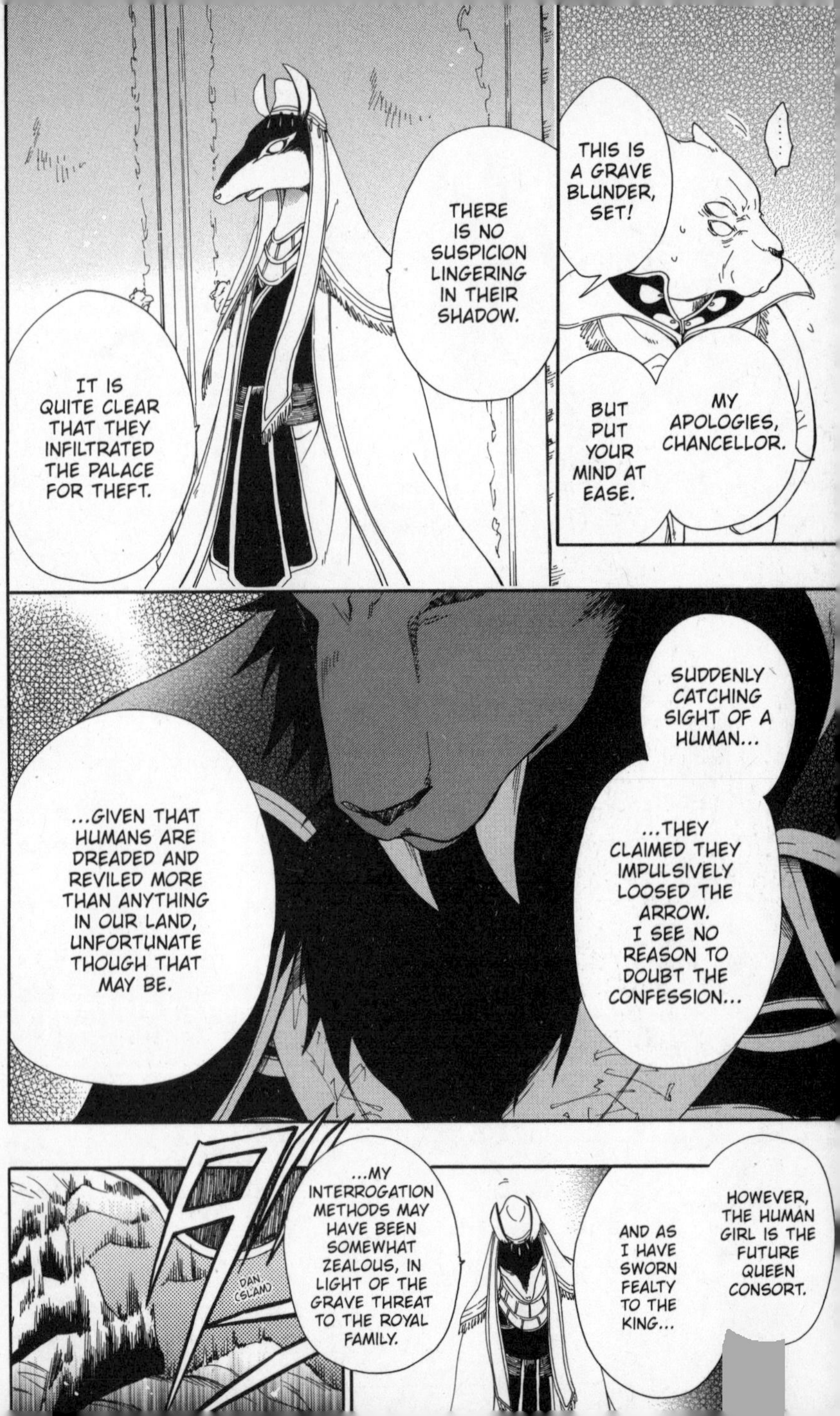
...
THIS IS A GRAVE BLUNDER, SET!
MY APOLOGIES, CHANCELLOR.
BUT PUT YOUR MIND AT EASE.
THERE IS NO SUSPICION LINGERING IN THEIR SHADOW.
IT IS QUITE CLEAR THAT THEY INFILTRATED THE PALACE FOR THEFT.
SUDDENLY CATCHING SIGHT OF A HUMAN...
...THEY CLAIMED THEY IMPULSIVELY LOOSED THE ARROW. I SEE NO REASON TO DOUBT THE CONFESSION...
...GIVEN THAT HUMANS ARE DREADED AND REVILED MORE THAN ANYTHING IN OUR LAND, UNFORTUNATE THOUGH THAT MAY BE.
HOWEVER, THE HUMAN GIRL IS THE FUTURE QUEEN CONSORT.
AND AS I HAVE SWORN FEALTY TO THE KING...
...MY INTERROGATION METHODS MAY HAVE BEEN SOMEWHAT ZEALOUS, IN LIGHT OF THE GRAVE THREAT TO THE ROYAL FAMILY.
DAN (SLAM)

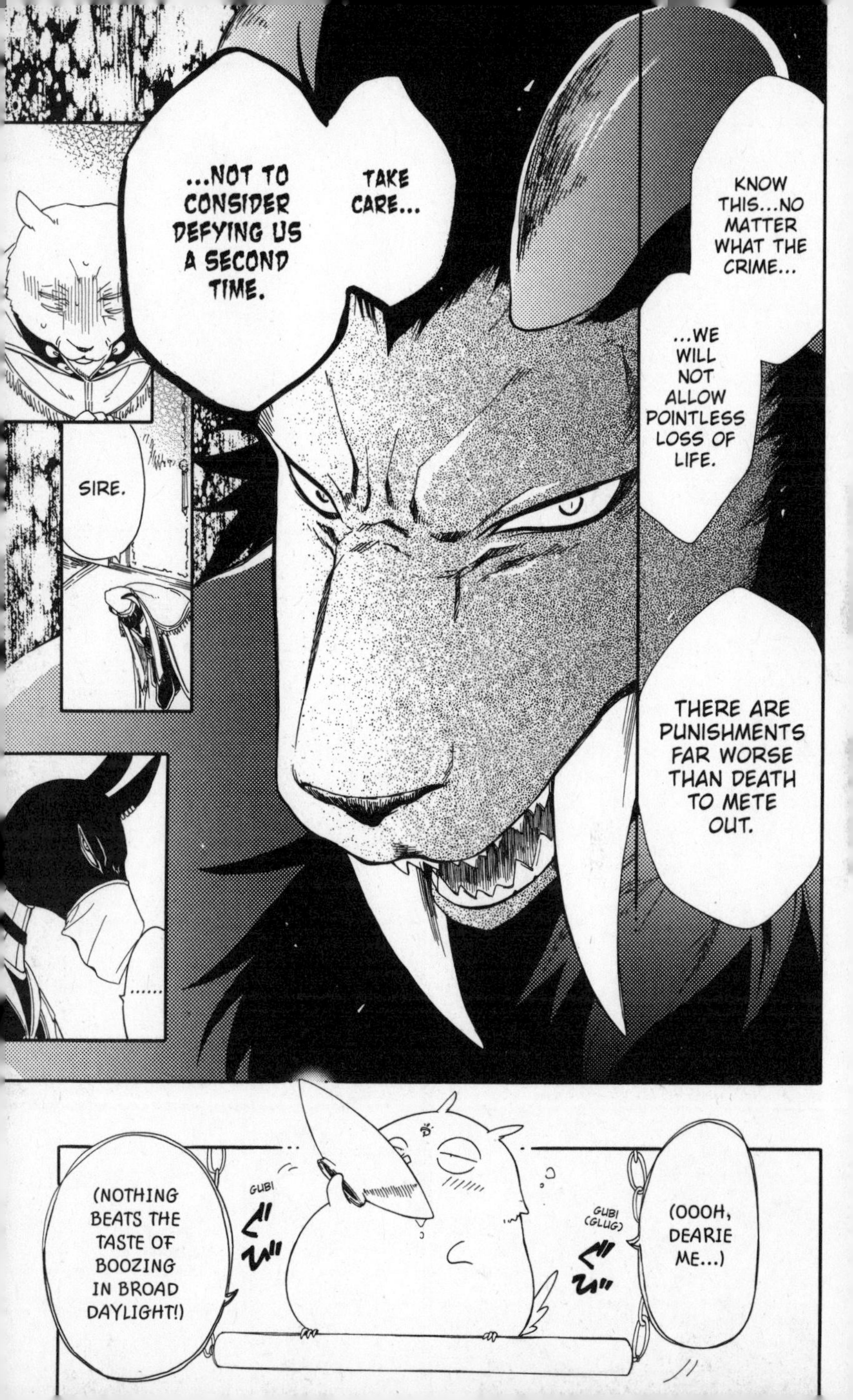
KNOW THIS...NO MATTER WHAT THE CRIME...
...WE WILL NOT ALLOW POINTLESS LOSS OF LIFE.
THERE ARE PUNISHMENTS FAR WORSE THAN DEATH TO METE OUT.
TAKE CARE...
...NOT TO CONSIDER DEFYING US A SECOND TIME.
SIRE.
......
(OOOH, DEARIE ME...)
GUBI (GLUG)
ぐび
GUBI
ぐび
(NOTHING BEATS THE TASTE OF BOOZING IN BROAD DAYLIGHT!)

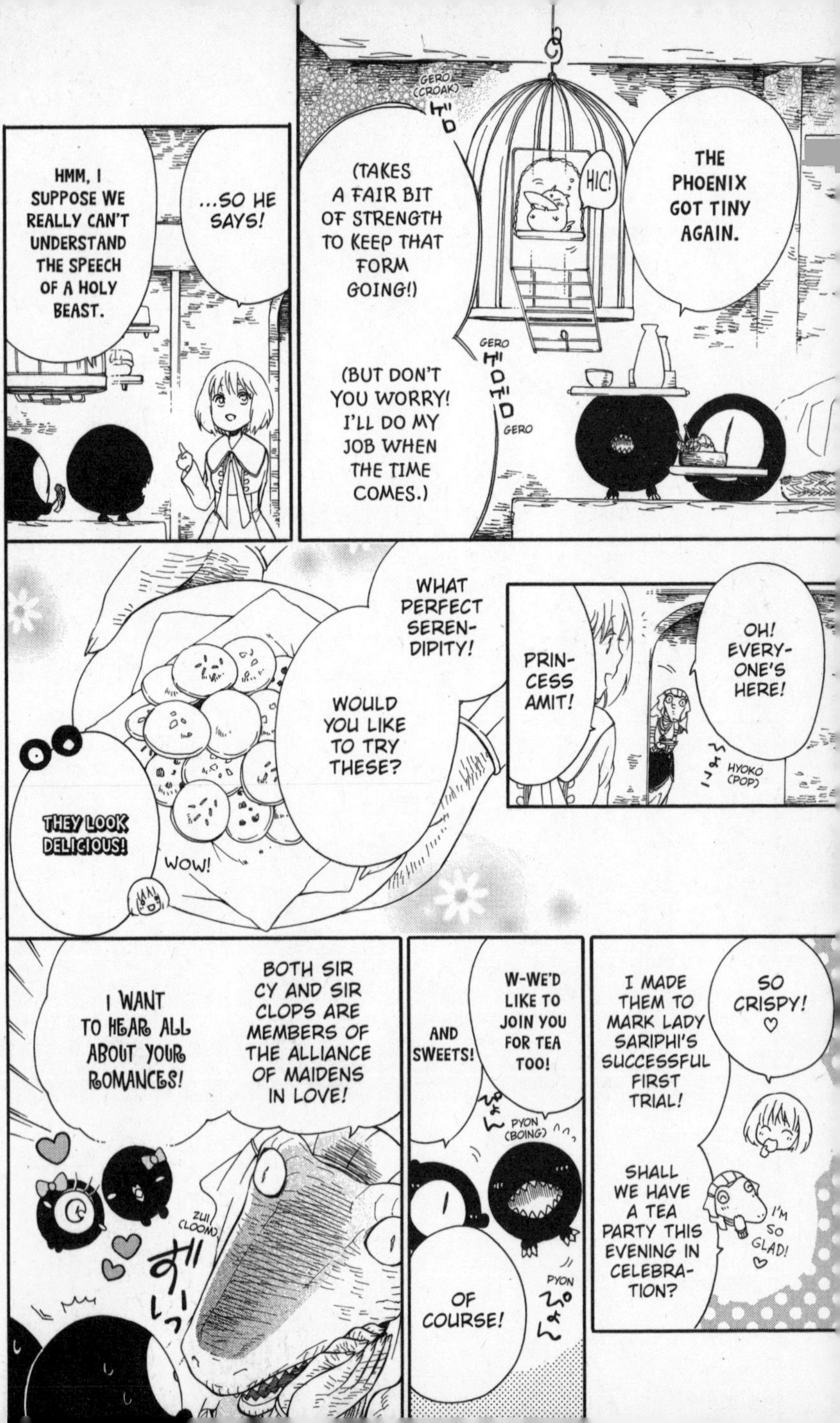
THE PHOENIX GOT TINY AGAIN.
HIC!
GERO (CROAK)
ゲロ
(TAKES A FAIR BIT OF STRENGTH TO KEEP THAT FORM GOING!)
GERO
ゲロゲロ
GERO
(BUT DON'T YOU WORRY! I'LL DO MY JOB WHEN THE TIME COMES.)
...SO HE SAYS!
HMM, I SUPPOSE WE REALLY CAN'T UNDERSTAND THE SPEECH OF A HOLY BEAST.
OH! EVERYONE'S HERE!
ひょこ
HYOKO (POP)
PRINCESS AMIT!
WHAT PERFECT SERENDIPITY!
WOULD YOU LIKE TO TRY THESE?
WOW!
THEY LOOK DELICIOUS!
SO CRISPY! ♡
I MADE THEM TO MARK LADY SARIPHI'S SUCCESSFUL FIRST TRIAL!
I'M SO GLAD! ♡
SHALL WE HAVE A TEA PARTY THIS EVENING IN CELEBRATION?
W-WE'D LIKE TO JOIN YOU FOR TEA TOO!
AND SWEETS!
ぴょん
PYON (BOING)
OF COURSE!
PYON
ぴょん
BOTH SIR CY AND SIR CLOPS ARE MEMBERS OF THE ALLIANCE OF MAIDENS IN LOVE!
I WANT TO HEAR ALL ABOUT YOUR ROMANCES!
ZUI (CLOOM)
ずいっ

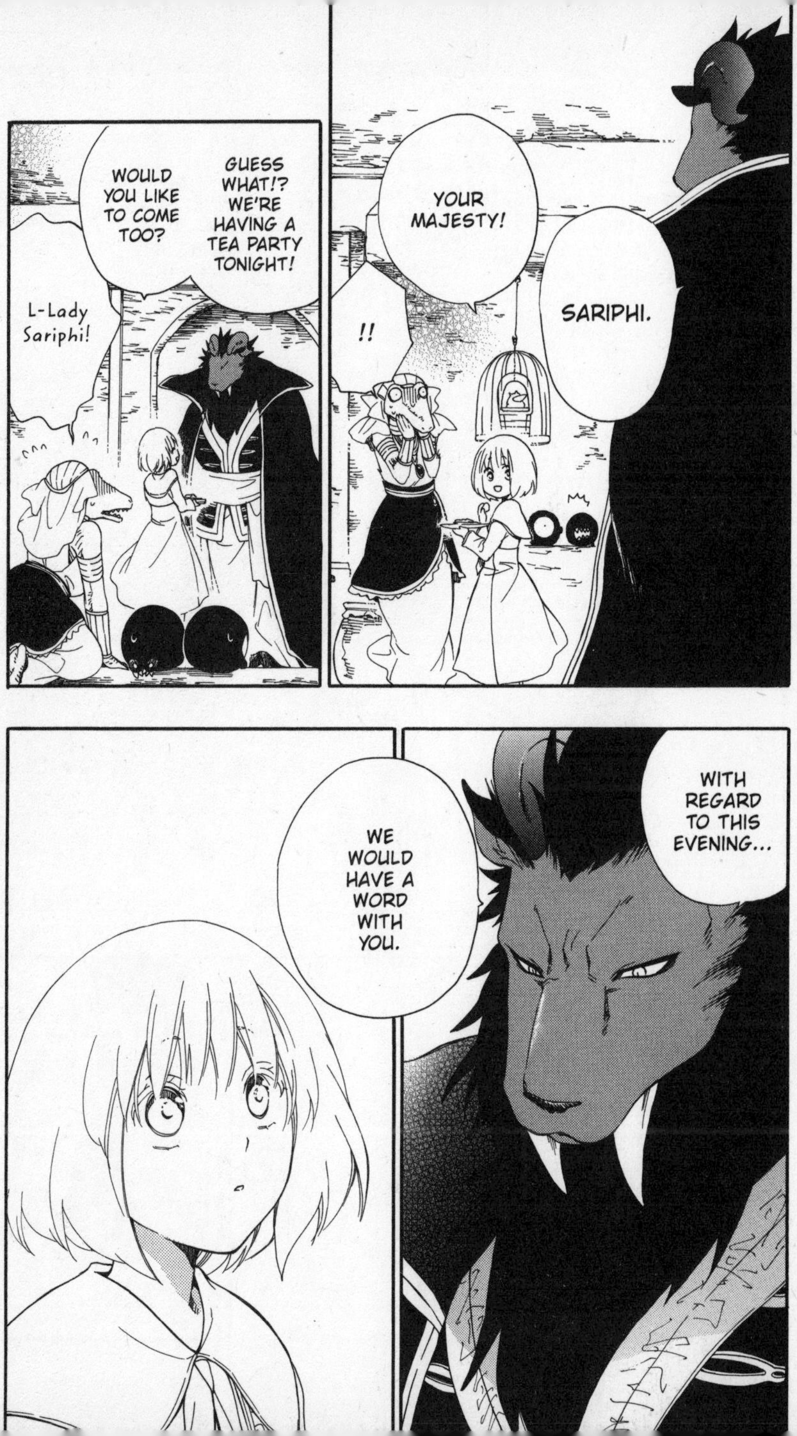
SARIPHI.
YOUR MAJESTY!
!!
GUESS WHAT!? WE'RE HAVING A TEA PARTY TONIGHT!
WOULD YOU LIKE TO COME TOO?
L-Lady Sariphi!
WITH REGARD TO THIS EVENING...
WE WOULD HAVE A WORD WITH YOU.

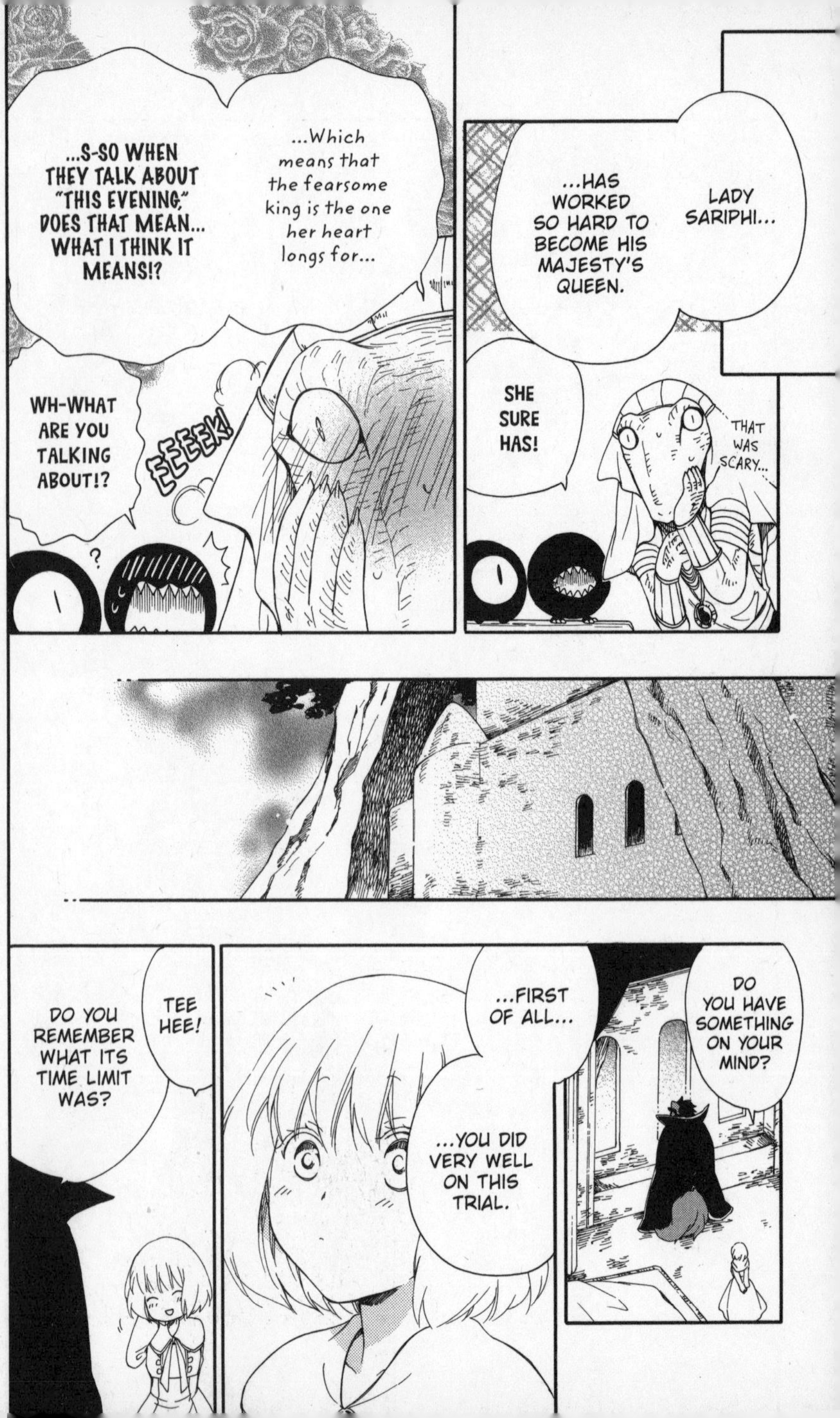
LADY SARIPHI...
...HAS WORKED SO HARD TO BECOME HIS MAJESTY'S QUEEN.
SHE SURE HAS!
THAT WAS SCARY...
...Which means that the fearsome king is the one her heart longs for...
...S-SO WHEN THEY TALK ABOUT "THIS EVENING," DOES THAT MEAN... WHAT I THINK IT MEANS!?
EEEEK!
WH-WHAT ARE YOU TALKING ABOUT!?
DO YOU HAVE SOMETHING ON YOUR MIND?
...FIRST OF ALL...
...YOU DID VERY WELL ON THIS TRIAL.
TEE HEE!
DO YOU REMEMBER WHAT ITS TIME LIMIT WAS?

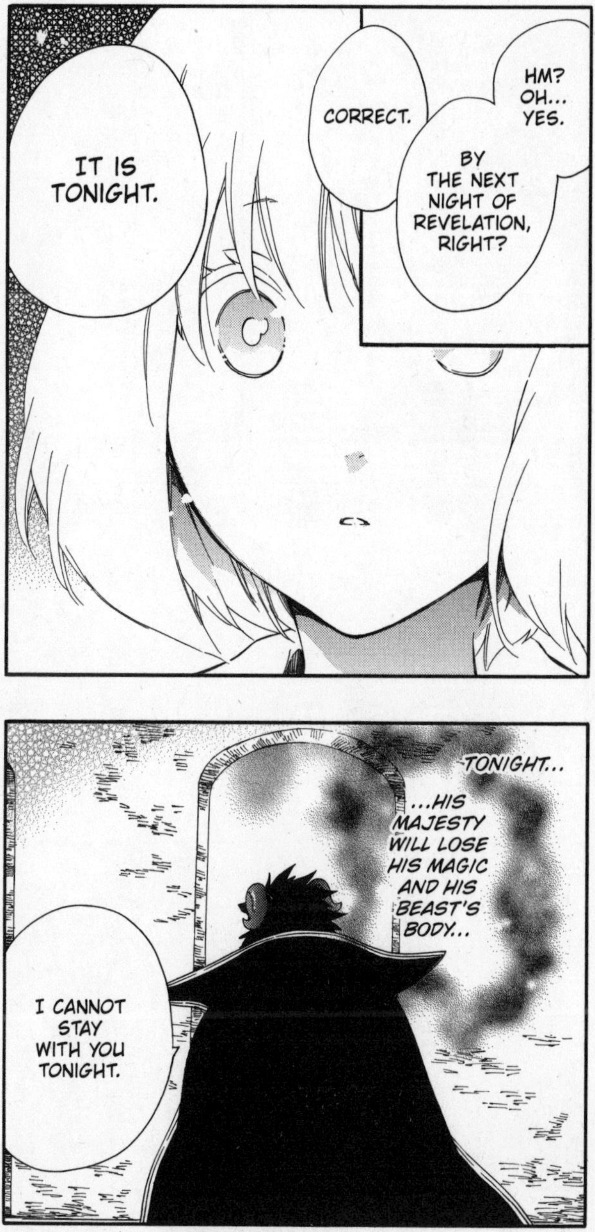
HM? OH... YES.
BY THE NEXT NIGHT OF REVELATION, RIGHT?
CORRECT.
IT IS TONIGHT.
TONIGHT...
...HIS MAJESTY WILL LOSE HIS MAGIC AND HIS BEAST'S BODY...
I CANNOT STAY WITH YOU TONIGHT.

WHEN I FIRST DREW THIS STORY AS A SHORT, I COULD NEVER HAVE IMAGINED GETTING THE CHANCE TO FINISH TWO WHOLE VOLUMES! STARTING WITH CHAPTER 8 OF THE SERIALIZATION, I GOT TO WORK WITH AN ASSISTANT FOR THE FIRST TIME, SO IT'S A VOLUME OF FIRSTS FOR ME. I'VE BEEN HELPED BY SO MANY PEOPLE SINCE MY DEBUT—MY FAMILY, MY EDITOR, MY ASSISTANT, AND THE READERS WHO SUPPORT MY WORK. THANK YOU ALL SO VERY MUCH!

I HOPE THAT WE'LL MEET AGAIN IN VOLUME 3!

THERE'S A BONUS AT THE END TOO!

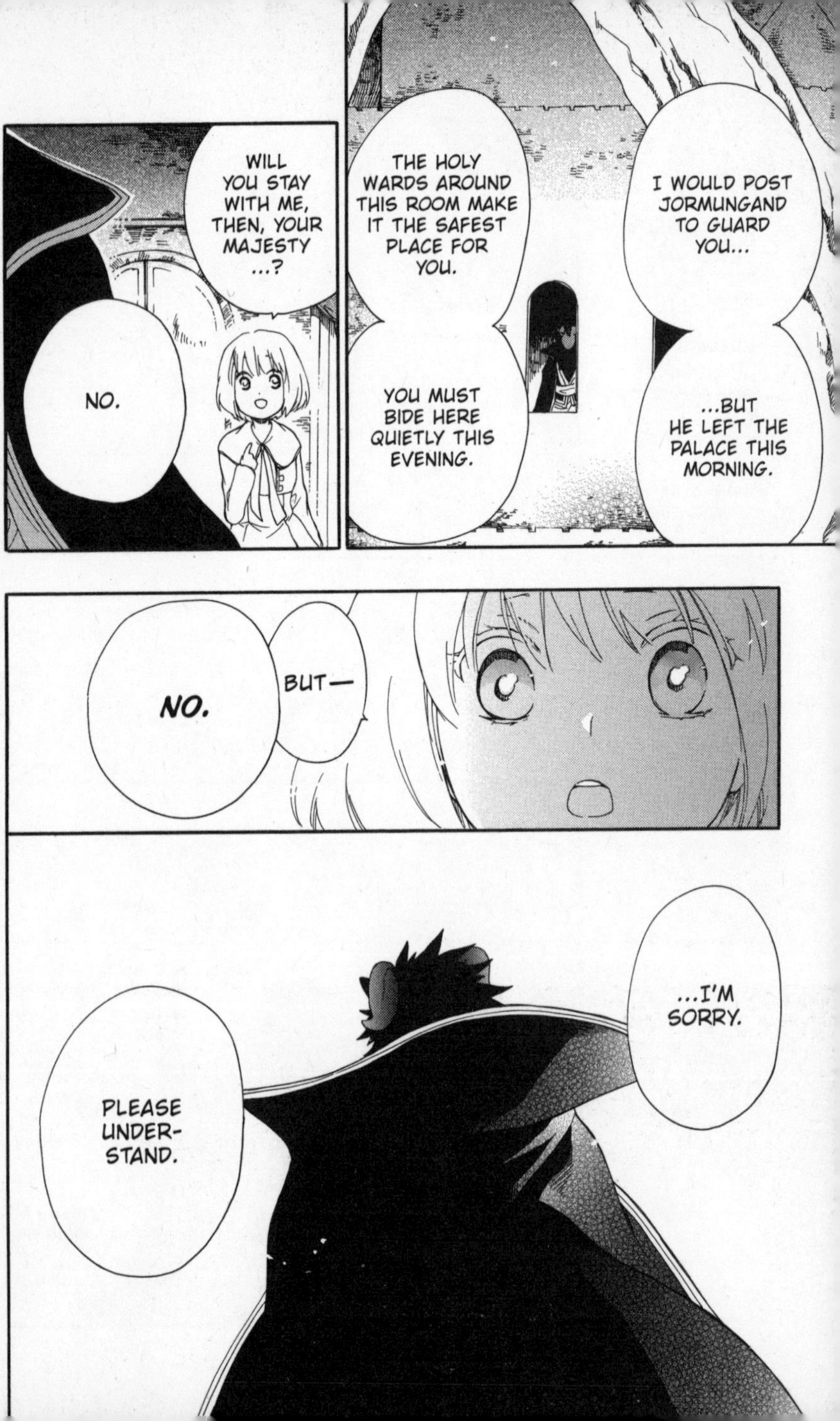
I WOULD POST JORMUNGAND TO GUARD YOU...
...BUT HE LEFT THE PALACE THIS MORNING.
THE HOLY WARDS AROUND THIS ROOM MAKE IT THE SAFEST PLACE FOR YOU.
YOU MUST BIDE HERE QUIETLY THIS EVENING.
WILL YOU STAY WITH ME, THEN, YOUR MAJESTY ...?
NO.
BUT—
NO.
...I'M SORRY.
PLEASE UNDER-STAND.

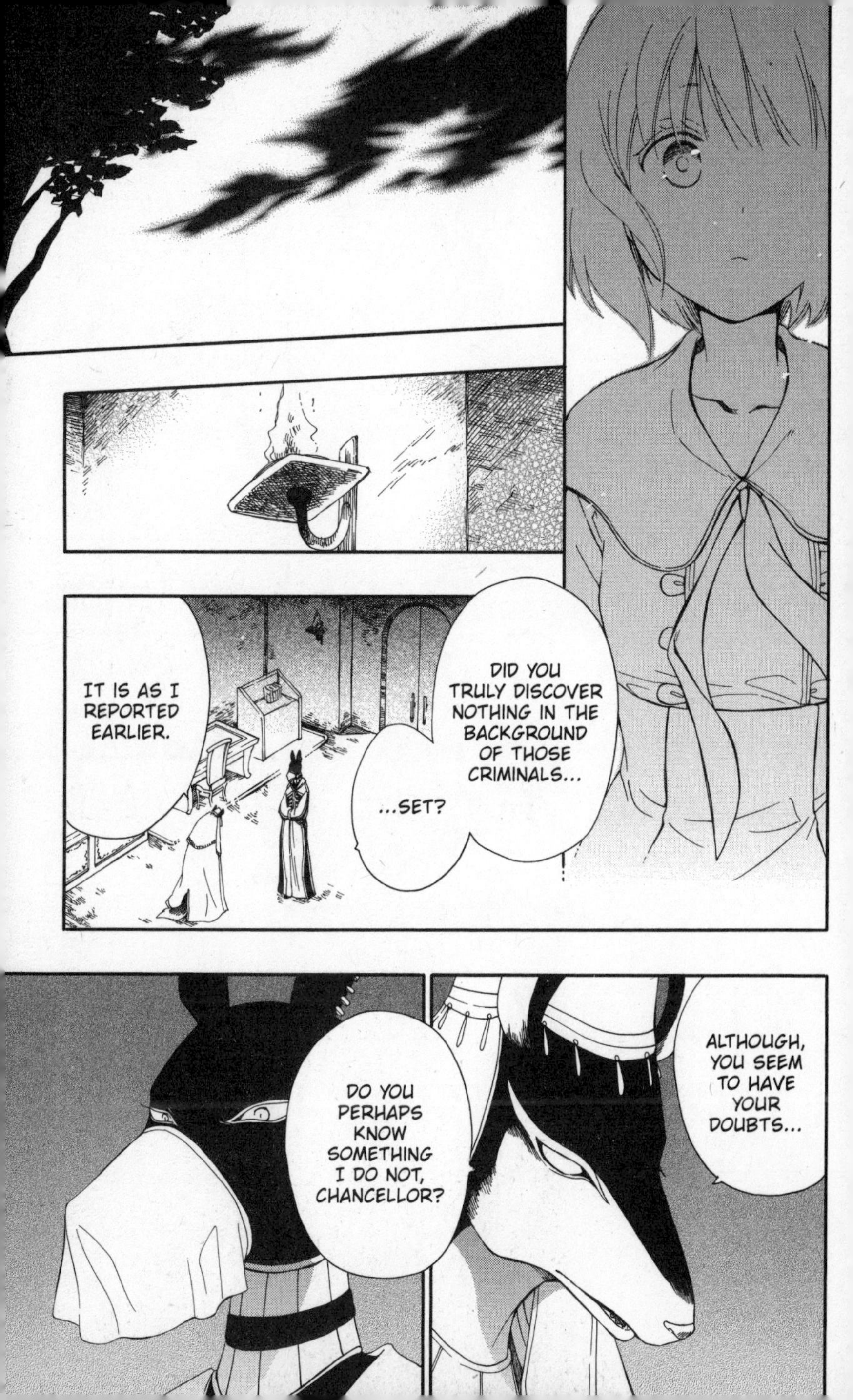
DID YOU TRULY DISCOVER NOTHING IN THE BACKGROUND OF THOSE CRIMINALS...
...SET?
IT IS AS I REPORTED EARLIER.
ALTHOUGH, YOU SEEM TO HAVE YOUR DOUBTS...
DO YOU PERHAPS KNOW SOMETHING I DO NOT, CHANCELLOR?

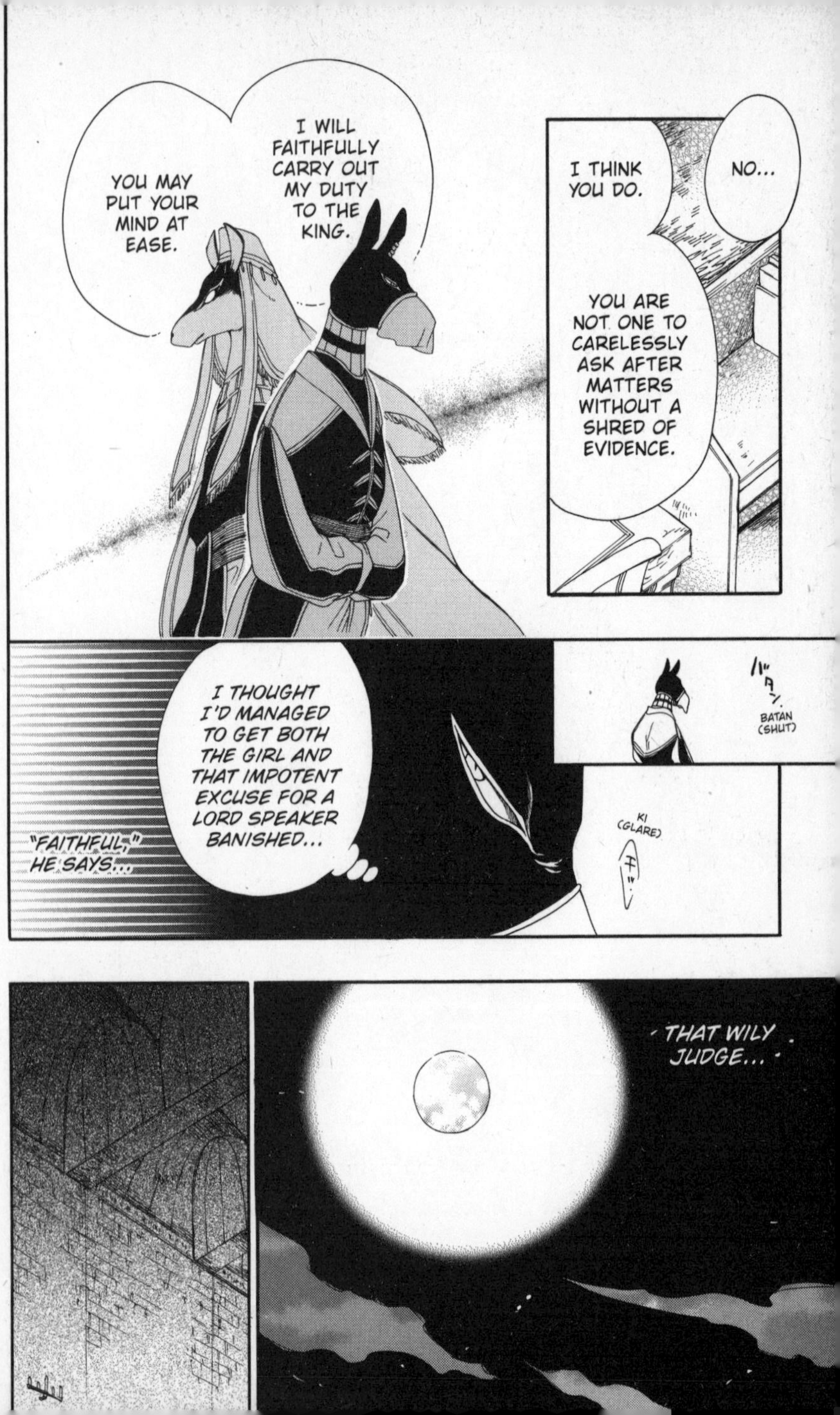
NO...
I THINK YOU DO.
YOU ARE NOT ONE TO CARELESSLY ASK AFTER MATTERS WITHOUT A SHRED OF EVIDENCE.
I WILL FAITHFULLY CARRY OUT MY DUTY TO THE KING.
YOU MAY PUT YOUR MIND AT EASE.
バタン
BATAN (SHUT)
KI (GLARE)
キッ
I THOUGHT I'D MANAGED TO GET BOTH THE GIRL AND THAT IMPOTENT EXCUSE FOR A LORD SPEAKER BANISHED...
"FAITHFUL," HE SAYS...
THAT WILY JUDGE...

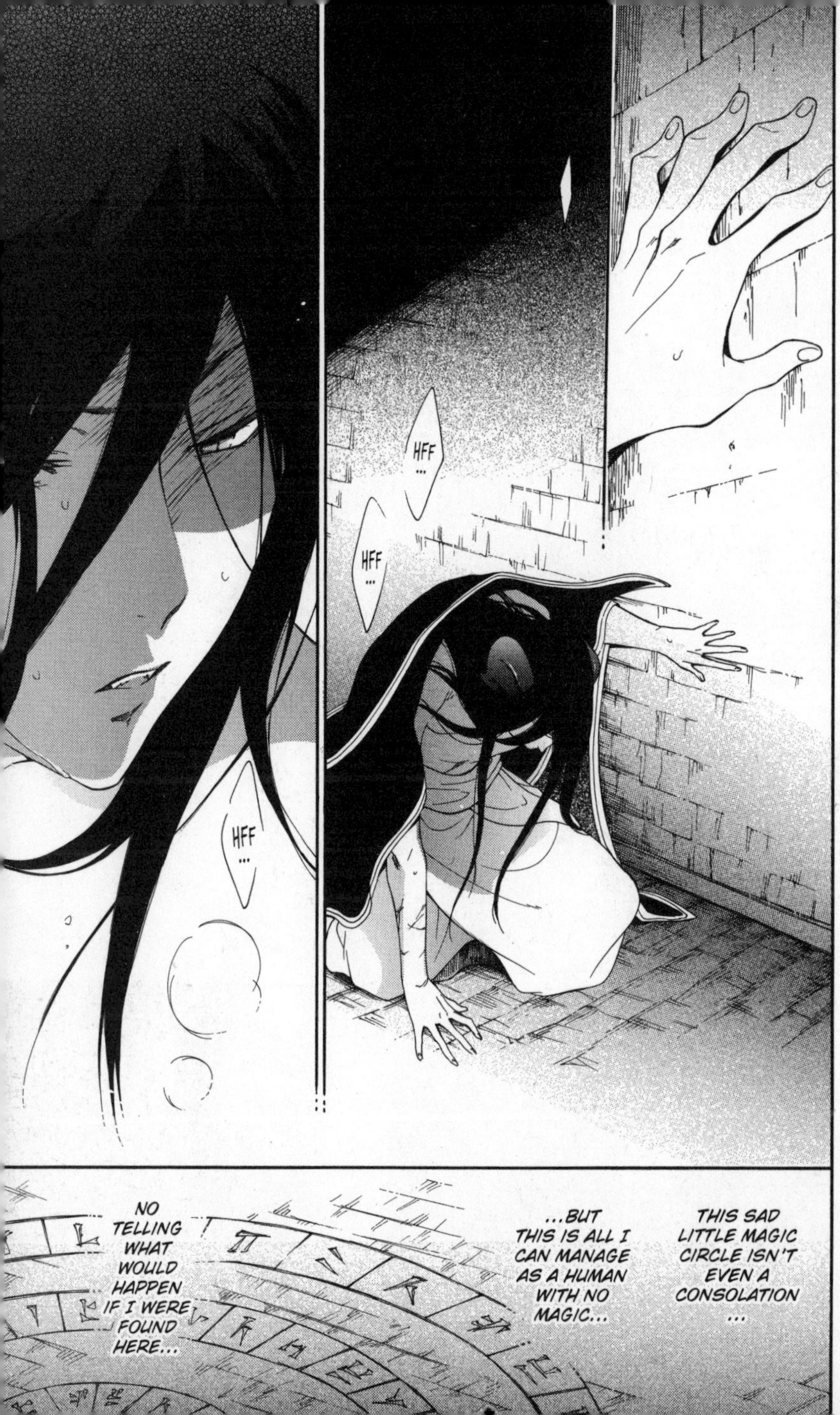
HFF...
HFF...
HFF...
THIS SAD LITTLE MAGIC CIRCLE ISN'T EVEN A CONSOLATION...
...BUT THIS IS ALL I CAN MANAGE AS A HUMAN WITH NO MAGIC...
NO TELLING WHAT WOULD HAPPEN IF I WERE FOUND HERE...

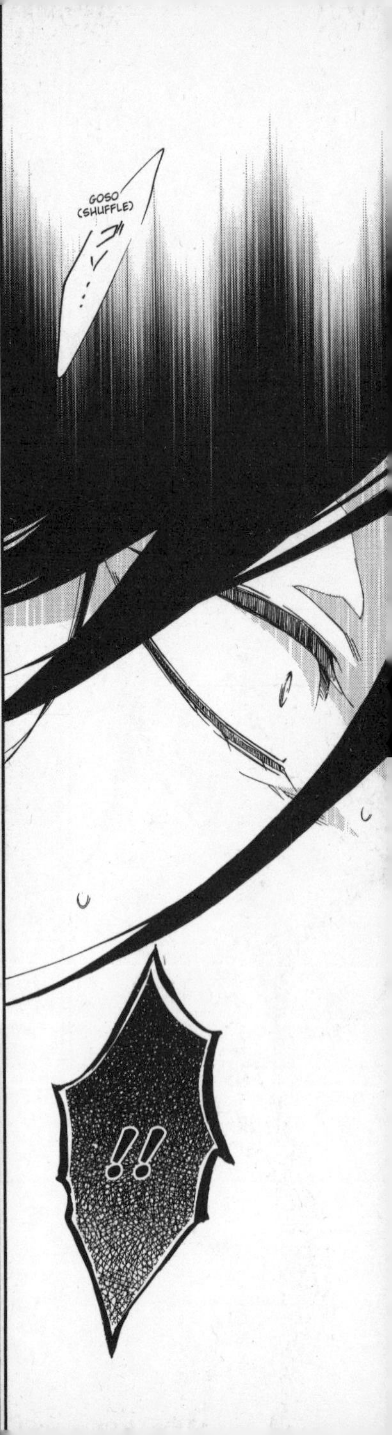
GOSO (SHUFFLE)
!!
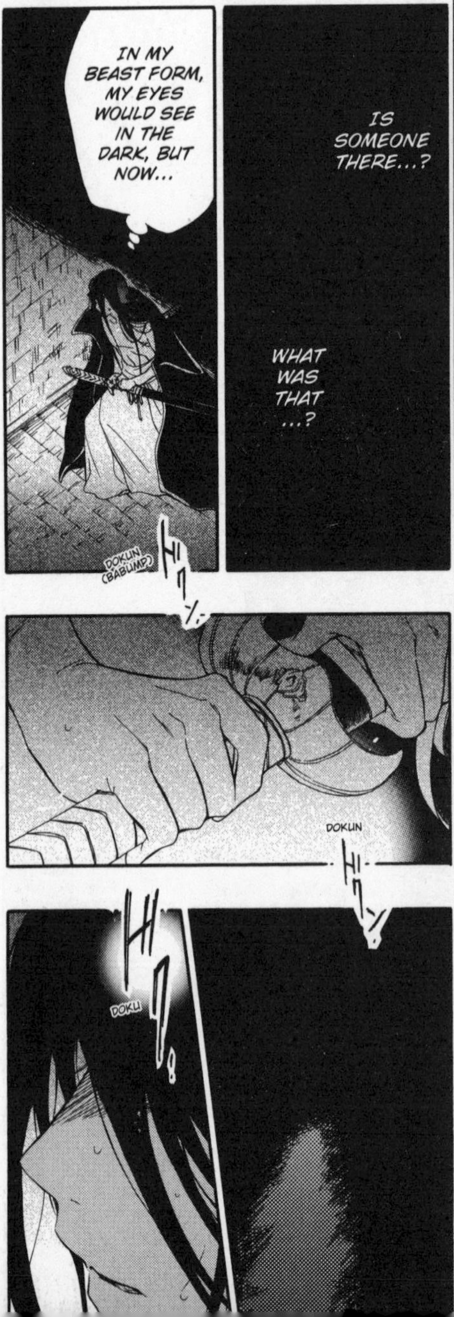
IS SOMEONE THERE...?
WHAT WAS THAT ...?
IN MY BEAST FORM, MY EYES WOULD SEE IN THE DARK, BUT NOW...
DOKUN (BABUMP)
DOKUN
DOKU

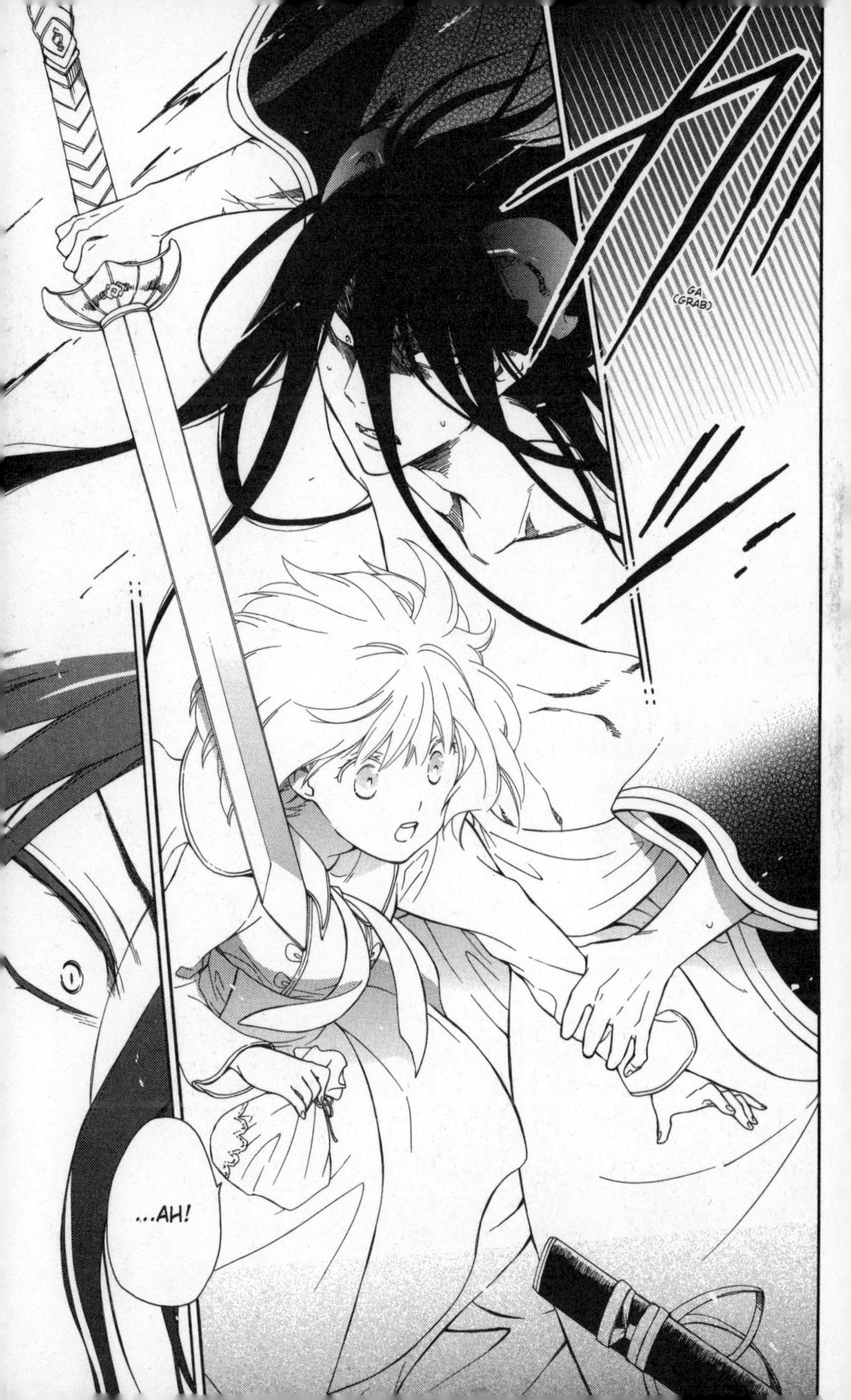
GA
(GRAB)
...AH!

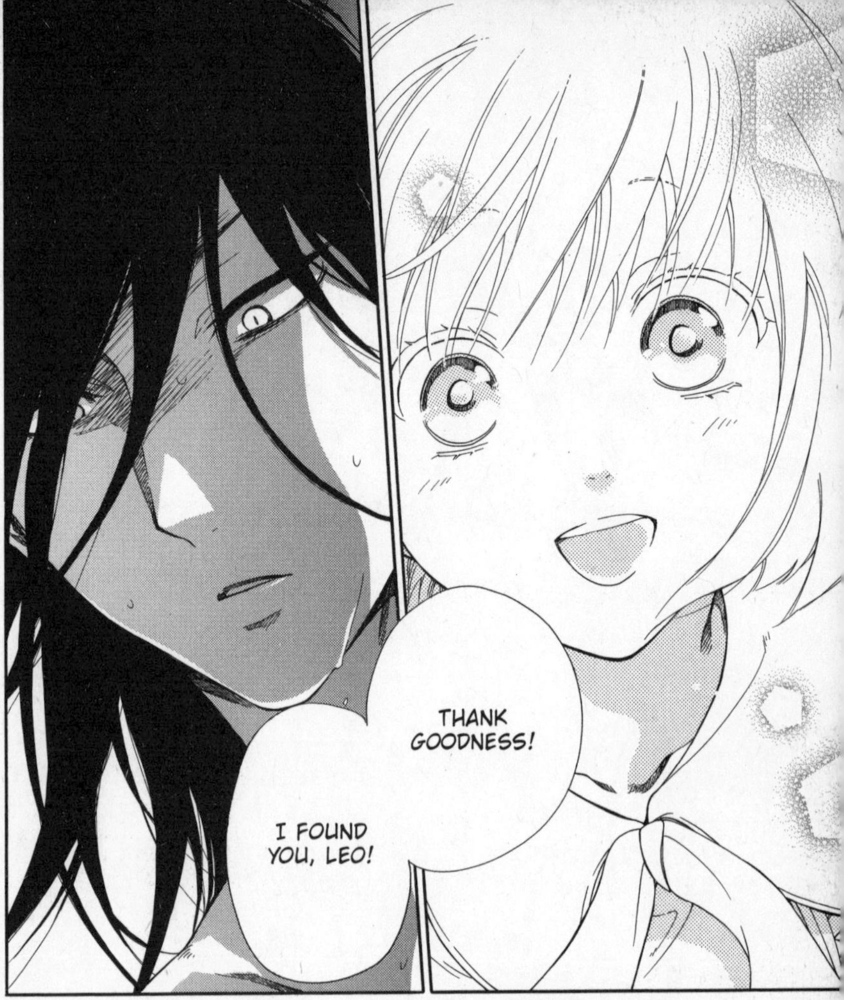
THANK GOODNESS!
I FOUND YOU, LEO!

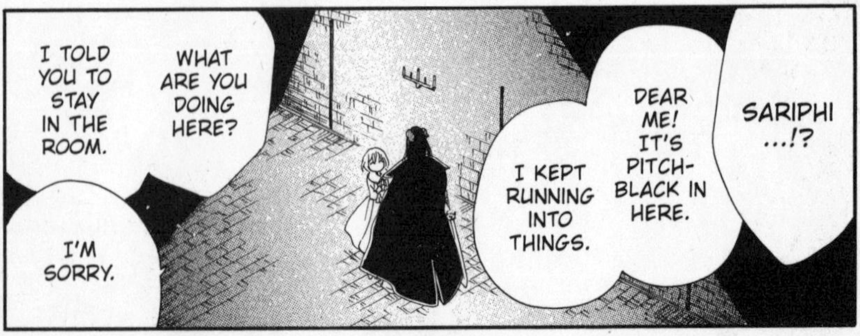
SARIPHI ...!?
DEAR ME! IT'S PITCH-BLACK IN HERE.
I KEPT RUNNING INTO THINGS.
WHAT ARE YOU DOING HERE?
I TOLD YOU TO STAY IN THE ROOM.
I'M SORRY.

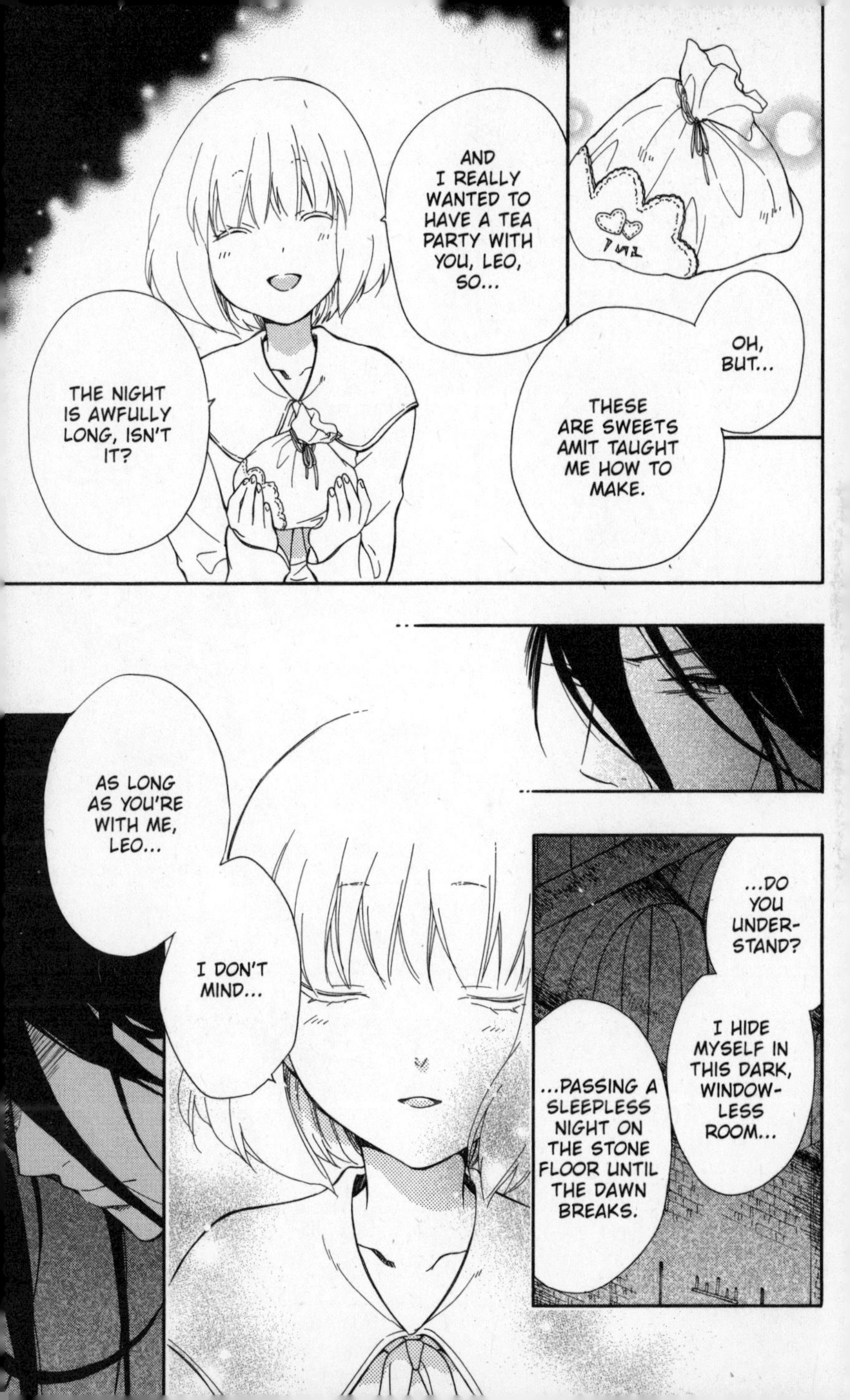
OH, BUT...
THESE ARE SWEETS AMIT TAUGHT ME HOW TO MAKE.
AND I REALLY WANTED TO HAVE A TEA PARTY WITH YOU, LEO, SO...
THE NIGHT IS AWFULLY LONG, ISN'T IT?
...DO YOU UNDER-STAND?
I HIDE MYSELF IN THIS DARK, WINDOW-LESS ROOM...
...PASSING A SLEEPLESS NIGHT ON THE STONE FLOOR UNTIL THE DAWN BREAKS.
AS LONG AS YOU'RE WITH ME, LEO...
I DON'T MIND...

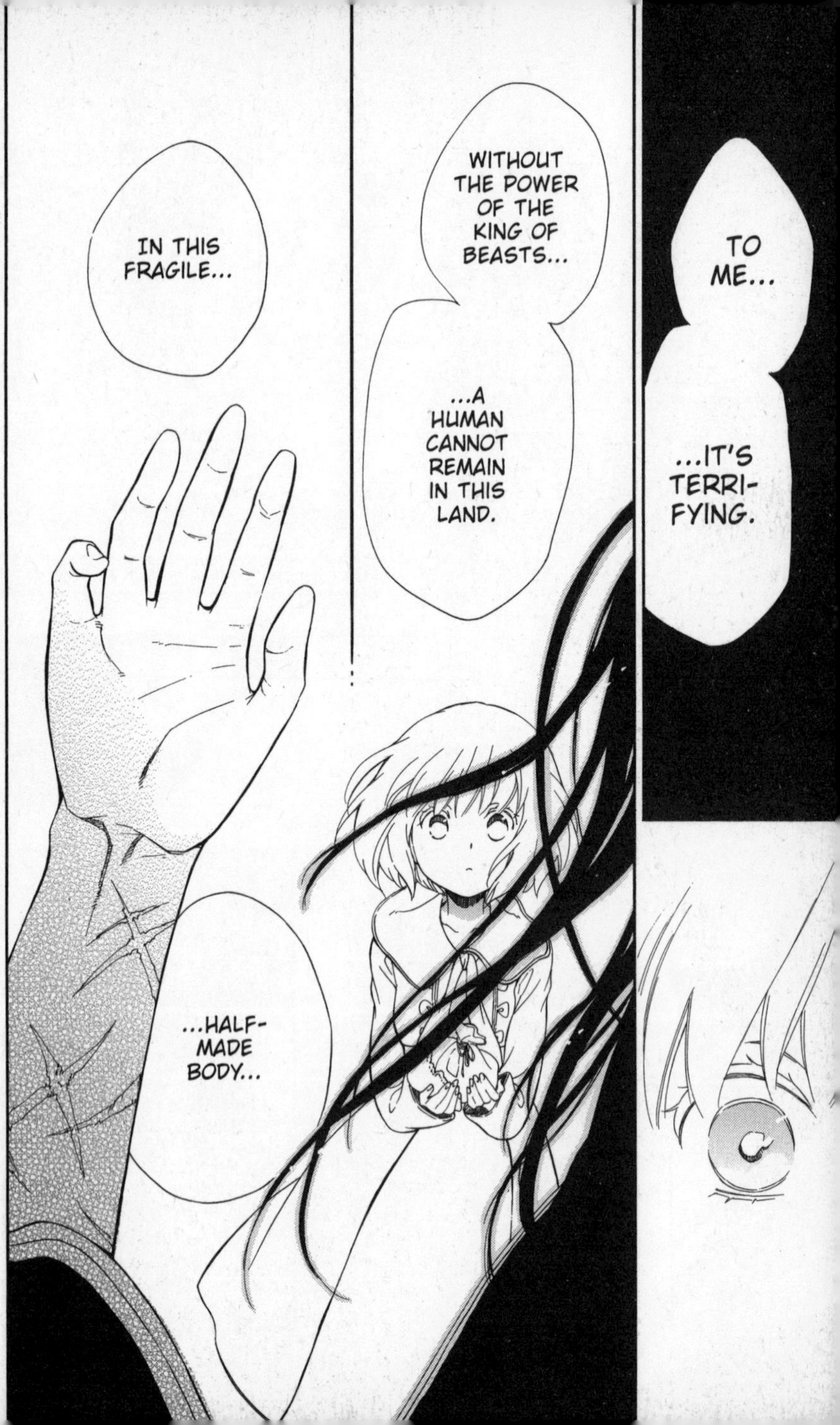
TO ME...
...IT'S TERRI-FYING.
WITHOUT THE POWER OF THE KING OF BEASTS...
...A HUMAN CANNOT REMAIN IN THIS LAND.
IN THIS FRAGILE...
...HALF-MADE BODY...

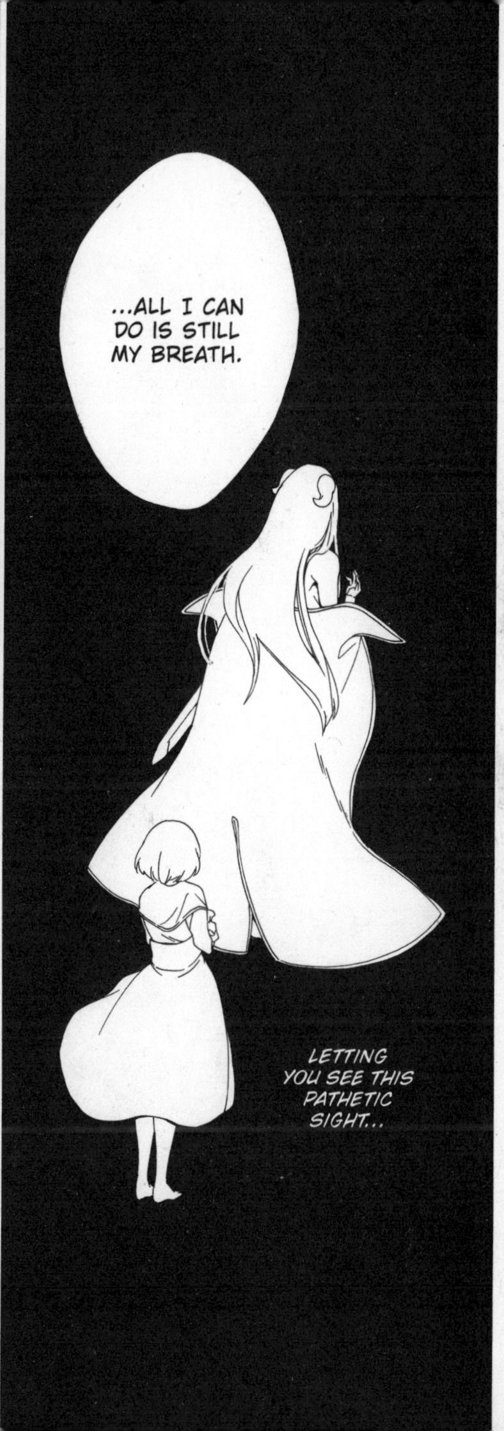
...ALL I CAN DO IS STILL MY BREATH.
LETTING YOU SEE THIS PATHETIC SIGHT...
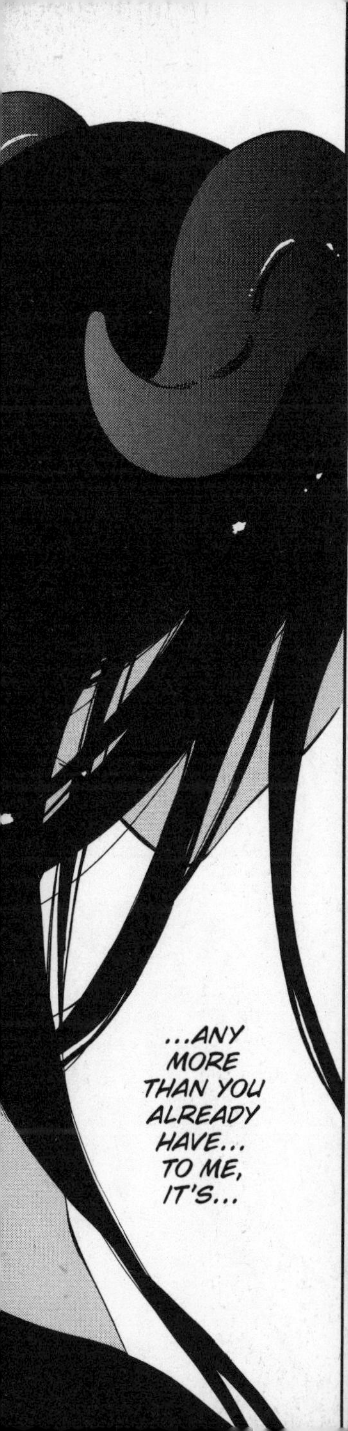
...ANY MORE THAN YOU ALREADY HAVE... TO ME, IT'S...

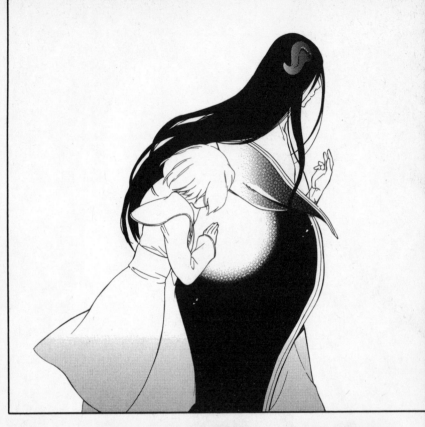

LEO...

I...

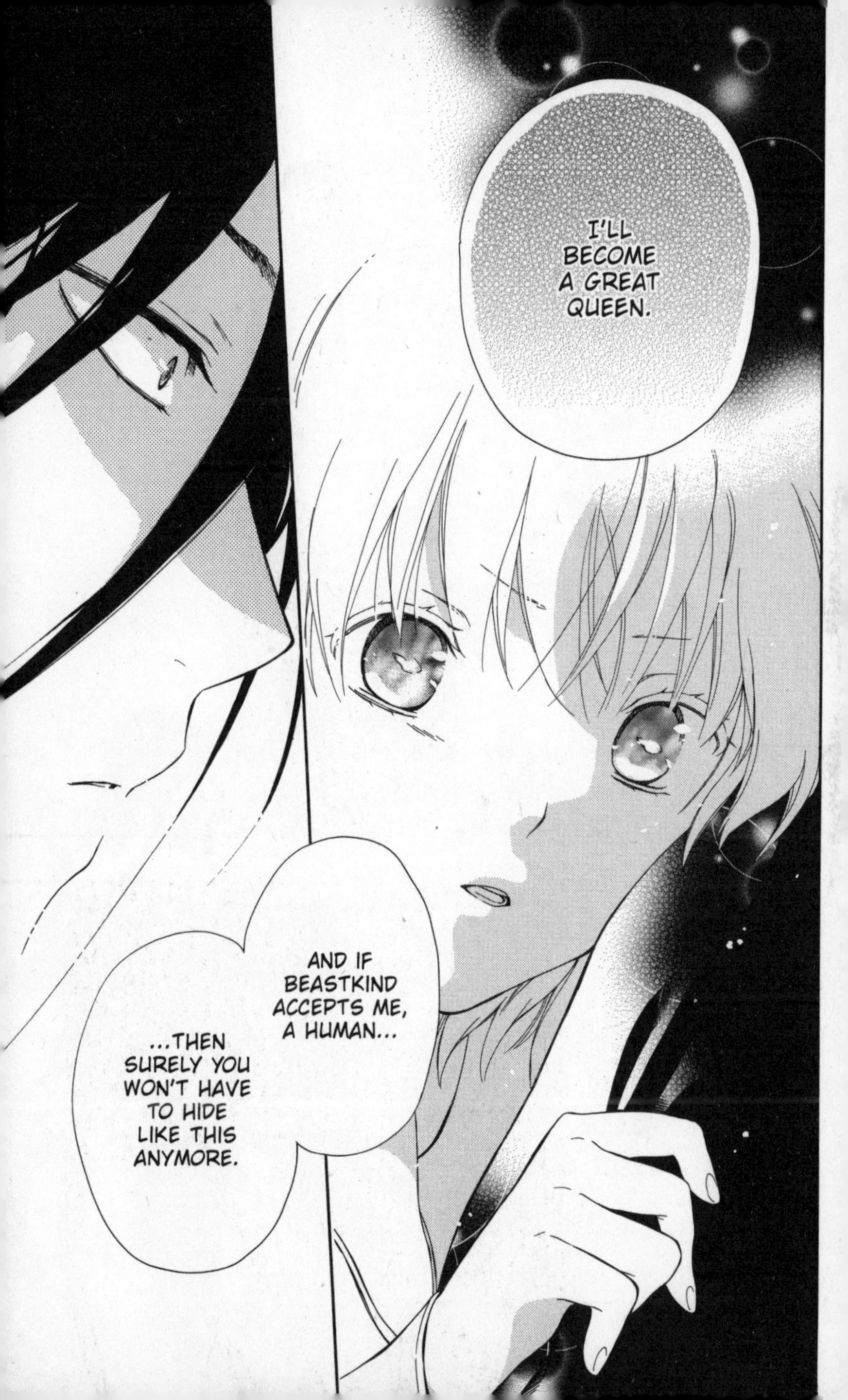
I'LL BECOME A GREAT QUEEN.
AND IF BEASTKIND ACCEPTS ME, A HUMAN...
...THEN SURELY YOU WON'T HAVE TO HIDE LIKE THIS ANYMORE.

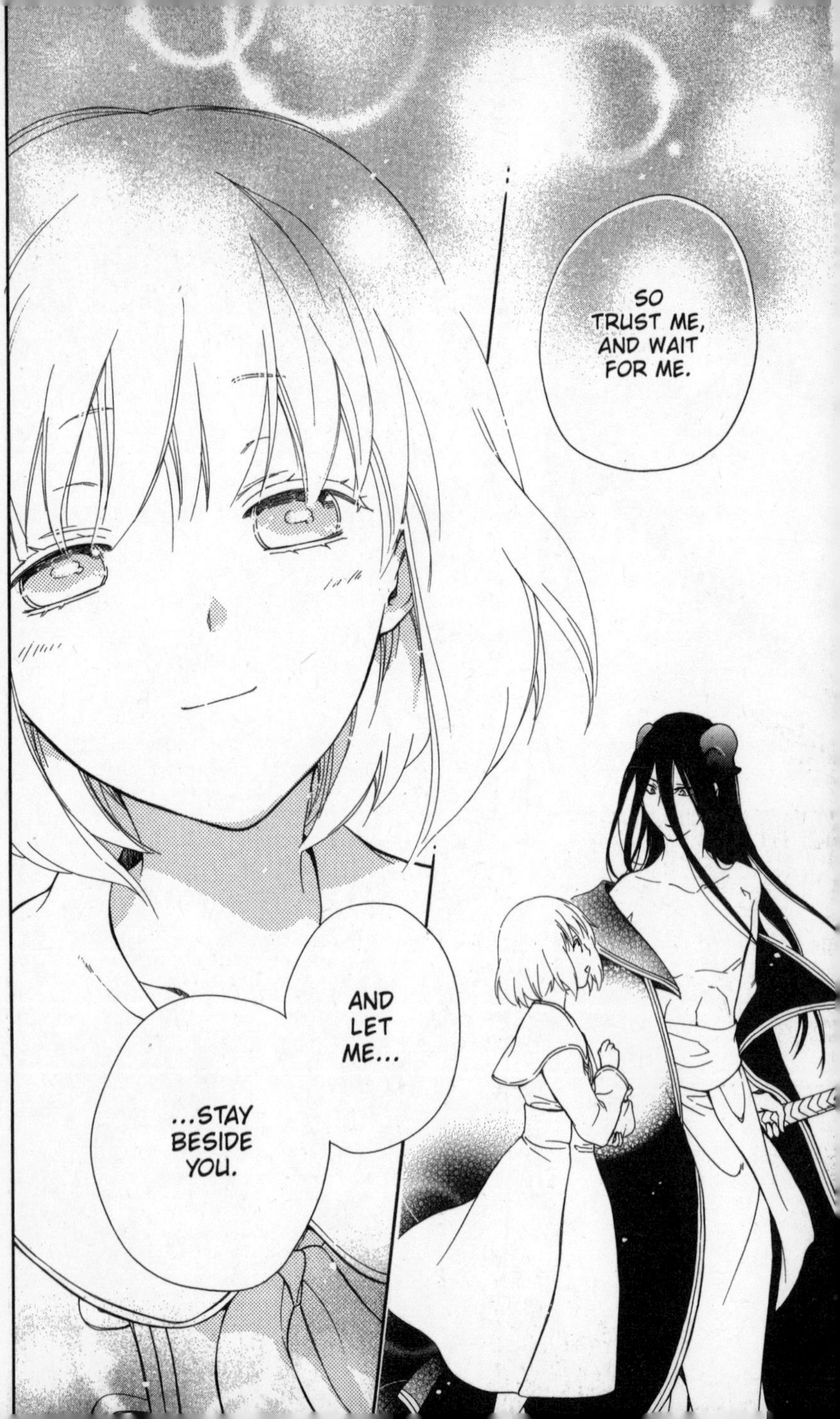
SO TRUST ME, AND WAIT FOR ME.
AND LET ME...
...STAY BESIDE YOU.

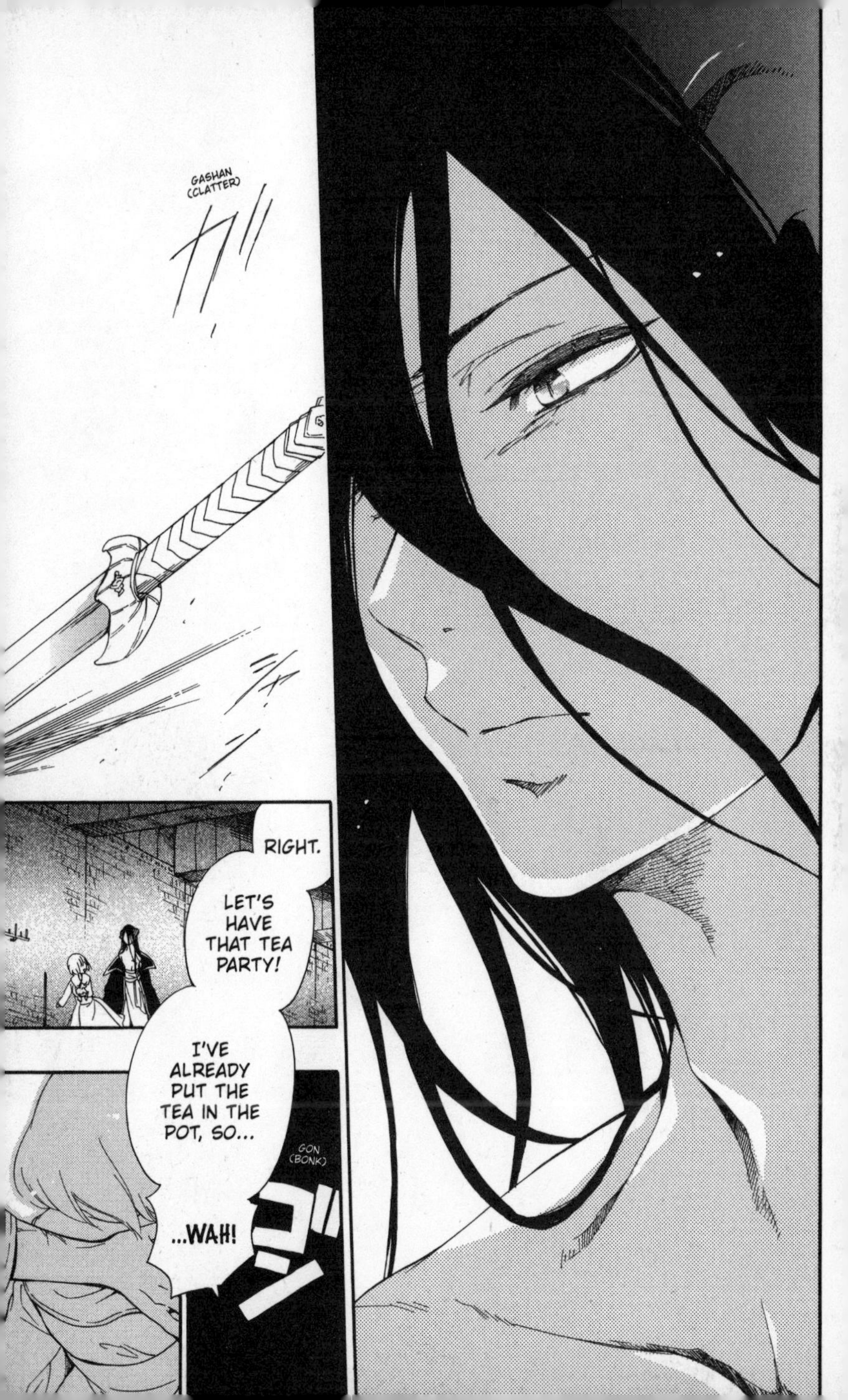
GASHAN (CLATTER)
RIGHT.
LET'S HAVE THAT TEA PARTY!
I'VE ALREADY PUT THE TEA IN THE POT, SO...
GON (BONK)
...WAH!

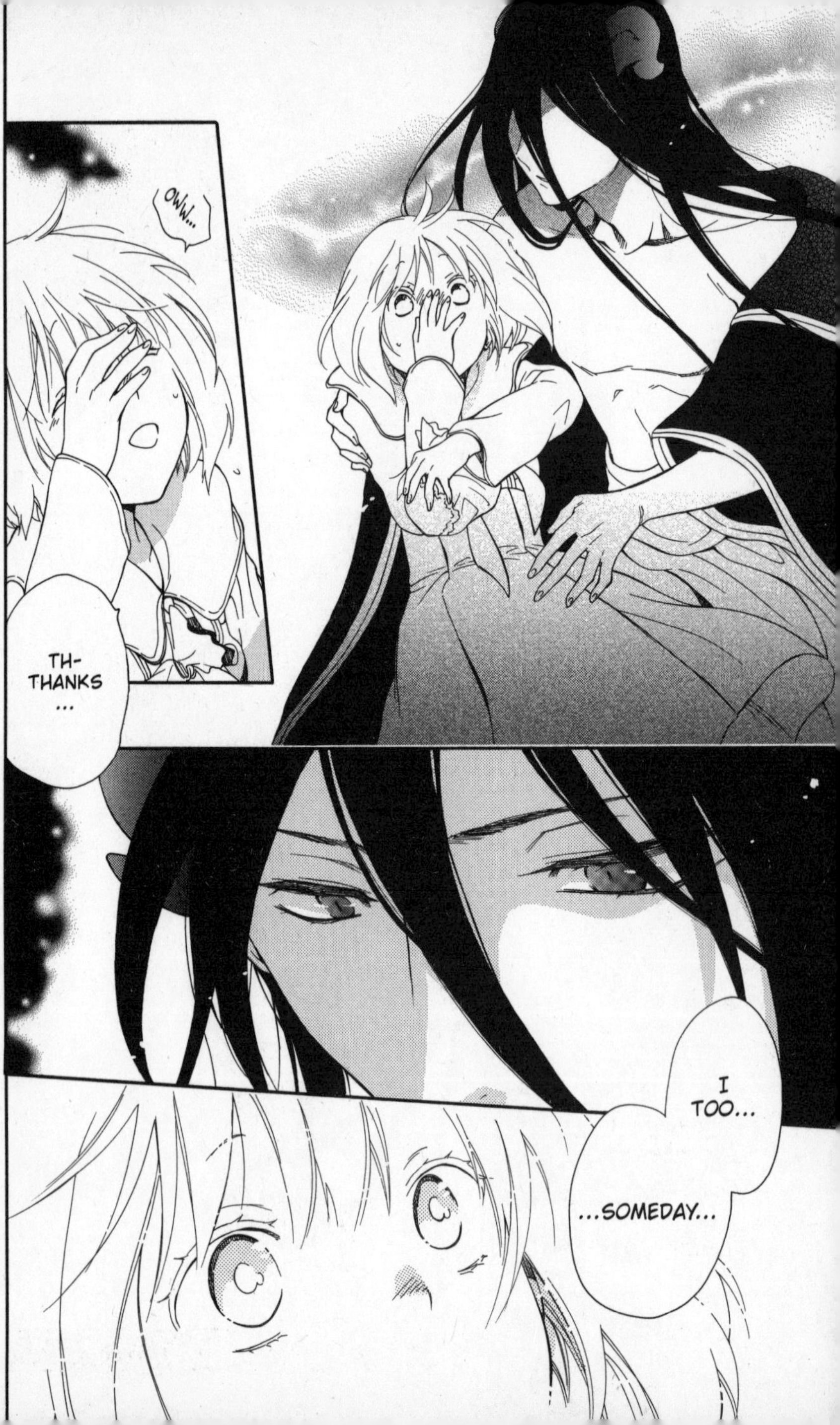
OWW...
TH-THANKS...
I TOO...
...SOMEDAY...

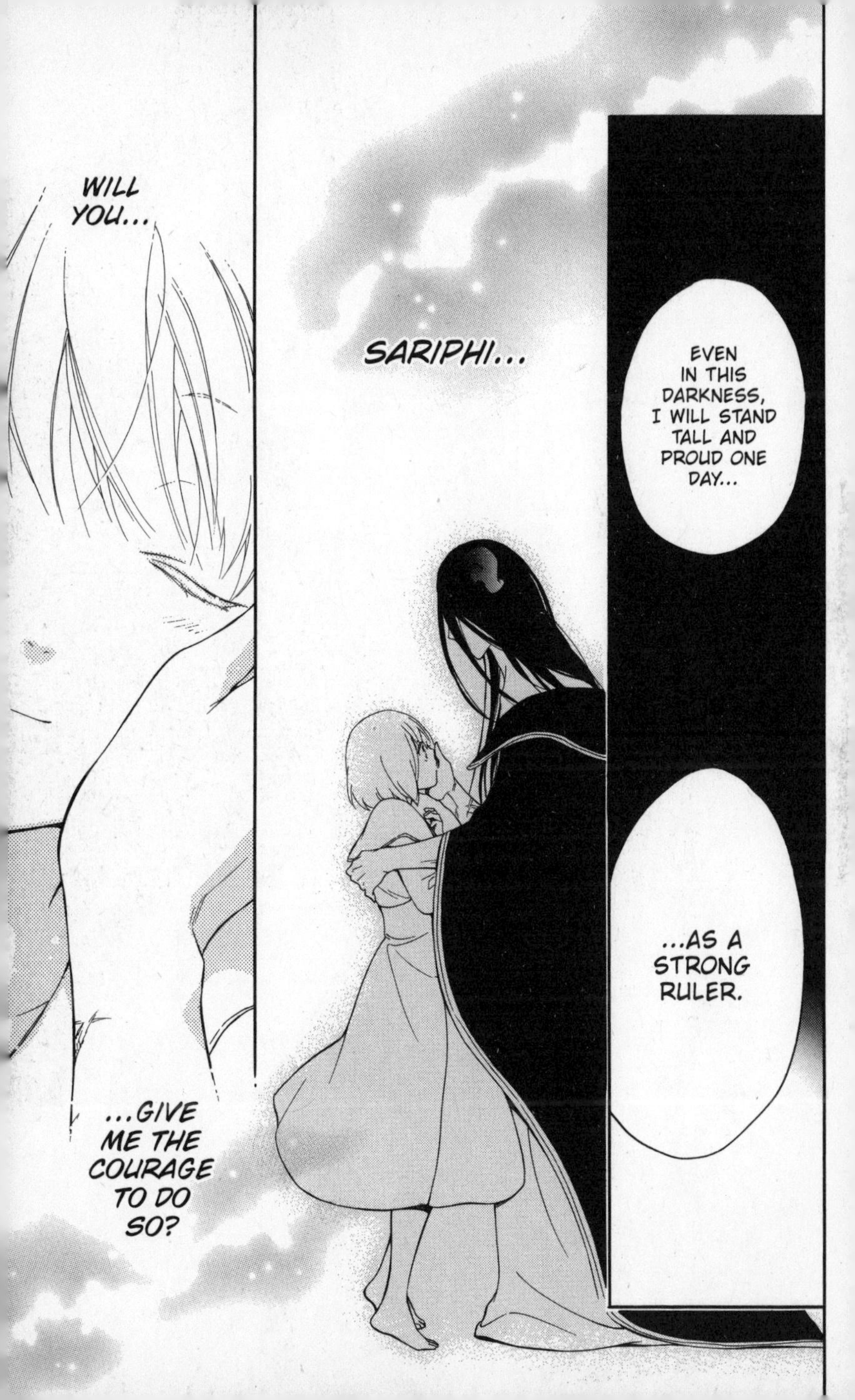
EVEN IN THIS DARKNESS, I WILL STAND TALL AND PROUD ONE DAY...
...AS A STRONG RULER.
SARIPHI...
WILL YOU...
...GIVE ME THE COURAGE TO DO SO?

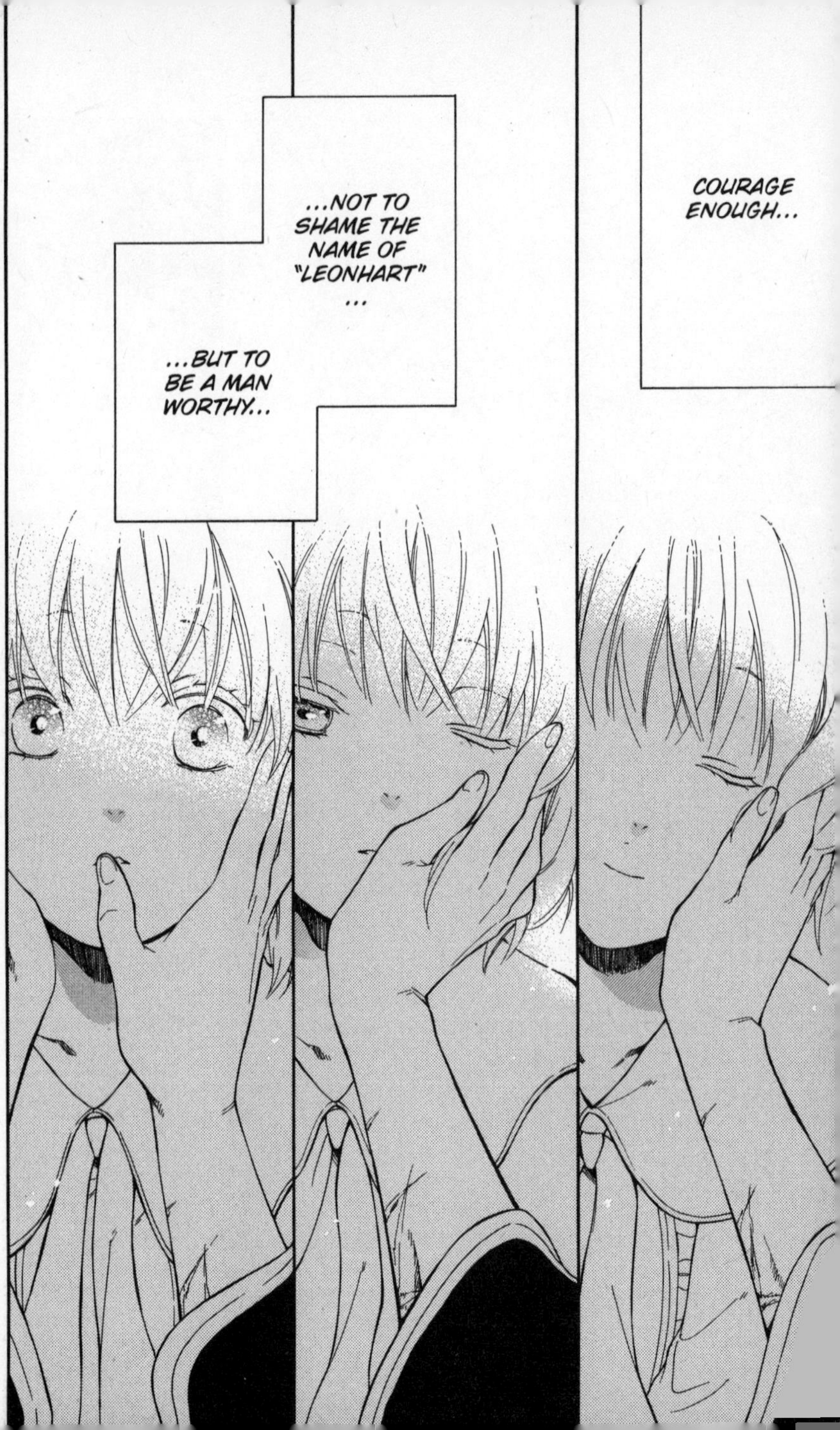
COURAGE ENOUGH...
...NOT TO SHAME THE NAME OF "LEONHART" ...
...BUT TO BE A MAN WORTHY...

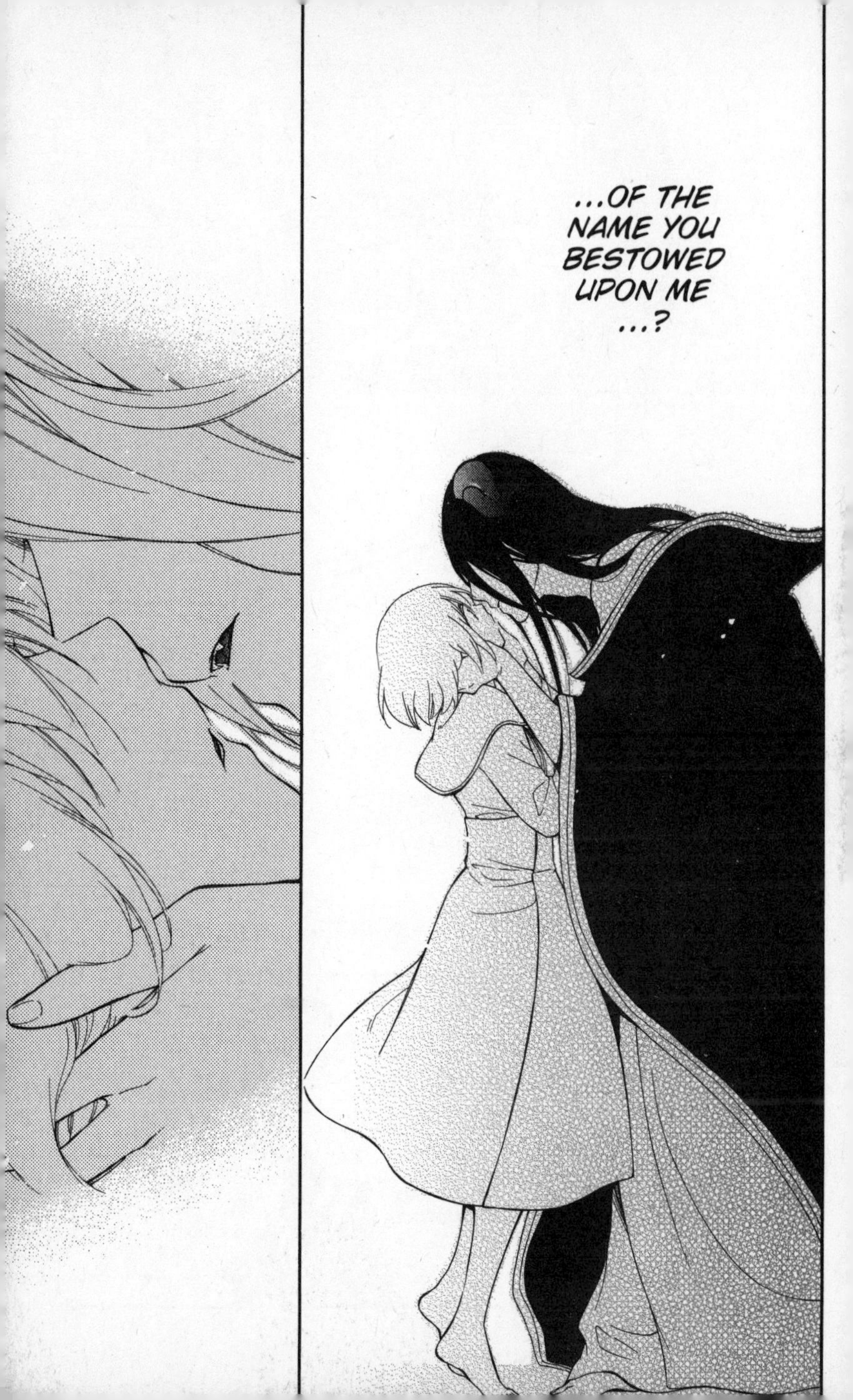
...OF THE NAME YOU BESTOWED UPON ME ...?

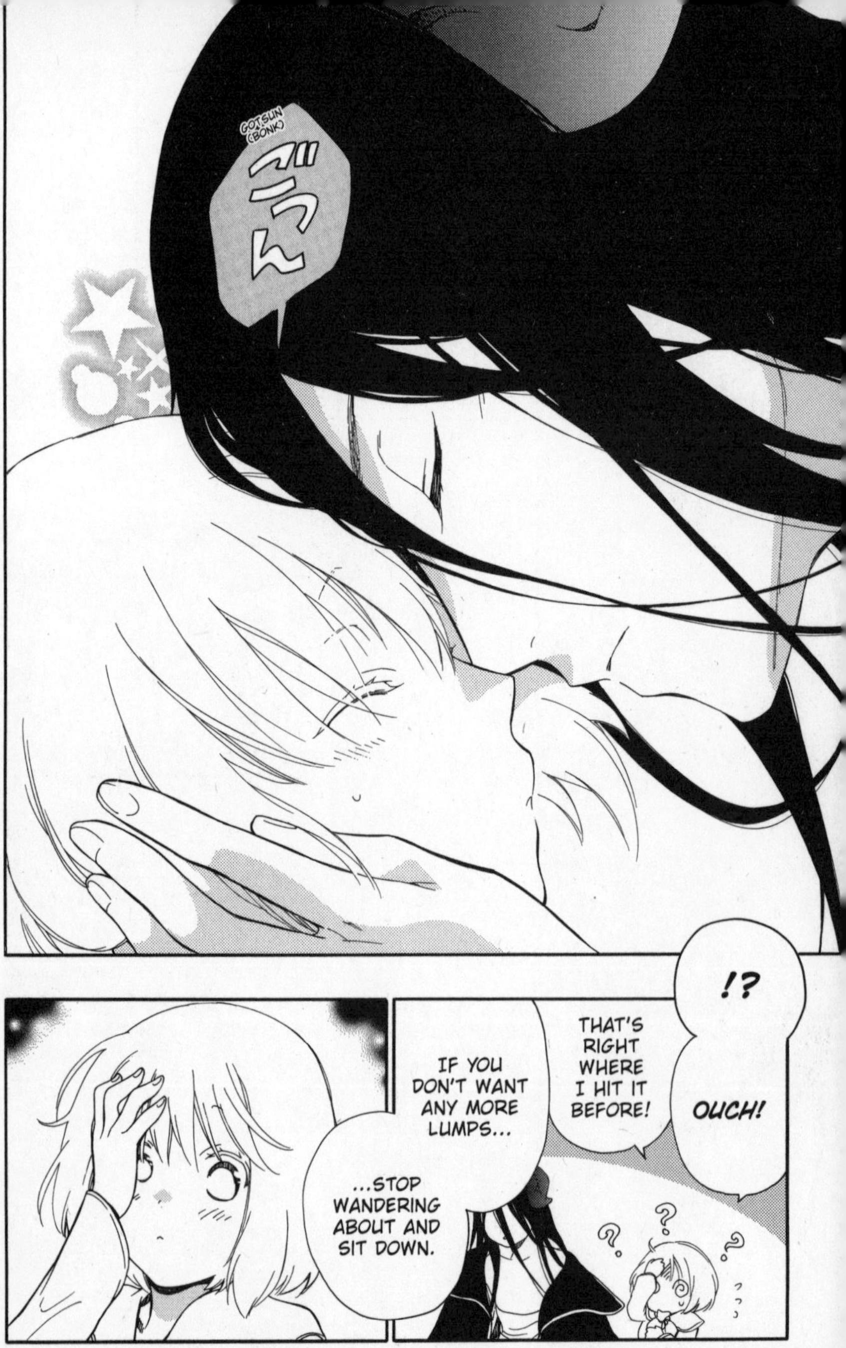
ごつん
GOTSUN (BONK)
!? OUCH!
THAT'S RIGHT WHERE I HIT IT BEFORE!
IF YOU DON'T WANT ANY MORE LUMPS...
...STOP WANDERING ABOUT AND SIT DOWN.

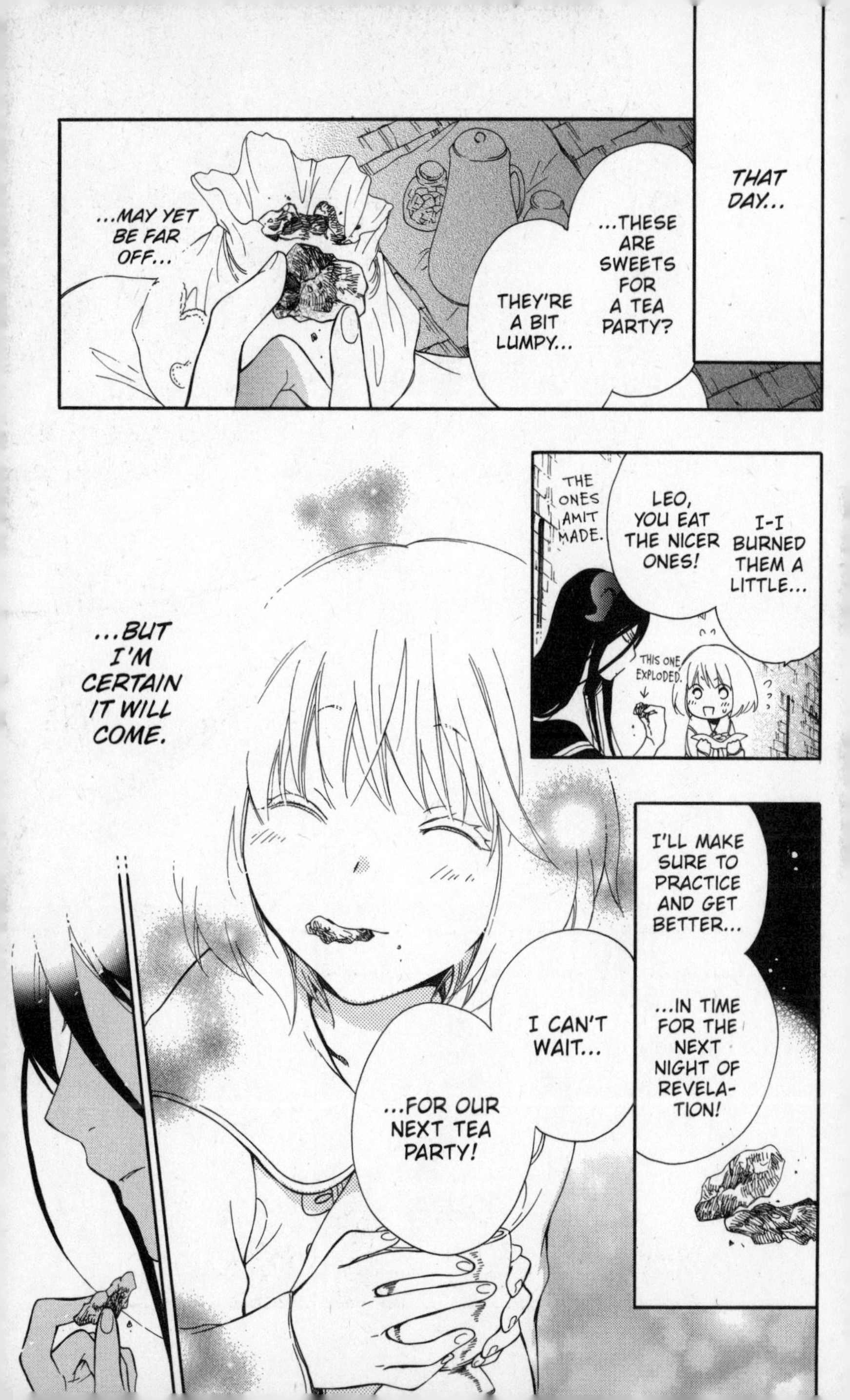
THAT DAY...
...THESE ARE SWEETS FOR A TEA PARTY?
THEY'RE A BIT LUMPY...
...MAY YET BE FAR OFF...
I-I BURNED THEM A LITTLE...
LEO, YOU EAT THE NICER ONES!
THE ONES AMIT MADE.
THIS ONE EXPLODED.
I'LL MAKE SURE TO PRACTICE AND GET BETTER...
...IN TIME FOR THE NEXT NIGHT OF REVELA-TION!
...BUT I'M CERTAIN IT WILL COME.
I CAN'T WAIT...
...FOR OUR NEXT TEA PARTY!

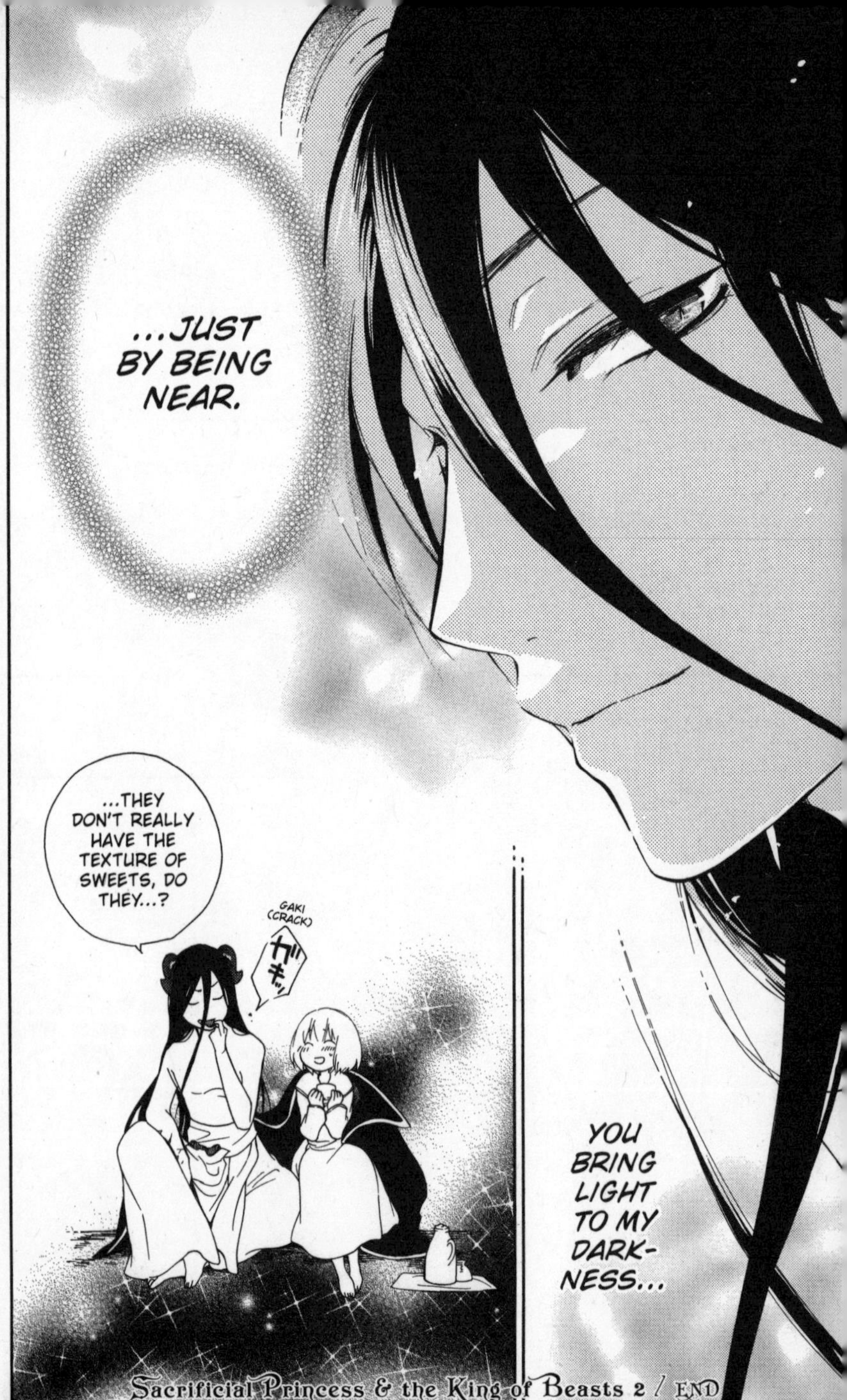
...JUST BY BEING NEAR.
YOU BRING LIGHT TO MY DARKNESS...
...THEY DON'T REALLY HAVE THE TEXTURE OF SWEETS, DO THEY...?
GAKI (CRACK)
ガギッ

Sacrificial Princess & the King of Beasts 2 / END

The Beast Princess and the Regular King

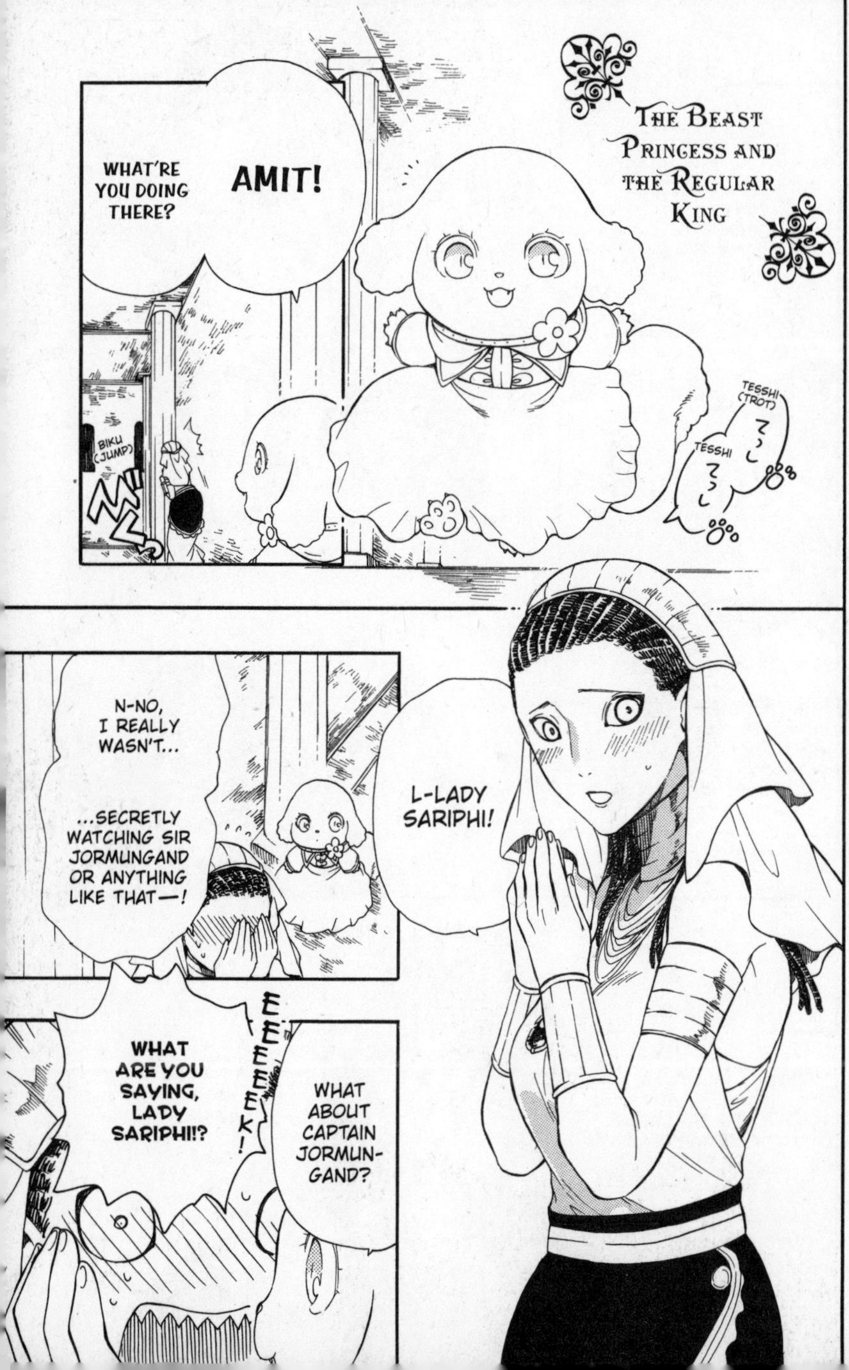
TESSHI (TROT)
TESSHI
AMIT!
WHAT'RE YOU DOING THERE?
BIKU (JUMP)
L-LADY SARIPHI!
N-NO, I REALLY WASN'T...
...SECRETLY WATCHING SIR JORMUNGAND OR ANYTHING LIKE THAT—!
WHAT ABOUT CAPTAIN JORMUNGAND?
EEEEEEK!
WHAT ARE YOU SAYING, LADY SARIPHI!?

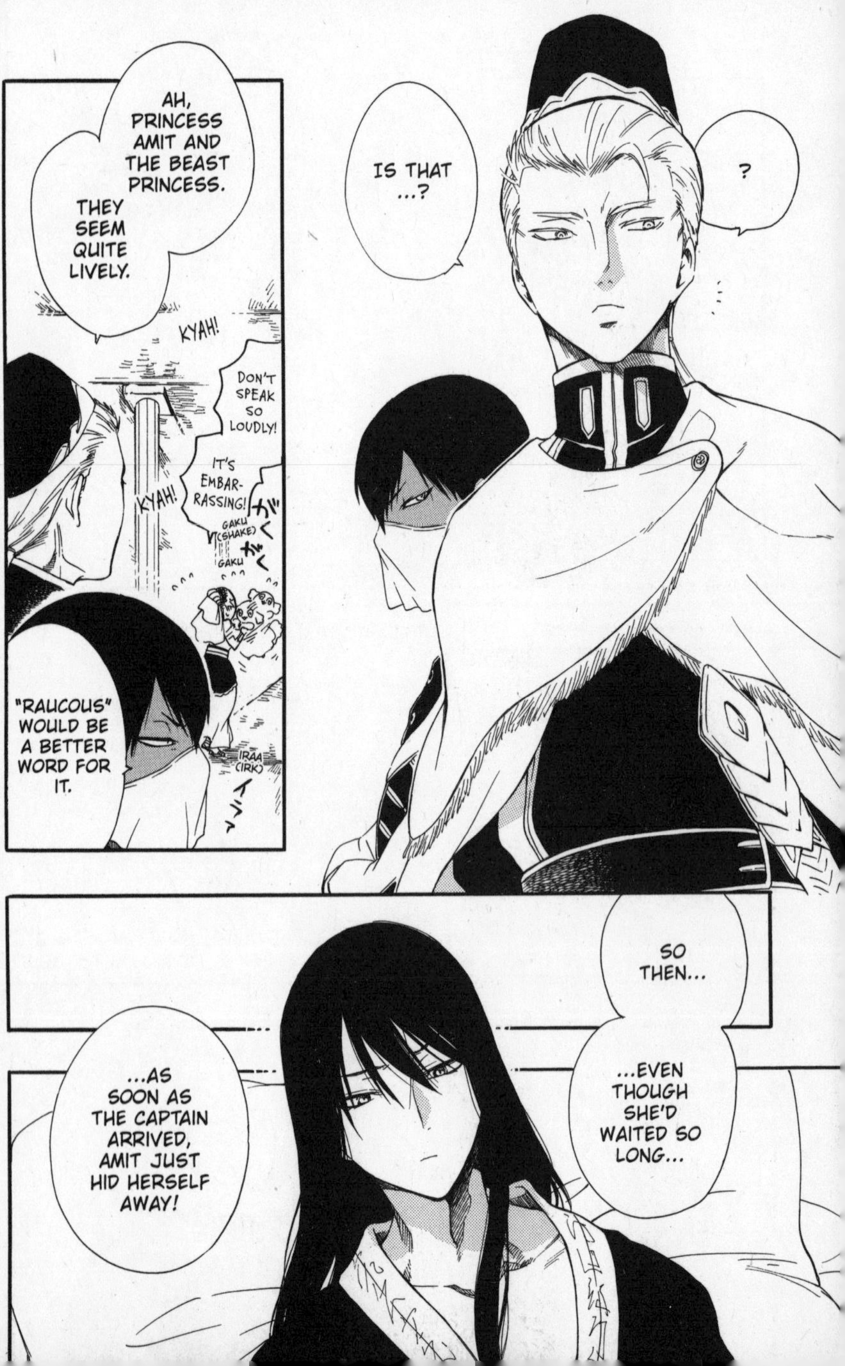
?
IS THAT ...?
AH, PRINCESS AMIT AND THE BEAST PRINCESS.
THEY SEEM QUITE LIVELY.
KYAH!
DON'T SPEAK SO LOUDLY!
IT'S EMBARRASSING!
KYAH!
GAKU (SHAKE)
GAKU
"RAUCOUS" WOULD BE A BETTER WORD FOR IT.
IRAA (IRK)
SO THEN...
...EVEN THOUGH SHE'D WAITED SO LONG...
...AS SOON AS THE CAPTAIN ARRIVED, AMIT JUST HID HERSELF AWAY!

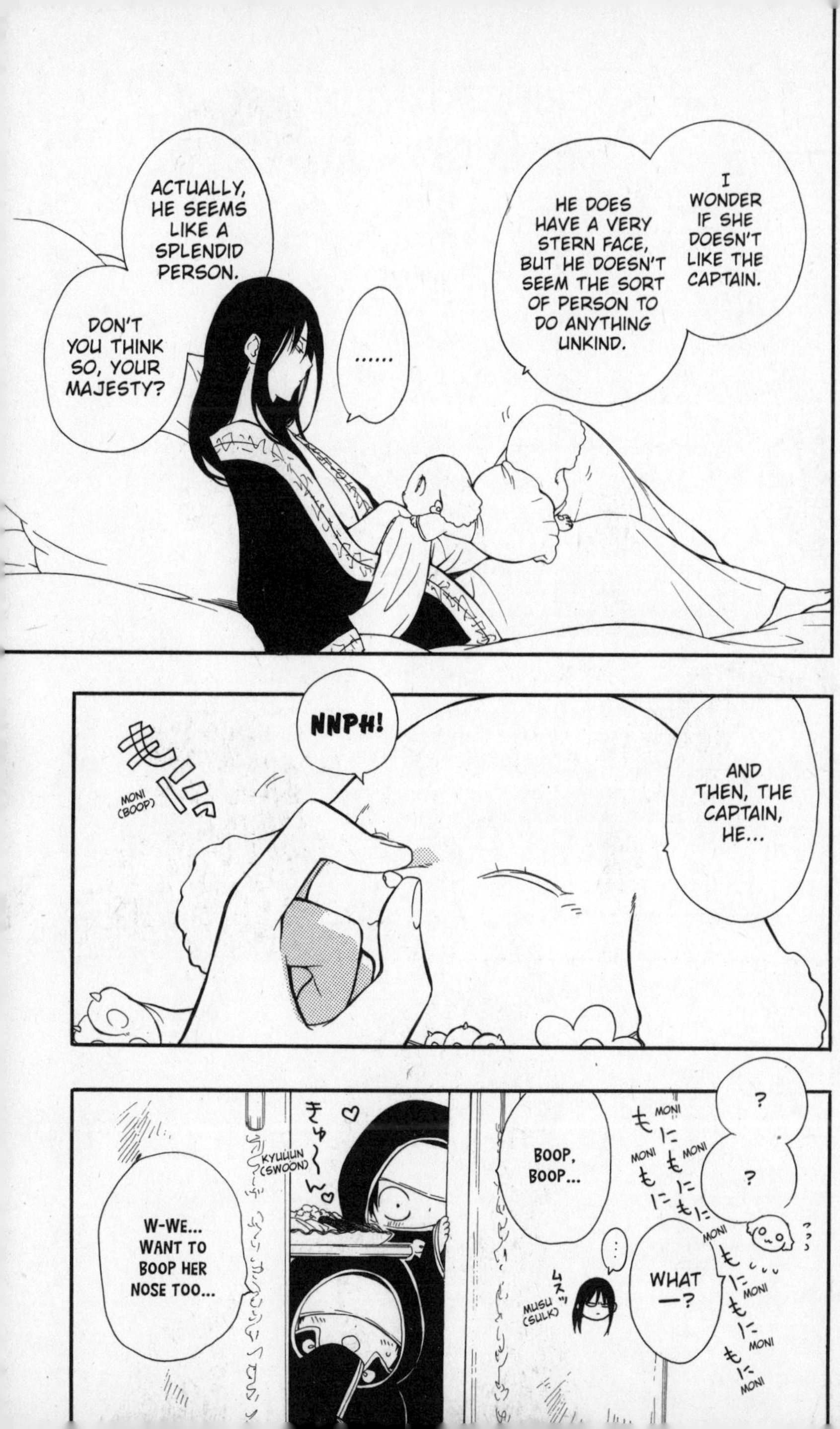
I WONDER IF SHE DOESN'T LIKE THE CAPTAIN.
HE DOES HAVE A VERY STERN FACE, BUT HE DOESN'T SEEM THE SORT OF PERSON TO DO ANYTHING UNKIND.
......
ACTUALLY, HE SEEMS LIKE A SPLENDID PERSON.
DON'T YOU THINK SO, YOUR MAJESTY?
AND THEN, THE CAPTAIN, HE...
NNPH!
もにっ
MONI (BOOP)
?
?
もにもにもに
MONI MONI MONI
もにもにもに
MONI MONI MONI
WHAT—?
...
ムスッ
MUSU (SULK)
BOOP, BOOP...
きゅ〜ん♡
KYUUUN (SWOON)
W-WE... WANT TO BOOP HER NOSE TOO...

SACRIFICIAL PRINCESS AND THE King of Beasts

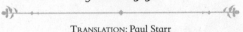

2

Yu Tomofuji

TRANSLATION: Paul Starr

LETTERING: Lys Blakeslee

This book is a work of fiction. Names, characters, places, and incidents are the product of the author's imagination or are used fictitiously. Any resemblance to actual events, locales, or persons, living or dead, is coincidental.

NIEHIME TO KEMONO NO OH by Yu Tomofuji
© Yu Tomofuji 2016
All rights reserved.
First published in Japan in 2016 by HAKUSENSHA, Inc., Tokyo.
English language translation rights in U.S.A., Canada and U.K. arranged with HAKUSENSHA, Inc., Tokyo through Tuttle-Mori Agency, Inc., Tokyo.

English translation © 2018 by Yen Press, LLC

Yen Press, LLC supports the right to free expression and the value of copyright. The purpose of copyright is to encourage writers and artists to produce the creative works that enrich our culture.

The scanning, uploading, and distribution of this book without permission is a theft of the author's intellectual property. If you would like permission to use material from the book (other than for review purposes), please contact the publisher. Thank you for your support of the author's rights.

Yen Press
1290 Avenue of the Americas
New York, NY 10104

Visit us at yenpress.com ❧ facebook.com/yenpress ❧ twitter.com/yenpress
yenpress.tumblr.com ❧ instagram.com/yenpress

First Yen Press Edition: July 2018

Yen Press is an imprint of Yen Press, LLC.
The Yen Press name and logo are trademarks of Yen Press, LLC.

The publisher is not responsible for websites (or their content) that are not owned by the publisher.

Library of Congress Control Number: 2018930817

ISBNs: 978-0-316-48099-4 (paperback)
978-0-316-48100-7 (ebook)

10 9 8 7 6 5 4 3 2 1

WOR

Printed in the United States of America